"Berinsky has brought together a world-class group of scholars working on cutting edge puzzles in the causes and consequences of public opinion. The book is an excellent resource for students, containing foundational insights about measurement and research design, electoral dynamics, and campaign media strategy. The largest contribution of this volume, however, may be the treasure trove of ideas for future research on the impact of group attitudes and identities in structuring our politics."

—*Nicholas A. Valentino, University of Michigan*

"With its new and updated chapters, the second edition of *New Directions in Public Opinion* improves upon what was already an extremely valuable collection of essays from an impressive group of leading scholars. Berinsky's masterful structuring of the book will allow it to be used as either a main text or a supplementary reader in a wide variety of courses. With just the right mix of analytical depth and topical breadth, this text will provide a solid grounding in six decades of public opinion research while also engaging and exciting students with its timely essays on pioneering new developments in the field."

—*Matthew Jacobsmeier, West Virginia University*

"In the latest edition of Berinsky's *New Directions in Public Opinion*, leading scholars of public opinion have written engaging chapters that survey recent research. Berinsky's volume continues to be the best overview of the topic, perfect for students who want to learn about new developments."

—*Gabriel Lenz, University of California-Berkeley*

New Directions in Public Opinion

The field of public opinion is one of the most diverse in political science. Over the last 60 years, scholars have drawn upon the disciplines of psychology, economics, sociology, and even biology to learn how ordinary people come to understand the complicated business of politics. But much of the path-breaking research in the field of public opinion is published in journals, taking up fairly narrow questions one at a time and often requiring advanced statistical knowledge to understand these findings. As a result, the study of public opinion can seem confusing and incoherent to undergraduates. To engage undergraduate students in this area, a new type of textbook is required.

The second edition of *New Directions in Public Opinion* brings together leading scholars to provide an accessible and coherent overview of the current state of the field of public opinion. Each chapter provides a general overview of topics that are at the cutting edge of study as well as well-established cornerstones of the field. Each contributor has made substantive revisions to their chapters, and three chapters have been added on genetics and biology, immigration, and political extremism and the Tea Party. Suitable for use as a main textbook or in tandem with a lengthier survey, this book comprehensively covers the topics of public opinion research and pushes students further to explore critical topics in contemporary politics.

Adam J. Berinsky is Professor of Political Science at Massachusetts Institute of Technology and Director of the MIT Political Experiments Research Lab.

New Directions in American Politics

The Routledge series *New Directions in American Politics* is composed of contributed volumes covering key areas of study in the field of American politics and government. Each title provides a state-of-the-art overview of current trends in its respective subfield, with an eye toward cutting edge research accessible to advanced undergraduate and beginning graduate students. While the volumes touch on the main topics of relevant study, they are not meant to cover the "nuts and bolts" of the subject. Rather, they engage readers in the most recent scholarship, real-world controversies, and theoretical debates with the aim of getting students excited about the same issues that animate scholars.

Titles in the Series:

New Directions in American Political Parties
Edited by Jeffrey M. Stonecash

New Directions in the American Presidency
Edited by Lori Cox Han

New Directions in Campaigns and Elections
Edited by Stephen K. Medvic

New Directions in Congressional Politics
Edited by Jamie Carson

New Directions in Public Opinion
Edited by Adam Berinsky

New Directions in Judicial Politics
Edited by Kevin McGuire

New Directions in Media and Politics
Edited by Travis Ridout

New Directions in American Politics
Edited by Raymond J. La Raja

New Directions in Interest Group Politics
Edited by Matt Grossmann

New Directions in Public Opinion (Second Edition)
Edited by Adam Berinksy

New Directions in Public Opinion

Second Edition

Edited by
Adam J. Berinsky

NEW YORK AND LONDON

First published 2016
by Routledge
711 Third Avenue, New York, NY 10017

and by Routledge
2 Park Square, Milton Park, Abingdon, Oxon OX14 4RN

Routledge is an imprint of the Taylor & Francis Group, an informa business

British Library Cataloguing in Publication Data
A catalogue record for this book is available from the British Library

Library of Congress Cataloging in Publication Data
New directions in public opinion / edited by Adam J. Berinsky. – Second
edition
pages cm.—(New directions in American politics)
Includes bibliographical references.
1. Public opinion—United States. 2. United States—Politics and government—
Public opinion. I. Berinsky, Adam J., 1970–
HN90.P8N49 2016
303.3'80973–dc23
2015021302

ISBN: 978-1-138-77465-0 (hbk)
ISBN: 978-1-138-77466-7 (pbk)
ISBN: 978-1-315-77436-7 (ebk)

Typeset in Minion Pro and Gill Sans
by Florence Production Ltd, Stoodleigh, Devon, UK

Contents

Illustrations

Figures

Tables

Contributors

Matt A. Barreto is Professor of Political Science and Chicana/o Studies at UCLA, the co-founder of the polling and research firm Latino Decisions, and has served two terms on the Board of Advisers of the American National Election Study. His research focuses on public opinion and attitudes towards racial and ethnic minorities in the U.S. and he is the co-author (with Christopher Parker) of the book *Change They Can't Believe In: The Tea Party and Reactionary Politics in America* (2013).

Matthew Baum is the Marvin Kalb Professor of Global Communications and Professor of Public Policy at Harvard University's John F. Kennedy School of Government and Department of Government. His research focuses on delineating the effects of domestic politics on international conflict and cooperation in general and American foreign policy in particular, as well as on the role of the mass media and public opinion in contemporary American politics. His research has appeared in over a dozen leading scholarly journals, such as the *American Political Science Review*, *American Journal of Political Science*, and the *Journal of Politics*. His books include *Soft News Goes to War: Public Opinion and American Foreign Policy in the New Media Age* (2003), *War Stories: The Causes and Consequences of Public Views of War* (2009, co-authored with Tim Groeling), and *War and Democratic Constraint: How the Public Influences Foreign Policy* (forthcoming 2015, co-authored with Phil Potter). He has also contributed op-ed articles to a variety of newspapers, magazines, and blog sites in the United States and abroad. Before coming to Harvard, Baum was an associate professor of political science and communication studies at UCLA.

Adam J. Berinsky is Professor of Political Science at MIT. Berinsky received his PhD from the University of Michigan in 2000. He is a specialist in the fields of political behavior and public opinion. He is the author of *In Time of War: Understanding American Public Opinion from World War II to Iraq* (2009) and *Silent Voices: Public Opinion and Political Participation in America* (2004) and has published articles in the *American Journal of Political Science*, *Journal of Politics*, *Political Behavior*, *Political Psychology*, *Public*

Opinion Quarterly, Quarterly Journal of Political Science, American Politics Research, and *Communist and Post-Communist Studies*. He has won several scholarly awards, is the recipient of grants from the National Science Foundation, and was a fellow at the Center for Advanced Study in the Behavioral Sciences.

Ted Brader is Professor of Political Science at the University of Michigan and Research Professor in the Center for Political Studies at the Institute for Social Research. He is a Principal Investigator of the American National Election Studies and Associate Principal Investigator for Time-sharing Experiments for the Social Sciences. His research focuses on the role of emotions in politics, political partisanship, media effects on public opinion, experimental and survey methods, and other topics in political psychology. He is the author of *Campaigning for Hearts and Minds* (2006) and numerous articles in journals, such as *American Journal of Political Science, Journal of Politics, Public Opinion Quarterly, Political Behavior, Political Psychology, Comparative Political Studies*, and *Comparative Politics*. He received his PhD from the Department of Government at Harvard University in 1999.

Nancy Burns is the Warren E. Miller Collegiate Professor of Political Science, Chair of the Department of Political Science, and Research Professor at the Center for Political Studies at the University of Michigan. Her work focuses on gender, race, public opinion, and political action. She is the co-author with Kay Lehman Schlozman and Sidney Verba of *The Private Roots of Public Action: Gender, Equality, and Political Participation* (2001) and the author of *The Formation of American Local Governments: Private Values in Public Institutions* (1994). Her work has appeared in the *American Political Science Review*, the *American Journal of Political Science*, the *Journal of Politics, Political Analysis, Politics & Gender, Studies in American Political Development*, and the *Annual Review of Political Science*, among other outlets. Burns served as Principal Investigator of the National Election Studies from 1999 to 2005. She is a Fellow of the American Academy of Arts and Sciences.

Andrea Louise Campbell is Professor of Political Science at the Massachusetts Institute of Technology. Her research interests include American politics, political behavior, public opinion, and political inequality, particularly their intersection with social welfare policy, health policy, and tax policy. She is the author of *Trapped in America's Safety Net: One Family's Struggle* (2014); *The Delegated Welfare State: Medicare, Markets, and the Governance of Social Provision*, with Kimberly J. Morgan (2011); and *How Policies Make Citizens: Senior Citizen Activism and the American Welfare State* (2003). She is also completing a book manuscript on public opinion and taxes in the United States. Her research has been supported by the National Science Foundation, Russell Sage Foundation, and Robert Wood Johnson Foundation. She holds a PhD from the University of California, Berkeley.

David E. Campbell is Professor of Political Science and Director of the Rooney Center for the Study of American Democracy at the University of Notre Dame. He is the author of *Why We Vote: How Schools and Communities Shape Our Civic Life* (2008); *American Grace: How Religion Divides and Unites Us* (2012, with Robert Putnam) and, most recently, *Seeking the Promised Land: Mormons and American Politics* (2014, with John Green and J. Quin Monson). In addition to publishing in scholarly journals such as the *American Journal of Political Science* and the *Journal of Politics*, his work has been featured in the *New York Times, Wall Street Journal, Economist, USA Today* and many other general media outlets.

Erica Czaja is a Robert Wood Johnson Foundation Scholar in Health Policy Research at the University of California, Berkeley. Her research interests span American politics, political psychology, inequality, and public policy. She is particularly interested in the effects of empathy and other emotions on public opinion and political behavior. Dr Czaja is a recipient of numerous grants and awards, including the National Science Foundation Doctoral Dissertation Research Improvement Grant, the Distinguished Junior Scholars Award from the American Political Science Association Political Psychology section, the Center for the Study of Democratic Politics Graduate Student Research Grant (Princeton University), and the Mamdouha S. Bobst Center for Peace and Justice Graduate Student Research Grant (Princeton University). Dr Czaja received her PhD in Politics and Social Policy (2013) and MA in Politics (2011) from Princeton University. She also earned her MA in the Social Sciences (2006) at the University of Chicago and her BA with High Distinction in Psychology (2003) at the University of Michigan, Ann Arbor. She has also worked on the survey research staff at the RAND Corporation in Santa Monica, CA.

Christopher M. Federico is Associate Professor of Psychology and Political Science at the University of Minnesota. His research focuses on the psychological foundations of ideology and belief systems. He is the recipient of numerous awards, including the International Society of Political Psychology's 2007 Erik Erikson Award for Early Career Achievements and the International Society for Justice Research's 2009 Morton Deutsch Award. His work has appeared in the *Journal of Personality and Social Psychology*, the *Personality and Social Psychology Bulletin, Public Opinion Quarterly*, and the *American Journal of Political Science*.

Martin Gilens is Professor of Politics at Princeton University. His research examines representation, public opinion, and mass media, especially in relation to inequality and public policy. Professor Gilens is the author of *Affluence & Influence: Economic Inequality and Political Power in America* (2014) and *Why Americans Hate Welfare: Race, Media and the Politics of Antipoverty Policy* (1999), and has published on political inequality, mass media, race, gender, and welfare politics in the *American Political*

Science Review, the *American Journal of Political Science*, *The Journal of Politics*, the *British Journal of Political Science*, *Public Opinion Quarterly*, and the *Berkeley Journal of Sociology*. He holds a PhD in sociology from the University of California, Berkeley, and taught at Yale University and UCLA before joining the faculty at Princeton. His research has been supported by the Russell Sage Foundation, the National Science Foundation, the Institute for Advanced Study, and the Social Science Research Council.

Frank J. Gonzalez is a PhD candidate in the department of Political Science at the University of Nebraska–Lincoln. He received a Master of Arts in Political Science at UNL, and a Bachelor of Arts in Psychology from the University of Delaware in 2011. His research interests include intergroup dynamics, race-based policy attitudes, and the social, cognitive, and affective underpinnings of political attitudes. His current work involves using biological and psychological methods to understand how people place themselves in groups in society, and the impact of group-related traits on attitudes toward issues such as affirmative action, racial profiling, national identity, and transnational policies.

John C. Green is Distinguished Professor of Political Science and director of the Ray C. Bliss Institute of Applied Politics at the University of Akron as well as a Senior Research Advisor for the Pew Forum on Religion & Public Life. He has written extensively on religion and American politics, including *Seeking the Promised Land: Mormons and American Politics*, *The Assemblies of God: Godly Love and the Revitalization of American Pentecostalism* (2010), and *The Faith Factor* (2007).

Jake Haselswerdt is an Assistant Professor in the Political Science Department and the Truman School of Public Affairs at the University of Missouri. He is currently on leave as a Robert Wood Johnson Foundation Scholar in Health Policy Research at the University of Michigan. His research focuses on tax policy, health policy, and public opinion.

Susan Herbst is the President of the University of Connecticut, where she is also Professor of Political Science. She is author of several books on public opinion including *Numbered Voices: How Opinion Polls Have Shaped American Politics* (1993), *Politics at the Margin: Historical Expression Outside of the Mainstream* (1994), *Reading Public Opinion: Political Actors View the Democratic Process* (1998), and, most recently, *Rude Democracy: Civility and Incivility in American Politics*. She has held academic positions at Northwestern University, Temple University, and the University at Albany.

Marc Hetherington is Professor of Political Science at Vanderbilt University. He is the author of three scholarly books, the most recent of which is *Why Washington Won't Work: Polarization, Political Trust, and the Governing Crisis* (with Thomas Rudolph) (2015). In addition, he has published numerous articles in scholarly journals such as the *American Political Science*

Review, American Journal of Political Science, Journal of Politics, Public Opinion Quarterly, and *British Journal of Political Science.* He was also the recipient of the Emerging Scholar Award from the American Political Science Association's section on Elections, Public Opinion, and Voting Behavior.

John R. Hibbing is the Foundation Regents Professor of Political Science and Psychology at the University of Nebraska–Lincoln, where he studies the interaction of biology and politics and co-directs the Political Physiology Lab. His articles have appeared in journals such as *Science, Behavioral and Brain Sciences, Current Biology,* and the *American Political Science Review,* and he is the co-author, with Kevin Smith and John Alford, of *Predisposed: Liberals, Conservatives, and the Biology of Political Differences.* He has been named a NATO Fellow in Science, a Fellow in the American Association for the Advancement of Science (AAAS), and a Guggenheim Fellow.

Matthew V. Hibbing is an Assistant Professor of Political Science at the University of California, Merced. His research focuses on American political behavior, with emphasis on public opinion, political psychology, and biology and politics. He has published research in a number of journals, including *Science, American Political Science Review, Legislative Studies Quarterly, British Journal of Political Science, Journal of Politics, Political Behavior,* and *Political Psychology.*

D. Sunshine Hillygus is Associate Professor of Political Science at Duke University and director of the Duke Initiative on Survey Methodology (DISM). Her research and teaching specialties include public opinion, political behavior, campaigns and elections, and survey methodology. She is co-author of *The Hard Count: The Social and Political Challenges of the 2000 Census* (2006) and *The Persuadable Voter: Wedge Issues in Political Campaigns* (2008). She has also published articles in *Public Opinion Quarterly, Political Analysis, American Journal of Political Science, Journal of Politics, Statistical Science,* and *Political Behavior,* among others. She holds a PhD from Stanford University and previously taught at Harvard University.

Ashley E. Jardina earned her PhD from the University of Michigan in 2014, and she is currently an Assistant Professor of Political Science at Duke University. Her research interests include race and politics, public opinion, gender and politics, and more broadly, understanding the way in which group identities and group conflict influence individuals' political behavior and preferences.

Jane Junn is Professor of Political Science at the University of Southern California. She specializes in U.S. political behavior and public opinion, with emphasis on race, ethnicity and the politics of immigration. She has published three books on political participation in the United States. Her first book, *Education and Democratic Citizenship in America* (1996, with

Norman H. Nie and Kenneth Stehlik-Barry), won the Woodrow Wilson award from the American Political Science Association for the best book published that year.

Donald Kinder is the Phillip E. Converse Collegiate Professor of Political Science at the University of Michigan. He has held fellowships from the Guggenheim Foundation and from the Center for Advanced Study in the Behavioral Sciences and is a member of the American Academy of Arts and Sciences. His books include *News that Matters* (1987), *Divided by Color* (1997), *Us against Them* (2009), and *The End of Race?* (2011).

Geoffrey C. Layman is Professor of Political Science at the University of Notre Dame. His research specialties are political parties, public opinion, voting behavior, and religion and politics. Layman is the author of *The Great Divide: Religious and Cultural Conflict in American Party Politics* (2001). He has published articles in a variety of academic journals, including the *American Political Science Review*, *American Journal of Political Science*, *Journal of Politics*, *British Journal of Political Science*, and *Public Opinion Quarterly*. His current research focuses on the growth of partisan issue polarization in the U.S., the political causes and consequences of growing non-religion and secularism, and changes in the character of American party activism.

Tali Mendelberg studies inequality and politics. Her book *The Race Card: Campaign Strategy, Implicit Messages, and the Norm of Equality* (2001), won the American Political Science Association's Woodrow Wilson Foundation Award for "the best book published in the United States during the prior year on government, politics or international affairs." *The Silent Sex: Gender, Deliberation and Institutions* (2014, co-authored with Chris Karpowitz), has also won distinctions. Earlier versions of its parts received the APSA Paul Lazarsfeld Award for the best paper in Political Communication (twice), the APSA Best Paper Award in Political Psychology (twice), the Carrie Chapman Catt Prize for Research on Women and Politics (honorable mention), and were in the top-ten most downloaded APSR articles in 2013. She was awarded the Erik H. Erikson Early Career Award for Excellence and Creativity in the Field of Political Psychology. She has published articles in the *American Political Science Review*, *American Journal of Political Science*, *Journal of Politics*, *Public Opinion Quarterly*, *Perspectives on Politics*, *Political Behavior*, *Political Psychology*, and *Political Communication*. Her work has been supported by grants and fellowships from the National Science Foundation, the University of Pennsylvania, Harvard University, the Center for Advanced Study in the Behavioral Sciences, Princeton University Center for Human Values, and The Mamdouha S. Bobst Center for Peace and Justice. She holds a PhD from the University of Michigan. Her areas of specialization are political communication, gender, race, class, public opinion, political psychology, and experimental methods.

Jeffery J. Mondak is James M. Benson Chair in Public Issues and Civic Leadership in the Department of Political Science at the University of Illinois at Urbana-Champaign. Mondak's research has examined numerous aspects of American and cross-national political behavior. His most recent work focuses on the political significance of personality traits. Mondak is the author of *Personality and the Foundations of Political Behavior* (2010) and *Nothing to Read: Newspapers and Elections in a Social Experiment* (1995), and co-editor of *Fault Lines: Why the Republicans Lost Congress* (2009). Mondak's articles have appeared in numerous journals, including the *American Political Science Review*, the *American Journal of Political Science*, the *British Journal of Political Science*, *Cognitive Brain Research*, the *Journal of Politics*, *Political Psychology* and *Public Opinion Quarterly*.

Christopher S. Parker is an Associate Professor in the department of political science at the University of Washington. A graduate of UCLA and the University of Chicago, Parker also served in the United States Navy. He is the author of *Change They Can't Believe In: The Tea Party and Reactionary Politics in America* (2013), and *Fighting for Democracy: Black Veterans and the Struggle Against White Supremacy in the Postwar South* (2009). He resides in Seattle.

Molly E. Reynolds is a Fellow in the Governance Studies Program at the Brookings Institution. Her research focuses on Congress and legislative politics, with an emphasis on how legislative rules and procedures affect domestic policy outcomes. She received her PhD in political science and public policy from the University of Michigan, where her dissertation examined the causes and consequences of majoritarian procedural change in the U.S. Senate with a focus on the budget reconciliation process. Her work has been published in the *Journal of Politics*.

Elizabeth Rigby is an Associate Professor in the Trachtenberg School of Public Policy and Public Administration at George Washington University where she teaches courses on the role of politics in the policymaking process. Her research examines the interplay of politics, policy, and social inequality in the contemporary United States and has been published in a range of journals including: *American Journal of Political Science*, *Political Research Quarterly*, *Journal of Policy Analysis and Management*, *Policy Studies Journal*, and *Health Affairs*. Professor Rigby holds a PhD (with distinction) from Columbia University. In addition, she received post-doctoral training in population health at the University of Wisconsin-Madison as a Robert Wood Johnson Health and Society Scholar and is currently serving as an APSA Congressional Fellow on the minority staff of the Senate Finance Committee.

Deborah J. Schildkraut is Professor of Political Science at Tufts University. She is the author of *Americanism in the Twenty-First Century: Public Opinion in the Age of Immigration* (2011), winner of the Robert E. Lane award for the best book in Political Psychology. She also wrote *Press "One" for English: Language Policy, Public Opinion, and American Identity* (2005), co-authored *The Challenge of Democracy: American Government in Global Politics* (13th edition, 2015), and published several research articles.

David O. Sears received his AB in History (Stanford University, 1957), his PhD in Psychology (Yale University, 1962), and then was appointed as Assistant Professor in Psychology at UCLA (1961) and Professor of Psychology and Political Science (1971). He has served as Dean of Social Sciences and Director of the Institute for Social Science Research at UCLA, and as President of the International Society of Political Psychology. He has co-authored *Public Opinion* (with Robert E. Lane, 1964), *The Politics of Violence: The New Urban Blacks and the Watts Riot* (with John B. McConahay, 1973), *Tax Revolt: Something for Nothing in California* (with Jack Citrin, 1982), 12 editions of *Social Psychology* (with Shelley E. Taylor and L. Anne Peplau, 1970–2005), *Obama's Race: The 2008 Election and the Dream of a Post-Racial America* (with Michael Tesler, 2010), and co-edited *Political Cognition* (with Richard Lau, 1986), *Racialized Politics: The Debate about Racism in America* (with Jim Sidanius and Lawrence Bobo, 2000), and the *Oxford Handbook of Political Psychology* (with Leonie Huddy and Robert Jervis, 2003).

John Sides is Associate Professor of Political Science at George Washington University. He studies political behavior in American and comparative politics. He is a co-author of *The Gamble: Choice and Chance in the 2012 Election* (with Lynn Vavreck) and *Campaigns and Elections: Rules, Reality, Strategy, Choice* (with Matt Grossmann, Keena Lipstiz, and Daron Shaw). His work has also appeared in various scholarly journals, including the *American Political Science Review, American Journal of Political Science*, and *Journal of Politics*. He helped found and contributes to The Monkey Cage, a political science blog.

Kevin B. Smith is Professor and Chair of the Department of Political Science at the University of Nebraska–Lincoln. His research focuses on the biology and psychology of attitudes and behaviors. His research has been published in *Science, Behavioral and Brain Sciences, Physiology and Behavior*, the *American Political Science Review*, the *American Journal of Political Science* and the *Journal of Politics*.

Carly Wayne is a PhD student in political science at the University of Michigan. Her main areas of research lie at the intersection of the fields of political psychology and decision-making in the context of war and conflict. Specifically, she is interested in the cognitive, emotional and motivational biases in foreign policy decision-making. She has served as senior editorial assistant for the journal *Political Psychology*. She is co-author of *The Polythink Syndrome: U.S. Foreign Policy Decisions on 9/11, Afghanistan, Iraq, Iran, Syria, and ISIS* (2015) as well as several chapters and articles in journals such as *Journal of Conflict Resolution* and *The European Psychologist*.

Acknowledgments

An edited volume is only as good as the chapters it contains. Every one of the authors who contributed to this volume produced an excellent chapter. The final product is a testament to their hard and careful work. Above all, I am grateful to them. I am also grateful to Michael Kerns who approached me to write the first edition of this manuscript and guided it seamlessly through the editorial process. He was also tremendously supportive of creating the second edition of this book. Seth Dickinson and Timothy McKinley both provided outstanding research assistance for the first edition. Daniel Guenther provided outstanding help for the second edition. Gabe Lenz, Michele Margolis, and Michael Sances provided helpful comments on drafts of the introduction. This book is dedicated to my former advisors Don Kinder and Nancy Burns, who sparked my interest in public opinion while I was a graduate student at Michigan (and provided a timely chapter for this volume to boot).

Introduction

Adam J. Berinsky

Why do some citizens approve of same-sex couples having the right to marry, while others are vehemently opposed? Why can't Democrats and Republicans seem to agree on anything? Should we trust opinion polls? Are some polls better than others? How much does the average American really care about politics anyway? These are the types of important questions that are central to the study of public opinion.

The field of public opinion is one of the most diverse in political science. Over the last 60 years, scholars have drawn upon the disciplines of psychology, economics, sociology, and even biology to answer these questions and more. As a field we have learned a great deal about how ordinary people come to understand the complicated business of politics.

This diversity makes the study of public opinion an especially interesting area of political science, but diversity comes with a cost. Much path breaking research in the field of public opinion is published in professional journals, whose target audience is professors and advanced graduate students. These papers take up fairly narrow questions one at a time and often require advanced statistical knowledge to understand. As a result, the study of public opinion can seem confusing and incoherent to novices and specialists alike.

This book is the second edition of *New Directions in Public Opinion*—a revised and expanded version of the original volume. As with the first edition, it is intended to expand the audience for cutting-edge public opinion research by providing an accessible and coherent overview of the current state of the field. In this volume, I have brought together leading scholars of public opinion to provide an understandable introduction to new and exciting research. Each of the authors of the chapters in this volume both provide an overview of their field of specialization as well as a lively review of their own research. In order to stimulate interest among readers and students, these examples focus on contemporary and ongoing political controversies. My hope is that this book will serve as a comprehensive introduction to the field, while at the same time piquing the interest of students to further explore the frontiers on their own. Each chapter is intended to be self-contained, but together, this volume serves as a gateway to the study of public opinion.

The Measure and Meaning of Public Opinion

Before we can begin to study public opinion, we need to have some sense of what we mean by "public opinion." As you might expect, this is easier said than done. As the eminent political scientist V.O. Key aptly noted 50 years ago, "To speak with precision of public opinion is a task not unlike coming to grips with the Holy Ghost."[1] Indeed, the term has long been used to mean many different things. The ancient Greeks assessed opinion through public rhetoric and oratory, embracing a notion of public opinion that befit their restrictive notions of citizenship.[2] With the emergence of expanded male suffrage throughout the nineteenth century, a notion of public opinion as an aggrega-tion of the preferences of individuals began to take hold. But this view did not go unchallenged. In the 1940s, sociologist Herbert Blumer argued that public opinion was a purely collective phenomenon. Public opinion emerged through the communication and clash of group interests and, as a result, could not be gauged through individual survey responses. It was, instead, "the product of a society in operation."[3] It is no surprise then, that a review of the academic literature on public opinion in the 1960s uncovered scores of different defini-tions of this central concept.[4]

While it may be difficult to come to a consensus on a single definition of public opinion, Key ultimately arrived at a working view of public opinion—one that is a useful starting point for this book: "Those opinions held by private persons which governments find it prudent to heed."[5] Key's definition is an expansive one. Public opinion is a property of individuals, but acquires its power in the public sphere. Moreover, there is a place both for the strongly formed, crystallized opinions of citizens that we might think of as reasoned public opinion and the lightly held beliefs and transient preferences that are decried by politicians and journalists as fickle judgments, but which sometimes guide government.

Once we have defined public opinion, we must figure out how best to measure it. Almost certainly, the most familiar technique for the readers of this volume is opinion polls or surveys. Over the course of the twentieth century, polls emerged as an important tool to measure the public will. Today, polls pervade the political scene. Indeed, writing for the 50th anniversary of the leading journal for public opinion research, *Public Opinion Quarterly*, noted political scientist Philip Converse (whose crucial contributions to the field are discussed below) argued that opinion polls *were* public opinion. This view is at least implicitly shared by nearly all scholars of public opinion. Indeed, in this volume, when scholars speak of public opinion, they almost always mean the results of polls.

There are, however, dissenting views. Opinion polls have only existed for 80 years, but scholars and practitioners of politics have been talking about public opinion for centuries. Before the development of polls, as Susan Herbst argues in her excellent book *Numbered Voices*, there were many ways that interested parties could measure public opinion.[6] Citizens could listen in at coffeehouses or follow the partisan press. Politicians could attend to public speeches or follow mail from their constituents. In Chapter 1, Herbst expands this argument, both reviewing the history of opinion expression and looking forward to possible changes in the years to come. Over time, she reminds us, public opinion has meant many things to many different people. In the future, it may change again. An exclusive focus on polls provides us with a restricted and perhaps incomplete picture of the public will.

But given that polls are the dominant way to measure opinion, practitioners should be careful about how they conduct surveys—and citizens should be careful about how they interpret them. In Chapter 2, D. Sunshine Hillygus describes the key challenges that face those who wish to conduct and use surveys as a measure of public opinion. Above all, Hillygus reminds us that we need to pay close attention to the quality of the data gathered by particular surveys.

Data quality is especially important in the twenty-first century, because we are undergoing great changes in the way we measure opinion through surveys. In the early days of surveys, pollsters went door-to-door to interview survey respondents. Beginning in the 1970s, the industry started conducting polls by telephone, a cheaper and more convenient form of data collection that facilitated an explosion in the number of polls in the United States. In recent years, however, this model of data collection has been threatened on several fronts. For one, the rise in the use of cell phones puts the representativeness of phone polls at risk. Over forty percent of all Americans have dropped their land lines in favor of a cell-phone and these numbers are growing, especially among younger Americans. As of June 2014, more than two-thirds of Americans aged 25 to 29 lived in households that had a cell phone but no traditional land line telephone.[7] Polling exclusively through land lines will therefore miss a large portion of the citizens that comprise the mass public. In addition, the Internet holds promise as a method of data collection but, as Hillygus notes, it is difficult to translate the time-tested mechanics of collecting opinions to this new medium. For instance, it is almost impossible to define the universe of Internet users, making it a challenge to draw representative samples.

With the future of opinion polling uncertain, scholars and practitioners must be even more careful about how they collect and report measures of public opinion. Consider, for example, the reporting of poll results by the media. Traditionally, media outlets such as the *New York Times* and the *Washington Post* (in conjunction with CBS and ABC, respectively) maintained polling units that would conduct polls across the course of a campaign. In the last few election cycles, websites that aggregate *all* available polling information—such as Real Clear Politics, Mark Blumenthal's Pollster.com (now under the umbrella of the Huffington Post) and Nate Silver's FiveThirtyEight (now published under the banner of ESPN)—have become extremely popular. These sites provide polling consumers with a vast array of information. But this information is not all of equal quality. Some surveys, Hillygus reminds us, are more worthy of trust than others. In the end, as Hillygus argues, no survey is perfect, but by making the decisions that go into collecting survey data more transparent, it is possible for policymakers, journalists, and ordinary citizens to decide how much faith to put into any single measure of the public will.

The Question of Democratic Competence

Even if we draw a high-quality sample and conduct our poll to minimize survey errors, sometimes it is not clear what it is that we can measure with opinion polls. If, as Walter Lippmann once wrote, politics is a "swarming confusion of problems," can ordinary people make sense of it?[8] Perhaps, when confronted with a complex world, ordinary citizens simply *don't* think about politics in a coherent manner—or even at all.

Lippmann did not have much faith in the common man. And he was not alone in his beliefs: for most of American history politicians and commentators have been skeptical that the mass public is—or ever could be—engaged enough with the political world to make reasonable and temperate political decisions. There was a reason, after all, that the founders established a *representative* democracy rather than let citizens directly govern themselves.

However, it was not until the early twentieth century that the capability of the citizenry became a pressing concern. In the early republic, the political sphere was restricted in numerous ways to keep "undesirables" away from the political process. But gradually more and more citizens were brought into the political sphere. With the expansion of the franchise to women in 1920, all Americans (at least nominally) had the right to vote. The capacity of the mass public, then, became a critical subject of interest to politicians and scholars alike. A. Lawrence Lowell, for example, argued that individual differences in political knowledge must be taken into account when determining the proper role of the public in the process of government—some people, according to Lowell, *should* count more than others.[9] To return to Key's conception of public opinion, Lowell's worry was that without some mechanism to filter opinion, public opinion would reflect *only* lightly held views and ill-thought-out transient demands.

The early days of opinion polling confirmed the worst suspicions of the skeptical. Survey researchers in the 1930s and 1940s painted a rather bleak picture of the capabilities of the mass public. Summing up the findings of one of the first large-scale academic studies of voter decision-making in the 1948 election, Bernard Berelson, Paul Lazarsfeld, and William McPhee wrote that their surveys "reveal that certain requirements commonly assumed for the successful operation of democracy are not met by the behavior of the 'average' citizen."[10] For instance, in 1947, one-quarter of the public could not even name the Vice President and 40 percent did not know who controlled the Senate, essentially failing a multiple choice question with two options. The passage of time has done little to alleviate these concerns. Even with a remarkable increase in the educational attainment of the average American and the rapid development of the mass media since the 1940s, American citizens remain largely ignorant of the goings-on in the political world. Moreover, survey researchers have consistently found that even minor differences in the wording of questions can dramatically change the shape of opinions expressed in polls. Americans support "assistance to the poor" but reject spending on "welfare." It is a legitimate question, then, whether American citizens hold meaningful policy preferences worthy of serving as the basis of democratic governance.

Martin Gilens addresses this very question in Chapter 3. As he concedes, much evidence suggests that citizens lack the knowledge or motivation to form sensible policy preferences. Few Americans, for example, understand the content of complex legislation like the recent health care reforms under President Obama. But, as Gilens notes, individuals do not navigate the political world on their own. For instance, citizens can draw on cues from prominent politicians to help them form meaningful attitudes. And while any individual might fall short of the democratic ideal, groups of citizens can be drawn together into a meaningful aggregate. As James Stimson has argued, once we think of public opinion as the property of whole electorates, rather than individuals, it appears orderly and functions as a sensitive barometer to events in the political world.[11]

Aggregation does not, however, solve all the problems of public opinion. The aggregation of disparate preferences may lead to a rational and reasonable opinion, but in practice not all individuals have an equal voice. For instance, Gilens finds that the policies enacted by government reflect aggregate public preferences, but these policies are strongly biased toward the preferences of the most economically advantaged Americans. Still, Gilens does not blame the public; the inequality in democratic responsiveness, he concludes, results not from a failure of the broader public to form meaningful preferences, but from the failure of the political decision makers to take those preferences into account.

The Foundations of Political Preferences

That said, the opinions of individual members of society remain a critical object of study. Shifting the focus to the aggregate level, as Gilens argues we should, might address some of the concerns raised by critics of direct democracy, such as Berelson and his colleagues. But it remains a fact that even if the American public, taken as a whole, can reason effectively, individual citizens are often distracted by more pressing concerns. Setting aside the noble impulse to accept the wisdom of the collective, to fully understand the relationship between the mass public and politicians, we must not lose our focus on individual citizens. After all, as Christopher Achen aptly noted, if individuals do not possess even meaningful attitudes, let alone well-defined policy preferences, then "democratic theory loses its starting point."[12] A great deal of public opinion research therefore tries to understand exactly how people *do* reason about politics. Answering this question is the task of the second section of this book.

Ideology and Political Reasoning

For the first few decades of the academic study of public opinion, the search for the principles that shaped public opinion did not stray far from ideology. From the 1950s through the 1970s, scholars were occupied by the search for a single overarching belief system that could guide political opinions. The seminal work in this tradition was Philip Converse's 1964 chapter, "The Nature of Belief Systems in Mass Publics." Converse defined a belief system as "a configuration of ideas and attitudes in which the elements are bound together by some form of constraint or functional interdependence."[13] Political ideology, as commonly conceived, is a belief system with a broad range of political objects serving as referents for the ideas and attitudes in the system. Ideology therefore provides a relatively abstract and far-reaching structure for a large variety of political attitudes and preferences.

Converse argued that very few citizens thought of politics in an ideological manner. Analyzing survey data from the 1950s, Converse found that the vast majority of citizens did not use ideological terms, such as "liberal" or "conservative," when talking about politics. Moreover, their opinions were largely unconnected across different issues and seemed to vary in random ways across time.

Converse's work is perhaps the most provocative piece of public opinion scholarship of the last fifty years. It is provocative not only because it focused researchers on questions central to the functioning of democracy, but also because it generated a tremendous amount of reaction—most of it trying to rehabilitate the picture of the general public. For instance, in the 1970s, Norman Nie, Sidney Verba, and John Petrocik published *The Changing American Voter*. These authors found that "constraint"—the correspondence between attitudes on related issues examined by Converse—suddenly increased in 1964. Nie, Verba, and Petrocik attributed this change to a shift in the larger political context—from the placid Eisenhower era of the 1950s to the ideologically charged events of the 1960s. These findings, however, turned out to be largely illusory. Both Converse and Nie, Verba, and Petrocik examined data collected by the American National Election Study (ANES). While the ANES is careful to preserve the continuity of its survey questions, at times the ANES does change its wordings. One important such change in question wording was . . . in 1964! It turns out that the ANES shifted from asking questions in a form where respondents were given a statement that asked if they agreed or disagreed with it, to a format where they were asked to choose between a pair of competing alternatives. In a series of clever experiments, John Sullivan, James Pierson, George Marcus, and Stanley Feldman demonstrated that most of the change found by Nie, Verba, and Petrocik could be attributed to these changes in question wording.[14] By the end of the 1970s, the field was in many ways back where it started in the 1950s—with the dismal findings of the early days of survey research at the forefront.

Was there, then, nothing left to say about public opinion? Perhaps the answer was to ask different kinds of questions. In the early 1980s, Donald Kinder made a call to reframe the study of public opinion from the search for a single overarching principle to a finer grained investigation of what, exactly, *does* structure the political thought of ordinary Americans.

This call to expand the study of public opinion beyond a debate over the power of ideology has been taken up to good effect. Indeed, the chapters in this book on the role of race, religion, emotion, personality, and other topics provide testament to the fruitfulness of this research agenda. However, what may have gotten somewhat lost in the renaissance of the last 30 years is that ideology is still an important topic, as demonstrated by Christopher Federico's contribution to this volume. In Chapter 4, Federico presents evidence that ideology has deep roots in citizens' social circumstances, their psychological characteristics, and perhaps even in biology. Federico also notes that there are conditions under which ideology is a powerful determinant of citizens' opinions on the matters of the day. Admittedly, not all citizens are able to reason in an ideological manner—they must possess both political information and a strong desire to appraise things as "good" or "bad" in order to think ideologically and express ideologically-consistent opinions. Among these citizens, though, ideology is a powerful force.

Moving Beyond Ideology

That said, Kinder's call to move beyond ideology has greatly expanded the scope of the field of public opinion. For those citizens who do not reason in an ideological manner, there are many other possible bases of political reasoning. Perhaps the most obvious determinant of public opinion is partisanship—the degree to which individual citizens identify with one of the major political parties in America. Republicans and Democrats, after all, differ greatly on the major issues of the day. For instance, a poll taken right after the 2010 midterm election by CBS News demonstrated that Americans were evenly split on the question of whether Congress should try to repeal the health care bill passed in March of 2010. Forty-five percent of respondents supported repeal, 45 percent opposed repeal, and another 10 percent were undecided. This seemingly balanced judgment, however, concealed a strong divide between the parties; 76 percent of Republicans favored repeal, compared with 19 percent of Democrats. These stark partisan differences extend to evaluations of major political figures. In that same poll, 78 percent of Democrats approved of the way Barack Obama was handling his job as president, but only 10 percent of Republicans expressed support.[15] Such divisions extended through the 2014 election. A December

2014 poll conducted by ABC News/Washington Post yielded nearly identical results to the CBS poll—75 percent of Democrats approved of the way Barack Obama was handling his job as president, compared to only 10 percent of Republicans.[16]

Given the magnitude of these differences it might surprise today's readers to learn that for much of the history of the field, the power of partisanship was not a given. In fact, if this book had been written 25 or 30 years ago we would be bemoaning the death of parties. While the heyday of the literature on the decline of parties occurred in the 1970s and 1980s—with works such as David Broder's 1972 book, *The Party's Over* and William Crotty's 1984 book, *American Parties in Decline*—Martin Wattenberg's seminal work, *The Decline of American Political Parties* was updated several times into the late 1990s. Ironically, at the precise moment that political scientists were writing about the decline of parties and attachments to parties as a central determinant of public opinion, parties were beginning a steep ascent. Examining the votes that occur on the floor of the House and the Senate, Keith Poole and Howard Rosenthal have found that beginning in the mid-1970s Democrats and Republicans began voting in more unified and distinct ways. Over time, the emergence of these distinct ideological positions among politicians began to trickle down to the level of ordinary citizens.

In Chapter 7, Marc Hetherington chronicles the rise in the importance of party identification over the last thirty years. He first describes the different ways in which political scientists have conceived of party identification. Some scholars have argued that party identification is akin to a summary judgment about the current state of the political world. If times are good when a Democrat is in power as they were in the early 1960s, individuals are more likely to think of themselves as Democrats. If times are bad—think, for instance, 2010—they are less likely to identify as Democrats. The more dominant view, however, is to think of party identification as an intense attachment to a political group. Over a lifetime, party identification is generally stable for most people. Identification with a particular party therefore provides even casually engaged citizens with a useful shortcut to arrive at an understanding of a complicated political world. This seemingly simple fact, though, has important political implications. Over the last thirty years, the beliefs, preferences, and even knowledge of politically relevant facts, among Republicans have increasingly diverged from those of Democrats. Hetherington details these changes and explores their significance for the study of public opinion.

The Importance of Groups

Attachments to political parties are not the only group connections that matter in American politics. As noted above, Converse's landmark work on belief systems is primarily remembered for its conclusions regarding the limits of ideological thinking among members of the mass public. But Converse did not merely document the shortcomings of the citizenry; he also considered the ways that individuals could come to reasoned political decisions, even in the absence of an overarching guiding ideology. Chief among these were social groups.

Converse claimed that visible groups in a society provide structure to individual political judgments, mentioning race, religion, and nationality as clear referents on the political scene in the 1950s. Converse placed a great deal of weight on the power of groups because they were relatively simple concepts, requiring a lower threshold of sophistication than needed to employ abstract concepts, such as ideology. As Converse argued, to make use of group-based reasoning, citizens need only "be endowed with some cognitions of the group and with some interstitial 'linking' information indicating why a given party or policy is relevant to the group."[17] Converse concluded that reference group cues could serve as the foundation of "ideology by proxy," creating meaningful patterns in the attitudes and behaviors of ordinary citizens.[18]

In America, for better or for worse, race has long served as such a guide. The political implications of the relationships between Blacks and Whites have a long history in this country, from pre-Civil War debates about the role of slavery, through today. But racial politics is not simply about these relationships. As America becomes a more diverse society, other racial groups have risen in prominence. For instance, over the last thirty years, the percentage of the population that is Hispanic has increased greatly. Moreover, the "multi-racial" population—individuals who identify with more than one racial group—is among the fastest-growing groups in America. Thus, as Erica Czaja, Jane Junn, and Tali Mendelberg remind us, racial politics in the United States is in flux. In Chapter 5, they argue that the contours of the relationships between racial group identity, racial group consciousness, and public opinion—especially for Latinos and Asian Americans—are particularly challenging for scholars. In their chapter, they try to make sense of these diverse measurements by focusing on individual-level measurements of psychological attachment to groups, namely group identity and consciousness, which are critical intervening variables between racial group classification and the formation of political preferences.

Czaja, Junn, and Mendelberg are primarily concerned with the consequences of attachment to particular groups for public opinion. This in-group identification is indeed an important component of political attitudes. But also important are an individual's relationships with other groups in society. In Chapter 6, Nancy Burns, Ashley Jardina, Donald Kinder, and Molly Reynolds explicitly take up both these concerns in the context of gender. Specifically, they consider how the groupings of "man" and "woman" matter for politics. As a mental category, gender provides an important guide to how we think about ourselves and others. Like race, gender is a source of persistent and serious inequality in America. However, in practice, race and gender have very different effects on opinion. Examining a wide range of policy attitudes, Burns, Jardina,

Kinder, and Reynolds find that the differences between men and women in the domain of gender policy are present, but often quite small. The reason for this common ground is straightforward: women spend much of their lives in close relationships with men: as daughters, sisters, and mothers. As a matter of course, women acquire interests and values in common with the men whose lives they share. That said, there are times when gender differences can help shape political views. Burns, Jardina, Kinder, and Reynolds use the case of attitudes towards Hillary Clinton to show how changes in Clinton's identity—from First Lady to Presidential candidate—shaped the gender basis of her personal support. Through these examples, Burns, Jardina, Kinder, and Reynolds remind us that the power of group identity is in many ways contextually dependent. Different aspects of group identity may come into play in different ways depending on the particular social and political circumstances that create, shape, and activate that identity.

Race and gender do not exhaust the scope of groups that matter in American politics. Another set of groups that Converse mentioned, almost in passing, were religious organizations. Despite a constitutional provision against state religion, throughout American history religion and politics have been inter-twined. In Chapter 11 David Campbell, Geoffrey Layman and John Green examine the religious bases of public opinion. Today, when commentators speak of religion and politics, they often mean the growing link between evangelical denominations and conservative politics. Indeed, as Layman has convincingly demonstrated elsewhere, through the 1980s and into the 1990s members of evangelical denominations became increasingly Republican in partisanship and conservative in political orientation relative to mainline denominations.[19]

However, a devotion to a religious identity does not always shift opinion to the right; it can also move attitudes in a liberal direction. While, today, religiosity is strongly correlated with conservative attitudes on "sex and family" issues like abortion, there are many more issues where religion has no effect. And there are a few issues—like the death penalty—where higher religiosity leads to a more liberal position.

Finally, Campbell, Layman and Green demonstrate that religion may also function as a guide for those individuals who reject religious affiliation. Even as religion has emerged as an increasingly important factor in politics, the number of Americans who do not identify with a particular religious sect has risen as well. Identification as a religious "none" therefore has important implications for public opinion.

The New Psychological Foundations of Opinion

In addition to political and group attachments, there are a host of other factors that help to shape public opinion. An important new direction in recent years is the incorporation of insights from psychology and biology about the roots of public opinion. One line of research concerns the role of emotion in shaping political preferences. At the forefront of this fast-growing subfield is Ted Brader, who, with his co-author Carly Wayne, provides an overview of the emotional foundations of democratic citizenship in Chapter 10. While emotions are a complex set of reactions to external circumstances, individuals experience emotions via their gut reactions to particular stimuli. Thus, as Brader and Wayne note, emotions are best understood as the processes that generate feelings, and serve as a motivation for action. For instance, a feeling of fear causes individuals to become more alert and focused on external threats. People therefore shift from the status quo to actively reconsider their options.

While emotions are not explicitly political, such feelings often have important political implications. Of the plethora of emotional reactions, scholars have found that three stand out: fear, anger, and enthusiasm. These emotions affect public opinion by altering whether and how citizens pay attention to political events, learn about political developments, think through their decisions, and act on their opinions. For example, in his work on campaign advertising reviewed in Chapter 10, Brader has found that campaign ads that elicit fear—through the use of ominous music and unsettling images—cause voters to reconsider their standing decisions and make decisions based on their assessment of a candidate's issue positions and leadership qualities.

A second area of research that has gained steam in recent years is of the relationship between personality and politics. Personality played an important role in some early studies of political behavior—for example, Herbert McClosky's work on personality and ideology.[20] But this line of research largely went dormant in the 1960s, perhaps because the lack of standard measures and concepts led the field of personality and psychology to acquire, as Paul Sniderman aptly puts it, "a jerry-built appearance," one without a coherent theory or set of findings.[21] The last 15 years, however, has seen a resurgence of this line of work. Beginning in the mid-1990s, scholars such as Stanley Feldman and Karen Stenner began exploring the power of authoritarianism.[22] This research harkens back to work done in the wake of the Second World War that sought to tie the rise of fascism in Europe to a particular "authoritarian" personality type, one prone to intolerance and obedience to authority.[23] While the early work had a number of measurement flaws that were quickly discovered and debated, this more recent work demonstrated that with a more careful eye towards questions of validity, the intersection of personality and politics could prove a fruitful and important area of inquiry.

More recent work has built on developments in basic measurement from psychology. In Chapter 8, Jeffery Mondak and Matthew Hibbing focus on the "Big Five" approach developed in personality psychology. This approach represents personality trait structure via attention to five trait dimensions: openness to experience, conscientiousness, extraversion, agreeableness and emotional stability. They then present original survey research that demonstrates the importance of these personality traits on a wide range of political attitudes ranging from basic political ideology to specific attitudes on moral policies, such as same-sex marriage.

In Chapter 9, Frank Gonzalez, Kevin Smith, and John Hibbing turn to the related question of the role of biology in politics. The authors who are some of the leading figures in the new field of biopolitics begin by exploring the importance of non-conscious information processing and then describe the important work that they and others are doing at the intersections of biology and politics. Some of this research studies how genetics can shape (though not determine) political attitudes. Other research explores brain activity during the process of political reasoning through functional Magnetic Resonance Imaging (fMRI). This work is still in its early stages, and studies of biology and politics have generated a great deal of controversy—as the authors note in their chapter. However, this is certainly a promising and interesting area that remains to be explored in the years to come.

The Public and Society

Understanding the structure of public opinion is an important step in assessing its political significance. But it is also important to actually detail the role it plays in the political world. The last section of this book explicitly examines how public opinion is shaped by political events and the rhetoric of politicians and how, in turn, public opinion shapes and guides the conduct of politics.

In Chapter 15, Matthew Baum explores how changes in the media environment have revolutionized the ways in which politicians reach out to the mass public when building support for their policies and programs. With the rise of the Internet, social media, and the fragmentation of the television audience among a growing number of cable channels, politicians can no longer mobilize the public through a single source. Instead, the changing media landscape means they must work harder to communicate with citizens, and be far more precise in tailoring their messages to particular sub-constituencies who might otherwise dismiss what they hear. As the media become more specialized—and as voters flock to different sources that share their pre-existing political views, in line with the rise of partisanship as a motivating force (as discussed by Hetherington in Chapter 7)—politicians face a difficult task. The opportunities to mobilize to action those citizens who already agree with a politician by "preaching to the choir" have increased as the media have become more specialized. However, opportunities to "convert the flock"—actually persuade citizens who are not inclined to share the preferences and political stances of a politician—are in increasingly short supply. Thus, while a common civic space for public affairs has not entirely disappeared, the potential for reaching across the partisan aisle through the media has certainly been shrinking in recent years.

Another important topic of research is the dynamics of democratic elections. Though the study of campaigns and elections is itself a thriving subfield in political science, it has been deeply informed by insights from the field of public opinion. In fact, many of the fundamental insights about the nature of public opinion discussed in this book came out of data collected on voter reactions to political campaigns in the 1940s and 1950s. Consider the Columbia studies led by Berelson, Lazarsfeld, and McPhee, discussed above. These scholars went into their study expecting that voters during a campaign would treat candidates as something akin to products in a supermarket—citizens would shop around, consider (and reconsider) their options, and finally arrive at a choice on Election Day. In fact, the Columbia researchers found something very different. Most people did not change their preferences. The campaign, it seemed, had little effect on voters' decisions.

In Chapter 12, John Sides and Jake Haselswerdt begin by observing that what was true in 1948 is true today. Months before an election, political scientists can predict election results. For instance, at a meeting of political scientists held over Labor Day weekend in 2012—even before the start of the Democratic National convention—a panel of political scientists each presented a forecast of the final vote tally. Almost all of them predicted the outcome within a few percentage points. The average of their predictions was a narrow Obama win of 50.2 percent two-party vote share for the Democrats, just 1.5 percent below the national percentage of the vote Barack Obama received on Election Day.

At the same time, there are lots of reasons to think that campaigns should matter. Journalists focus incessantly on the ups and downs of campaigns and analyze each day's events in the search for critical turning points. Furthermore, polls are variable, changing from day to day and week to week. This leads to an important question. How is it possible that elections are so predictable even amidst the apparent volatility of the campaign?

The answers to this question can, in part, be found in the other chapters in this volume. Voters, Sides and Haselswerdt remind us, almost never arrive at a campaign as a blank slate, devoid of ideas about politics or the candidates. In most elections, voters can draw on their long-standing political identities to guide their choices, even without any detailed information about the candidates. These identities include race, ethnicity, socioeconomic status, religion, and— above all—partisanship. The predictability of elections stems from how these fundamental factors affect how citizens vote and, by association, who wins the election. Put another way, campaign outcomes are predictable because preexisting ties to particular choices are so strong.

This, of course, is not to say that campaigns serve no function in a democratic society. True, most voters can draw on social and partisan identities to make decisions about candidates, but there will still be some citizens who are uncertain about or unfamiliar with the candidates. For these citizens, campaigns can serve a critical function. Moreover in primary or nonpartisan elections, voters cannot draw on familiar heuristics and decisions rules, such as straight-party voting.

Here too, campaigns can matter greatly. In the second half of their chapter, Sides and Haselswerdt therefore detail *how* campaigns can reinforce some existing decisions and change others' minds.

In Chapter 13, Deborah Schildkraut explores one of the most salient political controversies in recent years—public opinion concerning immigration policy. Taking a broad historical perspective, Schildkraut makes the case that American public opinion towards immigration is characterized by great ambivalence. On the one hand, while many citizens support creating a path to citizenship for undocumented immigrants, they also favor allowing law enforcement officers to check on the immigration status of aliens. In the aggregate, this has led to a situation in which there is no clear view of immigrants—half of Americans say that immigrants strengthen the country because of their hard work and talents, while 4 out of 10 Americans say that immigrants are a burden "because they take our jobs, housing, and healthcare." In this mix of competing views, many of the themes addressed elsewhere in this volume find expression, most notably the power of elite rhetoric to guide the public and the role of groups in shaping mass opinion.

Chapter 14 takes on the question of the effects of extremism in American politics. Matt Barreto and Christopher Parker use a detailed examination of the Tea Party movement—a loose amalgam of conservative groups across the nation—to explore the roots and effects of right-wing movements throughout American history. Drawing upon the long historical record, they describe the factors that motivate the reactionary right, and explore how such motivations inform the policy preferences and behavior of its constituents

Finally, in Chapter 16, Andrea Campbell and Elizabeth Rigby examine the relationship between public opinion and public policy, including processes of policy feedback. Political scientists have spent decades examining whether public opinion shapes the policies of government. But, as Campbell and Rigby note, an exclusive focus on the public opinion side of the equation paints an incomplete picture. On the one hand, the public's preferences influence policy outcomes, although this varies across time and across issues. Moreover, privileged and politically active groups are more likely to see their preferences fulfilled than others. But once policies are created, they acquire a life of their own. Thus, public policies themselves influence public opinion, so that existing policy shapes the political landscape and the possibilities for future policy. Opinion and policy move together, each influencing the other.

Campbell and Rigby use a case study of the Affordable Care Act (ACA)—the 2010 federal health reform bill nicknamed "ObamaCare"—to illustrate these effects. The ACA was one of the largest social policy reforms in generations. The political debate surrounding the passage of the bill illustrates many of the themes explored by Campbell and Rigby. On the one hand, public opinion can shape policy; differences in public support across the states influenced the pace of the implementation of the ACA. States where support was high, such as New York, were more likely to move forward to implement state-based health insurance exchanges, as specified in the federal legislation. States where support was relatively low, like Utah, were less likely to move forward. On the other hand, the case of the ACA also demonstrates that Americans' policy positions are shaped by the political discourse they encounter. For instance, survey questions that referred to the ACA as "ObamaCare" showed significantly less support for the reforms enacted by the ACA than did questions that did not.

Final Thoughts

Though I have tried to provide a comprehensive overview of the field of public opinion, this volume has only scratched the surface of the excellent research that is out there. Of necessity, there is a great deal of material that I could not cover. For instance, besides political and group attachments and personality and emotion, there are a host of other factors that help to shape public opinion. There is a large and rich literature on the power of core political values, such as subscription to principles of political equality or individualism.[24] Other scholars have explored the relationship between self interest and opinion.[25] For instance, some political scientists have examined whether those individuals with the greatest stake in a policy—parents who might be directly affected by policies designed to ensure school integration, for instance—are more likely to take a clear stance on questions relating to that policy. Here, the evidence is very mixed; somewhat surprisingly, the relationship between self interest and opinion is often quite weak. Recently, however, scholars have begun exploring other ways in which direct economic interests could matter for political choice.[26]

Beyond research on the structure of opinion, there is also a great deal of interesting work being done on the role of public opinion in society. For example, a number of researchers have explored the nature of social influence in opinion formation and dissemination, some of which harkens back to Blumer's work in the 1940s.[27] And even this work merely scratches the surface of the field.

But this book is intended to be just the starting point for most students. Hopefully, the chapters will pique your interests and give you the tools and motivation you need to go off and explore the field on your own.

Notes

1. Key, V. O., *Public Opinion and American Democracy* (New York: Alfred Knopf, 1963), p. 8.
2. Herbst, Susan, *Numbered Voices: How Opinion Polling has Shaped American Politics* (Chicago, IL: University of Chicago Press, 1993).
3. Blumer, Herbert, "Public Opinion and Public Opinion Polling," *American Sociological Review* 13 (1948): 542–549.
4. Childs, H., *Public Opinion* (Princeton, NJ: D. Van Nostrand, 1964).
5. Key (1963), p. 14.
6. Herbst (1993).

7. National Health Interview Study, "Wireless Substitution: Early Release of Estimates From the National Health Interview Survey," December 2014, retrieved from http://www.cdc.gov/nchs/data/nhis/earlyrelease/wireless201412.pdf.

8. Lippmann, Walter, *The Phantom Public* (New York: Macmillan Company, 1925), p. 24.

9. Lowell, Abbot Lawrence, *Public Opinion in War and Peace* (Cambridge, MA: Harvard University Press, 1922).

10. Berelson, Bernard, Paul Lazarsfeld, and William McPhee, *Voting* (Chicago, IL: University of Chicago Press, 1954), p. 207.

11. Stimson, James A., *Tides of Consent: How Public Opinion Shapes American Politics* (Cambridge: Cambridge University Press, 2004).

12. Achen, Christopher H., "Mass Political Attitudes and the Survey Response," *American Political Science Review* 69 (1975): 1227.

13. Converse, Philip, "The Nature of Belief Systems in Mass Publics," in *Ideology and Discontent*, ed. David Apter, p. 207.

14. Sullivan, John L., James Pierson, and George E. Marcus, "An Alternative Conceptualization of Political Tolerance: Illusory Increases, 1950s–1970s," *American Political Science Review* 73 (1979): 233–249.

15. CBS News, "Looking Ahead to the 112th congress," retrieved from http://www.cbsnews.com/stories/2010/11/11/politics/main7045964.shtml.

16. Washington Post, "Do You Approve or Disapprove of the Way Barack Obama is Handling His Job as President?" Washington Post-ABC News Poll December 11–14, 2014, retrieved from http://www.washingtonpost.com/page/2010-2019/WashingtonPost/2014/12/18/National-Politics/Polling/question_15172.xml?uuid=7Ke26IbIEeSrz1o9ezsguA.

17. Converse (1964), pp. 236–237.

18. Converse, Phillip, "Public Opinion and Voting Behavior," in *Handbook of Political Science,* ed. F. W. Greenstein and N. W. Polsby, Vol. 4 (Reading, MA: Addison-Wesley, 1975), pp. 75–169.

19. Layman, Geoffrey C., "Religion and Political Behavior in the United States: The Impact of Beliefs, Affiliations, and Commitment from 1980 to 1994," *Public Opinion Quarterly* 61 (1997): 288–316.

20. McClosky, Herbert, "Conservatism and Personality," *American Political Science Review* 52(1) (1958): 27–45.

21. Sniderman, Paul M., W. Russell Neuman, Jack Citrin, Herbert McClosky, and J. Merrill Shanks, "The Stability of Support for the Political System: The Impact of Watergate," *American Politics Quarterly* 3 (1975): 437–457.

22. Feldman, Stanley and Karen Stenner, "Perceived Threat and Authoritarianism," *Political Psychology* 18(4) (1998): 741–770; also, Stenner, Karen, *The Authoritarian Dynamic* (New York: Cambridge University Press, 2005). For more recent work in this vein, see Hetherington, Marc and Jonathan Weiler, *Authoritarianism and Polarization in American Politics* (New York: Cambridge University Press, 2009).

23. Adorno, T. W., E. Frenkel-Brunswik, D. J. Levinson, and R. N. Sanford, *The Authoritarian Personality* (New York: Harper and Row, 1950).

24. For an excellent review, see Feldman, Stanley, "Values, Ideology, and the Structure of Political Attitudes," in *Oxford Handbook of Political Psychology*, ed. David O. Sears, Leonie Huddy, and Robert Jervis (New York: Oxford University Press, 2003), pp. 477–508.

25. See, for example, Sears, David, O., Richard Lau, Tom Tyler, and Harris Allen, Jr, "Self-Interest vs. Symbolic Politics in Policy Attitudes and Presidential Voting," *American Political Science Review* 74(3) (1980): 670–684; also, Citrin, Jack, Beth

Reingold, and Donald Green, "American Identity and the Politics of Ethnic Change," *The Journal of Politics* 52 (1990): 1124–1154.

26. Gerber, Alan S. and Gregory A. Huber, "Partisanship, Political Control and Economic Assessments," *American Journal of Political Science* 54 (2010): 153–173.

27. See, for example, Huckfeldt, R. and J. Sprague, *Citizens, Politics, and Social Communication: Information and Influence in an Election Campaign* (New York: Cambridge University Press, 1995); Baybeck, Brady and Scott McClurg, "What Do They Know and How Do They Know It? An Examination of Citizen Awareness of Context," *American Politics Research* 33(4) (2005): 492–250; Mutz, Diana, *Hearing the Other Side: Deliberative versus Participatory Democracy* (New York: Cambridge University Press, 2006); Nickerson, David, "Is Voting Contagious? Evidence from Two Field Experiments," *American Political Science Review* 102(1) (2008): 49–57.

The Meaning and Measurement of Public Opinion

Chapter 1

The History and Meaning of Public Opinion

Susan Herbst

While the phrase "public opinion" was not formally coined until the eighteenth century, the concept has been with us since biblical times and the ancient Greek democracies. It seems that understanding the sentiment of common people is a chronic desire of leaders and citizens alike, no matter the form of government, nation in question, or moment in history.

In our day, the definition of public opinion seems more complex than ever before due to the intensity of global communication: changes in communication have upset all of our apple carts, making us question the value of opinion surveys, demonstrations, letters to the editor, punditry, and all of the other conventional vehicles for opinion expression and measurement we have become accustomed to. I will close this historical overview with a few reflections about the future of public opinion meaning and measures, based on the recent evolution of media like the Internet. But my central focus will be on the past, taking time to underscore pivotal eras and events, when the meaning of public opinion changed in significant ways.

The chapter is organized into four sections, reflecting my own periodization —designed for this volume—of public opinion history. First, however, a few notes of preface.

This is a Western history of public opinion with a focus on America, in part because of my own training, but primarily because we have little documentation of public opinion expression and assessment from Africa and Asia. This is not to say that popular sentiment was not important or interesting on those continents, but simply that we are challenged by the lack of a written historical record focused on public opinion before the twentieth century. Second, this chapter is most akin to intellectual history, due to the deficit of historical data that might better represent the perspectives of lower or middle class Europeans and Americans in a systematic way. Finally, my tour through hundreds of years is by nature a superficial one, and those wishing to explore different periods in more depth might begin with the bibliographic sources provided.

Public Opinion as Community: From Ancient Times to the Seventeenth Century

The phrase "public opinion" was not in common usage in ancient Greece or Rome (it was coined during the Enlightenment), but the vox populi was an intriguing phenomenon in both civilizations. We know far more about what the ancient Greeks believed, and it is clear that popular sentiment played a larger role than in Rome, where the public was called the "vulgus."[1]

In the Greek city-states, public opinion was a valued—if limited—dimension of the political sphere given the narrow definition of citizenship (confined to only a category of men), and the many contradictions of early democracy (e.g., slavery). Yet despite the limits, the Greeks were extraordinary in their attention to public opinion and its many forms—theater, rhetoric, oratory, festivals, juries, and the like.[2] These mechanisms for the expression and assessment of public opinion were abundant, creative, and very much in keeping with the outward expression of the period. If we were to gather clues about the meaning of public opinion, from these many forms of expression, they would add up to a sense of public opinion as *community*: people came together for entertainment, for debate, and even the goal of consensus. This is not to say that all participated on an equal footing or that the discourse was an inchoate model of strong democratic activity; we have far too little empirical evidence to draw such conclusions. But there is a sense that public opinion was very much tied to interpersonal networks, since ancient societies were small and built on kinship, friendship, and the face-to-face nature of tiny polities. This is a very different way of thinking about public opinion than we see in later centuries, where the scale of democracies makes an interpersonal model impossible to sustain. But suffice it to say that public opinion was formed through relationships, and expressed in much the same way, deeply embedded in social life—in the gathering of small groups, crowds, and even mobs.

The pre-eminent ancient philosophers debated public opinion, while the populace created it and went about their business.[3] Plato and Aristotle differed greatly in how they viewed public opinion, with Plato more skeptical of its role. The Aristotelian view likely matches better the hopes of at least the elite citizenry of early democracies, with their devotion to voting, juries, and political participation. Aristotle's view is worth quoting at length, the earliest and most profound view of public opinion as the aggregation of views within a community—a foreshadowing of polls and surveys to come much later:

> It is possible that the many, no one of whom taken singly is a good man, may yet taken all together be better than the few, not individually but collectively, in the same way that a feast to which all contribute is better than one given at one man's expense. For where there are many people, each has some share of goodness and intelligence, and when these are brought together, they become as it were one multiple man with many pairs

of feet and hands and many minds. So too in regard to character and the powers of perception. That is why the general public is a better judge of works of music and poetry; some judge some parts, some others, but their joint pronouncement is a verdict upon the whole. And it is this assembling in one what was before separate that gives the good man his superiority over any individual man from the masses.[4]

This view of public opinion is both ancient and very contemporary at the same time. It appeals to our current view of public opinion as the aggregation of individual opinions, yet embeds public opinion in everyday life. One gets the sense that—as Aristotle sees it—citizens can and should move from politics to art and music seamlessly, with valuable opinions on all.

My point is that early views and practices of public opinion were based in community in ways that are difficult to fathom in mass democratic societies of today. Put another way, the norms and values of a community *were* in fact its public opinion. This meaning of public opinion is the dominant one until the twentieth century, when societies grew larger and urban life dominated the political scene and the nature of intellectual life. Nonetheless, the notion of public opinion being deeply rooted in the values and day-to-day life of a community can still be found today when a polity or organization is tiny—a neighborhood, a PTA, or a place of business. And, as I mention in closing, threads of this definition of public opinion are also with us in Internet communication, as electronic communities form and social networking imitates at least some aspects of timeless community life.

The history of public opinion is nearly impossible to trace with much vigor between the ancient Greek and Roman states until the Renaissance, although of course the population grew and evolved during these centuries. Daily life was difficult, and citizens expressed their opinions in both older ways and newer ones, with petitions and bread riots characterizing the fifteenth and sixteenth centuries. I discuss these and other mechanisms elsewhere but, without question, the most important advance between the early democracies and the Renaissance was the development of the printing press, which transformed the notion of a public: while communities were often cohesive in previous centuries, the print tied people together across geography, made possible the diffusion of ideas, profoundly changed conceptions of democracy and citizenship.[5] The printing and distribution of bibles, books, pamphlets, and newspapers enabled the formation of attitudes, as well as the linear development of public thought, argument, and national identity. Print legitimated views and social groups, but most of all, led to the intensive and widespread cognitive engagement of people who previously had local conversation only to shape their world.

One last intellectual note about the pre-seventeenth century period that deserves mention is the appearance of Machiavelli's *The Prince*, one of the few compelling works on public opinion before the Enlightenment. As is well-known, the essays are written as advice to the prince, by a shrewd observer of politics, alliances, and people.[6] Machiavelli was a civil servant and warrior, but also a philosopher and advisor to political leaders. In *The Prince*, Machiavelli views people as fickle, greedy, and generally weak, hence the successful leader must adopt a kind and paternalistic style. Yet, as he notes, the populace must also be kept in line through fear, and a successful prince uses fear as his most powerful weapon, given the fragile power of love, hardly a way for a leader to maintain social control. With regard to public opinion, of course Machiavelli's views are undemocratic: the people are not capable of self-rule. Nonetheless, Machiavelli's perspectives are much in keeping with the conception of public opinion as based in community, in interpersonal networks, and reflect the norms and values of society at large. Most interesting for us, in our age where polling is so dominant, is what is missing in his thought: there is no trace of public opinion as the aggregation of individuals, or of the persuasion necessary to move them. Machiavelli's prince must persuade, but it is still his force and his power that moves public opinion, or better stated, keeps it unperturbed and in a relative state of ignorance.

Independent, Conversational Publics: From the Enlightenment to Early America

During the late seventeenth and early eighteenth centuries, we see the emergence of public opinion in a form far closer to what we understand it to be today. In fact, the phrase "public opinion" is often attributed to Jacques Necker, finance minister to King Louis XIV of France in the heady days before the revolution.[7] He coined the phrase to describe the talk of the salons and parlors of Enlightenment Paris, part of the "public sphere" identified by Jürgen Habermas in his narrative about the history of political communication.[8]

The decades before the French Revolution are without question the first truly important period in the intellectual and social history of public opinion, and so have received intensive scholarly treatment by historians and those with an interest in political development. While the ancient democracies and communities in the medieval period were defined by norms and interpersonal networks, the largely rural and agrarian economies meant that public opinion was largely under-developed as an idea and a reality. Print communication, often religious in nature, but eventually resulting in newssheets and newspapers, led to increased sophistication about citizenship and public expression that came to fruition in the decades of the Enlightenment. A few key modes of public opinion expression are worth exploring, since they led Necker to coin the phrase, but also exemplify what I mean by "conversational" public opinion.

Among the most important means of public opinion expression during the decades before the great revolutions, in Europe and America, were coffeehouses, salons, and taverns. Of course people have always gathered to eat, drink, and make merry, but these venues took on a far different character in the seventeenth and eighteenth centuries. By this era, printed news, pamphlets, and political tracts were commonplace, and read in public, given their cost (home delivery and individual subscription to newspapers is a late nineteenth century phenomenon). News was part of coffeehouse conversation—driving it, and being formed by it, since editors and journalists mingled with merchants and common folk in London coffeehouses. Information about politics, policy, commerce, and culture readily available through newspapers, and the urbanization of the population, led directly to a far more intense, dynamic, and coherent public opinion than had ever been imagined. As Habermas has noted, coffeehouses symbolize the emergence of a "public sphere"—an arena for free expression apart from the court and outside of the domestic realm. These profound changes in public life—indeed the emergence of a public life that had legitimacy and energy—would eventually lead to revolutions and the modern form of democracy.

Less democratic and open than the coffeehouse, but perhaps even more critical in the evolution of public opinion practice and philosophy, was the *salon* of pre-revolutionary Paris.[9] These were elite gatherings of statesmen, philosophers, writers, financiers, and other opinion leaders, typically held in the homes of wealthy and charismatic women. During these dinners, participants staged plays, argued about politics and the existence of God, tried out their theories of social life, and most important, sustained criticism of the king and his court. In fact, there is evidence that the king sent emissaries to the salons to report on conversations there, presumably to keep a finger on the pulse of public opinion. It might seem odd to us today, particularly in Western democracies, to view the salon as a vehicle for public opinion formation and expression, given the tiny number of privileged Parisians who took part. But the bulk of the population, even in a large and sophisticated city like Paris, was illiterate and too busy struggling to survive to have the time or opportunity for political theory.

This all changed with the onslaught of violent revolutionary fervor in France, the ideas of which were—somewhat ironically—developed in the salons of the elite. In an unusually direct mention of public opinion, the writer and literary critic Louis-Sébastien Mercier noted in 1782:

> Today, public opinion has a preponderant force in Europe that cannot be resisted. Thus in assessing the progress of enlightenment and the change it must bring about, we may hope that it will bring the greatest good to the world and that tyrants of all stripes will tremble before this universal cry that continuously rings out to fill and awaken Europe.[10]

In this period of public opinion development, expression of sentiment began energetically in salons and coffeehouses, was reflected in newspapers, and took on the occasional underclass formation of bread riots, strikes, and petitioning (during this period, petitions were presented both peacefully and violently).

These very same European-born techniques for the expression and assessment of public opinion take root, albeit in a different style, in the American revolution and early decades of the nation, described so well by Alexis de Tocqueville in his masterwork, *Democracy in America*. Tocqueville is quite interesting on this point, admiring public opinion and its democratic voice in a new nation, but seeing seeds of danger as well—the "tyranny of the majority", as he called it. As Leo Damrosch notes in his scholarly treatment of Tocqueville's travels of 1831:

> Only in hindsight could Americans appreciate the real force of Tocqueville's insight: public opinion was indeed the true danger, and prejudices might actually be strongest where expression was free. A self-governing people could internalize rigid attitudes and inhibitions, and in effect police its own behavior.[11]

To summarize this extraordinary period, from the inchoate public opinion of salons to the great revolutions and the birth of an American nation, we can detect some of the ancient threads—people still lived in communities that valued face-to-face relationships, conversation, kinship and friendship. The social imagination of most people—from elites to the lower classes—was largely a local one and public opinion took on this flavor. But it was becoming far more national and far reaching, with the development of print. Public opinion was suddenly a more powerful force to be reckoned with, whether an elite-driven revolution like the American one or a more proletariat French revolution. The power of public opinion, even if often illiterate and uneven, was clear and compelling, and theorists of the nineteenth century—Tocqueville, Marx, Bryce, Tönnies—recognized it with equal fervor. It was still a period characterized by human relations and towns, but the independent voice of the public had emerged never to be entirely silenced again, no matter the authoritarian intentions of a leader.

Numbered Voices and the Diffusion of Media: Mid-Nineteenth Century through the 1950s

While public opinion as a phenomenon is largely European in character, the accelerated development of the United States in the mid-nineteenth century made America the most interesting and complex site for the practice and philosophy of public opinion. In fact, Tocqueville and then the British visitor Lord Bryce, a few decades later, were among many European travelers drawn overseas. Many from the old world sought an understanding of democratic institutions, of political behavior, federalism, industry, and most of all, the strange and compelling force that is public opinion.

As is well documented by historians, the American nineteenth century was a confluence of profound changes in manufacturing, demographics,

communication, and transportation, all of which were reflected in the growth
and complexity of public opinion. Political parties evolved quickly, reflecting
and shaping the popular sentiment, through hand-to-hand combat in the urban
precincts and the highly partisan newspapers of the time. Immigration and
urbanization led to an extraordinarily stratified, even booming, population and
public opinion reflected the mobility and volatility of the time. Perhaps it was
inevitable that, in trying to understand the complex nature of public opinion,
journalists, statesmen, party operatives, and citizens themselves took to more
quantitative methods for opinion expression and measurement. In new larger-
scale democracies, where elections determined the course of a community and
a nation, the aggregation of individual opinions through counting and straw
polling was vital.

While voting and pre-election straw polling can be traced as far back as
biblical times, counting heads and opinions fit a growing democracy perfectly,
hence the explosion of these polls in the nineteenth century. As I note elsewhere,
citizens polled themselves and sent the counts into their local newspapers for
publication, journalists counted votes and opinions as they traveled the rails of
the Midwest, and of course party operatives polled in private, as they do today,
to get a sense of the prevailing winds. The intensity of polling, partisanship,
and campaigning was fierce by century's end and indeed many aspects of the
1896 U.S. presidential election reflect this change (the race was between William
McKinley and William Jennings Bryan). This particular election foreshadowed
the culture of politics we experience in the twenty-first century—highly emotional issues, new demographic coalitions of voters, wild campaign spending,
hyperbolic oratory, mud-slinging, and the extensive use of train travel to move
candidates and voters. For example, there was a fierce debate between the
candidates about the gold standard, which Bryan believed hurt rural working
people, deeply in trauma due to the 1893 economic downturn. He gave one of
the most famous speeches in American political history (the "Cross of Gold"
speech) at the 1896 Democratic Presidential Convention. It was one of the
earliest "rock star" type performances in our history, inspiring many and waging
class warfare in rhetorical terms. Bryan's populism was unique in its power and
formulation, and unforgettable in its effects on American politics even today.

Most of all, the election highlighted the centrality of public opinion—its
measurement and persuasion. After 1896, no campaign manager or candidate
would ever conceive of running without strategizing an approach to the ever-
evolving American public.

And everyone thought they owned the right to poll, from women in quilting
bees and college students to factory workers and drinking clubs. During the 1896
election, a railroad worker wrote a typical, colorful partisan polling report to
the *Chicago Tribune*:

> John J. Byrnes, General Passenger Agent and Auditor of the Southern
> California railroad, reached Chicago yesterday morning on a Santa Fe train

on which, among other passengers, were seventy-five Californians. Some one polled the denizens of the Far West and Bryan got fifteen votes. Just before Mr. Byrnes came East a large manufacturing plant in Los Angeles in which 1000 men are employed was polled, and McKinley was the choice of 997. Mr. Byrnes, who until this campaign has been a Democrat, is confident McKinley will carry California by a big majority.[12]

The nineteenth century was a period of tremendous quickening in the quantification of public opinion in the United States, in part because of the increasing intensity and partisanship, but also fed by the rise of the sciences, where measurement was central. If we could calculate the best ways to assess crop production or speed factory assembly lines, a booming industrial nation could also bring science to its democratic practices. Polling—unscientific though it was at the turn of the century—was as democratic as voting, and as satisfying, in a nation with so many people and opinions to count.

At the turn of the century and into the pre-war period, public opinion gained in thoughtfulness and sophistication due to a proliferation of print media, then eventually, radio. Most interesting was the explosion of magazines during these decades, the era when many periodicals still with us—*The New Republic, The Atlantic*, and *Harper's*—began or gained subscribers at an impressive pace. The rising literacy of the population enabled the appearance of thoughtful publications, leading to an even more engaged, serious public. As a result, polling the public became an extraordinarily attractive political and financial endeavor in the 1920s and 1930s. This is the period when a magazine called *The Literary Digest* began extensive polling of the public, and many of the polling firms still with us today were born. For example, George Gallup—a marketing expert—got his start as a pollster in the 1930s. In 1936, he correctly predicted victory for Franklin Roosevelt in his presidential bid against Alf Landon. The *Digest*, by contrast, had predicted a win for Landon, and so this year marked the ascendency of Gallup's more scientific methods. The *Digest* soon halted publication, and Gallup led the development of a far more sophisticated polling industry in the United States.[13]

As radio diffused in the early century and through the Second World War, a nation bound by communication was taken for granted: no one was out of reach, from the great plains to the depths of Appalachia. But what is interesting for our purposes here is the solidity of the notion of an *American public*, whose opinions could and would be counted.

From an Atomized Public to a Connected One: Broadcast Media and the Internet

By the 1950s, with the diffusion of television, Americans saw themselves as a diverse but unified public, brought together by culture, habits, media, the struggles of a depression, and two world wars of enormous consequence. We were never a cohesive nation, a fairy tale that no scholar can support. But by mid-century, the notion that publics could exist, even if momentarily, and that they could "speak", was as concrete as the massive skyscrapers of Chicago or the new highways that crisscrossed every state in the nation.

As so many have pointed out, television brought Americans together through shared programming, media events both planned and unexpected (e.g., the Kennedy assassination), but it also separated or atomized them. Even more compelling than radio, television in the United States was a domestic technology, one that drew viewers home and away from streets, bars, parks, and public space. Americans had been a people who, weather permitting, lived life in the open, from the giant torchlight political parades of the 1800s to amusement parks, movie theaters, urban street life of the tenements, and state fairs. Television began to affect this public culture, and some would argue, had a hand in abolishing it. While one could argue for multiple forces steering people toward the nuclear family, this turn inward was an undeniable reality in the latter half of the twentieth century to the present day.[14]

What did this type of cultural transformation mean for public opinion? With regard to measurement, it coincided with the rise of the sample survey, a systematic and scientific way to sample Americans' opinions either through visits to homes or phone calls to households.[15] So the "turning inward" of Americans, to their families, moving out of inner cities and toward the suburbs, fit squarely with a means of opinion measurement that relied on people sitting still: Americans were home and available to opine. The engagement of Americans with television, ever evolving and expanding in its offerings, focused them on the news and made the networks enormously powerful and influential. Politicians used the new medium, some better than others, but there was no question by the mid-1960s that visual electronic media would be the most dominant tool one could find to shape public opinion.

In terms of the four grand periods of this chapter, the televisual age drops much of the earlier sense—present in the three previous eras—that public opinion was based in interpersonal community and dialogue. With the advent of television, Americans were more closely tethered to the medium—to Walter Cronkite or Ed Sullivan—than they were to each other. The communities of ancient Greece, of the Enlightenment coffeehouses, of colonial taverns and the local gatherings so attractive to a visiting Tocqueville, were no longer interchangeable with the notion of public opinion. Public opinion in the twentieth century was based less in community norms, values, and exchange and more suitably defined as the aggregation of atomized households and their inhabitants. The conversational and interpersonal meanings of public opinion—the phenomena that prompted Necker to coin the phrase—no longer meant much in a modern world that lived in single family suburban houses or longed to.

Television had a profound effect on the nature of publics themselves—how they are formed and how they interact. And it still does: Americans get their news from cable television in great numbers and newer organizations like

MSNBC and Fox News are tremendously influential in shaping both opinion and public discourse. But try as they might to modernize, by reading Twitter messages on air or providing social networking opportunities, cable news programs are still very much in the "one to many" mode of early television. We don't interact with television hosts, they are not our friends, and we have no relationship with them.

Interestingly, the emergence of the Internet has brought us back around—although perhaps not full circle—to a more conversational mode of public opinion. I would argue that we live now in the most complex of times, with regard to the meaning of public opinion: all at once, it makes sense to define, express, and measure public opinion through traditional local means (local zoning board hearings), Facebook, opinion polls, demonstrations, Internet chat, and so many other means of communication. Perhaps Jacques Necker's meaning of public opinion—the wide-ranging, undisciplined, but engaging talk of the salons—fits America in the early twenty-first century?

The Return of the Repressed: Conversation and the Internet

It remains to be seen how American public opinion will be shaped by social networking, the abundance of political blogs, and upcoming forms of face-to-face chat that will make teleconferencing easy for the individual citizen. Much has changed already, as the Internet breaks down barriers and speeds the news cycle, forcing constant action and reaction by our candidates and leaders. Citizens try to keep up or not, but we all know that a world of debate about political and social issues awaits us at all hours on our screens, should we choose to lurk or actually participate. Internet literacy is booming, and young people know of no other way to learn of public opinion than the Internet, rich with data and full of serendipity. The immediacy of communication that we experience is perhaps the most gratifying aspect of all: there is no more trying to get one's modest letter to the editor published, or hoping in vain for a scene of the president on the basketball court. Images, ideas, debates, and screeds abound, and link us to a complex, but seemingly smaller world.

Public opinion—its dynamic and its meaning—evolves very slowly as my lengthy sweep of history demonstrates. Change seems to come at a faster pace now, but predicting the future of political discourse and popular sentiment would be a dangerous game. All that said, I close with three insights about public opinion in our current period, informed by history:

Citizens will have more control over the shape of public opinion and how it is measured. With the easy access afforded by the web, most people can express their opinions to large audiences, no matter their thoughtfulness, or accuracy of their facts. Whether this direct expression of public opinion—pursued without the gatekeepers and editors of previous periods—enhances the nature of free expression or the quality of public policy remains to be seen. But it is clear that we shall never return to a political realm where elites tightly regulate the nature and flow of popular beliefs. This is a profound change in the nature of public opinion, unique to the early twenty-first century and our technological environment. It is democratizing and it levels the communicative playing field, even if not the economic one.

Media organizations will need a fundamentally different business model. As has been pointed out repeatedly over the past few years, both advertising and subscriber-based models for sustaining a journalistic enterprise are failing even our most esteemed elite newspapers and networks. The future is unclear, but as more regional newspapers collapse or turn to shared wire services for content, a loss of professional, sophisticated reporting and investigative journalism will fundamentally change the nature of public opinion. A narrowing of news sources, and a media sphere where the same content is spread far and wide, will not enable the marketplace of ideas we hope for in a lively democracy. It is a dire moment for media professionals, and their organizational infrastructure matters immensely for the formation of intelligent public opinion.

Political participation is in danger of disappearing. Despite the abundance of information and opinions we now have, through our many Internet and broadcast sources, participation in politics has not risen in parallel. Turnout in presidential elections, for example, has not increased dramatically, nor do we see a rise in demonstrations or political participation at the local levels. While candidate fundraising has become easier, and there are some odd, media-induced political movements springing up (e.g., the Tea Party of 2010), it would be difficult to locate an uptick in actual political behavior. Perhaps the sociologists Robert Merton and Paul Lazarsfeld were right, in 1948, when they predicted that mass media (radio, in their time) would lull us into an *informed yet inactive state.* They wrote, famously:

> Exposure to this flood of information may serve to narcotize rather than to energize the average reader or listener. As an increasing meed [sic] of time is devoted to reading and listening, a decreasing share is available for organized action. The individual reads accounts of issues and problems and may even discuss alternative lines of action. But this rather intellectualized, rather remote connection with organized social action is not activated. The interested and informed citizen can congratulate himself on his lofty state of interest and information and neglect to see that he has abstained from decision and action. In short, he takes his secondary contact with the world of political reality, his reading and listening and thinking, as a vicarious performance. He comes to mistake *knowing* about problems of the day *for doing* something about them. His social conscience remains spotlessly clean. He *is* concerned. He *is* informed. And he has all sorts of ideas as to what should be done. But, after he has gotten through his dinner and after he has listened to his favored radio programs and after he has read

his second newspaper of the day, it is really time for bed. In this peculiar respect, mass communications may be included among the most respectable and efficient of social narcotics. They may be so fully effective as to keep the addict from recognizing his own malady.[16]

It seems a fine note on which to conclude this brief history of public opinion, as public opinion is not just a political phenomenon but a fundamental, endangered aspect of democracy. Without an unhindered yet intelligently engaged vox populi effective democratic institutions are elusive to us, hence the centrality of public opinion to the ambitions of both developed and developing nations around the world. Throughout human history, the popular sentiment has inevitably found vehicles and thousands of expressive forms. But it is fragile as well, crushed by many a dictator or authoritarian government. Public opinion as a practice and an ideal is very much in the hands of the people, should they choose to value it.

Notes

1. See Paul Palmer, "The Concept of Public Opinion in Political History," in *Essays in History and Political Theory in Honor of Charles Howard McIlwain* (New York: Russell & Russell, 1964).
2. An excellent starting point for learning about the history of public opinion is Wilhelm Bauer's "Public Opinion," in E. Seligman, ed., *Encyclopaedia of the Social Sciences* (New York: Macmillan, 1930).
3. See David Minar's brilliant intellectual history of public opinion, "Public Opinion in the Perspective of Political Theory," *Western Political Quarterly* 13 (1960): 31–44.
4. Aristotle, *The Politics*, ed. and trans. T.A. Sinclair (Baltimore, MD: Penguin Books, 1962).
5. See my *Numbered Voices: How Opinion Polling Has Shaped American Politics* (Chicago: University of Chicago Press, 1993). On the history of printing, see Elizabeth Eisenstein, *The Printing Press as an Agent of Change: Communications and Cultural Transformations in Early-Modern Europe* (Cambridge: Cambridge University Press, 1979).
6. Niccolò Machiavelli, *The Prince*, trans. N.H. Thompson (Buffalo, NY: Prometheus, 1986).
7. See Palmer, p. 238.
8. Jürgen Habermas, *The Structural Transformation of the Public Sphere: An Inquiry into a Category of Bourgeois Society* (Cambridge: MIT Press, 1989).
9. Much of the best work on Parisian salons is by Dena Goodman. See "Enlightenment Salons: The Convergence of Female and Philosophic Ambitions," *Eighteenth Century Studies* 22 (Spring 1989): 329–350.
10. Keith Baker, "Politics and Public Opinion Under the Old Regime," in J. Censer and J. Popkin, eds, *Press and Politics in Pre-Revolutionary France* (Berkeley: University of California Press, 1987).
11. Leo Damrosch, *Tocqueville's Discovery of America* (New York: Farrar, Straus and Giroux, 2010), p. 101.
12. *Chicago Tribune*, 11 August 1896, p. 4. McKinley lost narrowly in California that year.

13. See my *Numbered Voices* for more commentary on the *Digest*.
14. Robert Putnam, *Bowling Alone: The Collapse and Revival of American Community* (New York: Simon and Schuster, 2001).
15. For a history of academic and industry survey research, see Jean Converse, *Survey Research in the United States: Roots and Emergence, 1890—1960* (Berkeley, CA: University of California Press, 1987); also see Sarah Igo, *The Averaged American: Surveys, Citizens, and the Making of a Mass Public* (Cambridge, MA: Harvard University Press, 2007).
16. Paul Lazarsfeld and Robert Merton, "Mass Communication, Popular Taste, and Organized Social Action," in J.D. Peters and P. Simonson, *Mass Communication and American Thought: Key Texts 1919–1968* (Boulder, CO: Rowman and Littlefield, 2004), p. 235.

The Practice of Survey Research

Changes and Challenges

D. Sunshine Hillygus

After pre-election polls predicted the wrong winner of the 2008 Democratic primary in New Hampshire, a *Washington Post* headline asked "Can we ever trust the polls again?"[1] Concerns about the increasing methodological challenges facing survey research in recent years have undermined confidence in the entire survey enterprise. Surveys rely on the cooperation of people to check boxes and answer questions, yet people today are harder to reach, and when contacted they are less likely to answer questions. At the same time, there has been a proliferation in the amount of polling—from horserace numbers in the newspaper headlines to opt-in "polls" predicting sports outcomes on ESPN.com or judging celebrity outfits in *US Weekly* magazine. With so many polls, it is hard to figure out which ones are accurate and reliable.

It would be easy to blame the media for blurring the line between quality and junk polls. After all, many mainstream news organizations sponsor both open-access "straw polls" on their websites as well as traditional, scientific surveys—and fail to distinguish the methodological differences between the two. ABC News polling director Gary Langer chides the news media for indulging in "the lazy luxury of being both data hungry and math phobic."[2] Journalists value the credibility and authority that survey numbers add to a story, but they often fail to scrutinize those numbers for methodological rigor. The media, however, are not the only ones to blame. In academia, we have also seen increasing variability in survey quality. Surveys that would fail to meet the minimum quality standards of the top news organizations are currently being published in social science journals.[3] Some scholars justify their use by arguing that because all surveys are flawed it is just as valid to use inexpensive, opt-in samples. Others are simply unaware of how to evaluate survey quality or naive about the way survey design decisions can affect the validity of their research conclusions.

In this essay, I will outline some of the key methodological challenges in conducting, using, and evaluating surveys as a measure of public opinion. This essay has three "take-home" messages: first, I will explain why all surveys are not created equal. Some surveys should be trusted more than others, and, unfortunately, it is not sufficient to make assumptions about survey quality based on polling topic (say, politics rather than entertainment), sample size, or sponsorship. The total survey error perspective provides a framework for evaluating how various aspects of the survey method can influence the validity and reliability of the resulting survey statistics. Second, I hope this essay makes clear that NO survey is perfect. While there is significant variation in survey quality, not even our "gold standard" surveys like the American National Election Study should be immune from scrutiny. Finally, I will appeal for journalists and scholars at all levels to provide enough information about their survey methods for readers to assess the knowledge claims being made.

The Data Stork Myth

Despite increasing concerns about survey quality, surveys remain the cornerstone of research on economic, political, and social phenomena across academic, commercial, nonprofit, and government sectors. When properly designed, surveys can be a powerful tool for collecting information about the attitudes, characteristics, and behaviors of individuals, households, and organizations. Too often, however, scholars and journalists tend to treat survey data as if they have simply been delivered by a data stork, failing to question where they came from, how they were produced, and by what methodology. Yet a survey involves numerous steps and decisions, and with each one, error can be introduced into the resulting survey statistics.

A significant part of the difficulty in establishing survey quality standards is not that our scientific understanding of survey methodology is flawed or inadequate, but rather that scientific research in survey methodology has not permeated the broader community of survey consumers. In the survey methodology literature, scholars have adopted a total survey error perspective that recognizes the need to consider a variety of different types of error in evaluating survey quality.[4] Figure 2.1, reproduced from Herbert Weisberg's textbook *The Total Survey Error Approach*, summarizes these various sources of error in the survey process.[5] In this chapter, I discuss some of these—sampling error, coverage error, non-response error, and measurement error—highlighting specific challenges and controversies. I first provide an overview of the survey process and introduce some key terminology.

A high quality survey is one that tries to minimize all sources of error within the inevitable time and budgetary constraints of the project. The goal is to produce survey results that are *valid* and *reliable*, terms that have specific meaning and usage in scientific research. Validity refers to the accuracy of the results, while reliability refers to consistency or stability in the results if the survey were to be repeated in identical conditions. Archery offers a common analogy to clarify the difference between the concepts of validity and reliability. Research that is reliable but not valid is like an archer who always hits about the same place but not near the bullseye. Research that is valid but not reliable is like the archer who hits various places centered around the bullseye, but not very accurately. Again, the goal is to be both reliable and valid, like an archer who hits consistently close to the bullseye.

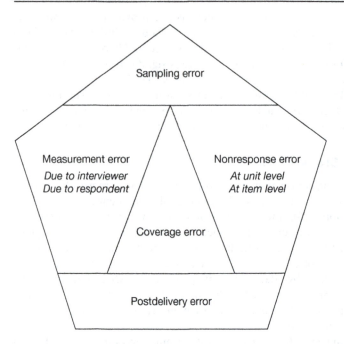

Figure 2.1 The Total Survey Error Perspective (source: Weisberg 2005).

Overview of the Survey Process

When we think of surveys, we often have in mind the resulting survey statistics. For example, a recent news story reported that 41 percent of Americans support legalizing marijuana, citing a CNN poll. This survey statistic about public opinion is the product of a very specific survey process that involves a series of consequential methodological decisions and assumptions. In small print at the end of the article, we find some of that methodological information: "Interviews with 1,010 adult Americans were conducted by residential telephone on September 21–23, 2011. The margin of sampling error is plus or minus 3 percentage points." In this section, I will outline the basic process involved in reaching conclusions about public opinion on the basis of a smaller sample of respondents.

The first step in the survey process is deciding on the *target population*; that is, the group to whom the survey is intended to generalize. The poll obviously did not ask all Americans their opinion on this issue; rather, they surveyed 1,010 individuals that they believed were representative of the broader American public. Their target population was the entire adult US population.[6] Pre-election polls, in contrast, typically want to generalize to the US voting population— adult citizens who will cast a ballot in the election (the so-called "likely voters"). Other surveys are interested in even more specialized populations; for example, a recent survey on alcohol and drug use at Duke University was meant to represent only those undergraduates currently enrolled at the university.

After determining the target population, the next step in the survey process is specifying a *sample frame*—lists or procedures that identify all elements of the target population. The sample frame may be a list of telephone numbers, maps of areas in which households can be found, or a procedure (like random digit dialing) that could identify the target population. At their simplest, sampling frames just list the phone numbers, addresses, or email addresses of individuals in the target population, such as the list of student email addresses for the Duke University student survey. In the case of the CNN poll, random digit dialing was likely used. In random digit dialing, a computer generates a random set of seven-digit numbers (in this case, excluding nonresidential and cellular exchanges). Compared to using a telephone book or other list of telephone numbers, an RDD sample frame has the advantage of including unlisted numbers.

Often, the list will not perfectly capture the entire target population. For example, the target population of the CNN poll is U.S. adults, but the sample frame excludes individuals living in households without landline telephones. This creates *coverage error*—the error that arises when the sampling approach does not include all of the target population. That is, when there is a failure to give some persons in the target population a chance of selection into the sample. If those included in the sample frame differ from those who are not, that coverage error can create coverage bias, affecting the accuracy of the resulting survey statistics. For example, there is a growing concern that the recent rise in the number of cell-only households threatens the generalizability of telephone surveys. Because cell-phone only respondents tend to be younger, lower income, and are more likely to be racial or ethnic minorities, there is concern that omitting them from pre-election polls leads to underestimation of Democratic candidate support.[7]

Once a sample frame has been identified, individual cases are randomly selected to be in the survey. Because the survey is administered to a sample, rather than all, of the target population, it is subject to random sampling error. This is the "margin of error" mentioned in the methodological disclosure of the CNN poll. Of course, these selected cases are just the people asked to be in the survey—many of them will be difficult to reach, will refuse to participate, or will drop out during the survey. *Nonresponse error* occurs when the individuals invited to take the survey are not interviewed. And the *respondents* are the subsample of the selected cases who actually complete the survey and on which the analysis is conducted.[8] Critically, if those who respond are different from those who do not (either because of coverage error or nonresponse error) the resulting survey statistics can be biased.[9]

Figure 2.2 illustrates the key steps in the survey sampling process using the CNN poll as an example. As shown in the figure, each step in the survey sampling process can introduce uncertainty and bias in the resulting survey

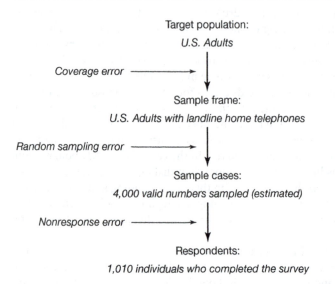

Target population:

U.S. Adults

Coverage error

Sample frame:

U.S. Adults with landline home telephones

Random sampling error

Sample cases:

4,000 valid numbers sampled (estimated)

Nonresponse error

Respondents:

1,010 individuals who completed the survey

Figure 2.2 Steps and Potential Error in Survey Sampling Process, CNN poll example.

statistics. These errors can threaten the ability to generalize from the sample to the target population.

Traditionally, survey users have focused on sampling error as the metric for evaluating survey quality. As mentioned, *sampling error* represents the uncertainty or imprecision in estimates based on random chance that occurs simply because we observe data from a sample of individuals in the population rather than every individual in the population. Sampling error is often reported as margin of error. In the case of the CNN poll, we should interpret the results as showing that public support for marijuana legalization is 41 percent +/- 3 percentage points. This tells us how precise we are in our estimate of public opinion on this issue—the larger the margin of error, the less confidence we have in our estimate. The literal interpretation of the margin of error is somewhat long-winded and awkward: if the survey were repeated many times, 95 percent of the samples of this size would be expected to produce a margin of error that captures the true percentage of Americans supporting the legalization of marijuana. [10]

Critically, the size of sampling error depends only on the size of the sample collected—the larger the sample, the less uncertainty in the estimate. Sampling error does not tell us about whether our estimates are biased or inaccurate. It is a measure of reliability. Thus, despite the traditional focus on sampling error, it may well be the *least* important aspect of survey error; for a survey of a given size sampling error simply "is what it is," whereas other sources of error— coverage error, nonresponse error, measurement error—can be minimized through various design decisions. [11]

The total survey error perspective highlights the need to take into account both sampling error and *nonsampling* error in evaluating survey quality. As such, we need to evaluate additional sources of error in the survey sampling process—coverage error and nonresponse error. At the same time, it recognizes that the substantive conclusions drawn from surveys also depend on the measurement process, in which scholars have to make decisions about how to operationalize and measure their theoretical constructs and then have to make decisions about how to code and adjust the resulting data. Nonsampling error is different from sampling error in that it can affect not only the reliability of the results, but also the accuracy. These errors can introduce bias in the survey results if they are systematic rather than random. In the remainder of this essay, I will use the total survey perspective to outline some of the key contemporary threats to survey quality.

Probability vs. Nonprobability Sampling

Surveys are typically conducted in order to make generalizations about a target population from data collected from a smaller subset—the sample. The ability to generalize from the sample to the population rests on the use of *probability sampling*. Probability samples are ones that use random selection. As pollsters like to joke, "If you don't believe in random sampling, the next time you have a blood test tell the doctor to take it all." Random selection of respondents means that errors—both those observed and unobserved—cancel out over the long run. In order to have a random selection method, it's necessary for each member of the target population to have a chance of being selected into the sample. With a random probability sample, the results will be close (within the "margin of error") to what we would have found had we interviewed the entire population. George Gallup liked to compare sampling public opinion to sampling soup—"as long as it was a well-stirred pot, you only need a single sip to determine the taste."

In contrast, *nonprobability samples* select respondents from the target population in some nonrandom manner, so that some members of the population have no chance of being selected. For example, many media organizations invite visitors to their websites to answer "straw polls." This type of nonprobability sampling is often called *convenience sampling* because members of the population are chosen based on their relative ease of access. A variant, *quota sampling*, identifies a set of groups (e.g., men, women, 18–25-year-olds, 26–40-year-olds, etc.) and specifies a fixed number of people to be recruited for each group. Interviewing then proceeds until the quota is reached for each group. For example, convenience samples might be designed so that they match the population proportions on age, gender, and socioeconomic status. Unfortunately, some people will be more likely to visit the website than others and some website visitors will be more likely to participate than others, so the results are not representative of any broader population—even if they look demographically similar because of quotas.

The *Literary Digest* polling fiasco of 1936 is the classic example of how nonprobability samples can lead to biased conclusions. The popular magazine had correctly predicted the winner in the previous five presidential elections, but in 1936 it incorrectly predicted that Alf Landon would beat FDR in that year's election by 57 to 43 percent (FDR won with 60.8 percent of the popular vote). The *Digest* had mailed over 10 million survey questionnaires to its subscribers and to names drawn from lists of automobile and telephone owners. More than 2.3 million people responded, but it turns out that, in 1936, those who owned automobiles, telephones, or had the disposable income to subscribe to a magazine were not a random cross-section of the voting public.

More recently, a *Scientific American* online poll illustrated the perils of nonprobability surveys. The popular science magazine's online poll asking their readers about climate change attracted the attention of climate skeptic bloggers who directed their own readers to participate in the poll. The resulting poll results found that 80 percent of respondents denied climate change and 84 percent answered that "The Intergovernmental Panel on Climate Change is . . . A corrupt organization, prone to groupthink, with a political agenda." Although it's not unusual for online polls to be hijacked by activists, these skewed polling results have since been reported in a *Wall Street Journal* editorial and included in Congressional testimony with no mention of the unscientific methodology.[12]

Probability sampling allows us to calculate sampling error so we can estimate how much our sample might differ from the target population (the margin of error). In nonprobability sampling, in contrast, the degree to which the sample differs from the population remains unknown and unknowable. Even if the sample looks demographically similar to the target population (as with quota sampling), we have no way to evaluate if the sample is representative on unobserved characteristics.

One of the key contemporary debates in public opinion research regards the quality of nonprobability-based online panel surveys. New technologies have both made probability sampling more difficult and made nonprobability sampling—especially with online panels—easy and inexpensive. The main concern with Internet based surveys is not just that they will miss those without Internet access—Internet usage rates are quickly approaching the same coverage rate of landline telephones. The key hurdle is that, in most cases, it is difficult to define an appropriate sample frame from which to draw a random sample that is a reasonable approximation of the target population.[13] In other words, there is typically no list of Internet users from which a random sample can be drawn. While not a problem in cases where a population list exists and is reachable online (e.g., email addresses of students at a university), for general population surveys, the nature of the Internet means that "frames of Internet users in a form suitable for sampling do not—and likely will not—exist."[14]

This issue is a source of confusion for academics and journalists alike. For one, not all Internet surveys are the same. In cases where the population list is known and reachable online (e.g., email addresses of students at a university or business CEOs), web surveys are appropriate—even preferable.[15] It is also possible to draw a probability-based sample using a traditional technique (such as RDD or address-based sampling), and then provide Internet access to those without it. This is the approach of the GFK KnowledgeNetworks Panel and the Rand American Life Panel, for example. But the majority of web-based surveys, including those by well-known firms like YouGov/Polimetrix, Harris Interactive, and Zogby Internet, rely on nonprobability online panels. In such cases the respondents are (nonrandomly) recruited through a variety of techniques: website advertisements, targeted emails, and the like.[16] Individuals are then signed up in an online panel in which they are regularly invited to answer surveys in exchange for financial incentives or other awards. Even if a given sample is randomly selected from this online panel, the pool of potential respondents are all people who initially "opted in" to the respondent pool so it is not representative of the general population.

A second source of confusion is that nonprobability samples are often claimed to be "representative" because the sample looks like the target population on a set of observed characteristics; often through adjustments (e.g., weighting and/or matching) of the opt-in sample to census benchmarks.[17] There are, however, only a limited number of benchmarks on which the sample can be compared, so these samples still require the untestable assumption that unmatched characteristics are ignorable.[18] And research has shown, for instance, that those who volunteer to participate in surveys are often more informed, knowledgeable, and opinionated about the survey topic even if they look demographically similar to the general population.[19] A recent taskforce of the American Association for Public Opinion Research (AAPOR), the leading professional organization of public opinion and survey research professionals in the U.S., tackled the issue of online panels and forcefully concludes that "There currently is no generally accepted theoretical basis from which to claim that survey results using samples from nonprobability online panels are projectable to the general population . . . Claims of 'representativeness' should be avoided." Pollsters Gary Langer and Jon Cohen offer a similar, if more colorful, conclusion:

> anyone following the polls is probably finding it increasingly difficult to separate signal from noise . . . .In reality, there are good polls and bad, reliable methods and unreliable ones. To meet reasonable news standards, a poll should be based on a representative, random sample of respondents; "probability sampling" is a fundamental requirement of inferential statistics, the foundation on which survey research is built. Surrender to "convenience" or self-selected samples of the sort that so many people click on the Internet, and you're quickly afloat in a sea of voodoo data. . . . Probability sampling has its own challenges, of course. Many telephone surveys are conducted using techniques that range from the minimally

acceptable to the dreadful. When it's all just numbers, these, too, get tossed into the mix, like turpentine in the salad dressing.[20]

To be sure, there is considerable variation in the quality of nonprobability samples, with some methods being better or worse depending on the particular outcome of interest. For example, Ansolabehere and Rivers (2013) offer a detailed overview of the YouGov methods and find only minor implications for studying vote choice.[21] There are also many research questions for which a probability sample will not be a priority. For example, scholars conducting survey experiments are often more concerned with internal validity (a clear causal effect) than external validity (generalizability). Likewise, focused exploratory research might use a nonprobability sample to generate hypotheses or pilot various measurements. There may also be times when the researcher simply wants to demonstrate that a particular trait occurs in a population. These are all cases in which the researcher does not intend to draw inferences to the broader population, so a nonprobability sample can be a cost effective method for the research goals.

In sum, the validity of inferences from a sample to a larger population rests on random probability sampling. In contrast, nonprobability samples—no matter their size—may not be generalizable; there is no way to know how respondents and nonrespondents might differ across an infinite number of characteristics related to the outcome of interest. Procedures such as quota sampling, matching, or weighting will ensure a convenience sample looks like the target population on a set of observed characteristics, but inherently assume that unobserved characteristics do not influence the phenomenon being studied—an often unrealistic, untestable and unstated assumption. This does not mean that nonprobability samples should never be conducted, but it is critical to be transparent about the methodology being used. AAPOR, for example, recommends the following wording when documenting surveys with nonprobability samples:

> Respondents for this survey were selected from among those who have [volunteered to participate/registered to participate in (company name) online surveys and polls]. The data (have been/have not been) weighted to reflect the demographic composition of (target population). Because the sample is based on those who initially self-selected for participation [in the panel] rather than a probability sample, no estimates of sampling error can be calculated. All sample surveys and polls may be subject to multiple sources of error, including, but not limited to sampling error, coverage error, and measurement error.

Unfortunately, there is a deep and growing schism in academia, journalism, and politics over the value of nonprobability samples. On one side are those who insist that statistical theory renders all nonprobability samples useless; on the other side are those who believe that nonprobability samples likely get us "close enough" to the right answer. Wherever one falls in this debate, we have an obligation to fully disclose the research methodology being used. At minimum, we should explicitly discuss the assumptions underlying our substantive conclusions.

Nonresponse Error

Nonresponse errors refer to errors introduced by the practical reality that surveys almost never collect data from all sampled cases. People are often difficult to reach or they refuse to participate. In fact, most of us have probably contributed to nonresponse in a survey if we have ever hung up the phone when we realized it was a pollster on the other end of the line interrupting our dinner. There has been considerable focus on nonresponse error in recent decades and rightfully so. In recent decades, response rates have declined precipitously across government, academic, and media surveys. Given the barrage of tele-marketing calls, spam, and junk mail, people are increasingly hesitant to participate in surveys. And technologies like voicemail and caller ID make it easier than ever to avoid intrusions from strangers. Nonresponse error will create nonresponse bias if those who respond are different from those who do not.

The most common marker for nonresponse error has traditionally been the survey response rate. In its most basic form, response rate is calculated as the number of people you actually surveyed divided by the number of people you tried to survey. Even high-budget "gold standard" academic surveys, such as the General Social Survey and the American National Election Study have seen sharp declines in response rates. For example, the ANES response rate declined from 74 percent in 1992 to less than 60 percent in 2008 to just 38 percent in 2012.[22] Moreover, much of the decline is attributable to increasing rates of refusal. The ANES refusal rate increased from less than 15 percent in 1972 to over 24 percent in 2004. Similarly, the GSS refusal rate jumped from 16.9 percent in 1975 to 25 percent in 2010.[23] Response rates for media polls have been especially hard hit by declining cooperation. Although the response rate was not reported for the CNN poll example, it is unlikely that a survey with a three day field period exceeded a 25 percent response rate (1,010/4,000). In reality, many media polls—especially those conducted as overnight "snapshot" polls on a salient topic that may have a limited number of callbacks—now have response rates that hover around 10 percent.

The question is whether these lower response rates actually lessen data quality. Certainly, low response rates of telephone polls are often used as justification for using nonprobability samples. Some argue that the bias introduced by those who "opt out" from survey requests (nonresponse) is no different from the bias introduced by people choosing to "opt in" to online nonprobability panels. An increasing body of research has evaluated the link between response rate and nonresponse bias, and, perhaps surprisingly, has concluded that low response rate by itself does not indicate the results are inaccurate.[24] Multiple studies have found that lower response rates do not significantly reduce survey quality.[25] Nonresponse bias depends not just on the rate of nonresponse but the extent to which those who answer are different from those who do not. So, a low response rate indicates a risk of lower accuracy, but does not guarantee it.

The reassuring news on response rates does not mean we can ignore nonresponse error. To the contrary, it remains a significant concern—we have just been using an incomplete metric for evaluating its impact. In thinking about nonresponse error, it's first worth clarifying that nonresponse can be classified in two different categories: unit and item nonresponse. Unit nonresponse is where an individual fails to take part in a survey. This is the basis of response rate calculations. Another type of nonresponse, item nonresponse, occurs when the individual answering the questionnaire skips a question, giving us incomplete data on an individual respondent. Questions on income, for instance, are often susceptible to item nonresponse. Once again, the key concern is with potential differences between nonrespondents and respondents. For instance, in his book *Silent Voices*, Adam Berinsky shows that item nonresponse in racially sensitive survey questions can reflect prejudicial sentiments.[26]

For both unit and item nonresponse, the most important step in reducing the potential for nonresponse bias is to create an appropriately designed survey in the first place. Many of the fundamental design decisions—including mode, interviewer characteristics, length of survey, question wording and response options—can directly affect the extent of nonresponse error. For example, research on the 2004 exit polls found that using college-aged interviewers resulted in higher rates of nonresponse among Republican voters compared to Democratic voters, thereby biasing estimates of vote choice.[27] Self-administered surveys (mail and Internet) have higher levels of item nonresponse than interviewer-administered surveys, but answers in self-administered surveys tend to be more accurate because of reduced pressures to give a socially desirable answer. Respondents are more likely to skip questions that are long, burdensome, confusing, vague, or that do not provide the preferred response, so it becomes especially important that the questionnaire itself follows best practice principles for the particular mode being used.

Again, while response rates are perhaps not the key marker of nonresponse bias, it is nonetheless important for those conducting surveys to try to minimize nonresponse error and those consuming surveys to consider the nature and extent of nonresponse bias in any reported data.

Coverage Error

One of the growing issues of concern about survey quality comes from coverage error. Coverage error is the failure to give some persons in a target population a chance of being selected into the sample, such as when those without Internet access have no chance of ending up in an Internet survey. The extent of bias resulting from coverage error depends both on the rate of noncoverage and the difference between those covered by the survey and those not. So, if Internet users were no different from non-Internet users on most dimensions then we might have coverage error, but our resulting estimates could still accurately reflect the characteristics of the target population we are interested in.

Much of the focus on coverage bias has concerned the impact of cell-only households on telephone surveys. It is widely recognized that there is a growing cellular only population, so that surveys that omit people who are exclusively or primarily reached through their cell phones may not be representative. Figure 2.3 shows the growth in cell-only households in the last few years. Cell phone usage is particularly prevalent among young people and minorities—38 percent of the U.S. population is cell-only, while 50 percent of Hispanics, and 54 percent of those aged 18–24 live in houses with wireless only telephones. It is also the case that cell-only respondents often hold different views to those with landline telephones. For instance, research from the 2008 presidential campaign found that cell-phone only respondents were significantly more likely to support Obama—60.5 percent of those with only a cell phone reported voting for Obama, compared to his actual vote share of 52.9 percent.[28]

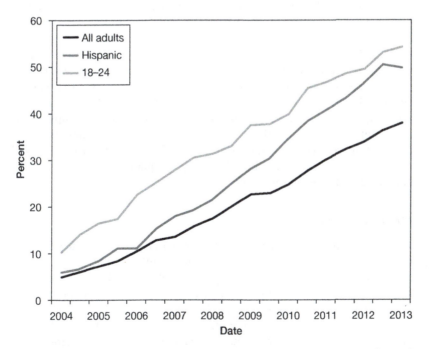

Figure 2.3 Trend in Cell-only Households (source: National Health Interview Surveys).

It is worth pausing to explain why cell phone numbers are often excluded from telephone surveys. Although there are some quality issues (e.g., blurry geographic associations, shorter questionnaires possible, lower response rates), mainly it's an issue of cost. Specifically, the 1991 Telephone Consumer Protection Act (TCPA) prohibits the use of automated dialers for all unsolicited calls to cell phones, including surveys. Pollsters typically use automated dialers—a device that automatically calls telephone numbers until reaching a live respondent—because it is much faster (and thus less expensive) than having interviewers manually dial the numbers.

To determine the extent of coverage bias introduced by excluding cell-only households we must take into account not only the difference in opinions between cell-only and landline respondents but also their expected proportion in the target population. For example, support for Obama was higher among cell-only individuals than the electorate at large, but those who relied solely on cell phones were also significantly less likely to vote. Thus, there was not as much bias in the polls as might otherwise be expected. Still, the problem is worsening, and a 2010 Pew Research Center study found that landline samples "tend to slightly underestimate support for Democratic candidates when compared with estimates from dual frame landline and cell samples in polling."[29] There is a related concern about the "cell phone mostly crowd," although there is limited research on this group to date. It is known that this group is nearly impossible to reach on a landline, and they look quite different—highly educated, white, homeowners, and married—from both the cell-only and the other landline crowds.

Returning to the example of the 2011 CNN poll, cell-only households were excluded from the sample frame. Because younger age groups tend to have more liberal positions on marijuana legalization, we might suspect that the poll actually underestimates public support for legalization because younger age groups might not be adequately represented. Given the clear implications of cell-only households on the generalizability of survey estimates, many top media organizations, including ABC News, CBS News, *New York Times*, and now CNN—have started routinely including cell phone respondents in their samples, despite the increased cost.

Measurement Error

Thus far, we have focused on sources of error that shape the ability to generalize from a sample of respondents to a population of interest. But the quality of a survey depends not only on the ability to generalize, but also on the ability to accurately measure the theoretical concepts of interest. Ideally, the survey questions result in measures that are both valid—they fully and accurately measure the concept that is supposed to be measured—and reliable—they measure the concept in a reproducible manner. Measurement error occurs when recorded responses to a survey fail to reflect the true characteristics of the respondents, and it can influence both the accuracy and reliability of our results.

There are many different sources of measurement error: the questionnaire, the data collection method, the interviewer, and the respondent. Questionnaire factors like question wording, question order, length of questions and questionnaire, number of response categories, presence of a "don't know" or middle response option can all influence measurement error. Even very small differences in question wording can generate very different findings. For example, asking about attitudes towards "assistance for the poor" generates much higher levels of support than a question asking about attitudes towards "welfare."[30] In another example, party identification questions that are otherwise identical besides the beginning phrase, either "In politics today" or "Generally speaking," result in entirely different conclusions regarding the stability of partisanship.[31]

Measurement error can also be affected by the mode of survey administration (e.g., telephone, in-person, mail). A survey that uses an interviewer in the administration, for example, can introduce measurement error from that interaction. Numerous studies have found that whites express more liberal racial attitudes to black interviewers than to white interviewers.[32]

Finally respondents themselves introduce error based on their comprehension or interpretation of the question in addition to any editing of the responses they might make because of fears of disclosure, concerns about privacy, or a desire to give a response that would be viewed favorably by others. People are especially reluctant to provide honest answers on sensitive topics, like sexual history, drug use, or racial attitudes. Voter turnout is another sensitive question—people tend to overreport voting because they want to appear to be good citizens. Thus, the ANES does not simply ask "Did you vote in the last election? (yes or no?)." Rather, they attempt to reassure the respondent that it really is okay to admit to not voting:

> In talking to people about elections, we often find that a lot of people were not able to vote because they weren't registered, they were sick, or they just didn't have time. Which of the following statements best describes you:
>
> 1. I did not vote (in the election this November)
> 2. I thought about voting this time—but didn't
> 3. I usually vote, but didn't this time
> 4. I am sure I voted.

For those conducting their own surveys, it is worth remembering that substantive expertise on a topic is *not* the only skill needed to conduct a survey. There is a rich body of research on the nature and extent of measurement error in surveys, and emerging best practices for reducing that error.[33] The single best way to improve measurement is to do extensive pretesting of the survey instrument.[34] For instance, *cognitive pretesting*, in which draft survey questions are administered for the purpose of collecting information about how people interpret and process the questions, can be used to identify any questions that are difficult to interpret or that can be interpreted in ways different from what the researcher intends. And for those introducing a new measure, it is especially important to explicitly evaluate the operationalization of that measure for validity and reliability. In this regard, political science as a field could take guidance from fields like psychology or education, where it is standard practice to take measurement seriously.

For those using secondary survey data, there is often a tendency to take for granted that the survey questions adequately measure the concepts of interest. However, many questions in major infrastructure surveys were written before the development of rigorous question-wording practices. Moreover, because over time inferences depend on having identical question wording, recurring surveys like the American National Election Study face a tension between the need for continuity in question wording and the need for innovation to keep up with developing knowledge in the field of survey methodology. Ultimately, we often must "work with what we got," but any analysis that uses survey research should pay careful attention to the potential for measurement error.

Disclosure

As the previous discussion highlights, there are many different threats to survey quality. Ultimately, the ability to assess survey quality—across all sources of survey error—rests on having sufficient information about the survey methodology. Although most academic journals and media organizations do not have formal disclosure requirements in place, there are increasing pressures on survey users to improve methodological transparency. In the last few years, there have been at least two well-publicized incidents in which survey firms appear to have made up or manipulated survey results. The liberal blog, DailyKos, discovered that weekly polling results they had paid for and featured from the organization Research 2000 (R2K) were "largely bunk."[35] Likewise, blogger Nate Silver of fivethirtyeight.com concluded that pollster Strategic Vision LLC was "disreputable and fraudulent."[36] AAPOR publicly reprimanded Strategic Vision for failure to disclose basic methodological information about the studies. Not long after, they announced a transparency initiative aimed at encouraging and making it as easy as possible for survey firms to be transparent about their research methods. Basic standards for minimal disclosure include reports of the following information about a survey:[37]

1. Who sponsored the survey, and who conducted it.
2. The exact wording of questions asked, including the text of any preceding instruction or explanation to the interviewer or respondents that might reasonably be expected to affect the response.
3. A definition of the population under study, and a description of the sampling frame used to identify this population.

4. A description of the sample design, giving a clear indication of the method by which the respondents were selected by the researcher, or whether the respondents were entirely self-selected.
5. Sample sizes and, where appropriate, eligibility criteria, screening procedures, and response rates computed according to AAPOR Standard Definitions. At a minimum, a summary of disposition of sample cases should be provided so that response rates could be computed.
6. A discussion of the precision of the findings, including estimates of sampling error, and a description of any weighting or estimating procedures used.
7. Which results are based on parts of the sample, rather than on the total sample, and the size of such parts.
8. Method, location, and dates of data collection.

With this basic information, readers can determine if the survey is a probability or nonprobability sample, and thus whether the sample is generalizable to the population of interest. It also offers some indication about the potential for nonsampling error, including coverage error, nonresponse error, and measurement error.

Full methodological disclosure should make clear that *every* survey is flawed in some way. There is no perfect survey design, in part because there are inevitable trade-offs involved in balancing the various sources of survey error. In reducing one source of survey error a researcher could inadvertently increase another source of error. For example, new technologies such as Interactive Voice Response (IVR) have the potential to reduce measurement bias introduced by the interactions of human interviewers, but they simultaneously increase nonresponse error or exacerbate coverage problems because people are less inclined to answer questions from a robocall. Likewise, best practices for measurement error would have multiple questions about each concept of interest, but doing so lengthens the survey and thus might increase the number of people who skip questions or drop out of the survey because of the time burden. Because no survey is perfect, every analysis of survey data should explicitly discuss how the results might or might not be affected by various survey errors.

Greater levels of transparency will give readers the ability to evaluate whether the knowledge claims being made are warranted given the methodology used. Increased transparency might also offer incentives to researchers to employ higher quality methods because it should make clear that not all survey methods are equal. Currently there seem to be two standards for surveys: gold and tin. The budgets of some of the most important federal and academic "gold standard" surveys are increasing dramatically in an effort to maintain the same levels of quality by traditional metrics; yet even these budgets are often not sufficient to maintain traditional metrics. At the same time, an extraordinary amount of research is currently conducted on modest budgets, yet falls dramatically short on many standards. A clearer understanding of the sources of survey errors and a full disclosure of survey methodology will help survey practitioners and consumers better understand and evaluate the potential trade-offs involved in using new or emerging technologies. Most importantly, it will make clear that there is no one answer to the question asked by the *Washington Post*, "Can we ever trust the polls again?"

Notes

1. George Bishop, "Why We Keep Getting Snowed by the Polls," *The Washington Post*, February 3, 2008, B03.
2. "Tracking Polls" transcript, On the Media, March 26, 2010. Accessed at http://www.onthemedia.org/transcripts/2010/03/26/04
3. Indeed, top media organizations are more likely than academic journals to have written to survey-quality standards. For example, The Associated Press, *The New York Times*, and ABC News, among others, have developed internal standards for judging whether or not they should report a survey. Media organizations often maintain a list of survey vendors—based on their methodology—that do not pass minimum quality standards.
4. Herbert Weisberg, *The Total Survey Error Approach: A Guide to the New Science of Survey Research* (Chicago: The University of Chicago Press, 2005); Robert Groves, F. J. Fowler, M. P. Couper, J. M. Lepowski, E. Singer, and R. Tourangeau, *Survey Methodology* (New York: John Wiley and Sons, 2004).
5. Weisberg, *The Total Survey Error Approach.*
6. We could even be more specific in defining the poll's target population—adults at home September 21–23, 2010.
7. Michael Mokrzycki, Scott Keeter, and Courtney Kennedy, "Cell-Phone-Only Voters in the 2008 Exit Poll and Implications for Future Noncoverage Bias," *Public Opinion Quarterly* 73 no. 5 (2009): 845–865.
8. Not mentioned are a number of other important steps, including choosing the precision level necessary, choosing the response mode, drafting the questionnaire, pretesting the instrument, data processing and analysis. These steps, too, can introduce error in the resulting statistics.
9. The distinction between error and bias is worth highlighting. Error can be either systematic or random; systematic error creates bias, decreasing the validity of survey estimates. Random error creates uncertainty, decreasing the reliability of the estimates.
10. The game of horseshoes offers an analogy for thinking about the correct interpretation of margin of error. Consider a blindfolded horseshoe champion who makes ringers 95 percent of the time. After a single pitch of the shoe, she doesn't know whether or not she made a ringer, but she is 95 percent confident that a ringer was made.
11. It is perhaps also worth noting that estimates of sampling error (margin of error; standard errors) almost always are calculated assuming the survey was collected using simple random sampling. Yet, most major data collections use a more complex probability sampling design such as clustered or stratified sampling. Although procedures exist in statistical packages like R and STATA for correcting the standard errors to account for complex designs, it is rarely ever done in political science. As such, published political science research often underestimates standard errors.

12. http://online.wsj.com/article_email/SB1000142405274870330540457561040211
6987146-lMyQjAxMTAwMDEwNjExNDYyWj.html; http://democrats.science.
house.gov/Media/file/Commdocs/hearings/2010/Energy/17nov/Michaels_Testimony.
pdf

13. There are also heightened concerns about data quality, particularly for Internet
panels. For a detailed overview, see M. Callegaro, R. P. Baker, J. Bethlehem, A. S.
Göritz, J. A. Krosnick, and P. J. Lavrakas (eds), *Online Panel Research: A Data
Quality Perspective* (New York: John Wiley & Sons, 2014).

    For instance, it can be difficult for researchers to verify that the person taking
the survey is the desired respondent. Some have found such respondents provide
"don't know" responses at a higher rate, are less likely to provide differentiated
responses across items, and are more likely to avoid responding to individual items
altogether.

14. Mick Couper and Peter Miller, "Web Survey Methods," *Public Opinion Quarterly*
72 (2008).

15. Indeed, the web, as a mode, has a number of unique advantages. For instance, web-
based surveys are convenient for both interviewers and subjects—respondents can
decide when to answer rather than having dinner interrupted by a phone survey.
Researchers have shown that the web-based mode is quite resistant to social
desirability biases. See Frauke Kreuter, Stanley Presser, and Roger Tourangeau,
"Social Desirability Bias in CATI, IVR, and Web Surveys," *Public Opinion Quarterly*
72 (2008); Don Dillman, "Why Choice of Survey Mode Makes a Difference," *Public
Health Reports* 121 (2006).

16. Researchers have evaluated the success rates from various recruitment strategies.
See R. Michael Alvarez, Robert Sherman, and Carla VanBeselaere, "Subject
Acquisition for Web-Based Surveys," *Political Analysis* 11 (2003). They found, for
instance, that their banner ad was displayed over 17 million times, resulting in
53,285 clicks directing respondents to the panel Web site, and ultimately 3,431
panel members.

17. The matching procedure might work as follows. First, the survey is administered
to a sample of opt-in respondents. Next, a random sample of individuals from
existing consumer and voter registration files is drawn, but not administered the
survey. Finally, a matching procedure is used to find the opt-in respondent (who
answered the survey) who most closely matches the randomly selected individual
(who did not answer the survey). Survey weighting is a post-survey procedure that
adjusts the sample to look more representative on some observed characteristics.
For example, if the sample of respondents is 60 percent female, 40 percent male,
but the target population is evenly split between the two, then we might weight each
man in the sample a bit more and each woman a bit less. See Ansolabehere and
Rivers (2013) for a more detailed description of the matching procedure used by
one survey firm.

18. A large number of studies—at least 19—have examined survey results with the
same questionnaire administered to probability samples and online to nonprobability samples. See, for instance Yeager et al., "Comparing the Accuracy of RDD
Telephone Surveys and Internet Surveys Conducted with Probability and Non-
Probability Samples," working paper (Knowledge Networks, 2009). Accessed at
www.knowledgenetworks.com/insights/docs/Mode-04_2.pdf. All but one found
significant differences in the results that could not be substantially reduced by
weighting. Unfortunately, most of these studies cannot adequately distinguish
differences due to sampling design effects and differences due to mode effects.

19. Mick Couper, "Web Surveys: A Review of Issues and Approaches," *Public Opinion Quarterly* 64 (2000); Jill Dever, Ann Rafferty, and Richard Valliant, "Internet Surveys: Can Statistical Adjustments Eliminate Coverage Bias?" *Survey Research Methods* 2 (2008); Linchiat Chang and Jon Krosnick, "National Surveys via RDD Telephone Interviewing versus the Internet: Comparing Sample Representativeness and Response Quality," *Public Opinion Quarterly* 73 (2009); Neil Malhotra and Jon Krosnick, "The Effect of Survey Mode and Sampling on Inferences about Political Attitudes and Behavior: Comparing the 2000 and 2004 ANES to Internet Surveys with Nonprobability Samples," *Political Analysis* 15 (2007).

20. Gary Langer and Jon Cohen, "5 Tips for Decoding Those Election Polls," *The Washington Post*, December 30, 2007, Sunday B03.

21. Stephen Ansolabehere, and Douglas Rivers, "Cooperative Survey Research," *Annual Review of Political Science* 16 (2013): 307–329. Although there remains some debate about the extent of bias in YouGov estimates of political engagement and knowledge, the point estimates and correlates of vote choice, in particular, appear quite comparable to that found in probability samples.

22. These response rates were computed according to AAPOR's "minimum response rate" (RR1). It is referred to as the "minimum" because it assumes that in all households at which the eligibility of residents was not determined, at least one eligible adult lived there. Numbers come from individual study year codebooks, available on the ANES website: http://www.electionstudies.org.

23. In contrast to the ANES, the GSS estimates are calculated based on AAPOR RR5, sometimes called the "maximum response rate," because it assumes that there are no eligible cases among the cases of unknown eligibility. Calculations come from James Allan Davis, Tom W. Smith, and Peter V. Marsden, *General Social Surveys, 1972–2008: Cumulative Codebook*. Chicago: National Opinion Research Center.

24. Emilia Peytcheva and Robert Groves, "Using Variation in Response Rates of Demographic Subgroups as Evidence of Nonresponse Bias in Survey Estimates," *Journal of Official Statistics* 25 (2009).

25. Scott Keeter, C. Kennedy, M. Dimock, J. Best, and P. Craighill, "Gauging the Impact of Growing Nonresponse on Estimates from a National RDD Telephone Survey," *Public Opinion Quarterly* 70 (2006); Penny Visser et al., "Mail Surveys for Election Forecasting? An Evaluation of the Columbus Dispatch Poll," *Public Opinion Quarterly* 60 (1996).

26. Adam Berinsky, *Silent Voices: Opinion Polls and Political Representation in America* (Princeton, NJ: Princeton University Press, 2004).

27. Warren Mitofsky, "Evaluation of Edison/ Mitofsky Election System of 2004," accessed 10-1-10, http://www.electionmathematics.org/em-exitpolls/Exit_Polls_2004_Edison_Mitofsky.pdf

28. Michael Mokrzycki, Scott Keeter, and Courtney Kennedy, "Cell Phone Only Voters in the 2008 Exit Poll and Implications for Future Noncoverage Bias," *Public Opinion Quarterly* 73 (2009).

29. Leah Christian, Scott Keeter, Kristen Purcell, and Aaron Smith, "Assessing the Cell Phone Challenge," Pew Research Center, May 20, 2010, accessed at http://pew research.org/pubs/1601/assessing-cell-phone-challenge-in-public-opinion-surveys

30. Tom Smith, "That Which we Call Welfare by any Other Name Would Smell Sweeter: An Analysis of the Impact of Question Wording on Response Patterns," *Public Opinion Quarterly* 51 (1987).

31. Paul Abramson, and Charles Ostrom, Jr., "Macropartisanship: An Empirical Reasessment," *American Political Science Review* 85 (1991); Paul Abramson et al., "Question Form and Context Effects in the Measurement of Partisanship:

Experimental Tests of the Artifact Hypothesis," *American Political Science Review* 88 (1994).

32. See, for example, Darren Davis, "Nonrandom Measurement Error and Race of Interviewer Effects among African-Americans," *Public Opinion Quarterly* 61 (1997).

33. Paul P. Biemer, R. M. Groves, L. E. Lyberg, N. A. Mathiowetz, and S. Sudman, *Measurement Errors in Surveys* (New York: John Wiley & Sons, 1991); Colm O'Muircheartaigh, *Measurement Error in Surveys: A Historical Perspective* (New York: John Wiley & Sons, 1997).

34. Mick Couper, S. Presser, J. M. Rothgeb, J. T. Lesser, E. Martin, J. Martin, and E. Singer, *Methods for Testing and Evaluating Survey Questionnaires* (New York: John Wiley & Sons, 2004).

35. For more complete discussion of the controversy and evidence, see http://www.dailykos.com/storyonly/2010/6/29/880185/-More-on-Research-2000

36. http://www.fivethirtyeight.com/search/label/strategic%20vision

37. http://www.aapor.org/AM/Template.cfm?Section=Standards_andamp_Ethics&Template=/CM/ContentDisplay.cfm&ContentID=2397

Chapter 3

Two-thirds Full?

Citizen Competence and Democratic Governance

Martin Gilens

The eminent political theorist Robert Dahl asserted that "a key characteristic of democracy is the continuing responsiveness of the government to the preferences of its citizens, considered as political equals."[1] This formulation implies first that citizens must have meaningful preferences for democratic government to be possible, and second that in order to gauge the democratic quality of any given government we must be able both to discern what its citizens' preferences are, and to assess how strongly and how equally government policy responds to those preferences.

The American public, it is often claimed, simply lacks the interest, motivation, or ability to form meaningful preferences on most political issues. Political issues in contemporary societies are numerous, complex, and often remote from citizens' everyday lives, while the ideal democratic citizen "is expected to be well informed about political affairs. He is supposed to know what the issues are, what their history is, what the relevant facts are, what alternatives are proposed . . . [and] what the likely consequences are."[2] Observers of American democracy have long questioned not only citizens' ability to meet this lofty goal, but citizens' ability to play any truly meaningful role in shaping government policy.

In this chapter I ask first whether American citizens hold meaningful policy preferences and whether such preferences, if they exist, are accurately reflected in surveys of political attitudes. I argue that despite the limited political knowledge and engagement typically displayed by the American public, public preferences—at least in the aggregate—are "enlightened enough" to serve as a reasonable basis for guiding government decision makers on a wide range of issues. Given this positive evaluation, I then ask how the preferences of the public are related to the policy decisions of the national government, and how equally influence over government policy extends to more and less well-off Americans.

To evaluate the link between public preferences and government policy, I rely on a dataset consisting of over two thousand survey questions in which random samples of Americans were asked whether they favored or opposed specific changes in government policy. Some of these proposed changes were extremely popular (like confiscating money from bank accounts linked to terrorism), others were quite unpopular (like reducing Social Security benefits), and some were favored by the poor but opposed by the affluent or vice versa. In each case, I determined whether the change in government policy posed in the survey question took place. Using these data, I assess how much the probability of a proposed policy change being adopted depends on the extent to which that change is favored or opposed, and how this association between preferences and policies differs for poor, middle class, and affluent Americans.

Conflicting Views of Citizen Competence

The proper role for citizens in a democracy has been debated for millennia. Some contemporary scholars believe that citizens can be fashioned into something resembling the "ideal democratic citizen" described above through deliberative processes and institutions. Proponents of deliberative democracy argue that a more enlightened public can be cultivated by providing citizens with the opportunity to learn about issues and to interact in an egalitarian forum with others who bring alternative information and perspectives.

At the other end of the spectrum lie proponents of minimalist democracy who view citizens as fundamentally limited in their interest and ability to form sensible preferences on questions of public policy. However, democratic minimalists believe citizens can still play a role in democracy by assessing whether their own wellbeing has improved or declined while the incumbent has been in office. If they feel they are better off, they can reelect the incumbent candidate or party; if not, they can "throw the bums out."

Yet even this minimalist conception of citizens' democratic role is more demanding than it may seem. First, voters disagree about what constitutes a desirable outcome on many important issues. Everyone may want a prosperous economy, but some want more government regulation of industry and others less, some favor pro-choice and others pro-life policies on abortion. Gun control, tax progressivity, environmental policy, school prayer, foreign military engagements all generate contentious disagreements about desirable policies and outcomes. On these sorts of issues, judging the incumbent's performance requires that citizens have *both* a policy preference *and* an assessment of whether the incumbent has helped to advance their desired outcome.

Even consensus issues like a robust economy or a low crime rate require that citizens distinguish between their personal experience and that of the country. If a voter has lost his or her job, and the unemployment rate has gone up, throwing out the incumbent seems straightforward. But what if they've lost their job while the overall unemployment rate has declined? In that case, the voter must attempt to assess the tie between their own personal situation and that of the broader society.

In sum, it is difficult to see how even minimalist democracy could function successfully if voters were unable to form issue preferences that reasonably reflected their underlying values and interests. Whether Americans are in fact able to do this has been a subject of considerable debate among public opinion scholars.

Scholars of public opinion can be roughly divided into two schools of thought. One concludes that Americans' low level of political knowledge and apparent lack of clear and consistent policy preferences shows that the public is incapable of providing meaningful guidance to government decision makers on policy matters. The other school of thought acknowledges the gap between the traditional expectations of democratic citizens and the public's performance, but believes that compensatory mechanisms allow citizens to form meaningful preferences, at least in the aggregate, even in the face of low information levels and considerable inconsistency in survey responses.

In his seminal paper "The Nature of Belief Systems in Mass Publics," Philip Converse[3] painted a bleak picture of the American public as largely lacking coherent political preferences. Converse observed that survey respondents were apt to express different preferences when presented with the identical question on different occasions, that preferences on one policy issue were at best weakly associated with questions on seemingly related issues, and that broad organizing principles like liberalism or conservatism were poorly understood by most Americans. Confronted with this evidence, Converse concluded that the preferences respondents report on surveys consist largely of "non-attitudes" and that "large portions of [the] electorate do not have meaningful beliefs, even on issues that have formed the basis for intense political controversy among elites for substantial periods of time."[4]

Many subsequent assessments of Americans' political preferences have been only slightly more hopeful. After examining hundreds of survey measures of political information, for example, Michael Delli Carpini and Scott Keeter conclude that

> More than a small fraction of the public is reasonably well informed about politics—informed enough to meet high standards of good citizenship. Many of the basic institutions and procedures of government are known to half or more of the public, as are the relative positions of the parties on many major issues of the day.[5]

But the flip side of this coin is that a large proportion of the public does not rise to this level. "[L]arge numbers of American citizens are woefully under-informed," Delli Carpini and Keeter write, and "overall levels of knowledge are modest at best."[6]

These two analyses address the two most troubling aspects of public opinion that cast doubt on the feasibility of meaningful democratic government: the public's lack of knowledge about political affairs and the seeming randomness of policy preferences expressed on surveys as reflected in their lack of stability over time, and the weakness of associations between related issues or across similar formulations of the same policy issue.

Scholars who take a more sanguine view of the quality of citizens' policy preferences point to three aspects of mass political attitudes to explain how a public with minimal political information can nevertheless form meaningful issue preferences. First, citizens with modest levels of information might turn to more knowledgeable others for "cues" about the desirability of alternative policies or politicians. Second, individual citizens are not equally interested in the full range of political issues in play at any given time but tend to "specialize" in a subset of issues about which they are more knowledgeable and have more stable and well thought out preferences. The division of citizens into these "issue publics" means that the ability of any individual citizen to meaningfully participate in shaping government policy should be judged relative to the set of issues that that individual cares about; all citizens need not hold equally well developed preferences on all issues for the public to fulfill its role in democratic governance. Finally, the fickle element of individual citizens' policy preferences will, to some degree at least, tend to cancel out when preferences are aggregated across the public as a whole (or across distinctive subgroups of the public). Aggregate opinion, by this reckoning, will typically be more stable, with a higher "signal to noise ratio" than the individual opinions that make it up.

Cue Taking as a Basis for Political Preferences

Given the stringent standards for "the ideal democratic citizen" noted above, it is not surprising that these authors view the American public as falling short. Political opinions, they write, are more frequently "matters of sentiment and disposition rather than 'reasoned preferences' . . . characterized more by faith than by conviction and by wishful expectation rather than careful prediction of consequences."[7] Yet Berelson and his coauthors believed that despite the public's general lack of politically relevant information and poor quality of reasoning about policy matters, the ignorant many are able to leverage the expertise of the well-informed few who are politically knowledgeable and engaged. If most citizens are indifferent to and uninformed about public affairs, it is nevertheless true that some are absorbed in the world of politics and policy. Moreover, social networks, they maintain, allow for a division of labor in which more informed "opinion leaders" provide policy insights and endorsements to their less informed friends and acquaintances. "The political genius of the citizenry," they conclude, "may reside less in how well they can judge public policy than in how well they can judge the people who advise them how to judge public policy."[8]

Taking cues from more knowledgeable elites or acquaintances is a sensible strategy for citizens who lack the ability or inclination to gather the information needed to formulate a preference on a given policy issue. Anthony Downs, writing shortly after Berelson, Lazarsfeld and McPhee, notes that the average citizen "cannot be expert in all the fields of policy that are relevant to his decision. Therefore, he will seek assistance from men who are experts in those fields, have the same political goals he does, and have good judgment."[9]

A substantial literature has developed over the past decades which identifies the wide range of cue-givers that citizens can rely on in forming political judgments.[10] Most cue-taking models posit that citizens adopt the policy positions expressed by "like minded" elites (judged on the basis of partisan or ideological compatibility, or the more specific affinities associated, for example, with a citizen's religious, union, or professional organization) and either ignore those of the "non-like minded" or adopt the opposite position from the one that they espouse.[11] Cue-givers of this sort can be either social leaders whose views are transmitted through the media, or individual acquaintances who are perceived as comparatively well informed on the issue at hand.

The strategy of turning to those with greater knowledge when faced with a challenging decision is hardly limited to political novices. Even citizens who follow politics closely will inevitably lack sufficient information (or technical expertise) to form opinions "from scratch" on many issues. In a modern nation, there are simply too many detailed and technical issues for even the most motivated members of the public to possibly keep abreast of. Indeed, even elected representatives who have abundant informational resources and who "follow politics" for a living turn to experts in specific issue areas for advice and take cues from other representatives in their own party who "specialize" in particular issue domains.[12]

Issue Publics

Cue taking is one mechanism by which citizens may be able to form meaningful preferences on issues despite a lack of knowledge and expertise, and the relationship between cue taker and cue giver highlights the large differences in political knowledge held by different members of the public. At the same time, however, any given individual's knowledge may differ greatly from one policy issue to another. Among the many enduring contributions of Converse's seminal paper was the concept of issue publics—the obvious but often overlooked fact that different people care about different political issues. In order to participate in democratic governance, citizens must be able to form meaningful preferences on the policy issues that government addresses. But that does not mean that every citizen must have a preference on every issue. Given the broad range of backgrounds, interests, and situations that citizens in a large and diverse society face, it would be surprising if there were not substantial variations in the specific political issues that different citizens care about and attend to.

Converse based his negative assessment of the mass public's political preferences in part on the substantially stronger inter-correlations of preferences on related issues among the political elites he surveyed. (Converse's sample of political elites consisted of candidates for the U.S. Congress, arguably an unrealistically sophisticated comparison group.) Nevertheless, when Converse restricted his analysis of the public's policy positions in a given issue domain like foreign aid or racial policy to those respondents who he judged to be members of a given issue public,[13] he found that the inter-correlations among ordinary Americans resembled those among his political elites. "[R]emoval from analysis of individuals who, through indifference or ignorance, lie outside the issue publics in question serves to close much of the gap in constraint levels between mass and elite publics."[14]

Subsequent analyses confirm Converse's insight regarding issue publics.[15] Jon Krosnick, for example, sorted survey respondents into issue publics on the basis of the level of importance they attached to a dozen different political issues.[16] Krosnick reported that the greater the importance a respondent attached to a given policy issue, the more likely they were to mention that issue as a reason for liking or disliking the presidential candidates, the less likely they were to change their issue preference in response to persuasive communications, and the more stable their reported issue preference was over time.

Another technique for identifying issue publics is to rely on demographic group membership on the assumption that members of particular groups are, at least on average, more interested in some issues than others. Vincent Hutchings, for example, identifies union members and people living in union households as more likely to have an interest in labor issues while abortion policy is likely to be of greater interest to women and religious conservatives.[17] Consistent with these expectations, he finds that members of these groups are more attentive to Senate and gubernatorial campaigns when "their" issues were raised and more likely to base their Senate votes on their Senator's record on the particular issues associated with their group.

Research on issue publics suggests that assessments of the quality of public preferences that look only at the average level of knowledge, preference stability, or other measures across the public as a whole may strongly understate the degree to which a typical citizen holds meaningful policy preferences. True, the typical citizen may attend to only a few of the many issues facing the country at any point in time. But if citizens have sensible, stable, and reasonably informed preferences on the subset of issues that they care most about, and if they use those issues disproportionately as a basis for choosing among parties and candidates, then the public can fulfill its assigned role in democratic governance, even if most citizens lack meaningful opinions on most issues.

The "Magic of Aggregation" and the Quality of Public Preferences

Cue taking suggests that even citizens with minimal information may be able to form meaningful preferences by relying on others who share their general outlooks or political orientations, and the division of the citizenry into issue publics suggests that meaningful participation in democratic governance does not require all citizens to hold meaningful preferences on all issues. A third factor relevant to the assessment of the public's role in democracy is that the aggregate preferences of the public as a whole have different characteristics than the individual preferences that make them up.

The eighteenth century French philosopher and mathematician Condorcet explained in his famous "jury theorem" that if each individual in a group has even a modest tendency to be correct, the group as an aggregate can have a very high probability of reaching the correct decision (and the larger the aggregate, the higher the probability that the collective judgment will be correct). This insight has been applied to the political attitudes expressed on surveys to suggest that the "errors" in respondents' reports of their own preferences will, at least under some circumstances, tend to cancel out, resulting in a measure of aggregate opinion that is more stable and more reliable than the individual opinions that make it up.[18]

But how can respondents be "wrong" about their own preferences? Two different kinds of "errors" in survey-based measures of policy preferences can be distinguished. First, even if respondents had perfectly fixed and certain views on a particular policy option, the reports of those views as captured on surveys would contain some degree of error. The ambiguities of question wording, the difficulty in matching a specific sentiment to the available response options, and mistakes in reading or hearing the survey question or recording the respondent's answer will all introduce some degree of "measurement error" (see Chapter 2 of this volume).

Second, most respondents are not likely to have perfectly fixed and certain views on most political issues. Current understandings of political attitudes suggest that citizens typically hold a variety of considerations relevant to a given policy issue and use those considerations to construct a position on a policy question when asked by a survey interviewer.[19] For example, if asked whether they favor cutting government spending on foreign aid, a survey respondent might consider his or her views about taxes and government spending, about humanitarian needs in developing countries, about waste and corruption in those countries, about competing domestic needs, and so on. This process of canvassing considerations and constructing positions is an imperfect one, however. Given the time and motivational constraints typical of a survey interview, only a subset of all possible considerations bearing on a particular question are likely to be brought to mind. Moreover, this subset of considerations may be biased toward those that are at the "top of the head" as a result of earlier questions in the survey, stories that have been in the news, recent experiences the respondent may have had, specific aspects of the question wording, or any number of other reasons.

From this perspective, most citizens cannot be said to "have attitudes" corresponding to a particular survey question on a political issue, in the sense that those attitudes existed in a crystallized form before the question was asked.[20] But individual citizens can be said to have "response tendencies" or "long-term preferences" which represent their (hypothetical) average opinion if it were to be ascertained repeatedly over time.[21] This Platonic "true attitude" is nothing more than the imperfectly revealed average of these hypothetical repeated preference constructions (in the same way that a "true circle" is a hypothetical shape that can only be approximated by any actual circle in the real world).

It is impractical, of course, to measure citizens' "long-term preferences" by repeatedly surveying the same individuals. But aggregating survey responses across many individuals will produce much the same result (without the problem of dealing with new information or changed circumstances which might alter the set of relevant considerations). To the extent that the biases in formulating a preference from a given set of considerations are randomly distributed across individuals they will balance out, just as the errors in individuals' judgments in a jury context cancel each other out. If randomly distributed idiosyncratic factors lead individual citizens to report preferences that differ from their "true" or "long-term" preferences, those errors will lead some citizens to under-report support for a policy while leading others to over-report support. With a large enough sample of citizens, these errors will cancel out resulting in aggregate preferences that closely match the average of the individuals' long-term preferences. Of course, not all factors that lead citizens to wrongly report their issue preferences will be random and therefore offsetting, a concern I'll return to below.

The most thorough examination of aggregate opinion toward public policy is Benjamin Page and Robert Shapiro's influential book *The Rational Public*.22 Page and Shapiro do not view aggregation as a cure for all of the shortcomings of public opinion. But they argue that collective preferences display a degree of stability and cogency that far exceeds the typical individual level preferences that make them up.

> While we grant the rational ignorance of most individuals, and the possibility that their policy preferences are shallow and unstable, we maintain that public opinion as a *collective* phenomenon is nonetheless stable (though not immovable), meaningful, and indeed rational . . . it is able to make distinctions; it is organized in coherent patterns; it is reasonable, based on the best available information; and it is adaptive to new information or changed circumstances.[23]

Moreover, they maintain, "surveys accurately measure this stable, meaningful, and reasonable collective public opinion."[24] The collective rationality of public opinion stems, Page and Shapiro argue, from the aggregation of individual opinions which cancel out both random measurement errors in surveys and temporary fluctuations in individuals' opinions. The aggregate preferences that result from this process tend to be quite stable, but also exhibit sensible responsiveness to changing conditions. For example, public support for unemployment assistance increases as unemployment rates rise, public support for defense spending increases when the threat of war goes up, public support for tax cuts declines when tax rates are lowered, and so on.

Two principal objections have been raised about the "miracle of aggregation." The first, which Page and Shapiro discuss at some length, is that "errors" in individuals' policy preferences will not always be randomly distributed. One source of non-random "error" in preference formation is misinformation that leads most or all members of the public to shift their policy preferences in the same direction. For example, John F. Kennedy and others claimed during the late 1950s that the U.S. was facing a nuclear "missile gap" with the Soviet Union. In retrospect it is clear that not only was there no missile gap (the U.S. had maintained a considerable advantage in nuclear missiles) but that good evidence was available at the time demonstrating the absence of such a gap. This sort of misinformation will inevitably "pervert" the preferences that the public would otherwise hold on related policy issues (in this case, defense spending and foreign policy).

Shared misinformation need not result from purposeful attempts to mislead the public. Sizeable misperceptions of changes in the crime rate, spending levels on foreign aid, the racial composition of the poor, and the typical length of time beneficiaries receive welfare have all been widespread among the American public at various points in time.[25] The extent of collectively held misinformation among the public is difficult to assess, in part because the truth about many politically relevant facts may not become known until later (if ever). After canvassing some of the sources and content of misinformation held by Americans, Page and Shapiro conclude

> we cannot hope to offer a precise or definitive account of the extent (or, for that matter, the nature) of information biases in the United States. But if we are on track concerning important instances of opinion manipulation and general patterns of biased and misleading information, these pose troubling implications for the workings of democracy.[26]

Just how troubled we should be about biased or misleading information is difficult to judge. To the extent that misinformation is universal (or nearly universal) among elites and the public at large, it is hard to see how any form of government could make optimal decisions. The consequences of misinformation that are unique to democracy, on the other hand, are those in which large numbers of citizens fall prey to *avoidable* misperceptions or biases. For example, if the preferences of the majority of citizens were influenced by misinformation that the best informed citizens knew to be untrue, then a democratic government that reflected the public's collective preference might do a poor job of serving the public's true interests. Misinformation always has the potential to bias preferences under any form of government, but the special challenge to democracy arises from situations in which the collective preferences of the public would look different if the public had the same level of relevant information that the most politically knowledgeable and engaged members of society hold.

In the following section, I will discuss the degree to which this sort of misinformation appears to bias public preferences and undermine democratic governance. But there is a second principled objection to the optimistic account of aggregate opinion that we must consider as well. As Scott Althaus explains, the notion that "errors" in the individual preferences reported on surveys will cancel out when those individual reports are aggregated rests on the assumption that preferences are measured in such a manner that errors in one direction and errors in the other direction are equally likely.[27] But this is not always the case. For example, consider questions with only two response options (in addition to "don't know"), such as those gauging support or opposition to some proposed policy change. Among citizens who "really" favor the proposed change, some proportion will mistakenly be recorded as opposing the change, because they misunderstood the question, because they were misinformed about the policy, or simply because the interviewer entered the wrong code. But if these sources of error are randomly distributed across the survey respondents, then (approximately) the same proportion of citizens who "really" oppose the policy will be recorded as favoring the policy.

It might appear that this balancing out of opposite errors will leave the aggregate preference on this policy as measured by this hypothetical survey question unchanged. But that is only the case if equal numbers of citizens support and oppose the policy. If "true" supporters outnumber opponents by, say, three to one, then the number of survey respondents erroneously counted as opponents will be three times as great as the number erroneously counted as supporters. In this example, if 20 percent of all respondents are misclassified then 15 percent of the respondents will be "erroneously" shifted from supporters to opponents (20 percent of 75) while 5 percent will be erroneously shifted from opponents to supporters (20 percent of 25). As a result, it will appear that 65 percent rather than 75 percent of respondents favor the proposed policy and 35 rather than 25 percent oppose it.[28]

More generally, random errors will shift the apparent distribution of preferences on questions with only two valid responses toward 50 percent. (If the true distribution of preferences on such an item is 50 percent, then random errors will in fact be equal and offsetting.) The same logic applies to survey questions with more than two valid response categories to the extent that the preferences of respondents who belong in the highest category can only be moved downward while those in the lowest category can only be moved upward. If the true distribution of long-term preferences is asymmetrical then random errors will not cancel out but will tend to move the recorded mean toward the center of the scale.

These sorts of non-offsetting errors on policy issues with asymmetric distributions of preferences will dampen the apparent extremity of preferences for the public as a whole. But the distortion of public opinion that results will be only one of degree, not of kind. The distribution of policy preferences will appear to be somewhat more "centrist" and less "extremist" than is really the case. Consequently the amount of opinion difference associated with a given change in the probability of a proposed policy change being adopted will appear somewhat smaller than it should (and the strength of the preference/policy link somewhat stronger than is really the case). In sum, the "magic of aggregation" cannot be assumed to cancel out all of the random error inherent in measures of political preferences. Highly popular policies will appear somewhat less popular and highly unpopular policies somewhat less unpopular than is really the case. But this "moderating bias" will have only a modest impact in strengthening the apparent association of government policy and public preferences.

How Well does Cue Taking and Aggregation Work?

To what extent do cue taking, preference aggregation, and issue publics ameliorate concerns about low levels of political information and the low quality of public preferences on political issues? No actual public in a large society is likely to meet the classical expectations of the well-informed citizen. But does the existing public display enough "wisdom" in its political preferences to recommend a system of governance that strongly reflects the preferences of the public?

We know that cue taking *can* be an effective strategy for forming policy preferences on complex issues. In one study, for example, respondents who were poorly informed about the details of five competing insurance-reform initiatives on a California ballot, but who knew where the insurance industry stood on each initiative, were able to closely emulate the voting behavior of their better-informed peers.[29] But just because cues *can* serve as effective shortcuts doesn't mean the necessary cues are always available or that citizens will make use of them when they are. One way to assess the quality of public preferences that emerge from the processes described above is to compare the actual preferences expressed on surveys to some hypothetical standard of "well-informed preferences" that citizens would hold if they had the ability, time, and inclination to gather the relevant information on a given set of policy issues.

The most straightforward way to assess how far actual preferences diverge from hypothetical well-informed preferences is to inform a representative group of citizens about some set of policy issues and see how their preferences shift as a result. James Fishkin and Robert Luskin have done just this in a series of "deliberative polls".[30] For example, the 1996 National Issues Convention brought 466 participants, selected at random from the U.S. population, to Austin, Texas for four days, during which time they read briefing materials on various economic, foreign policy, and family issues, discussed those issues in small groups, and participated in question-and-answer sessions with experts. When initially contacted, and once again at the end of their stay in Austin, participants answered identical questions concerning their policy preferences in these three issue areas. To provide a comparison group, members of the initial sample who elected not to come to Austin completed the same surveys.

The participants in the National Issues Convention did shift their preferences somewhat on many of the 48 political attitude questions they were asked. But the average change in aggregate preferences was not large and barely exceeded the aggregate change of preferences expressed by the control group which was not provided with the information or opportunity to deliberate. On a 100-point scale, the average net (i.e., aggregate) difference in pre-post preferences across these 48 issue questions was about five points for the deliberation group and about three points for the control group.[31] The four days of focused study and deliberation, it appears, resulted in a 2 percentage point greater aggregate change in policy preferences than would otherwise be expected by simply resurveying the same respondents with no intervening activity.

The results of the National Issues Convention study suggest that on the topics addressed, participants' pre-existing aggregate preferences closely resembled the "well-informed preferences" they expressed after four days of education and deliberation. But these conclusions hinge on the specific information provided to the deliberating respondents. If the information provided was not new to the participants, or was not different enough from what they already knew, or was not relevant enough to the policy judgments they were asked to make, then the possibility remains that different information might have shifted aggregate preferences to a greater degree. Nevertheless, since the organizers' goal was to provide just the sort of educational experience that critics of the quality of public opinion view as lacking, these results do lend some credibility to the notion that cue taking and aggregation result in collective judgments that differ little from what a well informed and engaged citizenry would express.

A very different way to compare actual to hypothetical "well-informed" preferences is to use statistical tools to simulate a well-informed citizenry. This approach takes advantage of the fact that, as Philip Converse observed, the mean level of political knowledge among the electorate is very low, but the variation in knowledge is very high.[32] By modeling the vote choices or policy preferences of the most well informed segment of the electorate, one can impute preferences for citizens who share a given set of characteristics but have lower levels of political information.

Larry Bartels, for example, compared the presidential votes of the most well informed respondents with those of less informed respondents of the same age, education, income, race, sex, occupational status, region, religion, union membership, urban residence, homeowner status, and labor force participation.[33] Bartels found an average individual deviation of about 10 percentage points between actual and "well-informed" votes for the six presidential elections between 1972 and 1992. Many of these deviations were off-setting, however—some poorly informed citizens reported casting a Republican vote when they would have been predicted to vote Democratic if well informed, but other poorly informed citizens "mistakenly" voted Democratic when they would have been predicted to vote Republican. The more relevant *aggregate* deviation between actual and well-informed presidential votes was only 3 percentage points.[34]

In an even more directly relevant study that used a similar methodology, Scott Althaus compared respondents' expressed preferences on 235 political opinion questions with imputed preferences calculated by assigning to each respondent the predicted preference of someone with the maximum level of political knowledge but otherwise identical in terms of education, income, age, partisan identification, race, sex, marital status, religion, region, labor force participation, occupational category, union membership, and homeownership.[35] Althaus found that in the aggregate, imputed "fully informed preferences" differed from expressed preferences by an average of about 6.5 percentage points. Not a trivial amount, but hardly enough to dismiss existing preferences as an unsuitable guide to government decision making.

Two lessons can be drawn from the research on "enlightened preferences." First, while heuristics or informational shortcuts might, in theory, be extremely effective at allowing citizens to reach the same preferences they would if they were more fully informed, in practice a gap remains between actual and hypothetical "well informed" preferences, whether those preferences are statistically imputed or arrived at after exposure to new information and deliberation. Second, the size of the aggregate gap is rather modest. The two most directly relevant analyses that focus on policy preferences find gaps of 2 and 6.5 percentage points, with a 3 percentage point gap in presidential voting. Differences of this size might be enough to swing a close election or to shift aggregate preferences from slightly favorable toward some policy option to slightly opposed. But the policy proposals I examine below range widely from strong opposition to strong support (about two-thirds of the proposed policy changes in my dataset were favored by under 40 or over 60 percent of the respondents). Thus, the relatively small differences in favorability that might be expected from a better informed, more "enlightened" citizenry, would be unlikely to lead to substantially different conclusions.

Question Wording and Framing Effects

Even casual consumers of survey data are aware that subtle differences in how a question is worded can sometimes produce large differences in responses. Advocacy groups sometimes take advantage of this phenomenon by asking "loaded" or "biased" questions which are designed to portray public sentiment as highly favorable toward the group's preferred policies. But many observers are skeptical that even careful and well crafted surveys can avoid this problem. One popular book aimed at explaining surveys and their use in American politics claims:

Even when the sponsor has no obvious ax to grind, question wording choices greatly influence the results obtained. In many instances, highly reputable polling organizations have arrived at divergent conclusions simply because they employed different (although well-constructed) questions on a particular topic.[36]

But just how ubiquitous and how consequential are such question wording effects? This is a difficult question to answer because there is no clear way to define the range of plausible question wordings on a given topic or the set of topics that should be considered. Some of the most frequently cited examples of question wording effects do raise doubts about the ability of survey measures to accurately capture the public's policy preferences. For example, Tom Smith reports that 64 percent of Americans thought the government was spending too little on "assistance to the poor" but only 22 percent thought too little was being spent on "welfare."[37] Howard Schuman and Stanley Presser found that in the 1970s two in five Americans felt that the United States should "not allow" public speeches against democracy, but only half that number felt that the United States should "forbid" public speeches against democracy.[38] Finally, George Quattrone and Amos Tversky found that 64 percent of their respondents preferred a program that would increase inflation somewhat while *reducing unemployment* from 10 percent to 5 percent, but only 46 percent made the same choice when the program was described as *increasing employment* from 90 percent to 95 percent.[39]

Each of these examples reveals substantial effects from apparently minor changes in the words used to describe a policy choice and each has been replicated numerous times, so we cannot dismiss them as statistical flukes. Yet their implications for how we understand citizens' policy preferences (or their lack of preferences), and our ability to gauge those preferences, are far from clear. For example, the greater appeal of "assisting the poor" over "welfare" has often been interpreted as indicating the sensitivity of the public to particular positively or negatively loaded terms. If the preferences expressed toward the same policy can be shifted so dramatically by calling it one thing rather than another, can we even say the public has a "real" and discernable preference toward that policy? Yet this example can be viewed another way entirely. There are many different government programs that assist the poor by providing medical care, housing subsidies, legal aid, child care, job training, and so on. For some respondents, all of these programs might be included under the rubric "welfare," but for many Americans welfare is understood as cash assistance to the able-bodied working-age unemployed poor. The public tends to be strongly supportive of these other anti-poverty programs, so the lesser appeal of "welfare" in comparison to "assisting the poor" can be understood not as a superficial response to an emotionally laden term, but as a sophisticated differentiation between different sorts of government anti-poverty programs.[40]

The broader lesson from this alternative perspective on the "welfare" question wording experiment is that much of what passes for question wording effects are in actuality differences in responses resulting from differences in the policy that respondents are asked to respond to. The same survey that showed more support for "assisting the poor" than for "welfare" also found greater support for "halting the rising crime rate" than for "law enforcement" and greater support for "dealing with drug addiction" than for "drug rehabilitation" (General Social Survey). But these alternative question wordings are not simply different formulations of the identical policies; they are references to different aspects of their respective issues.

In the second example above, which contrasts "forbid" and "not allow," the alternative wordings do appear to have identical meanings. The substantial differences in responses to these two formulations are a bit of a mystery, especially since the alternative question wordings sometimes produce dramatically different responses (like the case of "speeches against democracy" described above), sometimes modest differences (e.g., in a parallel experiment focused on "speeches in favor of communism"), and sometimes no differences at all (e.g., in questions about "showing x-rated movies" or "cigarette advertisements on television").[41] Sometimes respondents seem to react differently to "forbid" and "not allow" but at other times these alternative wordings seem to make no difference.

The third example above revealed different evaluations if a policy choice was presented in terms of its effect on the percent of the work force that would be *employed* or on the percent of the work force that would be *unemployed*. These sorts of mathematically equivalent alternative descriptions have been labeled "equivalency frames."[42] This example is explained by recognizing that people tend to evaluate differences in magnitude (like the employment or unemployment rates) at least partly in terms of ratios. The difference between 10 percent and 5 percent unemployment appears large because the former is twice as big as the latter. In contrast, the difference between 90 percent employment and 95 percent employment appears small because their ratio is close to one.[43]

These sorts of framing effects have led many scholars to doubt whether the public can plausibly be said to have preferences on the underlying policies. But other scholars point out that such framing effects in survey experiments take place under highly artificial conditions. In the real world alternative ways of characterizing a policy choice are typically encountered not in isolation (as in survey experiments) but simultaneously as part of the political debate. The availability of competing frames, and the give and take of political debate, have been shown to undermine framing effects, reducing or eliminating differences in responses.[44]

Question wording and framing effects potentially challenge the notion that the public holds meaningful preferences and that we can use survey interviews to discern what those preferences are. Yet the real world impact of these problems may be small, as two recent examples suggest. In the first example, opponents of the inheritance tax were said to have boosted their cause by relabeling it the "death tax".[45] But the best evidence suggests that the label made little difference. In a survey experiment using two alternative wordings administered to randomly selected halves of the sample, 69 percent of respondents favored doing away with the "estate tax" while 73 percent favored doing away with the "death tax".[46]

In a parallel example, observers have claimed that the label "climate change" generates greater concern among the public than "global warming".[47] But the only randomized survey experiment to pit these two formulations against each other found little difference: 57 percent of Americans believed that "global warming" would become a "very serious" or "extremely serious" problem if nothing was done, compared with 60 percent who felt that way about "climate change" and 58 percent about "global climate change."[48]

In sum, we cannot dismiss concerns about question wording and framing effects entirely. The evidence is strong that how a policy is described can have an impact on the level of support or opposition expressed toward that policy. These effects, however, do not imply that the public has no "real" attitudes toward these policies, or that we cannot know (at least approximately) what those attitudes are. As one expert who has himself conducted numerous studies of framing effects concludes "framing effects appear to be neither robust nor particularly pervasive. Elite competition and heterogeneous discussion limit and often eliminate framing effects."[49]

Feigned Attitudes and Feigned Non-Attitudes

Two additional problems are sometimes viewed as affecting survey measures of political attitudes. First, respondents who lack opinions may be reluctant to say "don't know" either out of embarrassment or in an effort to be "helpful" to the interviewer. In such cases, claims to support or oppose some policy represent "non-attitudes" which distort the observed measure of public preferences. In other cases, respondents who in fact do have relevant opinions nevertheless may answer "don't know" perhaps because they think their true preference is embarrassing or out of step with perceived social norms. In either situation, respondents who engage in these behaviors may be distinctive in ways that result in a misleading assessment of what the true distribution of preferences in the population looks like.

Scholars have examined both of these kinds of "mis-reported" attitudes. Respondents' tendency to feign preferences on issues on which they lack opinions has been assessed by asking respondents about wholly fictitious issues. For example, 24 percent of respondents in one survey expressed a preference on whether the "1975 Public Affairs Act" should be repealed and 39 percent offered an opinion on the "Agricultural Trade Act of 1984" despite the fact that neither of these supposed pieces of legislation existed.[50] This suggests that some of the opinion preferences collected by survey interviewers about policies (or potential policy changes) that really do exist are in fact "non-attitudes" reported by respondents who are reluctant to say "Don't Know." These sorts of findings are often seen as embarrassments undermining the notion that the surveys reveal meaningful preferences. Yet the 76 percent and 61 percent of respondents who did say "Don't Know" in response to these two questions about fictitious legislation is far higher than the percentage of respondents saying "Don't Know" to any of the real issues represented in the data I analyze below.

Since most respondents do seem able to resist the pressure to express a preference on an issue they have never heard of, most of the preferences that are expressed in response to the questions I examine in this study are likely real preferences, even if the respondents offering those preferences are only vaguely familiar with some of the issues they were asked about. Taking the "worst case scenario" above as a guide, if only 61 percent of those who really don't have an opinion on an issue say "Don't Know" and the rest offer a substantive preference anyway, the observed proportion of "Don't Knows" will be an underestimate of the true proportion. Thus if we observed that 5 percent of respondents said "Don't Know" (about the average for my data) we could infer that the real percentage of respondents who lack an opinion is about 8.2 percent (since 61 percent of 8.2 is 5.0).

The "hidden" non-attitudes in the example above consist of the 3.2 percent of respondents who gave a substantive answer despite having no real opinion. Of course, if the question concerned a more obscure policy on which a larger percentage of the respondents in fact had no opinion, the size of the hidden non-attitudes group would be proportionately larger. Since few of the policy questions in my data set produce observed "Don't Know" rates of greater than 10 percent, the extent of such hidden non-attitudes is simply too small to seriously distort the real information contained in the substantive survey responses that form the basis of my analyses.[51]

The second threat to the validity of survey data mentioned above is the opposite of hidden non-attitudes. In this second scenario, respondents who in fact hold opinions nevertheless give "Don't Know" responses. Adam Berinsky offers the most extensive analysis of this phenomenon. Berinsky hypothesizes that survey questions on political attitudes are most likely to elicit "Don't Know" responses from people who in fact do have opinions if the issue being discussed is either complex or if the respondent's views run counter to perceived social norms.[52] In the former case, for example, a question about tax policy might require considerable effort from respondents to connect the proposed policy to their own interests and preferences on taxes. Rather than engage in this effortful processing, respondents may simply say "Don't Know." In the latter case, a respondent who opposes laws protecting homosexuals from discrimination may prefer to avoid the risk of embarrassment or social sanction by saying "Don't Know" instead.

Berinsky tests this theory with a series of questions about race, social welfare policy, and the Vietnam war. Of concern here is the extent to which observed measures of policy preferences are distorted by respondents with real attitudes saying "Don't Know." Using a sophisticated statistical model to impute preferences to respondents who said "Don't Know," Berinsky finds virtually no such distortion for questions that lack complexity and have no clear socially normative answer. In contrast, he does find distortions on questions with one or the other of these qualities. But like the impact of hidden non-attitudes, the size of the distortions uncovered in Berinsky's analysis is quite small. The largest distortions occur on racial policy questions asked during the 1990s for which he estimates that opposition to school integration would appear three to five percent higher if the hidden attitudes of respondents saying "Don't Know" were statistically taken into account. The distortions on the other questions hypothesized to produce hidden attitudes are even smaller: observed preferences on social welfare policy in the 1990s and on the Vietnam war in the 1960s never differ from the estimated true preferences by more than 2 percentage points.

Survey questions are imperfect measures of public preferences in many ways. The question for scholars and others interested in what the public thinks is whether the distortions inherent in survey data are small enough that such data can be relied on to gauge public sentiments. With regard to both of the potential threats to validity examined above, it appears that these distortions are minor. Neither hidden attitudes nor hidden non-attitudes appear to be substantial enough to significantly impact the value of survey-based preference measures for analyzing Americans' preferences on matters of public policy.

Public Preferences and Government Responsiveness

If the policy preferences expressed by the mass public are meaningful (at least in the aggregate) and reflective of Americans' genuine attitudes toward alternative government actions, then one criterion for assessing the degree of democratic legitimacy is the strength of the association between public preferences and policy outcomes. Of course we would not expect or desire a perfect match between majority preferences and government policy. First, there are issues of minority rights to be considered. Second, the public is not capable of guiding policy on all questions that come before the government. Issues like alternative high-definition TV standards, or which government regulatory agency should be responsible for agricultural futures trading, are simply too obscure for most citizens to have meaningful preferences on. Finally, one subset of the public might care intensely about a particular issue while another is fairly indifferent. If I care deeply about foreign policy and am indifferent to education, and you care strongly about education and not foreign policy, a government that responds to my preferences on foreign policy and yours on education would make us both happier than one that took each of our views equally into consideration in both issue domains.

These considerations notwithstanding, it remains true that a government that responds only weakly or not at all to the preferences of the governed, or that systematically responds to some citizens but ignores others, has but a weak claim to being considered a democracy. The association of government policy with public preferences measured by surveys is only one basis for judging government responsiveness, but it is a useful starting point for assessing the nature and degree of representation.

To estimate the association between public preferences and government policy I make use of the dataset mentioned briefly above. These data consist of 2,245 survey questions asked between 1964 and 2006.[53] Each question asked whether respondents favored or opposed some specific change in federal government policy. In my dataset, I collected the responses to these questions separately for respondents at different income levels in order to compare the strength of the preference/policy link for more and less well-off Americans.

As we would expect, the more support a given policy has among the public, the more likely it is that that policy will be adopted, and this pattern holds true for respondents at all income levels. Figure 3.1 shows this relationship separately for respondents at the 10th, 50th, and 90th income percentiles.[54] The far left side of the figure shows that policies with strong public opposition (with fewer than 20 percent favoring the proposed change) have a low probability of being adopted, with the probability of adoption increasing as support increases. However, the far right side of the figure shows that even policies with strong public support (at least 80 percent of the public favoring the proposed change) have a less than even chance of being adopted. This pattern suggests that the political system is responsive to public preferences, but with a strong status quo bias. Given that our federal government was designed by its framers to inhibit as much as facilitate lawmaking (with its separation of powers, multiple veto points within congress, supermajority requirements in the Senate, and so on), this status quo bias should not be surprising.

Figure 3.1 also shows that the probability of a policy being adopted is somewhat more strongly related to the preferences of the affluent than those of the middle class or the poor: the solid line, representing respondents at the 90th income percentile, is somewhat steeper than the lines for the 50th and 10th income percentiles. But the differences among income groups are modest, and at every level of income, favored policies are substantially more likely to be adopted than unfavored policies.

To better gauge the true influence over policymaking of Americans at different income levels, we need to take into account the fact that poor and well-off Americans agree on many policy questions. If affluent Americans are better able to influence policy outcomes than the less well-off, the association of policy outcomes with the preferences of the poor or the middle class shown in Figure 3.1 may simply reflect those proposed changes on which Americans at all income levels agree.

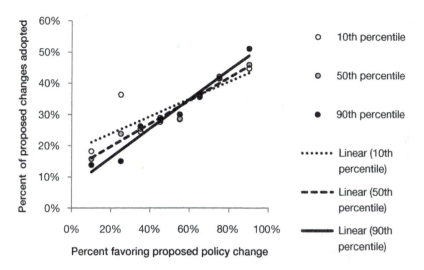

Figure 3.1 The Preference/Policy Link for Respondents at the 10th, 50th, and 90th Income Percentiles.

Note: Based on 2,245 survey questions concerning proposed policy changes asked between 1964 and 2006.

Figure 3.2 shows the same relationships shown in Figure 3.1, but restricted to proposed policy changes for which low- and high-income Americans' preferences, or middle- and high-income Americans' preferences, diverge by at least 10 percentage points. Here we see a very different picture: the preference/policy link for the affluent remains strong, but when the preferences of less well-off Americans diverge from those at the top of the income distribution, the preferences of the less well-off appear to have virtually no relationship with policy outcomes. In other publications I explore these relationships in greater detail. I find that the basic pattern shown in figure 3.2 is similar with regard to foreign policy, economic policy, social welfare, and moral or religious issues and cannot be explained by the higher levels of voting among the affluent, or a lack of strong preferences among the middle class or the poor.[55]

A number of different factors may contribute to the influence over policy exerted by affluent Americans and the lack of influence among the less well-off, but they all relate directly or indirectly to the importance of money in the political system. The well-off contribute to parties, candidates, and interest organizations at far higher rates than the middle class or the poor. In addition, they tend to share the policy preferences of an even smaller and more powerful group of truly rich Americans who help determine who runs for and wins public office (and therefore what sorts of policies they subsequently pursue). Finally, government policymakers are themselves far better off economically than the average American, and their own policy preferences are more likely to reflect those of their economic peers than of less well-off citizens.

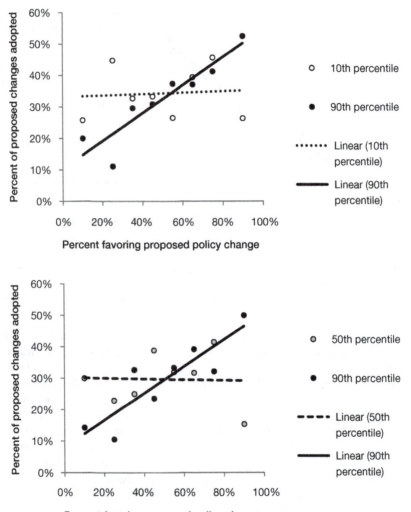

Figure 3.2 The Preference/Policy Link when Preferences at the 10th or 50th Income Percentiles Diverge From the 90th Income Percentile.

Note: Based on the 932 and 414 survey questions on which the preferences of people at the 10th and 90th and 50th and 90th income percentiles diverged by at least 10 percentage points.

Conclusions

The American public's knowledge of political issues and understanding of the policy choices government faces is clearly limited. And studies of framing and question wording show the potential difficulties of measuring public preferences. Yet on balance, the evidence indicates that framing and question wording effects in the real world are infrequent, and that aggregate preferences as measured by surveys reflect much the same set of attitudes that a more fully informed and engaged public would express. This evidence, I suggest, is sufficient to conclude that survey measures of public opinion are sensible bases on which to judge the extent to which government policy reflects the preferences of the governed.

Based on the findings described briefly above, American democracy is found wanting. The problem lies not in the failure of the public to form meaningful policy preferences, but in the failure of policymakers to respond to the public. Affluent Americans appear to have substantial influence over policy outcomes, but when less well-off Americans' preferences diverge from those of the affluent, government policymakers appear to take into account only the desires of the most economically advantaged.

In every society the well-off have more influence over government than the less economically advantaged. But the degree of inequality in how government responds to its citizens is a fundamental gauge of how truly democratic a society is. In this regard, we have a long way to go before we can claim to be a democracy characterized by "the continuing responsiveness of the government to the preferences of its citizens, considered as political equals."[56]

Notes

1. Robert A. Dahl, *Polyarchy: Participation and Opposition* (New Haven: Yale University Press, 1971), p.1.
2. Bernard R. Berelson, Paul F. Lazarsfeld, and William N. McPhee, *Voting: A Study of Opinion Formation in a Presidential Campaign* (Chicago: University of Chicago Press, 1954), p. 308.
3. Philip E. Converse, "The Nature of Belief Systems in Mass Publics," in *Ideology and Discontent*, ed. David E. Apter (New York: Free Press, 1964).
4. Ibid., p.245.
5. Michael X. Delli Carpini and Scott Keeter, *What Americans Know About Politics and Why It Matters* (New Haven: Yale University Press, 1996), p.269.
6. Ibid., p.270.
7. Berelson, Lazarsfeld, and McPhee, *Voting: A Study of Opinion Formation in a Presidential Campaign*, p.311.
8. Ibid., p.109.
9. Anthony Downs, *An Economic Theory of Democracy* (New York: Harper Collins, 1957), p.233.
10. Samuel L. Popkin, *The Reasoning Voter: Communication and Persuasion in Presidential Campaigns* (Chicago: University of Chicago Press, 1991); Paul M. Sniderman, Richard A. Brody, and Philip E. Tetlock, *Reasoning and Choice:*

Explorations in Political Psychology (Cambridge: Cambridge University Press, 1991); Arthur Lupia, "Shortcuts Versus Encyclopedias: Information and Voting Behavior in California Insurance Reform Elections," *American Political Science Review* 88, no. 1 (1994); Arthur Lupia and Mathew D. McCubbins, *The Democratic Dilemma: Can Citizens Learn What They Need to Know?* (Cambridge: Cambridge University Press, 1998); Martin Gilens and Naomi Murakawa, "Elite Cues and Political Decision-Making," in *Research in Micropolitics*, ed. Michael X. Delli Carpini, Leonie Huddy, and Robert Y. Shapiro (Oxford: Elsevier, 2002); Richard R. Lau and David P. Redlawsk, "Voting Correctly," *American Political Science Review* 91, no. 3 (1997); Richard R. Lau and David P. Redlawsk, *How Voters Decide: Information Processing During Election Campaigns*, Cambridge Studies in Public Opinion and Political Psychology (Cambridge; New York: Cambridge University Press, 2006); John R. Zaller, *The Nature and Origins of Mass Opinion* (Cambridge: Cambridge University Press, 1992); Edward G. Carmines and James H. Kuklinski, "Incentives, Opportunities, and the Logic of Public Opinion in American Political Representation," in *Information and Democratic Processes*, ed. John A. Ferejohn and James H. Kuklinski (Urbana, IL: University of Illinois Press, 1990).

11. Arthur Lupia, "Who Can Persuade?: A Formal Theory, a Survey and Implications for Democracy" (paper presented in Chicago, 1995).

12. E.g., John W. Kingdon, *Congressmen's Voting Decisions*, 3rd ed. (Ann Arbor: University of Michigan Press, 1989).

13. Converse assessed issue public membership by dint of the consistency of responses to the same questions over time.

14. Converse, "The Nature of Belief Systems in Mass Publics", p.246.

15. Shanto Iyengar et al., "Selective Exposure to Campaign Communication: The Role of Anticipated Agreement and Issue Public Membership," *Journal of Politics* 70, no. 1 (2008); Amy R. Gershkoff, "How Issue Interest Can Rescue the American Public" (Doctoral dissertation, Department of Politics, Princeton University, 2006); Jon A. Krosnick, "Government Policy and Citizen Passion: A Study of Issue Publics in Contemporary America," *Political Behavior* 12, no. 1 (1990).

16. Krosnick, "Government Policy and Citizen Passion: A Study of Issue Publics in Contemporary America."

17. Vincent L. Hutchings, *Public Opinion and Democratic Accountability: How Citizens Learn About Politics* (Princeton, N.J.: Princeton University Press, 2003).

18. Nicholas R. Miller, "Information, Electorates, and Democracy: Some Extensions and Interpretations of the Condorcet Jury Theorem," in *Information Pooling and Group Decision Making*, ed. Bernard Grofman and Guillermo Owen (Greenwich, CT: JAI, 1986); Benjamin I. Page and Robert Y. Shapiro, *The Rational Public: Fifty Years of Trends in Americans' Policy Preferences* (Chicago: University of Chicago Press, 1992); Philip E. Converse, "Popular Representation and the Distribution of Information," in *Information and Democratic Processes*, ed. John A. Ferejohn and James H. Kuklinski (Urbana: University of Illinois Press, 1990); Christopher H. Achen, "Mass Political Attitudes and the Survey Response," *American Political Science Review* 69, no. 4 (1975).

19. Zaller, *The Nature and Origins of Mass Opinion*; John Zaller and Stanley Feldman, "A Simple Theory of the Survey Response: Answering Questions Versus Revealing Preferences," *American Journal of Political Science* 36, no. 3 (1992).

20. Larry M. Bartels, "Democracy with Attitudes" in *Electoral Democracy*, ed. M.B. MacKuen and G. Rabinowitz (Ann Arbor: University of Michigan Press, 2003), pp. 48–82.

21. Page and Shapiro, *The Rational Public: Fifty Years of Trends in Americans' Policy Preferences*.

22. Ibid.

23. Ibid., p.14.

24. Ibid., p.14.

25. Martin Gilens, "Political Ignorance and Collective Policy Preferences," *American Political Science Review* 95, no. 2 (2001); J. H. Kuklinski, P. J. Quirk, J. Jerit, D. Schwieder, and R. F. Rich, "Misinformation and the Currency of Democratic Citizenship," *Journal of Politics* 62, no. 3 (2000); Martin Gilens, *Why Americans Hate Welfare: Race, Media, and the Politics of Antipoverty Policy* (Chicago: University of Chicago Press, 1999).

26. Page and Shapiro, *The Rational Public: Fifty Years of Trends in Americans' Policy Preferences*, p.381.

27. Scott L. Althaus, *Collective Preferences in Democratic Politics: Opinion Surveys and the Will of the People* (New York: Cambridge University Press, 2003).

28. With 20 percent of respondents reporting the "wrong" preference, the true 75 percent favoring is reduced by 15 percentage points (75 × .20) who are recorded instead as opposing. The true 25 percent who oppose is reduced by 5 percentage points (25 × .20) who are recorded instead as favoring. Thus the total percentage recorded as favoring is 75 − 15 + 5 = 65 and the total percentage recorded as opposing is 25 − 5 + 15 = 35.

29. Lupia, "Shortcuts Versus Encyclopedias: Information and Voting Behavior in California Insurance Reform Elections."

30. Robert C. Luskin and James S. Fishkin, "Deliberative Polling, Public Opinion, and Democracy: The Case of the National Issues Convention" (Paper presented at the American Political Science Association Annual Meetings, Boston, 1998); James S. Fishkin and Robert C. Luskin, "Bringing Deliberation to the Democratic Dialogue," in *A Poll with a Human Face*, ed. Max McCombs and Amy Reynolds (1999); James S. Fishkin and Robert C. Luskin, "Experimenting with a Democratic Ideal: Deliberative Polling and Public Opinion," *Acta Politica* 40, no. 3 (2005).

31. See Gilens and Murakawa, "Elite Cues and Political Decision-Making," for an analysis of these results.

32. Philip E. Converse, "Assessing the Capacity of Mass Electorates," *Annual Review of Political Science* 3 (2000).

33. L. M. Bartels, "Uninformed Votes: Information Effects in Presidential Elections," *American Journal of Political Science* 40, no. 1 (1996).

34. Ibid., table 3.

35. Althaus, *Collective Preferences in Democratic Politics: Opinion Surveys and the Will of the People.*

36. Herbert B. Asher, *Polling and the Public : What Every Citizen Should Know*, 7th ed. (Washington, DC: CQ Press, 2007), p.56.

37. Tom W. Smith, "That Which We Call Welfare by Any Other Name Would Smell Sweeter: An Analysis of the Impact of Question Wording on Response Patterns," *Public Opinion Quarterly* 51 (1987).

38. Howard Schuman and Stanley Presser, *Questions and Answers in Attitude Surveys* (San Diego: Academic Press, 1981), p.277.

39. George A. Quattrone and Amos Tversky, "Contrasting Rational and Psychological Analyses of Political Choice," *American Political Science Review* 82, no. 3 (1988).

40. Gilens, *Why Americans Hate Welfare: Race, Media, and the Politics of Antipoverty Policy.*

41. Schuman and Presser, *Questions and Answers in Attitude Surveys*, pp.281–283.

42. James N. Druckman, "The Implications of Framing Effects for Citizen Competence," *Political Behavior* 23, no. 3 (2001).

43. Quattrone and Tversky, "Contrasting Rational and Psychological Analyses of Political Choice", p.728.
44. James N. Druckman, "Political Preference Formation: Competition, Deliberation, and the (Ir)Relevance of Framing Effects," *American Political Science Review* 98, no. 4 (2004); Paul M. Sniderman and Sean M. Theriault, "The Structure of Political Argument and the Logic of Issue Framing" in Studies in Public Opinion: Attitudes, Nonattitudes, Measurement Error, and Change, ed. W.E. Saris and P.M. Sniderman (Princeton, NJ: Princeton University Press, 2004).
45. Michael J. Graetz and Ian Shapiro, *Death by a Thousand Cuts: The Fight over Taxing Inherited Wealth*, 1st ed. (Princeton, N.J.: Princeton University Press, 2005).
46. Larry M. Bartels, *Unequal Democracy: The Political Economy of the New Gilded Age* (Princeton: Princeton University Press, 2008). Whether Americans would still object to the estate tax if they knew how few estates were actually subject to the tax is uncertain. Bartels, *Unequal Democracy*, and Joel Slemrod "The Role of Misconceptions in Support for Regressive Tax Reform," *National Tax Journal* 59, no. 1 (2006) offer evidence that misinformation about the breadth of the estate tax's impact contributes only modestly to public opposition. In contrast, Ilyan Kuziemko, Michael I. Norton, Emmanuel Saez, and Stefanie Stantcheva, "How Elastic Are Preferences for Redistribution? Evidence from Randomized Survey Experiments," NBER Working Paper no. 18865 (2013), find a substantial impact.
47. Katy Butler, "George Lakoff Says Environmentalists Need to Watch Their Language," *Sierra Magazine* 89, July/August (2004).
48. Ana Villar and Jon A. Krosnick, "Global Warming Vs. Climate Change, Taxes Vs. Prices: Does Word Choice Matter?" *Climate Change* (2010), available at https://woods.stanford.edu/sites/default/files/files/WarmingVsChange.pdf
49. Druckman, "Political Preference Formation: Competition, Deliberation, and the (Ir)Relevance of Framing Effects," p.683.
50. George F. Bishop, Alfred J. Tuchfarber, and Robert W. Oldendick, "Opinions on Fictitious Issues: the Pressure to Answer Survey Questions," *Public Opinion Quarterly* 50, no. 2 (1986).
51. Ninety-one percent of the proposed policy change questions in my dataset elicited no more than 10 percent "Don't Know" responses; 97 percent of the questions elicited no more than 15 percent "Don't Know" responses.
52. Adam J. Berinsky, *Silent Voices: Public Opinion and Political Participation in America* (Princeton, New Jersey: Princeton University Press, 2004).
53. For reasons explained in Martin Gilens, "Paying the Piper: Economic Inequality and Democratic Responsiveness in the United States" (unpublished book manuscript, Princeton University, n.d.), only survey questions asked during 1964–68, 1981–2002, and 2005–06 were included.
54. Figures 3.1 and 3.2 show the mean proportion adopted for policies favored by less than 20 percent, 20–30, 30–40, 40–50, 50–60, 60–70, 70–80, and 80 percent of respondents or more (for respondents at the 10th, 50th, and 90th income percentiles). See Martin Gilens, "Inequality and Democratic Responsiveness," *Public Opinion Quarterly* 69, no. 5 (2005) for an explanation of how preferences at different income percentiles are calculated.
55. Gilens, "Inequality and Democratic Responsiveness"; Martin Gilens, "Preference Gaps and Inequality in Representation," *PS: Political Science and Politics* 42, no. 2 (2009); Martin Gilens, "Policy Outcomes and Representational Inequality," in *Who Gets Represented?*, ed. Peter K. Enns and Christopher Wlezien (New York, NY: Russell Sage Foundation, 2011); Gilens, "Paying the Piper: Economic Inequality and Democratic Responsiveness in the United States." (Unpublished manuscript, Princeton University).
56. Dahl, *Polyarchy: Participation and Opposition*, p.1.

Part II

Foundations of Political Preferences

Chapter 4

The Structure, Foundations, and Expression of Ideology

Christopher M. Federico

Few concepts in the study of public opinion have attracted as much attention as that of ideology. While social scientists have always shown a keen interest in the nuts and bolts of belief systems, the resurgence of bitter divisions between the left and right has brought the topic back to the forefront of scholarship and lay discussion alike. In this chapter, I review past and present work on the nature of ideology and its consequences for public opinion. I begin by addressing the definitional question of *what* ideology actually is. Next, I provide an overview of several decades' worth of research on *what attracts* individuals to different ideological postures like liberalism and conservatism and *when* individuals think and make judgments about issues and candidates in ways that reflect ideology. As we shall see, these two aspects of ideology do not always go hand-in-hand. While most citizens willingly identify themselves as "liberals" or "conservatives," only those who have absorbed a great deal of information from political leaders think about politics in terms of these ideological categories and express opinions that are consistently liberal or conservative. Finally, I expand on the question of when citizens rely on ideology by suggesting that information is not the whole story. To this end, I review evidence suggesting that citizens must possess both political information and a strong desire to appraise things as "good" or "bad" in order to think ideologically and express ideologically-consistent opinions.

What Is Ideology?

While the concept of ideology has a familiar ring to it, students of public opinion—including political scientists, sociologists, and psychologists—have struggled to settle on a common definition of what it is.[1] As a result, those who dive into the topic may find themselves adrift on a sea of competing inter-pretations. Nevertheless, in public-opinion research, the most important working definitions of ideology do repeatedly converge on a number of crucial claims.[2] First, ideologies are *belief systems* or frameworks of inter-related ideas. That is, they consist of opinions, values, and beliefs about the nature of social reality that can be grouped together under some common social theme, e.g., moving society in the direction of greater justice and equality. In the language of psychology, this claim suggests that ideologies are *schemas*—i.e., organized clusters of ideas about social and political life that have been stored away in long-term memory.[3] Second, ideologies are shared by and reflect the life situations of groups of individuals. In this respect, a given ideology is typically not idiosyncratic; it is held in common by a group of people living in a particular social and historical context and it expresses the opinions, values, and concerns they have developed as a result of the challenges and opportunities present in that context. Third, ideologies are both descriptive and prescriptive in nature. That is, they both provide an interpretation of society as it currently exists and offer normative guidelines about how society should ideally be organized and the acceptable means for attaining political goals.

Thus, ideologies can be thought of as shared belief systems that reflect some group's understanding of the social world and its vision of what that world should ideally look like. However, this definition tells us very little about how ideological belief systems are organized. On this point, there has also been a good bit of debate among scholars about the nature of the ideological beast. On one hand, the standard assumption is that ideological positions can be ordered according to the familiar "left–right" spectrum. This perspective suggests that ideological phenomena can be boiled down to a single belief dimension anchored by preferences for equality and openness to social change on the left end of the spectrum and by preferences for hierarchy and preservation of the status quo on the right end.[4] In this usage, the terms "left" and "right" date back to seating arrangements in the French National Assembly during the revolutionary era, which placed the more conservative factions on the right side of the hall and the more radical factions on the left.[5]

This understanding of the structure of ideology continues to inform current scholarship, and it receives support from a number of sources. To begin with, use of a single left–right spectrum is clearly the norm among those most involved in political action and political decision-making, i.e., "political elites" in government, party and activist organizations, the media, and academia.[6] Similarly, the most well-informed and politically active members of the general public also rely strongly on the basic left–right dimension in their thinking and political judgments—a tendency which has grown stronger in recent decades as elites from the Democratic and Republican parties have ideologically diverged.[7] Finally, a great deal of evidence suggests that individuals who place themselves at different positions on the left–right spectrum tend to adopt correspondingly different opinions about issues connected with the core distinctions of equality versus inequality and openness to change versus the *status quo*, especially if they are politically well-informed.[8] That is, self-described liberals are more likely to take liberal positions on specific issues, whereas self-described conservatives are more likely to take conservative stances on the same issues.

Of course, ideological self-placement and the general liberalism or conservatism of one's issue preferences rarely align in a simple one-to-one fashion. In this regard, researchers have been careful to distinguish between *symbolic* (or *philosophical*) ideology and *operational* ideology.[9] Symbolic ideology refers to whether one generally identifies oneself as a "liberal," "conservative," or some moderate position in between; while operational ideology refers to one's average left–right position across issues, especially those relevant to government spending. Importantly, evidence suggests that these two types of ideology do not coincide for many citizens. An example of this is Free and Cantril's classic finding that many Americans living in the middle of the twentieth century were simultaneously "philosophical conservatives" and "operational liberals," opposing "big government" in the abstract but offering strong support for the individual programs that made up "big government."[10] More recently, Ellis and Stimson have noted that over two-thirds of those who identify as symbolic conservatives are operational liberals on the issues.[11] Thus, even in situations where citizens do appear to rely on a single left–right spectrum, their belief profiles may differ at the levels of general identification and actual judgments about issues. We return to this point about the lack of concordance between left–right self-placement and issue opinions below.

While the notion of a single ideological dimension is simple and consistent with a great deal of evidence, other scholars have argued that citizens' ideological views may have more than one dimension. "Multidimensional" approaches of this sort come in a number of forms, but the most common variant argues that ideology can be characterized in terms of two different content dimensions.[12] Broadly speaking, the first dimension reflects one's preference for equality versus inequality in social life, while the second dimension reflects one's preference for openness versus social order. These "dual-process" models suggest that the two dimensions are governed by distinct but related sets of psychological processes, and that the dimensions may operate somewhat independently.[13] Thus, while the notion of a single left–right spectrum implies that a "right-wing" orientation on one dimension (e.g., a preference for inequality) should be accompanied by a right-wing orientation on the other (e.g., support for social order), the dual-process approach suggests that one's views on the two dimensions need not be perfectly congruent with one another.

Indeed, two dimensions of this sort appear to recur repeatedly in analyses of various kinds of social and political beliefs. For example, researchers interested in *human values*—abstract beliefs about desirable social goals or modes of conduct—suggest that the former can be arrayed according to two such dimensions.[14] The first dimension deals with "self-transcendence versus self-enhancement," and it reflects one's concern for power and rank. This dimension is anchored by values like benevolence and universal concern for others at one end and values like power and achievement at the other. The second deals with "openness versus conservation," and it reflects one's concern for security and order. This dimension is anchored by values like self-direction at one end and tradition and conformity at the other. Similar dual dimensions have been identified in studies of political extremism, which suggest that ideologies can be distinguished in terms of their level of support for equality versus inequality, on one hand, and their level of intolerance for alternative points of view, on the other.[15] The dual-process approach also finds an echo in public-opinion research suggesting that there are distinct dimensions corresponding to attitudes about "economic" issues (e.g., the extent to which government should regulate business, how much should the government spend on social welfare, etc.) and "social" issues (e.g., should the government protect gays and lesbians from discrimination, should access to abortion be increased or decreased, etc.).[16] A similar dichotomy manifests itself at the level of differences between political parties across nations, with research suggesting that parties compete with one another for votes along two dimensions corresponding to concern for equality and preferences regarding tradition versus change.[17]

So, which of these perspectives is correct? Is ideology best thought of in terms of a single left–right dimension, or multiple dimensions corresponding to preferences regarding equality and social openness? While the bulk of the data suggests that two dimensions of ideology are in fact present, it is also clear that these dimensions are not completely independent of one another and that they may be very highly aligned among the politically engaged.[18] In this vein, a number of theorists have suggested that having multiple dimensions of political evaluation makes many political decisions more difficult.[19] Many common political choices—such as who to vote for or which party to affiliate with—are dichotomous in nature: there is a left-wing option and a right-wing option. If one's preferences on the two dimensions are not aligned, political choices become more fraught with conflicts and tradeoffs. This implies that individuals who are most involved in political decision-making—including not just political professionals, but also the most informed and politically-involved segments of the mass public—would benefit most from a belief system in which the two dimensions of ideology overlap with one another to form a single left–right axis.

Consistent with this argument, attitudes associated with the equality and openness dimensions are more likely to be aligned with one another among the highly informed and involved and among elected officials.[20] Research also suggests that intensified political competition may lead multiple ideological dimensions to collapse more cleanly into a single left–right dimension. For example, cross-national comparisons reveal that the equality and openness dimensions are more likely to be positively correlated in countries with established systems of party competition with distinct left-wing and right-wing options.[21] Moreover, once a second dimension of ideological competition arises in a political system, it tends to become aligned with the existing dimension, such that parties and politicians that support equality also tend to support openness and freedom.[22] Thus, while there may be multiple dimensions of ideology, they are seldom fully independent of one another—and the need to effectively organize political competition and decision-making may lead to considerable overlap between the dimensions among those most engaged in politics.

What Attracts People to Different Ideological Positions?

Having discussed the issue of what ideology is, I turn to the question of what attracts people to various ideological positions. Working from a variety of theoretical perspectives, political scientists, psychologists, and sociologists have brought a great deal of data to bear on this question. From this welter of research a number of answers have emerged. While some of these answers have a decidedly "social" feel and center on features of an individual's social environment, such as his or her social position and group memberships, other focus more on processes within individuals, such as their psychological needs, personality traits, moral emphases, and even their genetic makeup. At a glance, Figure 4.1 summarizes some of the most important factors that attract people to particular ideological positions. Below, I review these factors in more detail.

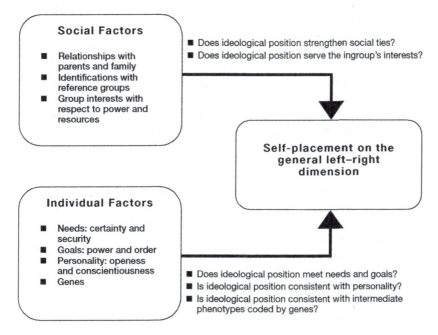

Figure 4.1 What Attracts People to Different Ideological Positions? (source: author creation).

Identifications and Relationships

As one might expect, social relationships—both with other individuals and with groups—are a major influence on citizens' ideological inclinations. In general, we tend to adopt the views of those we like, identify with, or otherwise have some social connection to. For example, psychological research suggests that activating a desire for closeness to a significant other leads individuals to align their own social and political opinions more closely with the perceived views of the other. In turn, this increased similarity in opinions produces a "shared reality" that helps solidify the relationship in question.[23]

Research on political socialization—the process by which individuals learn about the political world and acquire their opinions and views from others—also illustrates the role of relational influences on the acquisition of ideological positions.[24] In this vein, decades of research suggest that ideological positions are likely to be transmitted from parents to children, especially if both parents have similar beliefs and discuss politics frequently and if bonds within the family are close.[25] Similarly, reference groups— groups that people use as a standard for evaluating themselves and their behavior—also have a strong influence on ideological affinity.[26] That is, we tend to adopt the views of groups we relate to in some way. This was famously demonstrated by Theodore Newcomb in his study of female undergraduates at Bennington College.[27] Newcomb's undergraduates were largely conservative in their views when they first arrived at Bennington, having come from fairly well-off Eastern families. However, the Bennington environment itself—consisting of faculty and older students—was largely liberal. Accordingly, Newcomb's undergraduate subjects moved further and further to the left the longer they were at Bennington, as they came to identify more with the campus social environment; the only exceptions were undergraduates who remained unusually close to their families while at college. Naturally, these reference-group effects are not limited to one's college environment. They are also quite evident with respect to a number of more politically-relevant group identities, such as one's religion, region, or occupational category.[28]

These relational influences on ideology also appear to be stronger at some times than at others. In general, parents, peers, and reference groups have their strongest effects on ideological affinity during late adolescence and early adulthood, before a person's identity is fully fleshed out.[29] Moreover, the resulting identifications tend to persist as long as a person's pattern of relationships with other individuals and groups does not change markedly. For example, this pattern was notably evident in Newcomb's Bennington study: while Newcomb observed profound changes in his subjects' attitudes over the course of college, follow-up interviews later in their adult lives revealed little additional change.

Group Interests

Another relational influence on ideological affinity follows from identification with groups, namely, the pursuit of those groups' collective political interests.

In general, a long line of theorizing—derived mainly from economics—suggests that individuals should make political choices that reflect self-interest. However, a wide variety of research suggests that personal self-interest has only a minor effect on what people believe ideologically; that is, calculations about one's own economic interests or the interests of one's family have little influence on political attitudes.[30]

Nevertheless, the perceived collective interests of the social groups one identifies with do tend to influence ideology, especially when people are highly aware of their identity as a member of a particular group. Generally speaking, members of groups with low social status, less power, and/or fewer resources tend to be more egalitarian and left-wing in their political outlook, while members of more privileged groups gravitate toward the right.[31] However, this effect is not a simple "reflective" one: not all individuals who identify with a group adopt group-interested ideological positions. In fact, for some members of less well-off groups, the group-interest motive may be countered by other motives, such as the need to avoid the uncertainty or insecurity that might come from challenging the political status quo.[32] Thus, the effect of group interest— while often present—is rarely total.

Psychological Needs

Moving away from the level of broader social influences on ideological affinity, a great deal of research suggests that one's preference for the left versus the right may be heavily shaped by various psychological needs. In particular, attraction to different positions on the left–right spectrum is not random but systematically rooted in one's underlying level of comfort with uncertainty and threat. This body of work finds that strong needs for certainty and security correlate with greater conservatism—as support for the status quo allows individuals to stick with what is known, familiar, and safe—whereas weaker needs for certainty and security are associated with greater liberalism. This argument was first and perhaps most famously made by the authors of *The Authoritarian Personality*, who suggested that attraction to far-right ideological positions (as opposed to liberal or left-leaning positions) was driven by an "authoritarian personality" type consisting of nine interrelated tendencies, such as rigid moral conventionalism, aggressiveness, submission to idealized leaders, and a preoccupation with power and toughness.[33] In turn, this intolerant type was explained using some of Sigmund Freud's ideas about the management of anxiety. Specifically, Adorno and his colleagues argued that harsh childrearing led authoritarians to "repress" hostility toward their parents and other traditional authorities and "project" it outward onto the scapegoats and outsiders often targeted by right-wing political ideologies (e.g., minorities, those who desire social change, etc.). This need-based perspective was echoed by other early theorists as well.[34]

While these models—and the Adorno et al. model in particular—were later the subject of numerous theoretical and methodological criticisms[35], the notion that ideological affinity may be rooted in some underlying feature of psychological functioning has persisted. In this vein, psychologist Bob Altemeyer has updated the authoritarianism construct, re-labeling it *right-wing authoritarianism* (RWA) and characterizing it more simply as a learned constellation of three attitudes: conventionalism, "authoritarian submission" to traditional social authorities, and "authoritarian aggression" toward disliked outgroups.[36] Others have reduced the concept even further, boiling it down to a general hostility toward diversity.[37] More recently, John Jost and his colleagues— echoing the scholars mentioned above—have reiterated and provided much new evidence for the view that support for the right is associated with the need for certainty and security, whereas support for the left is associated with greater tolerance for uncertainty and potential social danger.[38]

Other psychological approaches have suggested that different sets of needs may account for preferences in different domains of political belief. As noted above, many researchers have suggested that ideology may consist of two dimensions—one corresponding to one's preference for equality versus inequality and the other corresponding to one's preference for openness versus order. In turn, these two dimensions may each be related to a distinct set of psychological needs. For example, Duckitt and Sibley argue that the equality dimension reflects one's orientation toward social hierarchy and depends on the value one places on superiority, achievement, and power, while the openness dimension reflects one's orientation toward traditional morality and social conformity and depends on the value one places on order and security in social life.[39] Moreover, each dimension may be connected with a distinct worldview— either the extent to which one believes that the world is a competitive, violent place, in the case of the equality dimension, or the extent to which one believes that it is a dangerous place, in the case of the openness dimension. People who see the world as a dangerous place tend to prefer order, conformity and security, which attracts them to conservative positions on social issues related to religion, gender, and social convention. In comparison, people who see the world as highly competitive place a premium on social hierarchy and social dominance, which attracts them to those aspects of conservatism which favor inequality, particularly in the economic realm. Thus, the needs for certainty and security highlighted by the "classic" models of ideological affinity reviewed earlier may actually be pertinent to only some of the political concerns that distinguish the left from the right—namely, those dealing with openness and freedom versus tradition and order.

Personality Characteristics

Another set of psychological approaches to ideology have focused on how individual differences in personality might account for variation in ideological sympathies. By "personality," these approaches refer to a set of characteristics possessed by a person that uniquely shape his or her thoughts, feelings, and behaviors across various situations.[40] Speculation about links between personality traits and politics has long been a preoccupation among psychologists. For example, several of the scholars discussed earlier—including the authors of *The Authoritarian Personality*—were interested not only in how needs for certainty and security might shape political sympathies, but also in how these needs might be shaped by enduring personality differences between individuals.[41] However, the dominant framework for examining the relationship between personality and ideology in recent years has been the "Big Five" model of personality traits.[42] Using analyses of personality adjectives found in everyday language, this model boils variation in personality down to five key dimensions. These include *extraversion*, one's level of sociability and assertiveness; *agreeableness*, one's level of altruism and concern for others; *conscientiousness*, one's level of concern for social duty, responsibility, and impulse control; *emotional stability*, one's level of even-temperedness or freedom from negative emotion; and *openness to experience*, one's level of interest in novelty, complexity, and originality.

Numerous studies by psychologists and political scientists alike have examined relationships between these five dimensions and support for the left versus the right. This impressive body of work is reviewed in detail elsewhere in this volume,[43] so I will touch only on its key findings. In this regard, the Big Five dimensions that have the most consistent relationships with ideological affinity are openness to experience and conscientiousness. While openness is typically associated with greater support for the left, conscientiousness is usually associated with greater support for the right.[44] The relationships between each of these dimensions and ideology are not negligible in size; indeed, they are similar in magnitude to the relationships between ideology and key demographic variables like education and income. In contrast, the relationships between the other three Big Five dimensions and ideology are far less consistent across studies, and they also tend to vary across issue domains (i.e., economic issues versus social issues) and social groups (e.g., blacks versus whites).[45]

Morality

Noting the highly moralistic tone of many contemporary ideological disputes, other perspectives argue that left–right differences may be rooted in divergent moral sensibilities. A recent proponent of this view is the psychologist Jonathan Haidt, who suggests that moral judgment rests on five intuitive moral foundations: avoidance of harm to others, concern for fairness, group loyalty, respect for authority, and purity from contamination. The first two foundations are considered *individualizing*: they function to protect individual rights. The other foundations—related to loyalty, authority, and purity—are considered *binding*: their function is to protect the integrity and cohesion of social groups. Importantly, Haidt and his colleagues have shown that liberals and conservatives differ in their relative emphasis on these two sets of concerns: conservatives tend to emphasize all five foundations equally, whereas liberals emphasize the two individualizing foundations and downplay the importance of the three binding ones.[46]

This pattern is echoed by research on ideology and human values, some of which was discussed previously. Specifically, studies on this topic indicate that those who identify with the left place a greater emphasis on self-transcendence values like benevolence and universal concern for humanity, while those who identify with the right emphasize conservation values focused on security, order, and tradition.[47] Thus, evidence from a variety of quarters suggests that ideology may at least in part reflect deeper individual differences in moral understanding.

The Role of Genetics

Finally, researchers in a number of disciplines have begun to explore the possibility that ideological sympathies may at least in part be genetically shaped and transmitted.[48] This view is a sharp departure from most work on ideology in public-opinion research, which has traditionally assumed that ideological affinity is socially learned from parents, peers, and important social groups. This line of work generally relies on what is known as the "classic twin design" in order to estimate what proportions of the variation among individuals in political opinion are due to genes, common environmental influences (i.e., those shared by members of a family) and unique environmental influences (i.e., those not shared by family members).[49] The method does this by comparing the attitudes of identical twins, who effectively share 100 percent of their genetic makeup; and fraternal twins, who share roughly 50 percent of one another's genetic heritage. This fixed difference between identical and fraternal twins in genetic relatedness, along with the assumption that a given pair of twins—whether identical or fraternal—is subject to similar environmental influences, allows the researcher to tease apart the relative impact of genes and environment.

Studies using this and other related methods have found strikingly large effects of genes on ideological opinions. Research on this topic is reviewed more comprehensively elsewhere in this volume[50], so I only discuss the most important of its findings here. Specifically, some 40 percent to 50 percent of the variability in left–right political opinions among individuals appears to be attributable to genetic differences as opposed to differences in social environment.[51] Interestingly, however, genetics does not appear to contribute to differences in partisanship, although it may have an influence on the strength of people's partisan identifications.[52] Although much work remains to be done, research does not suggest that the influence of genes on political attitudes is direct; rather, genes are believed to influence intermediate phenotypes or observable traits related to social behavior (e.g., orientations toward threat or social order), which then affects specific attitudes in the domain of politics (e.g., social conservatism). Thus, while social influences on ideological affinity are undoubtedly important, at least some portion of what people believe politically may be linked to their genetic makeup. Not surprisingly, this conclusion has been controversial, given political scientists' traditional emphasis on the social and institutional sources of political attitudes. Among other things, the validity of the assumption that identical and fraternal twins are subject to the same environmental influence has come in for criticism. Nevertheless, statistical corrections for potential differences in environment across types of twins fail to rule out environmental effects, suggesting that biological influences must be considered by any full treatment of the bases of ideology.[53]

When Do People "Use" Ideology?

Thus far, I have discussed ideology primarily in terms of attraction to particular ideological identities or positions along the left–right spectrum. However, as noted at the outset, ideologies are belief systems. Besides some crowning posture or identity—like liberalism or conservatism—they consist of an interlocking web of opinions, values, and interpretations of existing social reality that go along with that posture. For example, an identification with the political left implies a wide range of issue opinions across a variety of domains—support for welfare spending, support for gay rights, support for diplomacy over the use of force in international relations, and so on. Moreover, it implies support for general value postures (e.g., preferences for equality and self-direction) as well as certain beliefs about the nature of the social world (e.g., inequality stems from structural factors like discrimination as opposed to an individual lack of ability or effort). Indeed, as we have seen, the general ideological label a person adopts typically has consequences for their opinions about specific issues: those who identify themselves as conservatives tend to adopt conservative issue positions, while those who identify themselves as liberals tend to adopt liberal issue positions.

But where do these broader belief packages come from? Public opinion researchers have long noted that the sheer force of logic is not sufficient to explain why certain issue positions get linked together as part of an ideological whole; as just one example, there is no apparent reason why opposition to legal abortion should go together with support for lower taxes as part of the contemporary "conservative" belief package. As such, most scholars have come to regard ideologies as products of convention—or more specifically, the culture of the groups that share the ideology.[54] Nevertheless, most perspectives on ideology suggest that the social activities which give rise to ideological content are disproportionately the province of narrow elites within the groups that share different ideologies—usually powerful and unrepresentative ones. This emphasis is perhaps most evident in the classical sociological tradition and in Marxist approaches to social science, both of which have argued—albeit with different evaluative implications, depending on the writer—that the discursive content of ideologies should disproportionately represent the interests of powerful groups and justify states of affairs the latter benefit from. Other approaches have placed a similar emphasis on the construction of belief packages by small, highly-involved segments of the population. However, in these models, the focus is less on the role of dominant groups whose interests color the content of ideologies and more on the role of the "political elites" discussed earlier—the politicians, activists, and media figures whose activity develops the constellations of positions, values, and interpretations of reality that make up different ideological positions.[55] From this perspective, groups of political elites in competing political parties adopt belief packages reflecting particular interests and values—belief packages that are often articulated ahead of time by intellectuals and transmitted to party elites by activists and other "intense policy demanders."[56] These opposed packages of opinions and positions then serve to psychologically "anchor" the ends of the left–right spectrum in a particular context; they make up the ideological "menu" from which members of the mass public typically make their political choices (e.g., votes).

The flip side of this notion of "elite opinion leadership" is that the beliefs held by citizens at the mass level are typically not constructed by the citizens themselves. Rather, the content associated with different ideological positions is acquired by members of the mass public when they "take cues" about what to believe from political figures that share their basic partisan and ideological identifications.[57] Thus, for most people, the packages of issue opinions, values, and views associated with a particular ideological posture are learned from those more highly involved in politics. This raises an important question: to what extent does the content associated with particular ideological positions fully diffuse to the broader public? By and large, decades of research suggest that most citizens do not learn the full set of "correct" opinions and views associated with the ideological identity they claim, even when they do claim a left–right position.[58] On one hand, at least 66 percent of individuals are willing to place themselves on the left–right spectrum and label themselves as liberals, conservatives, or something in between.[59] On the other hand, most citizens— even if they do adopt an ideological position—fail to pick up the broader systems of opinions and views associated with particular ideological positions in elite discussion.[60]

Perhaps the most important demonstration of this incomplete learning of ideology was provided by Philip Converse in a famous essay on "The Nature of Belief Systems in Mass Publics."[61] In this essay, Converse reviewed findings taken from large surveys of American political elites and everyday citizens conducted during the 1950s. To begin with, Converse demonstrated that most members of the general public showed what political scientists refer to as a low "level of conceptualization"—that is, only a minority typically characterized political parties and candidates in terms of ideological categories like liberalism and conservatism. Similarly, most people were not able to explain the philosophical differences between conservatism and liberalism, and they are not able to accurately indicate which issue positions "go along" with each of these two ideological categories. Moreover, most citizens showed relatively low levels of *ideological constraint*, i.e., they do not take consistently liberal or consistently conservative positions across different issues. Finally, the issue opinions of most citizens showed little stability over time—that is, they tend to fluctuate randomly over time, which is not what we would expect if opinions were more deeply anchored in an overarching ideological posture like liberalism or conservatism. Importantly, in each of these cases, Converse found that his samples of political leaders showed far more ideological sophistication: on average, they revealed a higher level of conceptualization, they understood the meaning of ideological labels better, and their issue opinions showed greater constraint and stability over time.

To Converse, this suggested that the issue opinions of a large portion of the general public were effectively "non-attitudes." That is, in most cases, survey respondents were neither interested in nor informed about the issues they were queried on, and they definitely did not use a common left–right standard when making judgments about them. Accordingly, they offered off-the-cuff, "doorstep" opinions that showed little structure, ideological or otherwise. Although there has been some debate about whether the public's apparent ideological innocence is really an artifact of imperfect measurement[62] and about the extent to which the average citizen makes greater use of ideology than in the past[63], much of the research in this area has followed Converse in concluding that most citizens' political preferences are not heavily structured by ideology.[64] Other lines of work have demonstrated a similar lack of ideological structure in citizens' opinions. For instance, to refer back to an example from earlier, recall that several researchers have noted a lack of concordance between symbolic and operational ideology—that is, there are many citizens who label themselves as "conservatives" while taking issue positions that lean toward the left.[65]

Naturally, the conclusions reached by Converse and others have somewhat negative implications for democracy, as they suggest that much of the citizenry is too disengaged from politics to form "real" opinions about crucial issues and organize their opinions in an ideological fashion. This has led many scholars to ask what factors allow citizens to think in ideological terms and adopt opinions that are consistent with the ideological positions they claim. At the mass level, the main factor governing the acquisition of ideological content is exposure to flows of information from leading political figures, which is highest among those with a strong interest in politics, the highly educated, those who see themselves as politically competent, and members of relatively privileged social groups.[66]

Individuals who receive a good deal of political information over time eventually build up elaborate political knowledge structures in long-term memory, leading to the development of *political expertise*.[67] As a result, highly informed citizens are more likely to have learned what goes with what politically, i.e., the specific issue positions and views about the world that go along with being a liberal, a conservative, or something in between. In turn, this knowledge results in patterns of thinking and opinion which more closely resemble those of political leaders. So, for example, well-informed citizens are more likely to make active use of concepts like liberalism and conservatism in explaining differences between parties and candidates,[68] and they show higher levels of ideological constraint in their opinions toward different issues.[69] They are also more likely to possess operational issue positions that match their symbolic ideological identifications.[70] Moreover, it even appears to be the case that the psychological needs commonly linked to ideology—such as needs for certainty and security—predict differences in ideological sympathies only among those who possess a great deal of political information.[71] Thus, information appears to be central not only to the learning of the full range of content associated with particular ideological positions, but also to the ability to "choose" the ideological position that best satisfies underlying psychological needs.

On the whole, the sheer volume of data suggesting that the well-informed are more likely to think and make judgments in ways that reflect a mastery of ideological content has had a profound effect on how public opinion researchers understand the phenomenon of ideology. Indeed, even a brief look at the literature on the topic makes it clear that researchers have adopted a largely information-based perspective on the use of ideology: the consensus view is that a given citizen will think about political actors in an ideological way and adopt an ideologically-consistent set of opinions to the extent that he or she has successfully received political information and stored it away in long-term memory in the form of an organized knowledge structure. While this focus on information has greatly improved our understanding of when ideology becomes relevant to the political behavior of the average citizen, it is not without its hazards. In particular, it sidesteps the question of whether citizens also have to be motivated to use political information in certain ways in order for that information to result in "ideological" patterns of thought and judgment.

I return to this key point below. At this juncture, though, it should be noted that the poor mastery of ideological content that follows from a lack of information does not make citizens incapable of being political. In this respect, other orientations that are not strictly ideological but which have some political content or relevance—like values and social group memberships—may serve many of the same functions as the more complex ideological belief systems discussed above: they provide cues about what positions to take on various political issues, justify one state of affairs over another, and so on.[72] Among others, these "proxies for ideology" include *core political values* such as egalitarianism, moral traditionalism, and self-reliance, which even information-poor citizens may be able to use in making political judgments.[73] Similarly, much evidence suggests that reference groups—like one's social class, racial or ethnic group, or religious affiliation—can be used as cues about what positions to take or how to vote by individuals at all levels of information.[74] Finally, standard surveys may not be able to detect discursive frameworks that differ from the ones offered by political leaders. Since these techniques are best used to detect "ideology" in the conventional left–right sense, they may miss idiosyncratic belief systems that are as elaborate and internally consistent as those offered by elites and which serve all of the important functions of ideology (e.g., organizing different opinions together under common themes, justifying political action, explaining the world, etc.). Indeed, in-depth interviews of citizens with low-to-average levels of political information have shown that normal conversation can reveal coherent "ideological" understandings of political reality that nevertheless depart from the left–right framework used by political elites.[75]

Information, Motivation, and the Use of Ideology

As noted above, public-opinion researchers generally regard the use of ideology as being an informational problem. As a wide range of research has shown, citizens are more likely to think about politics in ideological terms and express ideologically-consistent opinions about issues if they possess larger stores of political information. To the extent that citizens possess enough information to understand what goes with what ideologically, they are assumed to use that information. However, in psychology, a growing body of work suggests that key needs, goals, and wants determine if and how prior information is used to make judgments.[76] This trend suggests that public-opinion research on ideology might benefit from a closer look at the role of *motivation*—that is, a closer look at how people's needs or goals shape their use of political information pertinent to the content of ideology. In a series of studies over the last decade, I have attempted to fill this gap by proposing that information is more likely to predict ideologically-guided thinking and judgment when citizens are motivated to use political information for *evaluative* purposes.

Specifically, I argue that the relationship between information and reliance on ideology should depend on factors that strengthen people's tendency to evaluate people and things as "good" or "bad." Since ideology provides an overarching framework for the evaluation of many different objects, information about the content of various ideological positions should be of greater importance to those motivated to make evaluative judgments about the things they encounter—regardless of whether this motivation comes from personality traits, characteristics of the situation the individual finds himself or herself in, or a general interest in politics.[77]

This point leads to a simple hypothesis: citizens who possess large stores of political information will be particularly likely to think about politics in ideological terms and express ideologically-consistent issue positions when they also approach politics with a high level of evaluative motivation. The necessary "motive to evaluate" may come from a number of sources. For example, these include individual differences in personality like the *need to evaluate*, i.e., the extent to which an individual is motivated to spontaneously form evaluations of experiences, ideas, and social objects as either "good" or "bad."[78] While the need to evaluate is a very general motivation that encourages people to form more opinions—and stronger opinions—across a variety of domains, individuals with a high need to evaluate are particularly likely to be politically opinionated.[79] Other potential sources of evaluative motivation are more specific to politics, such as the extent to which the political domain itself is seen as important and relevant to the self (i.e., personal involvement).[80]

Regardless of its source, a motive to evaluate things should have important effects on how individuals think about politics and make judgments about political issues. As we have seen, ideology provides a common reference point that helps citizens reach a consistent set of conclusions about the nature of the social world and how to confront various political issues. Moreover, having a clear ideological position may simplify important political choices that are fundamentally evaluative in nature, like which party is the best one to join or which candidate is the best to vote for. This suggests that the understanding of ideology provided by political information may be more useful to those who feel the need to have opinions about the things they encounter. Since ideology offers a handy mental rubric for the evaluation of multiple issues, candidates, and political questions, information about the content of the left–right distinction should be more useful to people who want to form opinions. Consequently, well-informed citizens who are also high in evaluative motivation may be particularly inclined to rely on ideology, increasing the extent to which their political thinking is colored by ideological categories and the degree to which their issue opinions are ideologically consistent with one another. In contrast, information may make little difference among citizens who lack a strong evaluative motive. Instead of relying on their knowledge of the content of ideology, these individuals may make political judgments in a more frag-mented, episodic way. As such, their thinking and opinions may be influenced less by a common ideological reference point than by whatever is salient at the time. An overall representation of this model can be found in Figure 4.2; the dashed arrow pointing from evaluative motivation to the connection between information and the use of ideology indicates the aforementioned role of evaluative motivation in turning the influence of information on ideological thinking and judgment "on" and "off."

Using data from numerous surveys of American adults, I have provided a consistent body of evidence for this hypothesis. In particular, in several studies, I have used a short measure of the need to evaluate to assess evaluative motivation in terms of individual personality differences. Analyses using this measure repeatedly showed that politically well-informed survey respondents are more likely to think about politics in ideological terms and express ideologically-consistent issue opinions when they are also high in the need to evaluate. For example, using data from the 1998 and 2000 American National Election Studies (ANES), I found that political information more strongly predicted ideological constraint—the degree to which one expresses consistently liberal or consistent conservative issue positions—among those high in the

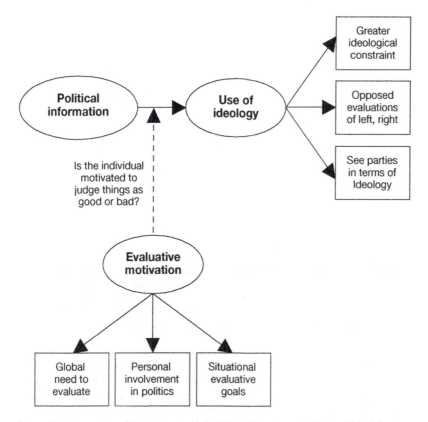

Figure 4.2 Information, Motivation, and the Use of Ideology: A General Model
(source: author creation).

need to evaluate.[81] As an example, Figure 4.3 presents the results of this analysis
for the 1998 ANES Pilot.

Moreover, in the 2000 and 2004 ANES, I have shown that expertise was more
strongly associated with a tendency to evaluate ideologically antagonistic groups,
candidates, and parties in opposite ways among those with a high need to
evaluate.[82] That is, the well-informed were more "consistent" in their evaluations
of competing actors—for example, evaluating conservatives and Republicans
positively if they evaluated liberals and Democrats negatively—if they were
also high in the need to evaluate. I have found similar patterns with respect to
other outcomes indicative of a strong reliance on ideology. For instance, in
another set of analyses using the 2000 ANES, I demonstrated that well-informed
survey respondents are more likely to explain the differences between the
Democratic and Republican parties in ideological terms when they are also high
in the need to evaluate.[83]

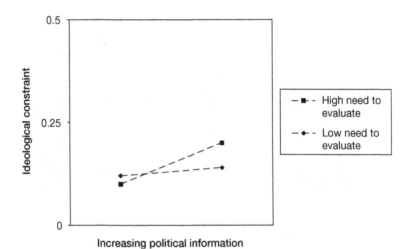

Figure 4.3 Information and the Need to Evaluate as Predictors of Ideological Constraint (source: Christopher M. Federico and Monica Schneider, "Political Expertise and the Use of Ideology: Moderating Effects of Evaluative Motivation," *Public Opinion Quarterly* 71 (2007): 221–252. Data for the graph are from the 1998 ANES Pilot).

In a more recent study, I have found similar results using other variables that should encourage individuals to form opinions.[84] As noted earlier, factors specific to the political domain—such as personal involvement in politics—should also strengthen the relationship between information and reliance on ideology. Accordingly, using data from the 2004 ANES and a national survey of my own construction, I found that political information more strongly predicted ideological constraint among respondents who were highly interested in politics and who indicated that their political attitudes were central to their sense of who they were. Similarly, a second indicator of personal involvement in politics—strength of partisanship—had a similar effect: information more strongly predicted constraint among those who identified as "strong" Democrats or Republicans.

Conclusion

As Philip Converse noted a half-century ago, ideologies have often "served as primary exhibits for the doctrine that what is important to study cannot be measured and that what can be measured is not important to study."[85] Since then, public-opinion research has made considerable progress not only in overcoming the difficulties inherent in studying ideology, but also in reinforcing the importance of ideology as an explanatory concept. In this chapter, I have attempted to provide the reader with an overview of this body of work.

Specifically, I have tried to address the questions of what ideology is, which social and psychological factors attract citizens to one ideological posture rather than another, and when citizens use the full range of content associated with various ideological postures in order to think about the political world and form opinions about major political topics.

As we have seen, ideologies—defined here as belief systems that reflect some group's understanding of the social world and its preferences about how that world should be ordered—are clearly relevant to mass opinion in certain respects. Ideologies of the left and right play a key role in the organization of opinion-holding and debate among political leaders and other elites. Moreover, under the influence of various identifications and interests, psychological needs and traits, and perhaps even their genetic inheritance, most members of the general public are sufficiently attracted to one ideological posture or another to place themselves on the left–right spectrum as liberals, conservatives, or something in between. However, at the mass level, far fewer citizens actually adopt the full range of views and opinions that "go along" with these postures. In an effort to explain this state of relative ideological innocence, researchers have focused in particular on the role of information received from political leaders, repeatedly observing that well-informed citizens are more likely to think about politics in ideological terms and express opinions that are ideologically consistent with one another. Building on this perspective, my own work suggests that the motivation to use information in a specifically evaluative way may also matter, such that well-informed citizens are more likely to think about politics ideologically and express ideologically-consistent issue opinions when they are also strongly driven to form opinions of things as good or bad. Thus, while ideology plays a key role in the organization of political discussion in the political system as a whole, its influence in the political lives of individual citizens depends heavily on how much they know about politics and how they are motivated to use that knowledge.

Notes

1. Converse, Philip, "The Nature of Belief Systems in Mass Publics," in *Ideology and Discontent*, ed. D. Apter (New York: Free Press, 1964); John T. Jost, Christopher M. Federico, and Jaime L. Napier, "Political Ideology: Its Structure, Functions, and Elective Affinities," *Annual Review of Psychology* 60 (2009): 307–337.
2. Arthur D. Denzau and Douglass C. North, "Shared Mental Models: Ideologies and Institutions," in *Elements of Reason: Cognition, Choice, and the Bounds of Rationality*, ed. Arthur Lupia, Matthew McCubbins, and Samuel L. Popkin (New York: Cambridge University Press, 2000).
3. Susan T. Fiske, Richard R. Lau, and Richard A. Smith, "On the Varieties and Utilities of Political Expertise," *Social Cognition* 8 (1990): 31–48; Charles M. Judd and Jon A. Krosnick, "The Structural Bases of Consistency Among Political Attitudes: Effects of Expertise and Attitude Importance," in *Attitude Structure and Function*, ed. Anthony Pratkanis, Steven Breckler, and Anthony Greenwald (Hillsdale, NJ: Erlbaum, 1989).

4. R. S. Erikson and K. L. Tedin, *American Public Opinion* (6th ed.) (New York: Longman, 2003); Jost et al., "Political Ideology"; Seymour M. Lipset, *Political Man* (New York: Doubleday, 1960).
5. N. Bobbio, *Left and Right* (Cambridge: Polity Press, 1996).
6. Angus Campbell, P. Converse, W. Miller, and D. Stokes, *The American Voter* (New York: Wiley, 1960); Converse, "The Nature of Belief Systems"; Nolan McCarty, Keith T. Poole, and Howard Rosenthal, *Polarized America: The Dance of Ideology and Unequal Riches* (Cambridge, MA: MIT Press, 2006); Hans Noel, *Political Ideologies and Political Parties in America* (New York: Cambridge University Press, 2013).
7. John Zaller, *The Nature and Origins of Mass Opinion* (New York: Cambridge University Press, 1992). On polarization, see Alan I. Abramowitz, *The Disappearing Center: Engaged Citizens, Polarization, and American Democracy* (New Haven, CT: Yale University Press, 2010); and Matthew Levendusky, *The Partisan Sort* (Chicago: The University of Chicago Press, 2009).
8. Erikson and Tedin, *American Public Opinion.*
9. Lloyd A. Free and Hadley Cantril, *The Political Beliefs of Americans* (New Brunswick, NJ: Rutgers University Press, 1967); James A. Stimson, *Tides of Consent: How Public Opinion Shapes American Politics* (New York: Cambridge University Press, 2004); Christopher Ellis and James A. Stimson, *Ideology in America* (New York: Cambridge University Press, 2012).
10. Free and Cantril, *The Political Beliefs of Americans.*
11. Ellis and Stimson, *Ideology in America*; see also Stimson, *Tides of Consent.* Note that the opposite pattern—a combination of symbolic liberalism and operational conservatism—is comparatively rare (only 2% of the population). As such, Ellis and Stimson argue that the relatively high proportion of symbolic conservatives with operationally-liberal beliefs may arise from political discourse that associates the "liberal" label with negative cultural connotations without calling for reductions in the most popular (and most expensive) government programs, such as Social Security, Medicare, and education spending.
12. Stanley Feldman, "Political Ideology," in *The Oxford Handbook of Political Psychology*, ed. David O. Sears, Leonie Huddy, and Jack Levy (New York: Oxford University Press, 2013).
13. John Duckitt and Christopher G. Sibley, "A Dual Process Model of Ideological Attitudes and System Justification," in *Social and Psychological Bases of Ideology and System Justification*, ed. John T. Jost, Aaron C. Kay, and Hulda Thorisdottir (New York: Oxford University Press, 2009).
14. Shalom H. Schwartz, "Universals in the Content and Structure of Values: Theoretical Advances and Empirical Tests in 20 Countries," *Advances in Experimental Social Psychology* 25 (1992): 1–65; Milton Rokeach, *The Nature of Human Values* (New York: Free Press, 1973).
15. Hans J. Eysenck, *The Psychology of Politics* (New York: Praeger, 1954); Rokeach, *The Nature of Human Values.*
16. e.g., Geoffrey Evans, A. Heath, and M. Lalljee, "Measuring Left-Right and Libertarian-Conservative Attitudes in the British Electorate," *British Journal of Sociology* 47 (1996): 93–112.
17. e.g., Seymour M. Lipset and S. Rokkan, *Party Systems and Voter Alignment* (New York: Free Press, 1967).
18. Jost et al., "Political Ideology."
19. Anthony Downs, *An Economic Theory of Democracy* (New York: Harper and Row, 1967); Paul M. Sniderman and John Bullock, "A Consistency Theory of Public Opinion and Political Choice: The Hypothesis of Menu Dependence," in *Studies in*

Public Opinion: Attitudes, Nonattitudes, Measurement Error, and Change, ed. Willem E. Saris and Paul M. Sniderman (Princeton, NJ: Princeton University Press, 2004).

20. On the informed and involved, see Abramowitz, *The Disappearing Center*, and Judd and Krosnick, "The Structural Bases of Consistency"; on elected officials, see Converse, "The Nature of Belief Systems" and McCarty et al., *Polarized America*.
21. Duckitt and Sibley, "A Dual Process Model."
22. Stimson, *Tides of Consent*.
23. For a discussion, see Jost et al., "Political Ideology," p. 322.
24. For a review, see David O. Sears and S. Levy, "Childhood and Adult Political Development," in *The Oxford Handbook of Political Psychology*, ed. David O. Sears, Leonie Huddy, and Robert Jervis (New York: Oxford University Press, 2003).
25. M. Kent Jennings and Richard G. Niemi, *Generations and Politics: A Panel Study of Adults and Their Parents* (Princeton, NJ: Princeton University Press, 1981).
26. Duane F. Alwin, R. L. Cohen, and Theodore Newcomb, *Political Attitudes Over the Life Span* (Madison, WI: University of Wisconsin Press, 1991).
27. Theodore M. Newcomb, *Personality and Social Change: Attitude Formation in a Student Community* (New York: John Wiley and Sons, 1943).
28. B. R Berelson, Paul F. Lazarsfeld, and W. N. McPhee, *Voting: A Study of Opinion Formation in a Presidential Campaign* (Chicago: University of Chicago Press, 1954); Campbell et al., *The American Voter*.
29. Alwin et al., *Political Attitudes Over the Lifespan*; Sears and Levy, "Childhood and Adult Political Development."
30. David O. Sears and Cary L. Funk, "The Role of Self-Interest in Social and Political Attitudes," *Advances in Experimental Social Psychology* 24 (1991): 1–91.
31. James R. Kluegel and Eliot R. Smith, *Beliefs about Inequality: Americans' Views of What Is and What Ought to Be* (New York: Aldine de Gruyter, 1986); Sears and Funk, "The Role of Self-Interest"; Mark J. Brandt, "Do the Disadvantaged Legitimize the Social System? A Large-Scale Test of the Status–Legitimacy Hypothesis," *Journal of Personality and Social Psychology* 104 (2013): 765–785.
32. Jost et al., "Political Ideology."
33. Theodor W. Adorno, Else Frenkel-Brunswik, D. J. Levison, and R. N. Sanford, *The Authoritarian Personality* (New York: Harper and Row, 1950). See also Mondak and Hibbing, "Personality and Public Opinion," this volume.
34. For reviews, see John T. Jost, Jack Glaser, Arie W. Kruglanski, and Frank J. Sulloway, "Political Conservatism as Motivated Social Cognition," *Psychological Bulletin* 129 (2003): 339–375; and Jost et al., "Political Ideology."
35. For a discussion of these criticisms, see Robert A. Altemeyer, *The Authoritarian Specter* (Cambridge, MA: Harvard University Press, 1996), pp. 45–47.
36. Altemeyer, *The Authoritarian Specter*.
37. Stanley Feldman, "Enforcing Social Conformity: A Theory of Authoritarianism," *Political Psychology* 24 (2003): 41–74; Karen Stenner, *The Authoritarian Dynamic* (Cambridge: Cambridge University Press, 2005); Marc Hetherington and J. D. Weiler, *Authoritarianism and Polarization in American Politics* (Cambridge: Cambridge University Press, 2009).
38. Jost et al., "Political Conservatism as Motivated Social Cognition."
39. Duckitt and Sibley, "A Dual Process Model."
40. See Mondak and Hibbing, this volume.
41. Jost et al., "Political Conservatism as Motivated Social Cognition."
42. Mondak and Hibbing, this volume.
43. Ibid.

44. Alan S. Gerber, D. Doherty, C. M. Dowling, and S. E. Ha, "Personality and Political Attitudes: Relationships Across Issue Domains and Political Contexts," *American Political Science Review* 104 (2010): 111–133; Mondak and Hibbing, this volume.
45. Gerber et al., "Personality and Political Attitudes."
46. For a review of this work, see Jonathan Haidt, *The Righteous Mind: Why Good People Are Divided by Politics and Religion* (New York: Pantheon, 2012).
47. Schwartz, "Universals in the Content and Structure of Values"; Paul Goren, *On Voter Competence* (New York: Oxford University Press, 2012).
48. For additional review, see Frank Gonzales, Kevin B. Smith, and John R. Hibbing, "No Longer 'Beyond Our Scope:'," this volume.
49. John R. Alford, Carolyn L. Funk, and John R. Hibbing, "Are Political Orientations Genetically Transmitted?" *American Political Science Review* 99 (2005): 153–167; John R. Hibbing, Kevin B. Smith, and John R. Alford, *Predisposed: Liberals, Conservatives, and the Biology of Political Differences* (New York: Routledge, 2014); Gonzales, Smith, and Hibbing, this volume.
50. See Gonzales, Smith, and Hibbing, this volume.
51. Ibid.
52. Peter K. Hatemi, J. R. Alford, J. R. Hibbing, N. G. Martin, and L. J. Eaves, "Is There a 'Party' in Your Genes?" *Political Research Quarterly* 62 (2009): 584–600.
53. For an example of such criticisms, see Evan Charney, "Genes and Ideologies," *Perspectives on Politics* 6 (2008): 299–319; for a response, see John R. Alford, Carolyn L. Funk, and John R. Hibbing, "Beyond Liberals and Conservatives to Political Genotypes and Phenotypes," *Perspectives on Politics* 6 (2008): 321–328.
54. Converse, "The Nature of Belief Systems."
55. Converse, "The Nature of Belief Systems"; Zaller, *The Nature and Origins of Mass Opinion.*
56. e.g., Sniderman and Bullock, "A Consistency Theory of Public Opinion." On the process by which ideological packages are transmitted by intellectuals and activists, see Noel, *Political Ideologies and Political Parties in America.*
57. Zaller, *The Nature and Origins of Mass Opinion.*
58. Converse, "The Nature of Belief Systems."
59. Erikson and Tedin, *American Public Opinion*; Stimson, *Tides of Consent.*
60. Zaller, *The Nature and Origins of Mass Opinion.*
61. Converse, "The Nature of Belief Systems."
62. Christopher H. Achen, "Mass Political Attitudes and the Survey Response," *American Political Science Review* 69 (1975): 1218–1223.
63. e.g., Norman H. Nie, Sidney Verba, and John Petrocik, *The Changing American Voter* (Cambridge, MA: Harvard University Press, 1976).
64. Michael X. Delli Carpini and Scott Keeter, *What Americans Know About Politics and Why it Matters* (New Haven, CT: Yale University Press, 1996); Judd and Krosnick, "The Structural Bases of Consistency"; Zaller, *The Nature and Origins of Mass Opinion.*
65. Ellis and Stimson, *Ideology in America*; Stimson, *Tides of Consent.*
66. Delli Carpini and Keeter, *What Americans Know About Politics*; Martin Gilens, "Two-Thirds Full? Citizen Competence and Democratic Governance," this volume.
67. Fiske et al., "On the Varieties and Utilities of Political Expertise."
68. Converse, "The Nature of Belief Systems."
69. See Delli Carpini and Keeter, *What Americans Know About Politics.* While these results suggest that most citizens do not learn the content of various ideologies in all their glorious detail, they should not be taken as a sign that the poorly informed are utterly devoid of ideological understanding. Rather, it is merely the case those

less exposed to political information flows understand and use the content of ideology less competently and with less elaboration than those who receive more information; on this point, see Jost et al., "Political Ideology."

70. Stimson, *Tides of Consent*.

71. Christopher M. Federico and Paul Goren, "Motivated Social Cognition and Ideology: Is Attention to Elite Discourse a Prerequisite for Epistemically Motivated Political Affinities?" in *Social and Psychological Bases of Ideology and System Justification*, ed. John T. Jost, Aaron C. Kay, and Hulda Thorisdottir (New York: Oxford University Press, 2009); Christopher M. Federico, Emily L. Fisher, and Grace Deason, "Political Expertise and the Link Between the Authoritarian Predisposition and Conservatism," *Public Opinion Quarterly* 75 (2011): 686–708.

72. Jost et al., "Political Ideology."

73. Goren, *On Voter Competence*. Here, "values" should be distinguished from ideologies in that the latter are usually more abstract and encompassing. In this respect, ideologies are usually thought of as tying together multiple values into a larger posture.

74. Berelson et al., *Voting*; Campbell et al., *The American Voter*.

75. Robert E. Lane, *Political Ideology* (New York: Free Press, 1962). There is one caveat worth mentioning in the context of this argument: it is not clear that all individuals who fail to show an understanding of the discursive content associated with the left–right distinction are in fact using their "own" ideologies. If this were the case, we would observe substantial attitude stability even in the absence of left–right understanding. However, such stability is rarely observed, and it tends to be higher among those who are politically well-informed; on this point, see Converse, "The Nature of Belief Systems," and Zaller, *The Nature and Origins of Mass Opinion*.

76. Howard Lavine, "Online versus Memory-Based Process Models of Political Evaluation," in *Political Psychology*, ed. Kristen R. Monroe (Mahwah, NJ: LEA, 2002).

77. W. Blair G. Jarvis and Richard E. Petty, "The Need to Evaluate," *Journal of Personality and Social Psychology* 70 (1996): 172–94.

78. Ibid.

79. Christopher M. Federico, "Predicting Attitude Extremity: The Interactive Effects of Schema Development and the Need to Evaluate–and Their Mediation by Evaluative Integration," *Personality and Social Psychology Bulletin* 30 (2004): 1281–94.

80. Christopher M. Federico and Corrie V. Hunt, "Political Information, Political Involvement, and Reliance on Ideology in Political Evaluation," *Political Behavior* 35 (2013): 89–112.

81. Christopher M. Federico and Monica Schneider, "Political Expertise and the Use of Ideology: Moderating Effects of Evaluative Motivation," *Public Opinion Quarterly* 71 (2007): 221–252.

82. Federico, "Predicting Attitude Extremity"; Christopher M. Federico, "Expertise, Evaluative Motivation, and the Structure of Citizens' Ideological Commitments," *Political Psychology* 28 (2007): 535–562.

83. Federico and Schneider, "Political Expertise and the Use of Ideology."

84. Federico and Hunt, "Political Information, Political Involvement, and Reliance on Ideology in Political Evaluation."

85. Converse, "The Nature of Belief Systems," p. 206.

Chapter 5

Race, Ethnicity, and the Group Bases of Public Opinion

Erica Czaja, Jane Junn, and Tali Mendelberg

Scholarship in political science on race and its impact on political preferences has undergone substantial transformation in the last quarter-century. Once defined racially by black and white, today the U.S. population is characterized by a multiplicity of racial and ethnic group divisions. Hispanics are now the largest minority population in the U.S., followed by African Americans and then Asian Americans and Native Americans.[1] The "multi-racial" population—a category formed by counting more than one racial group and allowed by the census since 2000—is among the fastest-growing groups.[2] The vast majority of the newest Americans are no longer from Europe as they once were in the nineteenth century. Instead, today's immigrants come primarily from Latin America and Asia. While black migrants from Africa and the Caribbean constitute a much smaller share of new immigrants, their presence creates important diversity within the racial category of black.[3]

In this chapter we take the increased racial and ethnic diversity of the United States as a starting point, and analyze the significance of race, ethnicity, and the group bases of political preferences. We begin with a discussion of categories of race and ethnicity in the U.S. and argue that these categories are based not in "objective" biological differences, but rather have been "socially constructed" or created by the institutions and practices of U.S. government and society, which have assigned different meanings and values to various racial categories.[4] Next we focus on individual-level measurements of psychological attachment to groups—group identity and consciousness—as critical intervening variables between racial group classification and the formation of political preferences. The contours of the relationships between racial group identity, racial group consciousness, and individuals' opinions, particularly for Latinos and Asian Americans, are especially challenging for public opinion researchers because these populations and their politics are in flux. Finally, we discuss additional factors that may differentially influence the political opinions of individuals, depending in part on their racial group classifications and attachments, including party identification and mobilization, interpersonal contact and the racial, economic, and political context, and perceptions of and experiences with discrimination.

Categorizing Race and Ethnicity

The practice of official racial classification in the U.S. dates to the nation's founding. The institution of slavery made information on racial categorization vital to the apportionment of legislative seats in the federal government. The now-infamous "Three-Fifths" compromise found in Article I Section 2 of the U.S. Constitution specifies that both taxes and the number of elected representatives be calculated by adding the number of free persons and three-fifths of all other persons, "excluding Indians not taxed" (U.S. Constitution). The free population was white while the enslaved population was black, hence the enumeration by slave status was also an enumeration by race.

In every decennial census since the first in 1790, race has been recorded for each person counted. Political scientist Melissa Nobles demonstrates how government agencies such as the U.S. Bureau of the Census constructed categories of race in order to meet social and political goals of the time.[5] It would take almost 100 years and a bloody civil war for the United States to abolish slavery, but by then the idea of race as a meaningful social distinction was embedded in the fabric of the polity. Skin color only has more meaning in politics than, for example, eye color or other arbitrary physical differences between people because political actors have given racial categories particular meanings in order to serve their purposes. This is what scholars mean when they say race is "socially constructed." The practices of categorizing people based on race and recording race have continued unabated through the present day.

Moreover, for the vast majority of the nation's history, racial categorization has gone hand in hand with preferential treatment for those recognized as white—from citizenship and property rights to eligibility to vote. Political scientists have documented clear patterns of the role of the American state in the maintenance and definition of racial categories, unequal treatment by race, and the accompanying white privilege.[6] These scholars argue that racial discrimination is deeply embedded in American political institutions and culture. Even when discrimination on the basis of racial categories was prohibited by law, as in the Fourteenth Amendment, state and local governments as well as private individuals have found creative ways to use ostensibly race-neutral practices and rules to exclude racial minorities from public life, beginning in the 1860s and continuing even today.[7] Some scholars draw an important distinction between systemic structures of discrimination, or institutionalized racism, such as election rules that prevented African Americans from voting, and individuals' feelings of racial antipathy, arguing both that the latter do not necessarily lead to the former and that institutionalized racism is what matters most for political outcomes.[8]

The long-standing patterns of racial categorization and white privilege in the United States have persisted at the same time that the categories themselves have undergone change. Individuals at any point in time may be designated as part of a racial group, not because they are objectively Latino or black but instead because of a combination of social and political constructions that work together to ascribe a specific category of race to the person. Especially relevant is the move among "white ethnics" during the period of mass immigration in the late-nineteenth and early-twentieth centuries to be classified by the government as white.[9] Some groups such as the Irish, Italians and Jews (once considered non-white) were successful. Others, including Asian Americans, were not able to get the courts to recognize them as white and thus eligible for the full privileges of U.S. citizenship.[10] Federal law prohibited Asian immigrants from naturalization until 1952, breaking more than 70 years of explicit Asian exclusion from the United States.[11] From the 1860s, local and state governments, as well as the national government of the United States, enacted laws targeting Asian Americans that barred property ownership, levied additional race-based taxes, and forcibly interned Americans of Japanese descent during the Second World War.[12] Claire Kim explains these dynamics in her theoretical description of Asian Americans in U.S. society as "triangulated" between blacks and whites. According to Kim, Asian Americans have been (and continue to be) valorized by whites as superior to African Americans on some cultural and racial dimensions but at the same time have been deemed forever foreign and unfit for assimilation and civic membership with whites. This triangulation racializes Asian Americans and African Americans in different ways and enables the majority racial group, white Americans, to maintain its dominant position over both minority groups simultaneously.[13]

Complicating matters further is the introduction by the federal government of a fourth major category, Hispanic or Latino ethnicity. While developed decades earlier, the requirement of reporting Hispanic/Latino ethnicity along with other racial categories was implemented by the federal Office of Management and Budget in the 1970s. The complexity of racial categories suggests that researchers of racial and ethnic groups must utilize the terms white, black, Latino, and Asian American carefully and with an awareness of the role that cultural norms and politics play in shaping individuals' ideas of race.

Key Concepts, Measurement, and Methodology

Key Concepts in the Study of Race and Groups

Researchers are concerned with three key concepts: *racial group membership*, or what we have referred to above as racial categorization, *racial group identity*, and *racial group consciousness*. According to Paula McClain and her colleagues and to a long tradition of research, simple membership does not tell us how strongly a person identifies with a group or whether she views politics as relevant to the group.[14] "Group identification refers to an individual's awareness of belonging to a certain group and having a psychological attachment to that group based on a perception of shared beliefs, feelings, interests, and ideas with other group members;" whereas

[g]roup consciousness is in-group identification *politicized* by a set of ideological beliefs about one's group's social standing, as well as a view that collective action is the best means by which the group can improve its status and realize its interests.[15]

The more strongly that society and politics define group members by their racial category, and the more isolated and discriminated against people are because of their assigned group membership, the more likely they are to identify with their assigned racial group. These conditions increase the likelihood that group members will view their unequal treatment as a result of politics as well as the likelihood that they will thus organize for political change. Paradoxically then, the very conditions that stifle individuals can facilitate political mobilization of the group.

The interactions between oppressive institutions and the politics of non-white minority individuals are well illustrated by another set of key concepts developed by Michael Dawson in the study of African American politics: *linked fate*, the *black counterpublic*, and the *black utility heuristic*.[16] Linked fate is the idea among African Americans that individual wellbeing is inextricably linked with the fate of the race as a whole; essentially, they believe that their success depends on the success of the group, so what is good for the race is good for the individual. According to Dawson, African Americans' unique history of racial subjugation and forced segregation has led to the transmission of notions of linked fate across generations, so that still today African Americans continue to receive messages that reinforce their sense of shared racial group interests through the black counterpublic—mainly, black media, predominantly black organizations, and the black church. Information shared in these segregated spaces, Dawson argues, enables and encourages African Americans to evaluate politics using a rational, mental shortcut that he calls the "black utility heuristic." That is, African Americans form their political opinions about political parties, candidates, and public policies by using their perceptions of what is best for the entire racial group instead of what they think is best for them individually. The sense of linked fate is so strong that it overcomes the force of class interests for the black middle class and the lure of cultural conservatism, which resonates with many African Americans. According to Dawson, linked fate explains why African Americans vote nearly unanimously for the Democratic Party in presidential and many lower-level electoral contests.

Researchers of Asian American and Latino politics are beginning to use both sets of concepts but, we argue, should do so with care because of the different historical and contemporary experiences of racial groups. Today, for example, Asian Americans and Latinos are typically much closer to the immigration experience that helps shape political incorporation. Michael Jones-Correa's study of first-generation Latino immigrants in Queens, New York suggests that there are important psychological and material costs in renouncing homeland citizenship that prevent some immigrants from becoming citizens.[17]

He argues that Latinos practice a "politics of in-between," being torn between two nations, neither fully politically engaged in their new homes nor in their homelands. However, beyond such individual factors, he as well as others also identified a lack of institutional mechanisms to aid in the incorporation of immigrants, including exclusive local party machines.[18] Latino organizations such as churches may be evolving to play an increasingly political role that could strengthen Latinos' identification with all Latinos rather than merely their national origin group (e.g. Mexicans) and enhance their sense of linked fate and group consciousness.

Measurement of Key Concepts

There are a number of important challenges in the measurement of racial group membership, identity, and consciousness, and we highlight two of the primary challenges here. The first challenge arises because, as detailed above, group identity and consciousness are flexible for individuals, depending on context. In addition, historical, political, and social forces shape what it means to be a member of particular racial and ethnic groups. In-person and telephone survey interviews are the most common ways to measure these concepts in the study of public opinion, but different individuals understand questions about race and ethnicity differently.[19]

Second, the survey questions that attempt to measure group-based identities vary widely in their wording across surveys, making comparisons between groups and at different time periods difficult. Furthermore, the context in which the survey is administered, such as whether the interview is conducted by a same-race interviewer or during an election campaign, can influence the racial identity and level of group consciousness that respondents report. In addition, there are a range of national origin groups that make up the pan-ethnic categories of Latino and Asian American, and therefore, whether respondents identify with their country of origin or with a broad pan-ethnic category depends upon the options given to respondents in surveys. While Mexican-Americans make up the largest share of the Latino population in the U.S., the category of Hispanic or Latino also includes Cubans, Caribbeans, Puerto Ricans, and people from other Latin American countries. Similarly, there are as many national origin and ethnicity groups within the pan-ethnic racial category of Asian American, with the six largest groups being Chinese, Asian Indian, Filippino, Vietnamese, Korean, and Japanese. Finally, while blacks demonstrate the highest degree of racial group consciousness, the internal diversity of this group is also in flux, with U.S.-born African Americans included in the same racial category as new arrivals from the African continent as well as large numbers of Afro-Caribbeans.

Thus, differences in the ways in which individuals understand the same questions, differences in the ways that survey questions are worded, and the contexts in which these questions are administered complicate the measurement and comparison of group membership, identity, and consciousness across racial groups.

Methodological Challenges in Survey Research

There are also methodological challenges in collecting data on racial groups in the United States, particularly those that heavily comprise immigrants. Geographic concentration and dispersion and the prevalence of speaking a language other than English characterize Latino and Asian American populations today, and reaching individuals for interviews requires innovative methods of survey research designed specifically for these respondents.

Asian Americans and Latinos, and immigrant groups more generally, have increasingly complex patterns of geographic mobility. Once heavily concentrated in the southwestern United States and large urban metropolitan areas such as Los Angeles and New York City, Latinos are moving in increasing numbers to the South, the mid-Atlantic and the plains states.[20] At the same time, Asian Americans, while once heavily concentrated in a handful of states, are beginning to disperse as well, with sizeable populations in states such as Virginia, Florida, and Nevada. Sampling these populations for survey interviews is challenging, but making sure that subjects are not drawn only from high-density locations is critical for obtaining survey samples that are representative of the population.

Similarly, because nearly three-quarters of Asian American adults[21] and approximately one in three Latino adults are foreign-born,[22] writing surveys in languages other than English and hiring interviewers who can speak in respondents' native languages greatly increase the likelihood of acquiring both a good sample and good data. While many immigrants speak English, it is a second language for many, and answering survey questions in their native language is preferable.[23]

Finally, given the high degree of internal heterogeneity within each of these groups, the size of the sample must be large enough to include sufficient numbers of respondents from specific national origin groups. For example, Mexican-Americans and Cuban-Americans not only have different migration histories to the United States, but they are also distinctive in their political beliefs.[24] National origin groups within the pan-ethnic rubric of Asian Americans demonstrate similar differences.[25]

Racial Group Identity and Racial Group Consciousness

There is no simple way to characterize the multiplicity of identities of Americans classified as racial minorities today. Moreover, the political influence of group identity and group consciousness may differ across racial categories and individuals. In this section, we examine the individual and contextual antecedents that impact racial group identity and consciousness as well as the ways in which racial identity and consciousness affect political attitudes.

Explaining Group Identity and Consciousness

Several recent studies demonstrate the contextual nature of both group identity and group consciousness and the ways in which they operate differently for different groups. First, with respect to group identity, the labels "Asian American" and "Latino" are the least frequent identifiers adopted by group members themselves: only 19 percent of Asians and 24 percent of Latinos say that they identify with these pan-ethnic labels, while 62 percent of Asians[26] and 51 percent of Latinos[27] self-identify with their country of origin.

These results might suggest that country of origin is more central to the group identities of Asians and Latinos living in the United States than the pan-ethnic identifiers of Asian American and Latino. However, in an earlier study, Pei-te Lien and colleagues found that when respondents who did not immediately self-identify as Asian American were asked the follow-up question, "Have you ever thought of yourself as an Asian American?" approximately 50 percent of respondents provided an affirmative response, illustrating that racial identification is a complex choice for group members, not a fixed, objective membership classification.[28] These results highlight the multiple identity options for Asian Americans, and minority groups more generally, as well as the possibility of adopting different identities at different times.

Second, with respect to racial group consciousness, the evidence suggests that environmental cues can play a role in whether one's racial group identity becomes politicized. Jane Junn and Natalie Masuoka conducted a survey experiment intended to uncover the potential effects of descriptive representation—that is, representation by an elected official who shares a particular demographic characteristic, in this case race—on African American and Asian American racial group consciousness.[29] In the experiment, half of the participants in each racial group were randomly assigned to a treatment condition in which they were exposed to photographs and brief biographies of U.S. presidential cabinet members who shared their race while the remaining participants in each racial group were not.

Junn and Masuoka hypothesized that African-Americans' typically high levels of group consciousness would be unlikely to increase much further as a result of cuing descriptive representation in the treatment condition. However, they expected Asian-Americans' group consciousness, though lower than that of African-Americans overall, to be more malleable in response to contextual cues that reminded them of "the political consequences of being Asian American," such as exposure to same-race political actors. They found Asian Americans who received the descriptive representation treatment scored significantly higher on measures of racial group consciousness than the control group of Asian Americans. Asian American respondents who were exposed to the treatment were more likely than control subjects to agree that their individual fates are linked to those of Asian Americans as a group and to say that being Asian/Asian American is at least "somewhat important" to their political identity and beliefs.[30] The treatment condition resulted in similar but weaker effects among African Americans, confirming Junn and Masuoka's expectations that African Americans would be difficult to move any further since this group is already highly race-conscious. These results support their contention that racial groups have very different levels of racial group consciousness and, as a result, are influenced by the political environment to varying degrees.

In his study of mayoral elections in five major U.S. cities, Matt Barreto provides evidence that a similar latent group consciousness may operate among Latinos.[31] He compared consecutive mayoral elections in Houston, Los Angeles, San Francisco, Denver, and New York—one in which a competitive Latino candidate was on the ballot and one in which a Latino candidate was not—in order to test whether Latino candidates would be more likely than non-Latino candidates to mobilize Latinos. He finds that "[p]recincts with larger proportions of Latino registrants were more likely to evidence high rates of turnout when a Latino candidate was running for office."[32] Ethnic and racial identity may be a critical factor enabling racial minorities to overcome their relative disadvantage in resources such as education, employment, and interest in politics, which have proven crucial for participating in politics.[33] Descriptive representation may activate and politicize these identities and help to level the political playing field.

Beyond candidate co-ethnicity, numerous other features of contemporary campaigns heighten Latino voters' awareness of their ethnic identity "in a way that directly connects Latino identity with politics."[34] Personalized mobilization of Spanish-surname voters, targeted ads stressing the immigrant experience, Spanish-language campaign materials, and candidate endorsements by well-known Latinos may all serve to mobilize and engage Latinos.[35] In addition, Barreto and Pedraza argue that a steady stream of immigration from Latin America anchors Latino identities in the immigrant experience and garners popular attention for Latinos, including negative attention in the form of discriminatory public discourse and policies.[36] All of this serves to further politicize Latino identity and elevate Latino group consciousness, an effect we noted earlier with regard to African Americans' experiences of racial discrimination.

Finally, the socioeconomic context in which racial and ethnic minorities live matters. For example, Gay found that the lower the quality of one's neighborhood in terms of the maintenance and value of homes, cleanliness and safety of streets, and accessibility of public and private services like reliable trash removal and grocery stores, the higher was African Americans' sense of racial group consciousness or linked fate.[37]

Diversity vs. Solidarity in Group Identity and Consciousness

Beginning with Michael Dawson's seminal work, *Behind the Mule*, the political impact of racial group consciousness, usually measured with questions about racial linked fate, has primarily been studied within the African American population.[38] Dawson's work has been used to explain the apparent homogeneity in political opinions within the black community across other lines of difference, such as class, and to explain African Americans' near universal support for the Democratic Party since the mid-1960s.

However, Cathy Cohen argues the notion of linked fate itself is limited and that

> a more accurate characterization of the political positioning of most black Americans is that of a *qualified linked fate*, whereby not every black person in crisis is seen as equally essential to the survival of the community, as an equally representative proxy of our own individual interests, and thus as equally worthy of political support by other African Americans.[39]

Cohen demonstrates the consequences of this qualified linked fate through her in-depth study of the African-American political response to the HIV/AIDS crisis in the 1980s and early 1990s. She focuses on the actions of black media, organizations, and leaders in New York City, and finds that, despite eventually acknowledging that AIDS severely affects many in the black community and attempting to provide services for afflicted individuals, these black elites ultimately failed to transform most African Americans' thinking about the disease. African Americans do not view AIDs as a "black issue," or an issue of primary importance to the black community, which Cohen calls "consensus issues." Nor are those living with AIDS in the black community "embraced and 'owned' as essential members of the group."[40]

Generalizing beyond the HIV/AIDS case, Cohen contends that black politics has historically been focused on consensus issues but, increasingly, cross-cutting issues relating to the particular concerns of vulnerable or stigmatized subpopulations within the black community—usually along the lines of class, gender, and sexuality—are competing for a place on the black political agenda.[41] Cohen's study challenges us to think more carefully about how racial minority groups address internal differences and inequality within the group, highlighting the complexities of politicized group consciousness and its dependency both on context for activation or development and on the subpopulation and issue area to which it is applied.

Building on Dawson's historical account of the heterogeneity of black ideological traditions,[42] Melissa Harris-Lacewell examines the adult socialization processes that occur in the contemporary black counterpublic—including social spaces like barbershops, churches, and media outlets. She demonstrates that ordinary African American citizens make sense of the world and form "identifiable patterns of public opinion that can be understood as ideologies" through processes of "everyday talk."[43] In the segregated spaces of the black counterpublic, African Americans can feel free to candidly talk to each other "beyond the gaze of racial others," particularly whites, and this conversation serves to socially (re)construct a variety of unique black worldviews.[44] Harris-Lacewell identifies four black political ideologies that continue to operate today: Black Conservatism, Liberal Integrationism, Black Feminism, and Black Nationalism. While there are similarities between these ideologies and the traditional liberal–conservative spectrum used in survey research (developed to understand white ideology), the relevant difference between the two overall frameworks is in whether there is a deliberate recognition of race as politically salient. Whereas the white ideological spectrum is, on its face, race-neutral, Harris-Lacewell argues that all of the black political ideologies are built upon a kind of black race consciousness or notion that being black matters politically, which she calls "black common sense."[45] Exactly *how* one believes that being black matters is proscribed by one's ideology.

Work on other racial groups also emphasizes the important types of diversity within each group. Abrajano, for example, argues that Latinos who speak English are more politically knowledgeable and orient more toward the substance of issues in political campaigns, while Latinos who speak only Spanish are more oriented toward easily digestible cues to their ethnic identity, such as Spanish language campaign materials and co-ethnicity of political candidates.[46] More generally, some scholars raise questions about the downside of group solidarity and political unanimity. Blacks have been called a "captured" group with the Democratic Party because they are the most loyal Democratic voters and their votes can be taken for granted. Thus, African Americans lack the influence that comes with the credible threat of switching their votes to the other party.[47] Latinos vote Democratic but in less consistent and uniform numbers, and this may give them leverage to get more of what they want from politics.[48] In addition, when group membership becomes a simplistic cue, it can sometimes produce support for co-ethnic leaders or for parties at odds with what voters would choose if they were fully informed and voting in their own best interests.[49]

What Influences Public Opinion?

Among the multiple facets of public opinion and factors influencing political attitudes, we focus on: 1) party identification and mobilization, 2) interpersonal contact and the racial and economic context, and 3) perceptions of and experiences with discrimination. It is crucial to consider how and why the same antecedents might work in distinctive ways for different groups.

Partisan Identification

Scholars have consistently identified partisanship as the most enduring, stable and powerful of all political predispositions.[50] For white Americans, party identification is produced through an early emotional attachment to one party or the other, often learned through childhood socialization in the home or other institutions.[51] The available evidence indicates that (overwhelmingly Democratic) partisanship is acquired through similar processes of institutional socialization for African Americans, though for this group partisanship appears to be more instrumental and group-interested than affective.[52]

It is unclear how immigrant-based racial groups acquire partisanship when often their early and even adult political socialization does not occur in the United States and, as demonstrated by the work of Rogers[53] and Jones-Correa,[54] they encounter numerous barriers to institutional incorporation once in the U.S. Wong[55] argues that the longer an immigrant resides in the U.S., the greater political exposure she will have, the more likely she is to become a citizen, and the more likely she is to learn English proficiently; thus, the more likely she will be to identify with one of the political parties.

Party mobilization (or lack of it) also seems to be a pivotal factor in whether and how immigrant groups are incorporated into the American polity. Being ignored or excluded by local political parties discourages naturalization,[56] which in turn depresses the acquisition of partisanship, while becoming a citizen and being brought into the fold by the political parties encourages immigrants to adopt a partisan identification, likely that of whichever party is most welcoming.[57]

Race Relations

Two primary hypotheses have been advanced to explain the impact of cross-racial exposure: the *threat hypothesis* and the *contact hypothesis*. Most basically, greater exposure between members of different races will increase negative attitudes and worsen race relations according to the threat hypothesis, but decrease prejudices and improve race relations under the contact hypothesis. Classical formulations of the threat hypothesis predict that dominant groups will perceive increasing threats to their political and economic privileges as the population of subordinate group members in the immediate environment increases; then, as threats to resources increase so do dominant group hostilities toward subordinate groups.[58] The contact hypothesis, on the other hand, predicts improved attitudes and cooperative relations through interpersonal contact as long as certain ideal conditions for the interactions are met, including equal status among individuals and shared goals.[59]

Welch et al. provide support for the contact hypothesis in their finding that integrated neighborhoods actually reduce racial hostilities by promoting interactions between members of different racial groups.[60] At the same time, the prevalence of racially segregated neighborhoods noted by Massey and Denton[61] calls the primary mechanism of both hypotheses into question. That is, whites are unlikely to live in neighborhoods with African Americans, so interracial contact resulting in improved race relations seems unlikely to occur;

similarly, because of the rarity of racially integrated neighborhoods, whites feeling threatened by the size of the black population and then becoming more hostile toward African Americans seems like a phenomenon that would occur only infrequently.[62] Oliver and Mendelberg speak to these issues, emphasizing that researchers must carefully consider environmental context and pay close attention to the relative size of groups at both the smaller neighborhood level and the larger city or metropolitan level.

Oliver and Mendelberg find that the size of the African American population is unrelated to white racial attitudes at the neighborhood level, though it is moderately related to whites' anti-black stereotypes at the metropolitan level. However, the strongest contextual effects come, not from racial composition, but from neighborhood educational composition, which they argue is a measure of white economic vulnerability. Whites living in economically vulnerable contexts are not only more prejudiced against African Americans but are also more anti-Semitic and authoritarian than less economically vulnerable whites. They attribute this generalized out-group hostility to the psychological stresses of living in economically vulnerable environments and suggest that in the specific racial context of the U.S., such generalized out-group hostility is perhaps most often directed at African Americans. Considering the rapidly changing racial topography of the U.S., future research should explore the impact of these psychological stresses on attitudes toward other racial minorities as well.

Contrary to Oliver and Mendelberg's findings in the case of whites and African Americans, Claudine Gay finds that the *overall* economic conditions of a neighborhood do not influence African Americans' expressions of anti-Latino prejudice.[63] Instead, it is the *relative* economic positions of the two racial groups that matter. That is, African Americans who shared neighborhoods with economically advantaged Latinos exhibited more prejudice against Latinos, were less supportive of "special preferences in hiring and promotion" for Latinos than they were for themselves, and agreed more with the statement "more good jobs for Latinos means fewer good jobs for blacks."[64] Both racial prejudice and unsupportive policy attitudes intensified somewhat as the size of the Latino population increased but only in contexts of Latino economic advantage. When African Americans are better off than or economically equal to their Latino neighbors, neighborhood economic conditions have no impact on blacks' attitudes toward Latinos. These results lend partial support to both the threat and contact hypotheses, demonstrating that exposure produces threat and worsens race relations under conditions of economic inequality and also suggesting that interpersonal contact may indeed only be effective at improving race relations under conditions of equality, as the contact hypothesis predicts.

Oliver and Wong take the research that can be used to adjudicate between the threat and contact hypotheses several steps further by using interview data taken from all four of the primary racial groups while analytically distinguishing between smaller neighborhood and larger metropolitan contexts.[65] They examined racial prejudices among these groups and found that—among whites,

African Americans, and Latinos—the more integrated the neighborhood (and thus the more opportunities for contact) the less hostility residents expressed toward racial out-groups. Furthermore, these effects were most apparent in metropolitan areas in which there were large populations of racial out-groups. For example, Oliver and Wong compared the attitudes toward Latinos of African American and white residents of Atlanta, where the population of Latinos is relatively small, and Los Angeles, where the population of Latinos is relatively large. They found that African Americans and whites living in less integrated, racially homogeneous neighborhoods in Los Angeles displayed much higher rates of anti-Latino sentiment than their counterparts in Atlanta, and they attribute this difference to the larger Latino population in the L.A. metropolis relative to Atlanta.[66]

Asian Americans in Oliver and Wong's study who were interviewed in English followed a similar pattern. However, Chinese and Korean respondents who were interviewed in their native languages reported greater prejudice when living in more integrated neighborhoods. The authors speculate that these findings may be related to the lower level of incorporation that non-English-speaking Asian Americans experience, or possibly to the violence in Los Angeles against Asian-American small businesses that occurred shortly before the survey was administered.

Finally, Daniel Hopkins extends research on the threat hypothesis to long-time residents' attitudes toward recent immigrants and highlights another important factor beyond the size of local and metropolitan populations: the role of the national media in drawing attention to and politicizing issues as threatening political problems. Hopkins advances and finds support for what he calls the "politicized places hypothesis," which predicts that residents of communities in which the number of immigrants has grown will perceive immigrants as threatening and adopt anti-immigrant attitudes primarily when there are threatening, anti-immigration cues in the national media environment.[67] Conversely, according to Hopkins' research, residents are not threatened simply by increasing numbers of immigrants in their local communities if increasing immigration has not been politicized as a problem by political elites at the national level.[68]

Research on the emotion of anxiety by Shana Gadarian and Bethany Albertson demonstrates how the effects of threat politicized by the national media might multiply. They find that once people are made to feel anxious about immigration, they will seek out threatening immigration news with greater frequency than people who are not anxious about immigration. In this way, biased information seeking among people who encounter threatening cues about immigration in the media likely further reinforces the negative effects on immigration attitudes identified by Hopkins.[69]

The results of all of these studies highlight the important role that is played by context—at the neighborhood, city, and national levels—in influencing the effects of integration and contact on relations between groups. Furthermore, not only do the relative sizes and geographic distributions of racial and ethnic groups in neighborhoods and cities matter, but economic conditions, the relative economic positions of groups, and national politics played out in the media all impact how people respond to the increased presence of out-group others in the neighborhoods and cities in which they reside.

Discrimination

Dennis Chong and Dukhong Kim's "theory of opportunities" echoes our theme that "[t]he assimilation of a minority group into American society depends not only on the actions of group members but also on the reception accorded that group by the majority population."[70] Specifically, Chong and Kim ask why members with higher economic status sometimes continue to have strong racial group consciousness. They find that the effects of class will depend upon racial group members' perceptions of opportunities for social mobility—beliefs about their chances of moving up in the world.[71]

At the group level—that is, looking at between-group differences among African Americans, Asian Americans, and Latinos—Chong and Kim find that economic status has the smallest effect on African Americans' levels of group consciousness. They find that support for policies that benefit the group is least affected by improved economic fortunes for African Americans, relative to other racial groups, because of frequent experiences with discrimination and perceptions that blacks have fewer opportunities relative to whites. In contrast, improved economic status for Asian Americans and Latinos is often accompanied by fewer experiences with discrimination and a more positive outlook on U.S. society, making increased economic status for these groups a significant predictor of diminished support for racial group interests.[72]

Chong and Kim find the same dynamic at work at the individual level. In other words, when they focus on the between-person differences within each of the three racial minority groups, they find that economic status has no effect on support for group interests for minority individuals who frequently experience discrimination and perceive unequal opportunities. On the other hand, among minority individuals who have little experience with discrimination and believe that U.S. society does offer equal opportunities for all, high economic status reduces support for group interests.[73]

Importantly, Chong and Kim's research contradicts earlier scholarship on black public opinion. Sigelman and Welch found that African Americans' perceptions of group discrimination influenced their views about the sources of racial disparities, and both these perceptions and explanations influenced the policy solutions that African Americans preferred to remedy racial inequality.[74] Furthermore, they found that African Americans perceived much higher levels of discrimination against blacks as a group than they reported experiencing personally, and as such, personal experiences with discrimination had little effect on their attitudes.

But why do personal experiences with discrimination impact African Americans' opinions in Chong and Kim's 2006 study but not in that of Sigelman and Welch in 1991? In answering this question, it is critical to look at the ways in which the different pairs of researchers measured personal discrimination. Chong and Kim used a combination of seven wide-ranging questions to measure respondents' levels of perceived discrimination, including questions that ask whether respondents have experienced discrimination in the past 10 years or have ever been "physically threatened or attacked" or "unfairly stopped by police."[75] Respondents in Chong and Kim's 2006 study were also asked about the frequency with which they have been given "less respect" and "poorer service" (while shopping or dining) than others, as well as about how often people insult or call them names or seem fearful of them because of their race. In contrast, Sigelman and Welch used four questions about basic "quality of life" issues, which they acknowledged were "fairly crude," including whether respondents had ever been discriminated against in getting "quality education" and "decent" housing, jobs, and wages.[76] Sigelman and Welch astutely note that their measurements "ignore possible discrimination in the daily routines of life," like shopping, eating at restaurants, and interacting with others in the community.[77] As Chong and Kim's measures highlight, Sigelman and Welch's research also fails to capture discrimination at the hands of state actors like the police.

The factors that influence others' perceptions of discrimination against out-group members are also important to understand because of the consequences these perceptions have for public opinion about policies intended to benefit racial minority groups. Whites' belief that blacks are discriminated against is positively correlated with white support for a range of policies that serve to ameliorate racial inequality, like affirmative action, as well as less race-conscious policies.[78] Believing that African Americans, Latinos, and Asian Americans continue to be discriminated against goes hand in hand with support for policies intended to benefit all racial minorities, including job training, educational assistance, and preferential hiring and promotion programs, among white, African American, Latino, and Asian American respondents.[79]

Concluding Remarks

We began our review of research in political science on race and the group bases of public opinion by describing the complexity and the socially constructed nature of racial categories in the United States. Despite the inherent difficulties in measuring these concepts, race and ethnicity remain among the most import-ant divisions in political attitudes among Americans. To better understand the group bases of public opinion, researchers have attempted to define, measure, and examine the three key concepts of *racial group membership* (what we have referred to as racial categorization), *racial group identity*, and *racial group consciousness*. Most scholarship has focused on one of the four primary racial groups: whites, African Americans, Latinos, and Asian Americans. Michael Dawson developed the concept of *linked fate* from the experiences of African Americans in U.S. politics. This idea has been influential in scholarship in racial and ethnic politics; however the extent to which the concept is applicable to other minority populations facing different political circumstances, including Asian Americans and Latinos, is not clear. Differences in the ways in which individuals understand the same questions on surveys, and the distinctive contexts in which surveys are administered, complicate the measurement and comparison of group membership, identity, and consciousness across groups.

We conclude that the contours of the relationships between racial group identity, racial group consciousness, and public opinion, particularly for Latinos and Asian Americans, are not well understood because of the dynamic nature of these populations and the still-early stage of systematic research. For members of these pan-ethnic racial groups, identification is a complex choice. For all racial and ethnic groups, membership and identity are fluid and primarily based on the forces of politics and the circumstances of society. They are not fixed or objective. Within all groups, there are important tensions between unity and difference, favored status and marginalization.

Finally, we reviewed three widely studied predictors of public opinion, including party identification, race relations, and perceptions of discrimination. In terms of race relations, the mixture of resident groups in neighborhoods and cities along with the local economic and national political contexts in which they occur are key to understanding public opinion related to racial and ethnic out-groups. In terms of discrimination, it is crucial to understand how the discriminatory treatment directed at a group member, and her interaction with society, vary systematically as a function of her group membership. The different historical and current circumstances of groups explain the varied outlooks their members adopt on individual opportunity.

Notes

1. "United States Census Bureau State & County QuickFacts," last modified July 8, 2014, http://quickfacts.census.gov/qfd/states/00000.html
2. Natalie Masuoka, "Political Attitudes and Ideologies of Multiracial Americans: The Implications of Mixed Race in the United States," *Political Research Quarterly* 61(2) (2008): 253–267; Kim M. Williams, *Mark One or More: Civil Rights in Multiracial America* (Ann Arbor, MI: The University of Michigan Press, 2006).
3. Reuel Rogers, *Afro-Caribbean Immigrants and the Politics of Incorporation: Ethnicity, Exception or Exit* (Cambridge, MA: Cambridge University Press, 2006); Yvette Alex-Assensoh, "African Immigrants and African-Americans: An Analysis of Voluntary African Immigration and the Evolution of Black Ethnic Politics in America," *African and Asian Studies* 8 (2009): 89–124.
4. Michael Omi and Howard Winant, *Racial Formation in the United States: From the 1960s to the 1990s* (New York: Routledge, 1994); Anthony W. Marx, *Making Race and Nation: A Comparison of the U.S., South Africa, and Brazil* (New York: Cambridge University Press, 1998); David Roediger, *The Wages of Whiteness: Race and the Making of the American Working Class* (New York: Verso Books, 1999).

5. Melissa Nobles, *Shades of Citizenship: Race and the Census in Modern Politics* (Stanford, CA: Stanford University Press, 2000).
6. Ira Katznelson, *When Affirmative Action Was White: An Untold History of Racial Inequality in Twentieth-Century America* (New York: W. W. Norton, 2005); Rogers Smith, *Civic Ideals: Conflicting Visions of Citizenship in U.S. History* (New Haven, CT: Yale University Press, 1997); Daniel J. Tichenor, *Dividing Lines: The Politics of Immigration Control in America* (Princeton, NJ: Princeton University Press, 2002).
7. Rachael V. Cobb, D. James Greiner, and Kevin M. Quinn, "Can Voter ID Laws Be Administered in a Race-Neutral Manner? Evidence from the City of Boston in 2008," *Quarterly Journal of Political Science* 7 (2012): 1–33.
8. Paul Frymer, *Black and Blue: African Americans, the Labor Movement, and the Decline of the Democratic Party* (Princeton, NJ: Princeton University Press, 2008).
9. Victoria Hattam, *In the Shadow of Race: Jews, Latinos, and Immigrant Politics in the United States* (Chicago, IL: The University of Chicago Press, 2007); Noel Ignatiev, *How the Irish Became White* (New York: Routledge, 1995); Matthew Frye Jacobson, *Whiteness of a Different Color: European Immigrants and the Alchemy of Race* (Cambridge, MA: Harvard University Press, 1999); Ariela Gross, *What Blood Won't Tell: A History of Race on Trial in America* (Cambridge, MA: Harvard University Press, 2008).
10. Ian Haney Lopez, *White by Law: The Legal Construction of Race*, revised and expanded edition (New York: New York University Press, 2006).
11. Roger Daniels, *Guarding the Golden Door: American Immigration Policy and Immigrants since 1882* (New York: Hill and Wang, 2004).
12. Mae Ngai, *Impossible Subjects: Illegal Aliens and the Making of Modern America* (Princeton, NJ: Princeton University Press, 2004).
13. Claire Kim, "The Racial Triangulation of Asian Americans," *Politics & Society* 27(1) (1999): 105–138.
14. Paula McClain, Jessica D. Johnson Carew, Eugene Walton, Jr., and Candis S. Watts, "Group Membership, Group Identity, and Group Consciousness: Measures of Racial Identity in American Politics?" *Annual Review of Political Science* 12 (2009): 471–485.
15. McClain et al., "Group Membership, Group Identity, and Group Consciousness: Measures of Racial Identity in American Politics?" *Annual Review of Political Science* 12 (2009): 474, 476, emphasis in original.
16. Michael Dawson, *Behind the Mule: Race and Class in African American Politics* (Princeton, NJ: Princeton University Press, 1994).
17. Michael Jones-Correa, *Between Two Nations: The Political Predicament of Latinos in New York City* (Ithaca, NY: Cornell University Press, 1998).
18. Jones-Correa, *Between Two Nations*, 1998; Rogers, *Afro-Caribbean Immigrants and the Politics of Incorporation*, 2006.
19. Taeku Lee, "Race, Immigration, and the Identity-to-Politics Link," *Annual Review of Political Science* 11 (2008): 457–478; Dennis Chong and Reuel Rogers, "Racial Solidarity and Political Participation," *Political Behavior* 27(4) (2005): 347–374.
20. Paula D. McClain, Niambi M. Carter, Victoria M. DeFrancesco Soto, Monique L. Lyle, Jeffrey D. Grynaviski, Shayla C. Nunnally, Thomas J. Scotto, J. Alan Kendrick, Gerald F. Lackey, and Kendra Davenport Cotton, "Racial Distancing in a Southern City: Latino Immigrants' Views of Black Americans," *Journal of Politics* 68 (2006): 571–584; Rogelio Saenz, "Latinos and the Changing Face of America," in *The American People: Census 2000*, eds Reynolds Farley and John Haaga (New York: Russell Sage Foundation, 2005).

21. Pew Research Center, "The Rise of Asian Americans, Updated Edition," *Pew Research Social and Demographic Trends* (2013), accessed November 6, 2014, http://www.pewsocialtrends.org/2012/06/19/the-rise-of-asian-americans/#fn-12979-11

22. Anna Brown and Eileen Patten, "Statistical Portrait of Hispanics in the United States, 2012," Pew Research Hispanic Trends Project (2014), accessed November 6, 2014, http://www.pewhispanic.org/2014/04/29/statistical-portrait-of-hispanics-in-the-united-states-2012/

23. Matt Barreto and Francisco Pedraza, "The Renewal and Persistence of Group Identification in American Politics," *Electoral Studies* 28 (2009): 595–605.

24. Barreto and Pedraza, "The Renewal and Persistence of Group Identification in American Politics," 595–605; Luis Ricardo Fraga, John A. Garcia, Rodney E. Hero, Michael Jones-Correa, Valerie Martinez-Ebers, and Gary M. Segura, *Latino Lives in America: Making it Home* (Philadelphia, PA: Temple University Press, 2010).

25. Pei-te M. Lien, Margaret Conway, and Janelle Wong, "The Contours and Sources of Ethnic Identity Choices Among Asian Americans," *Social Science Quarterly* 84(2) (2003): 461–481; S. Karthick Ramakrishnan, Janelle Wong, Taeku Lee, and Jane Junn, "Race-Based Considerations and the Obama Vote," *Du Bois Review* 6(1) (2009): 219–238.

26. Pew Research Center, "The Rise of Asian Americans."

27. Paul Taylor, Mark Hugo Lopez, Jessica Martinez, and Gabriel Velasco, "When Labels Don't Fit: Hispanics and Their Views of Identity," Pew Research Hispanic Trends Project (2012), accessed November 6, 2014, http://www.pewhispanic.org/2012/04/04/when-labels-dont-fit-hispanics-and-their-views-of-identity/

28. Lien et. al., "The Contours and Sources of Ethnic Identity Choices Among Asian Americans," 465.

29. Jane Junn and Natalie Masuoka, "Asian American Identity: Shared Racial Status and Political Context," *Perspectives on Politics* 6(4) (2008): 729–740.

30. Junn and Masuoka, "Asian American Identity: Shared Racial Status and Political Context," 737.

31. Matt Barreto, "Si Se Puede! Latino Candidates and the Mobilization of Latino Voters," *American Political Science Review* 101(3) (2007): 425–441.

32. Barreto, "Si Se Puede! Latino Candidates and the Mobilization of Latino Voters," 438.

33. Katherine Tate, *From Protest to Politics: The New Black Voters in American Elections* (New York: Russell Sage Foundation, 1993).

34. Barreto and Pedraza, "The Renewal and Persistence of Group Identification in American Politics," 599.

35. Marisa A. Abrajano and R. Michael Alvarez, *New Faces New Voices: The Hispanic Electorate in America* (Princeton, NJ: Princeton University Press, 2010)

36. Barreto and Pedraza, "The Renewal and Persistence of Group Identification in American Politics."

37. Claudine Gay, "Putting Race in Context: Identifying the Environmental Determinants of Black Racial Attitudes," *American Political Science Review* 98(4) (2004): 547–562.

38. Dawson, *Behind the Mule.*

39. Cathy Cohen, *The Boundaries of Blackness: AIDS and the Breakdown of Black Politics* (Chicago: University of Chicago Press, 1999): x–xi, emphasis added.

40. Cohen, *The Boundaries of Blackness*, 118.

41. Cohen, *The Boundaries of Blackness*, 8.

42. Michael Dawson, *Black Visions: The Roots of Contemporary African-American Political Ideologies* (Chicago: The University of Chicago Press, 2001).
43. Melissa Harris-Lacewell, *Barbershops, Bibles, and BET: Everyday Talk and Black Political Thought* (Princeton, NJ: Princeton University Press, 2004): xxiii.
44. Harris-Lacewell, *Barbershops, Bibles, and BET*, 9.
45. Harris-Lacewell, *Barbershops, Bibles, and BET*, 23.
46. Abrajano and Alvarez, *New Faces New Voices.*
47. Paul Frymer, *Uneasy Alliances: Race and Party Competition in America* (Princeton, NJ: Princeton University Press, 1999).
48. Adrian D. Pantoja, Ricardo Ramirez, and Gary M. Segura, "Citizens by Choice, Voters by Necessity: Patterns of Political Mobilization by Naturalized Latinos," *Political Research Quarterly* 54 (2001): 729–750.
49. James H. Kuklinski and Norman L. Hurley, "On Hearing and Interpreting Political Messages: A Cautionary Tale of Citizen Cue-Taking," *The Journal of Politics* 56(3) (1994): 729–51; Tasha Philpot, *Race, Republicans, and the Return of the Party of Lincoln* (Ann Arbor, MI: The University of Michigan Press, 2007); Jane Mansbridge and Katherine Tate, "Race Trumps Gender: The Thomas Nomination in the Black Community," *PS: Political Science and Politics* 25 (1992): 488–492.
50. Angus Campbell, Philip E. Converse, Warren E. Miller, and Donald E. Stokes, *The American Voter* (Chicago, IL: The University of Chicago Press, 1960).
51. Campbell, Converse, Miller, and Stokes, *The American Voter.*
52. Dawson, *Behind the Mule.*
53. Rogers, *Afro-Caribbean Immigrants and the Politics of Incorporation.*
54. Jones-Correa, *Between Two Nations.*
55. Janelle S. Wong, "The Effects of Age and Political Exposure on the Development of Party Identification among Asian American and Latino Immigrants in the United States," *Political Behavior* 22(4) (2000): 341–371.
56. Rogers, *Afro-Caribbean Immigrants and the Politics of Incorporation*; Jones-Correa, *Between Two Nations.*
57. Wong, "The Effects of Age and Political Exposure on the Development of Party Identification among Asian American and Latino Immigrants in the United States," 341–371; Pei-te Lien, Christian Collet, Janelle Wong, and S. Karthick Ramakrishnan, "Asian Pacific-American Public Opinion and Political Participation," *PS: Political Science & Politics* 34(3) (2001): 625–630.
58. V. O. Key, *Southern Politics in State and Nation* (New York: Knopf, 1984 [1949]); Hubert M. Blalock, *Toward a Theory of Minority-Group Relations* (New York: Wiley, 1967).
59. Gordon Allport, *The Nature of Prejudice* (Cambridge: Addison-Wesley Publishing Company, 1954).
60. Susan Welch, Lee Sigelman, Timothy Bledsoe, and Michael Combs, *Race & Place: Race Relations in an American City* (Cambridge: Cambridge University Press, 2001).
61. Douglas Massey and Nancy Denton, *American Apartheid: Segregation and the Making of the Underclass* (Cambridge, MA: Harvard University Press, 1993).
62. Eric J. Oliver and Tali Mendelberg, "Reconsidering the Environmental Determinants of White Racial Attitudes," *American Journal of Political Science* 44(3) (2000): 574–589.
63. Claudine Gay, "Seeing Difference: The Effects of Economic Disparity on Black Attitudes toward Latinos," *American Journal of Political Science* 50(4) (2006): 982–997.
64. Gay, "Seeing Difference," 990.

65. Eric J. Oliver and Janelle Wong, "Intergroup Prejudice in Multiethnic Settings," *American Journal of Political Science* 47(4) (2003): 567–582.
66. Oliver and Wong, "Intergroup Prejudice in Multiethnic Settings."
67. Daniel J. Hopkins, "Politicized Places: Explaining Where and When Immigrants Provoke Local Opposition," *American Political Science Review* 104(1) (2010): 40–60.
68. Hopkins, "Politicized Places."
69. Shana Kushner Gadarian and Bethany Albertson, "Anxiety, Immigration, and the Search for Information," *Political Psychology* 35(2) (2014): 133–164.
70. Dennis Chong and Dukhong Kim, "The Experiences and Effects of Economic Status among Racial and Ethnic Minorities," *American Political Science Review* 100(3) (2006): 336–337.
71. Chong and Kim, "The Experiences and Effects of Economic Status among Racial and Ethnic Minorities."
72. Chong and Kim, "The Experiences and Effects of Economic Status among Racial and Ethnic Minorities."
73. Chong and Kim, "The Experiences and Effects of Economic Status among Racial and Ethnic Minorities."
74. Lee Sigelman and Susan Welch, *Black Americans' Views of Racial Inequality: The Dream Deferred* (Cambridge: Cambridge University Press, 1991).
75. Chong and Kim, "The Experiences and Effects of Economic Status among Racial and Ethnic Minorities," 350.
76. Sigelman and Welch, *Black Americans' Views of Racial Inequality*, 55, 59.
77. Sigelman and Welch, *Black Americans' Views of Racial Inequality*, 59.
78. Donald Kinder and Lynn Sanders, *Divide By Color: Racial Politics and Democratic Ideals* (Chicago: The University of Chicago Press, 1996); David O. Sears, Jim Sidanius, and Lawrence Bobo (eds), *Racialized Politics: The Debate About Racism in America* (Chicago: The University of Chicago Press, 2000).
79. Linda Lopez and Adrian D. Pantoja, "Beyond Black and White: General Support for Race-Conscious Policies among African Americans, Latinos, Asian Americans and Whites," *Political Research Quarterly* 57(4) (2004): 633–642.

Chapter 6

The Politics of Gender

Nancy Burns, Ashley E. Jardina,
Donald Kinder, and Molly E. Reynolds

Much of what we know about how individuals interact with the political world lies in what we know about their place in society. Where one is situated is often a function of our universal human tendency to categorize. We place ourselves and others into groups based on our religions and nationalities, occupations and social class, the sports teams for which we cheer, and the colleges we attend. We organize people into "us" and "them," in-group members and out-group members, and we do so perhaps most readily when it comes to categories we generally believe to be immutable, like gender. In this chapter, we focus on the structure of such categorical thinking with respect to gender, and we describe some of the significant ways in which notions about gender factor into political attitudes and behavior.

While men and women may physically differ from one another in terms of average size and reproductive capacity, the roles, arrangements, and practices organized around these differences are socially constructed. In other words, the characteristics ascribed to each gender are well beyond any fixed, biological features that may distinguish these groups. And these socially assembled differences give rise to significant disadvantages for women—disadvantages that are pervasive and persistent. They are what Charles Tilly calls "durable inequalities"—ones that are repeated across generations and over time.[1] These inequalities have had a powerful impact on the extent to which women engage in the political world, and they have influenced the attitudes both men and women possess about the role of women in politics.

When we consider the place of women in the United States from the early twentieth century until the present, we can see quite clearly how women have experienced significant disadvantages that are still apparent today. Until the 1960s, women in the United States were routinely excluded from the majority of both white- and blue-collar occupations. When they sought careers, it was almost exclusively in the service sector, where they were maids, waitresses, or nannies. Middle-class, more educated women were mostly limited to working as nurses, secretaries, or teachers.[2] In recent decades, the labor market has opened considerably for women, but today they still earn, on average, less than men.[3] Furthermore, women in the United States have been repeatedly barred from non-civilian military service. They were not permitted into the U.S. military academy until 1976, and their role in combat was severely limited through the early 1990s. Women were banned from direct combat in 1994, and it was not until 2013 that this restriction was tentatively lifted.

These inequalities extend to the political sphere. For much of U.S. history, women were not permitted to vote; the Nineteenth Amendment granting women suffrage was not ratified until 1920. Until very recently, women participated noticeably less in politics compared to men, and far fewer women seek and win elective political office.[4] In 2014, women held only 18.5 percent of the seats in the U.S. House and 20 percent of the seats in the U.S. Senate. When Nancy Pelosi (D-CA) was elected Speaker of the House in 2007, she was the first woman to hold that position in the governing body's 218-year history, and she is, to date, the highest-ranking female politician in American history.

Put in these terms, gender disparities are striking. Often, however, the factors that produce these inequalities occur gradually and sometimes imperceptibly over the course of women's lives. This subtlety is exacerbated by the fact that gender relations are defined—and complicated by—contact and intimacy.[5] Men and women are intimately tied in their day-to-day lives. Women have fathers, brothers, husbands, and sons with whom they have close emotional and familial ties. These connections mean that the economic fates of men and women are inextricably linked, and because their roles as wives and mothers provide social status and protection, women may find traditional gender roles rewarding.[6]

This particular social arrangement—where women are both disadvantaged but integrated, where they experience significant inequality but are deeply valued in their roles as mothers and caretakers—has powerful implications for widespread beliefs about the definition of gender, the role of women, and the extent to which women identify with their gender or possess a sense of group solidarity. Below, we describe the elements of these widespread beliefs and examine their political implications.

Essentialism and Women's Place

A quality fundamental to individual notions about gender is essentialism—the belief that members of a particular category share inherent traits, and that differences between members of one category and another are natural and fixed. Children as young as five believe that women and men have essences.[7] Cognitive psychologists argue that this essentialism serves as a heuristic bias, or mental shortcut, to help us navigate our complex social interactions.[8] These seemingly fundamental beliefs make it difficult for women to achieve equality with men. Writing in 1977, Erving Goffman explains,

> Women may be defined as being less than men, but they are nonetheless idealized, mythologized, in a serious way through such values as motherhood, innocence, gentleness, sexual attractiveness, and so forth—

a lesser pantheon, perhaps, but a pantheon nonetheless. Moreover, many women—perhaps the vast majority in America even today—are profoundly convinced that however baleful their place in society, the official view concerning the natural characterological differences between themselves and men is correct, eternally and naturally so.[9]

Essentialism also serves to reinforce stereotypes about the nature and capabilities of women, and gender stereotypes developed around essentialism are related to what individuals believe is the proper place of women in the home, in society, in the workforce, and in politics. In fact, debates about gender in the United States have been centered largely on whether women should be relegated to the private sphere, primarily at home with a family. Scholars have traditionally measured opinion regarding the proper place of women using variants of what is called the Attitudes toward Women Scale (AWS).[10] Like much of the scholarship on gender roles, the AWS scale was developed in the early 1970s, when the women's rights movement brought significant attention to issues surrounding gender inequality. It comprises survey questions designed to assess individuals' beliefs about the roles, responsibilities, and rights of American women. The extremes of the scale represent the endorsement of traditional views about women's place at one end and modern views about the role of women at the other. Political scientists have used a version of this scale that usually includes questions assessing individuals' comfort with having a female boss, beliefs about the quality of the relationships working women can have with their children, opinion regarding the time men and women should spend on household chores, and attitudes about whether women should remain at home to take care of the household.

Since the mid-1970s, both men's and women's average placement on the AWS has moved increasingly toward the "modern" position of the scale. Generational replacement, women's increased participation in the labor force, and higher levels of educational attainment have pushed both genders toward the belief that men's and women's roles should be equal.[11] Yet, even in recent years, there remains a noteworthy divide between men and women in the extent to which they actually endorse equal roles, and a number of Americans still agree that the place of these groups should be fundamentally different. To illustrate this point, we draw on data from a piece of the 2012 Cooperative Congressional Election Study (CCES). As part of the study, a nationally representative sample of 1,000 Americans were asked variants of questions tapping these ideas about women's place. In Figure 6.1, we compare the distribution among men and women on four of these questions.

When we look at the distribution of responses to the individual items that comprise the Attitudes toward Women Scale, we can see that there remain noteworthy differences among both genders regarding the proper role of women. Most notably, we see that men tend to have somewhat more traditional views about women's place than do women. Especially when the issue directly

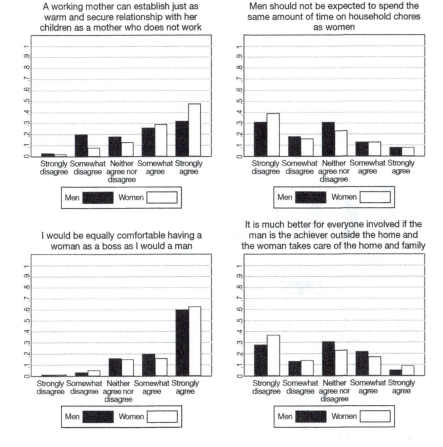

Figure 6.1 Distribution of Responses to Questions about Women's Place (source: 2012 Cooperative Congressional Election Study. [Module]. N = 463 men, 537 women).

involves children or work at home, men, on average, express more traditional views than do women.

When we combine these four items into a single measure by averaging them, we are able to obtain a general view of attitudes toward the role of women across the U.S. population. We present, in Figure 6.2, the distribution of the scale measured in the 2012 CCES. What the scale indicates is that today, a sizeable portion of both American men and women agree that members of each gender should have different roles. Scholars have argued that these attitudes regarding the role of women affect political ambition among women, discouraging them from either participating in or engaging with politics, and help to explain public opinion on a variety of issues, including federal support for day care centers,

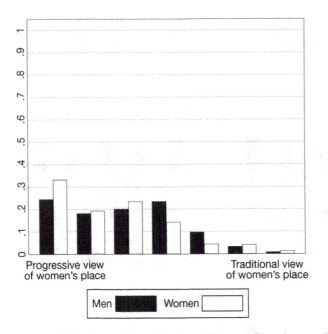

Figure 6.2 The Scale of Attitudes about Women's Place (source: 2012 Cooperative Congressional Election Study. [Module]. N = 463 men, 537 women).

permitting women to serve in military combat, attitudes toward parental leave, and endorsement of the ERA.[12]

Modern Sexism

Despite the notable variation in the extent to which Americans hold traditional views about the proper place of women, we know that subscriptions to gender essentialism are not as firmly held as they once were. In the wake of the Civil Rights era and the modern Women's Movement, gender essentialism began to fall somewhat out of fashion, and significant strides were made toward gender equality in the United States. As a result, some Americans now believe that gender discrimination is a relic of the past, and they feel antagonistic toward women who, in their view, are asking for special favors or making illegitimate political and economic demands. Swim et al. developed the Modern Sexism Scale to tap into these sentiments. [13] The scale assesses the extent to which individuals deny the existence of discrimination against women and resent both complaints from women regarding discrimination and any "special favors" directed to women in domains like education and the workplace.[14]

In Figure 6.3, we present the distribution of responses among men and women to variants of questions from the Modern Sexism Scale. Our data come from the 2012 American National Election Study (ANES), a nationally representative sample of 5,900 respondents. When we examine the distribution of the first item in the scale—whether women demanding equality are actually seeking "special favors"—we can see that 49 percent of women and 52 percent of men agree that this is true some of the time. Indeed, the majority of both men and women in the 2012 national sample believe that women are actually asking for special treatment under the guise of seeking equality. The vast majority of men and women also endorse the notion that when women complain about discrimination, they cause more problems than they solve. Only 10 percent of men and 9 percent of women believe that these complaints never cause more problems than they solve. Most men and women do believe, however, that discrimination against women does occur when employers are making hiring decisions. Examining the last graph in Figure 6.3, we can see that

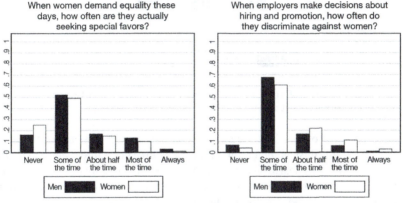

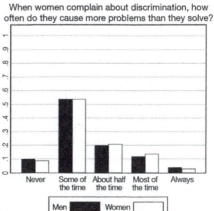

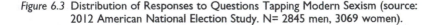

Figure 6.3 Distribution of Responses to Questions Tapping Modern Sexism (source: 2012 American National Election Study. N= 2845 men, 3069 women).

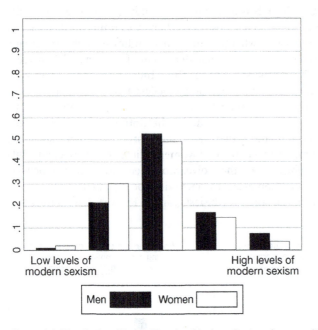

Figure 6.4 The Scale of Items Tapping Modern Sexism (source: 2012 American National Election Study. N= 2845 men, 3069 women).

only 7 percent of men and 4 percent of women believe that employers *never* discriminate against women. Combining these three items into a single measure yields the Modern Sexism Scale, the distribution of which we present in Figure 6.4. The bar graph makes clear that the majority of both men and women in the U.S. possess moderate to high levels of modern sexism.

Group Solidarity

The systematic discrimination women have experienced, in part through the maintenance of traditional beliefs about the role of women, has contributed to the development of another important predisposition—group solidarity. Sometimes groups that experience systematic disadvantages and pervasive discrimination develop a sense of group interdependence and solidarity. That is, individuals come to believe that their life outcomes are linked with the experiences and opportunities of their group.[15] They may also feel a sense of emotional interdependence with their group, reporting anger in response to the way group members are treated in society or pride in the accomplishments of their group.[16] Furthermore, individuals scoring high on group solidarity often subscribe to the notion that their group's position in society is a product of structural factors that systematically contribute to the discrimination and subordination experienced by group members. Because women are inextricably linked to men through contact and intimacy, however, women have not developed a politicized group identity or consciousness surrounding their gender as readily as other subordinate groups in the United States.

Gurin provided the first comprehensive examination of gender solidarity among women in the wake of the modern women's movement.[17] She finds that over the course of the 1970s, women did become somewhat more politically conscious, especially college educated, employed, unmarried women under 30. She also finds that men changed with women, becoming more likely to recognize women's deprivation and their own relative privilege and power.

In Figure 6.5, we consider gender solidarity among women in the present day using the 2012 CCES. Examining the first bar graph, we see that 51 percent of women believe that what happens to women in this country will affect their

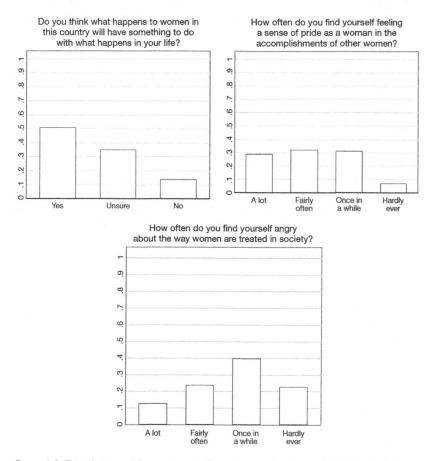

Figure 6.5 Distribution of Responses to Questions in the Group Solidarity Scale (source: 2012 Cooperative Congressional Election Study. [Module]. N = 537 women).

own life. When it comes to emotional interdependence, a majority of women (61 percent) claim that they feel pride in the accomplishments of other women at least fairly often. Furthermore, 37 percent claim that they have felt angry about the way women are treated in society fairly often or a lot.

Political Implications

The extent to which individuals adopt traditional views about the role of women, subscribe to modern sexism, or have a sense of gender solidarity has important implications for their political preferences. Here, we build on previous efforts and investigate the relationship between these aspects of gender ideology and women's preferences on policy. For this purpose, we examined women's opinion on three distinct policies: abortion rights; legislation protecting women from job discrimination; and the war on Iraq, all coded such that higher values of the variable reflect more conservative attitudes.[18] In each case, the analysis includes three principal explanatory factors: beliefs about women's place; attitudes about modern sexism; and feelings of gender solidarity. The analysis also includes several other factors that we expect might also predict policy attitudes (social class, beliefs about how active the federal government should be in solving society's problems, attitudes about the importance of equal opportunity in society, and partisanship).

Figure 6.6 summarizes the results of the three analyses, carried out by multiple regression. Our aim is to understand how closely related women's attitudes towards women's place, modern sexism, and gender solidarity are to policy views. Are they closely related to some policies and not to others? Along the left hand side of each graph are the three gender ingredients. Each bar indicates the predicted difference in the policy attitudes of an individual who holds the most traditional views on the respective ingredient with an individual who holds the most progressive ones. Each bar for women's place, then, shows the difference on each policy item between women holding the most and least traditional views. For modern sexism, it is the difference between women who agree with all of the modern sexism questions versus those who agree with none. For gender solidarity, finally, it is the difference between women who do not feel close at all to other women with those who feel extremely close. If a bar is to the right of zero, it indicates that more traditional views are associated with more conservative attitudes on the policy item, while if the bar is to the left of zero, it demonstrates that more progressive views correspond to less conservative opinions on policy.

If we begin with women's place, we can see that a more traditional perspective on the role of women in society is strongly related to opposition to abortion. The size of this effect—0.27—is roughly equivalent to moving from one of the four answer options—for example, "of rape, incest or when the woman's life is in danger"—to the next most conservative answer option, for example, "abortion should never be permitted"—for the average woman taking

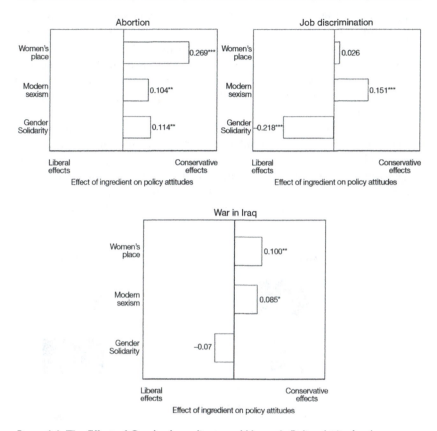

Figure 6.6 The Effect of Gender Ingredients on Women's Policy Attitudes (source: 2006 Cooperative Congressional Election Study. [Module]. N = 1615).
*** p<0.01, ** p<0.05, * p<0.1.

the survey.[19] Traditional attitudes on women's place are also associated with greater support for the war in Iraq, but the size of the effect is much smaller. Having more traditional views of women's place, then, is associated with being only slightly less likely, on average, to report thinking the war in Iraq was a mistake. Finally, there is no statistically significant relationship between attitudes towards the place of women in society and opinions on legislation prohibiting job discrimination against women. Not all gender policies are the same. Some tend to center on roles, and some tend to center on rights. Views on those that center on rights, as does the question of job discrimination, tend not to be about women's place, but rather tend to draw upon solidarity and sexism.

For modern sexism, meanwhile, we see that as women agree with more statements like "women demanding equality are actually seeking special favors," they also hold more conservative policy views on abortion, job discrimination legislation, and the war in Iraq. The effect of this ingredient is statistically significant and approximately the same size for abortion and the war in Iraq, and slightly larger for job discrimination legislation. Moving from the highest score on the Modern Sexism Scale to the lowest is associated with a move of about half of the way between answer options to the job discrimination question—i.e., about half of the way from "somewhat oppose" the legislation to "strongly oppos[ing]" it.

Finally, for gender solidarity, we can see that feeling closer to other women predicts more conservative attitudes on abortion, and much more liberal views on the job discrimination measure; it does not appear to have a statistically significant effect on attitudes to the war in Iraq. The size of the effect for abortion is relatively slight, but on job discrimination, it is notably larger. The average woman who feels the closest to other women reports attitudes on

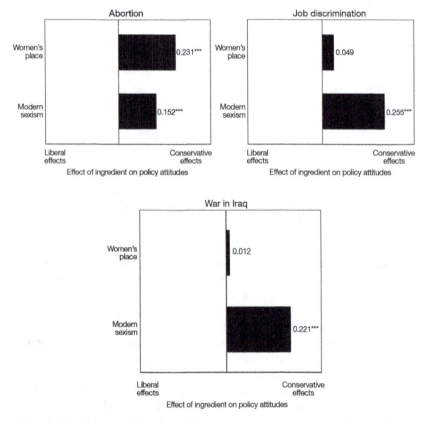

Figure 6.7 The Effect of Gender Ingredients on Men's Policy Attitudes (source: 2006 Cooperative Congressional Election Study. [Module]. N=1031).

*** p<0.01, ** p<0.05, * p<0.1.

legislation prohibiting job discrimination that are almost one full answer option more liberal—i.e., strongly supporting the bill instead of slightly supporting it—than the average woman who reports feeling no solidarity with other women.

While we are perhaps more interested in the way that gender ingredients structure *women's* policy attitudes, we have reason to believe that they might also affect men's policy preferences, especially on issues that we would consider "gendered" ones, like abortion and legislation protecting women from job discrimination. In Figure 6.7 above, we carry out the same analysis as above, omitting only the gender solidarity measure, but this time for men. The results for men bear a striking similarity to those for women. Traditional views on women's place are strongly related to more conservative views on abortion, though not on either job discrimination or the war in Iraq for men. Subscribing to modern sexism, meanwhile, is associated with more conservative opinions in all three policy areas. While men and women differ somewhat in the degree to which they subscribe to the individual gender ingredients, then, Figures 6.6 and 6.7 suggest that they use them similarly to structure their attitudes on policy issues.

The Gender Gap in Party Identification

Despite similarities in the extent to which these attitudes toward gender predict political preferences among both men and women, we *do* observe important, systematic, and persistent—though small—gender differences when it comes both to political party loyalties and to certain policy positions. In recent decades, women in the U.S. have been a little more inclined to identify with the Democratic Party, while men have been a little more aligned with the Republicans.

Figure 6.8 shows the difference in the proportion of men and women identifying as Democrats over time, as recorded by the American National Election Study. In the 1950s, the line for men is above that for women, indicating more men reported allegiance to the Democrats than women. Beginning around 1970, and consistently since then, women have become somewhat more Democratic. Many scholars have sought to explain this difference, especially the dynamics of its change over time. One explanation emphasizes party change.[20] Following a period of consensus on women's rights issues such as the Equal Rights Amendment (ERA) in the early 1970s, the parties began to polarize sharply and consistently on the matter. The Republican Party removed support for the ERA from its platform in 1980, and by 1992 convention observers indicated that party positions on women's rights were among the starkest points of contrast between the Democrats and Republicans.

Other accounts focus on the changes women have experienced over the past fifty years. One possible explanation rests in labor market changes, specifically the movement of women into more professional and managerial jobs.[21] An alternative focuses on the increasing numbers of single women, who may be particularly engaged with the kinds of social welfare policies promoted by the

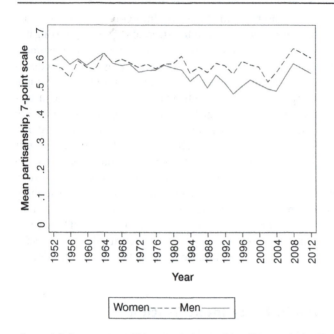

Figure 6.8 Proportion of Men and Women Identifying with the Democratic Party (source: American National Election Study Cumulative File).

Democratic Party due to their economic vulnerability.[22] Rising divorce rates, meanwhile, have also been offered as a reason for women becoming more liberal.[23]

This focus on changes in women's lives as a potential source of the gap is complicated by this fact: men have moved more quickly and farther into the Republican camp, while women have moved into the Democratic Party to a lesser extent.[24] As Miller put it in 1991: "The Republicans have not had a new problem with women: the Democrats have had a continuing problem among men."[25] Stoker and Jennings offer an intriguing clue here: when they analyze their parent–child socialization data, data that—conveniently—start with high school graduates in 1965 and continue with re-interviews until recently, Stoker and Jennings find that one group of women, in particular, resisted the move to the Republican Party over this period: unmarried white women.[26] These analyses point to the power of influence in marriage as a key factor in the difference between married and unmarried white women, as married white women have tended to follow their husbands into the Republican Party.

The Gender Gap over Policy

We turn now to the gender gap over policy. As the over-time graphs plotting men and women's average attitudes toward a range of policies presented below demonstrate, there are systematic differences in public opinion on policy questions between men and women. These are not always, however, the kinds of distinctions we would expect based on intuition alone. Women and men tend to have very *similar* attitudes on so-called "women's issues," like abortion, but differ notably on other policies, especially the use of military and police force or social welfare.[27]

Indeed, as Figure 6.9 shows, men and women have been largely indistinguishable from one another in their average levels of support for abortion. When we consider, in Figure 6.10, preferences on whether the U.S. should go to war measured across time, however, we see an obvious gap in opinion. From 1952 to the present, men have been markedly more supportive of going to war than women, though the gap has narrowed and overall support has decreased.

Figure 6.11, meanwhile, shows the generally persistent gap between men and women when it comes to federal spending on welfare. For the most part, women, on average, are noticeably more supportive of increasing federal spending on welfare than are men. Some have connected this "compassion gap" to views on racial issues. Hutchings et al. have gone so far as to suggest that the gap in party identification can be largely explained by differences on racial issues between men and women.[28] Specifically, they argue that the gap emerges because women react differently than men to cues from political candidates regarding how compassionate they are toward vulnerable social groups.

Figure 6.9 Mean Opinion on Support for Abortion Rights (source: American National Election Study Cumulative File).

Figure 6.10 Mean Opinion on Whether U.S. Should Have Gone to War (source: American National Election Study Cumulative File).

Figure 6.11 Mean Opinion on Increasing Federal Spending on Welfare (source: American National Election Study Cumulative File).

The Case of Hillary Clinton

Party identification and policy preferences are, of course, not the only relevant outcomes that may be affected by gender or for which gender ingredients may help structure attitudes. We turn here to one other outcome and ask whether gender and gender ingredients matter for how men and women view Hillary Clinton over time, focusing explicitly on the place of gender solidarity.

Clinton's place in public life and the extent to which she has drawn gender themes into her own rhetoric has evolved over time. In 1992, for example, she famously told an interviewer: "I suppose I could have stayed home and baked cookies and had teas, but what I decided to do was to fulfill my profession which I entered before my husband was in public life."[29] By the time Clinton was conceding the 2008 Democratic presidential primary to Barack Obama sixteen years later, however, her rhetoric was not couched in terms of traditional domestic roles. Rather, it was in the language of women's success in traditionally male-dominated endeavors, as she claimed, "we will someday launch a woman into the White House. Although we weren't able to shatter that highest, hardest glass ceiling this time . . . it's got about 18 million cracks in it."[30]

We ask whether women have evaluated Hillary Clinton on the basis of gender solidarity as a way to explore whether context matters in how women use our gender ingredients to think about politics.[31] Has this varied at different points in time? Has the context—the ways in which Clinton has or has not relied on a rhetoric incorporating gender—affected how women draw on their feelings of gender solidarity to evaluate Clinton? Clinton's place in American public life has clearly evolved over time; has the way women think about her followed suit? Clinton's prolonged prominence on the national scene makes her a ripe candidate for this kind of analysis, illustrated in Figure 6.12. Again, larger values of the dependent variable—feelings towards Clinton—are more favorable. We also control for the same additional factors that may influence attitudes towards Clinton as in the analyses above.

Rather than depicting the effect of gender solidarity on feelings towards Clinton, Figure 6.12 displays the *predicted ratings* of Clinton on the y-axis, holding all other variables in the analysis at their means. Put differently, each line demonstrates the rating of Clinton that we would expect for a woman who is average on all of our control variables (income, education, partisanship, etc.) at each different level of gender solidarity. We estimate these effects at three different points in time. The first, 1992 (from the 1992 ANES), was just as Clinton was emerging on the national scene as the wife of a presidential candidate and just before she played an unprecedented role in developing policy during the 1993–1994 health care reform debate.[32] The second, 2000 (from the Detroit–Atlanta Study), was during her campaign for U.S. Senate from New York. And the third, from the January 2008 wave of the Cooperative Campaign Analysis Project (CCAP), was during the heart of her campaign for the Democratic presidential nomination.

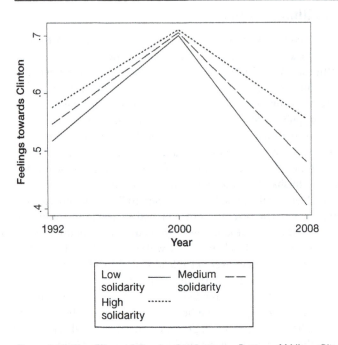

Figure 6.12 The Effect of Gender Solidarity on Rating of Hillary Clinton
(source: American National Election Study, 1992; Detroit-Atlanta Study,
2000; Cooperative Campaign Analysis Project, 2008).

What we see here is that women's identification with other women affected
their ratings of Clinton sometimes—when she was front and center on the
national stage, challenging long-held beliefs about the role of women in public
life—and not at others. In 2000, by contrast, women with high gender solidarity
evaluated Clinton in exactly the same way as did women with low gender
solidarity. In other words, in 2000, gender solidarity didn't matter much. By
contrast, in 1992 and 2008, it did matter to women's evaluations of Hillary
Clinton. The contrast between the effect in 1992, where women reporting high
solidarity rate Clinton about 6 percentage points more favorably than their low-
solidarity peers, and 2008, where the difference is nearly 16 percentage points,
is also telling. Defying expectations of how a presidential candidate's wife should
behave creates one kind of context for activating gender solidarity, but actually
running for the highest office in the land elevates gendered thinking to an
entirely different level. In 2000, by contrast, Clinton's Senate bid did not seem
to have had the same potential to upset the gender status quo.

Conclusion

When writing in 1985, Gurin asked,

> Do more women now recognize that they are objectively deprived economically and politically? Do more women believe that women are treated categorically? Have women become more aggrieved about their relative influence in the public arena? Have more begun to question the legitimacy of gender disparities, such as their continuing wage gap?[33]

She speculates that there is little reason to suspect change between the 1970s and the time of her writing, but since then the social and political landscape has changed dramatically. Women have surpassed men in college graduation rates, an even greater percentage of women have entered the labor market, and a number of women have emerged in high-profile political positions.

Our analysis provides some mixed answers to Gurin's provocative questions. Women do tend to hold more progressive views on women's place in the workplace relative to the home than men, and most women express at least a moderate amount of solidarity with other women; these findings suggest that perhaps women do recognize that their economic status is different than men's and view themselves as a unified, solidary group. At the same time, women's responses to the items on the modern sexism scale track those of their male peers very closely, and most individuals of *both* genders register moderate-to-high values on the scale. Even if women feel a sense of group identification with other women, then, they still believe that other women cause more-problems than they solve when they draw attention in the workplace to the kinds of issues Gurin highlights. The policy analyses provide similar mixed results. Clearly gender attitudes help structure women's policy preferences, with progressive gender attitudes corresponding to more liberal policy preferences. Women do not, however, express systematically different policy preferences from men on "gender issues," like abortion, suggesting that any recognition of gender disparities has not permeated all policy attitudes.

Our analysis of attitudes towards Clinton, finally, provides interesting insight into Gurin's claims about women in the public arena. Women on the whole, it seems, felt most positively about Clinton when she was doing the least to challenge traditional gender roles—when she was running for the U.S. Senate, a body that, in 2000, already contained nine women. When Clinton was openly questioning the lifestyle choices of other women, as she did during her husband's campaign in 1992, or working to break that "highest, hardest glass ceiling," as she was in 2008, women felt less positively towards her. This overall pattern suggests that perhaps Gurin was right; women have not become aggrieved about their place in the public arena. Indeed, they appear to support women, like Clinton, when they are doing less to break new ground. At the same time, however, the clear effect of gender solidarity on attitudes towards Clinton hints that things may also have changed some since the time of Gurin's writing.

To the extent that some women may begin to recognize their lack of influence in the public arena before others, we would expect those "first movers" to be women who feel closely connected to other women—exactly the group who, in each period, holds the most favorable attitudes towards Clinton.

Our portrait, then, of the place of gender in public opinion rests heavily on the sociological organization of gender, an organization that features hierarchy with intimacy, an organization that centers on the ways in which women's and men's lives are entwined. This sociological organization has, as we outlined, shaped the basic ingredients Americans have to think about gender. Gender is a sticky distinction, easily essentialized and not likely to go away as long as there are families and children.[34]

Notes

1. Charles Tilly, *Durable Inequality* (Berkeley, CA: University of California Press, 1998).
2. Maria Charles and David B. Grusky, *Occupational Ghettos: The Worldwide Segregation of Women and Men* (Palo Alto, CA: Stanford University Press, 2005); Barbara F. Reskin and Patricia A. Roos, *Job Queues, Gender Queues: Explaining Women's Inroads into Male Occupations* (Philadelphia, PA: Temple University Press, 1990).
3. Francine D. Blau, Mary C. Brinton, and David B. Grusky, *The Declining Significance of Gender?* (New York: Russell Sage Foundation, 2006); Claudia Goldin, "The Quiet Revolution That Transformed Women's Employment, Education, and Family" (National Bureau of Economic Research, Working Paper No. 11953, 2006); Ariane Hegewisch, Hannah Liepmann, Jeffrey Hayes, and Heidi Hartmann, "Separate and Not Equal? Gender Segregation in the Labor Market and the Gender Wage Gap" (Institute for Women's Policy Research, Briefing Paper #C377, 2010).
4. Nancy Burns, Kay Lehman Schlozman, and Sidney Verba, *The Private Roots of Public Action* (Cambridge, MA: Harvard University Press, 2001).
5. Erving Goffman, "The Arrangement between the Sexes," *Theory and Society* 4, no. 3 (1977); Mary R. Jackman, *The Velvet Glove: Paternalism and Conflict in Gender, Class, and Race Relations* (Berkeley, CA: University of California Press, 1994); Nicholas J.G. Winter, *Dangerous Frames: How Ideas about Race and Gender Shape Public Opinion* (Chicago: University of Chicago Press, 2008).
6. Patricia Gurin, "Women's Gender Consciousness," *Public Opinion Quarterly* 49, no. 2 (1985).
7. Susan A. Gelman, Marianne G. Taylor, Simone P. Nguyen, Campbell Leaper, and Rebecca S. Bigler, "Mother-Child Gender: Understanding the Acquisition of Essentialist Beliefs," *Monographs of the Society for Research in Child Development* 69, no. 1 (2004); Lawrence A. Hirschfeld, "Do Children Have a Theory of Race?" *Cognition* 54, no. 2 (1995): 209–252; Marianne G. Taylor, "The Development of Children's Beliefs about Social and Biological Aspects of Gender Differences," *Child Development* 67 (1996).
8. Douglas L. Medin and Andrew Ortony,"Psychological Essentialism," in *Similarity and Analogical Reasoning*, eds. S. Vosniadou and Andrew Ortony (New York: Cambridge University Press, 1989).

9. Goffman, "The Arrangement between the Sexes," p. 308.
10. Janet T. Spencer and Robert Helmreich, "The Attitudes toward Women Scale: An Objective Instrument to Measure Attitudes toward the Rights and Roles of Women in Contemporary Society," *JSAS Catalog of Selected Documents in Psychology* 2, no. 66 (1972).
11. Arland Thornton, Duane F. Alwin, and Donald Camburn, "Causes and Consequences of Sex-Role Attitudes and Attitude Change," *American Sociological Review* 48, no. 2 (1983): 211–227.
12. Katherine G. Robbins, "The Foundations of Political Ambition at the Intersection of Race and Gender" (Ph.D. Dissertation, University of Michigan. 2014); Nancy Burns and Donald R. Kinder, *Categorical Politics: Gender, Race, and the Pursuit of Equality in America* (forthcoming).
13. Janet K. Swim, Kathryn J. Aikin, Wayne S. Hall, and Barbara A. Hunter, "Sexism and Racism: Old-fashioned and Modern Prejudices," *Journal of Personality and Social Psychology* 68, no. 2 (1995). The Modern Sexism scale was developed in parallel to what scholars were describing as a similar shift in racial attitudes from the overt to the more subtle and covert attitudes that developed in the post Civil Rights era. For a theoretical account of this shift, see Donald R. Kinder and Lynn M. Sanders, *Divided by Color* (Chicago: University of Chicago Press, 1996).
14. Janet K. Swim and Laurie L. Cohen, "Overt, Covert, and Subtle Sexism," *Psychology of Women Quarterly* 21, no. 1 (1997).
15. Donald T. Campbell, "Common Fate, Similarity, and Other Indices of the Status of Aggregates of Persons as Social Entities," *Behavioral Science* 3, no. 1 (1958); Patricia Gurin and Aloen Townsend, "Properties of Gender Identity and Their Implications for Gender Consciousness," *British Journal of Social Psychology* 25, no. 2 (1986); Andrew H. Miller, Patricia Gurin, Gerald Gurin, and Oksana Malanchuk, "Group Consciousness and Political Participation," *American Journal of Political Science* 25, no. 3 (1981).
16. Pamela J. Conover and Virginia Sapiro, "Gender Consciousness and Gender Politics in the 1991 Pilot Study: A Report to the ANES Board of Overseers," ANES Pilot Study Report No. nes008197, 1992.
17. Patricia Gurin, "Women's Gender Consciousness," *Public Opinion Quarterly* 49, no. 2 (1985).
18. The specific questions are as follows:

    Abortion: "There has been some discussion about abortion during recent years. Which one of the opinions on this page best agrees with your view on this issue?"

    1. By law, abortion should never be permitted
    2. The law should permit abortion only in case of rape, incest or when the woman's life is in danger
    3. The law should permit abortion for reasons other than rape, incest, or danger to the woman's life, but only after the need for the abortion has been clearly established
    4. By law, a woman should always be able to obtain an abortion as a matter of personal choice

    Iraq: "Do you think it was a mistake to invade Iraq?"

    1. Yes
    2. No
    3. Not sure

Job Discrimination: "Do you favor or oppose laws to protect women against job discrimination?"

1.   Favor
0.   Oppose

"Is that strongly or not so strongly?"

2   Strongly
1   Not so strongly

19. In this context, "the average woman" means a female survey respondent who has the mean values in the survey sample for all the other variables included in the model, such as education and income.
20. Christina Wolbrecht, *The Politics of Women's Rights: Parties, Positions, and Change* (Princeton, NJ: Princeton University Press, 2000).
21. Jeff Maza and Clem Brooks, "The Gender Gap in US Presidential Elections: When? Why? Implications?" *American Journal of Sociology* 103, no. 5 (1998); Janet M. Box-Steffensmeier, Suzanna De Boef, and Tse-Min Lin, "The Dynamics of the Partisan Gender Gap," *American Political Science Review* 98, no. 3 (2004).
22. Box-Steffensmeier, De Boef, and Lin, "The Dynamics of the Partisan Gender Gap."
23. Lena Edlund and Rohini Pande, "Why Have Women Become Left-Wing? The Political Gender Gap and the Decline in Marriage," *Quarterly Journal of Economics* (2002): 917–961.
24. Alan I. Abramowitz and Kyle L. Saunders, "Ideological Realignment in the US Electorate," *The Journal of Politics* 60, no. 3 (1998); Warren E. Miller, "Party Identification, Realignment, and Party Voting: Back to the Basics," *The American Political Science Review* 85, no. 2 (1991); Warren E. Miller and J. Merrill Shanks, *The New American Voter* (Cambridge, MA: Harvard University Press, 1996); Vincent L. Hutchings, Nicholas A. Valentino, Tasha S. Philpot, and Ismail K. White, "The Compassion Strategy: Race and the Gender Gap in Campaign 2000," *Public Opinion Quarterly* 68, no. 4 (2004); Karen M. Kaufmann and John R. Petrocik, "The Changing Politics of American Men: Understanding the Sources of the Gender Gap," *American Journal of Political Science* 43, no. 3 (1999); Donald Wirls, "Reinterpreting the Gender Gap," *Public Opinion Quarterly* 50 (1986).
25. Miller, "Party Identification, Realignment, and Party Voting: Back to the Basics," p. 543.
26. Laura Stoker and M. Kent Jennings, "Political Similarity and Influence between Husbands and Wives," in *The Logic of Politics: Personal Networks as Contexts for Political Behavior*, ed. Alan S. Zuckerman. (Philadelphia, PA: Temple University Press, 2005).
27. Conover and Sapiro, "Gender, Feminist Consciousness, and War."
28. Hutchings, Valentino, Philpot, and White, "The Compassion Strategy: Race and the Gender Gap in Campaign 2000."
29. See "Making Hillary Clinton an Issue," *Nightline Transcripts* 26 March 1992, available at http://www.pbs.org/wgbh/pages/frontline/shows/clinton/etc/03261992.html
30. See "Transcript: Hillary Clinton Endorses Barack Obama," *New York Times* 7 June 2008, available at http://www.nytimes.com/2008/06/07/us/politics/07text-clinton.html?pagewanted=all
31. Ideally, we would evaluate whether women have evaluated Clinton based on their attitudes toward women's place and modern sexism. Unfortunately, we lack

comparable measures of those two ingredients at multiple points in time during Clinton's time in public life.

32. Nicholas J.G. Winter, "Framing Gender: Political Rhetoric, Gender Schemas, and Public Opinion on U.S. Health Care Reform," *Gender and Politics* 1, no. 3 (2005).

33. Gurin, "Women's Gender Consciousness," p. 144.

34. Future research will examine in more detail differences among women and men. While the picture we paint here holds for many groups of women and men, there are some differences to note, differences that have not been fully treated in the literature. For example, African-American women identify with other women at notably higher levels than do white women. And working class women have somewhat more conservative views about women's place than do women with more resources.

Chapter 7

Partisanship and Polarization in Contemporary Politics

Marc Hetherington

In 1950, believing that American political parties had become so ineffectual as to render them all but meaningless, a group of political scientists penned a document entitled "Toward a More Responsible Two Party System." They argued that policymakers needed to take steps to strengthen American parties, so they could do what parties do well, namely play a central role in structuring political conflict in government and, in turn, provide ordinary Americans with meaningful choices. American parties only grew weaker in the succeeding decades. Newspaper columnist David Broder even suggested in the early 1970s that American parties had died.[1]

Compare that situation with today. According to data collected by Keith Poole and Howard Rosenthal every Democrat in the U.S. House of Representatives is more liberal than every Republican, a stark departure from the past when liberal northeastern Republicans and conservative southern Democrats roamed the Capitol. And, those divisions in Washington are starting to spill over more into the electorate with voters supporting their party's representatives much more loyally than in the past. Sometimes the partisan heat seems to be boiling over. In the 2010 midterm election campaign, for example, fisticuffs broke out, once in the state of Washington and once in Kentucky, between Republican and Democratic candidate supporters. So much for the idea that ordinary Americans do not care much about party politics. More and more of them care a lot. Concerns about hyper-partisanship have replaced those decades of old concerns about weak parties. Perhaps political scientists should be careful what they wish for.

Increased party strength is evident at all levels of American politics. The national party organizations are in better financial shape than ever. The parties in Congress pursue ideologically distinct policy agendas, making it easier for the electorate to distinguish between them. And, as a consequence of this resurgence of parties among political elites, ordinary Americans now behave in a more partisan manner than they have for decades. In fact, in all three presidential elections running from 2004–2012, partisans were more faithful to their party's candidates than in any previous election in the history of polling.

In this chapter, I make sense of these profound changes in the American political universe, with a focus on the role that parties play for ordinary people. I start by explaining what scholars mean by party identification. In providing this conceptual sketch, I trace the development of the concept as well as detail the arguments that critics have leveled against its central importance. I then turn to an explanation of why partisanship is so important to understand. Finally, I trace the historical arc that has led us from party decline to party polarization, with a particular emphasis on the contemporary scholarly debate on party polarization.

What is Partisanship and Where Does it Come From?

The scholars who pioneered the concept of party identification hailed from the University of Michigan. The Michigan scholars thought of party identification in social psychological terms, defining it as an intense psychological attachment to a political group.[2] As evidence of its centrality to people's political lives, the authors of *The American Voter* asked the same people about their party identification at two year intervals, finding that very few people went from thinking about themselves as Democrats one year and Republicans two years later, or vice versa. Of all the political attitudes they studied, it was by far the most stable.

Most research suggests that people develop their party identification early in life, with parents playing an influential role in their children's identifications. If a child grows up in a household where Republicans are held in high esteem and Democrats are not, the child will typically grow up to be a Republican and vice versa. In that sense, people are born into a party, much as they are born into a religion. Like rooting for a sports team, this association tends to grow stronger through the life cycle. Once someone has decided that he roots for the Red Sox and not the Yankees, he does not easily change sides and, in fact, usually becomes a more ardent fan. Similarly, once someone decides that he is a Republican, he usually remains a Republican, and his identification tends to grow stronger over time.

Although parental party identification is important in understanding a person's party identification, it is not the only factor.[3] In fact, a fair number of people grow up in families where parents' party identification is not clear because politics is simply not an important part of family life. Other cues can be helpful for people in developing bonds with a political party. Over the last several decades, people have connected the two major parties with a remarkably consistent set of social groups. Americans tend to connect the Republicans with business interests and those higher in socioeconomic status, and Democrats with labor unions and the working class.[4] More recently, other group attachments have developed as well. For example, people increasingly connect the Republicans with social conservatism and especially evangelical religious groups and the Democrats with racial and ethnic diversity and irreligiousness.

These connections are important because people tend to identify themselves as belonging to different social groups as well. People can, in turn, use the groups they identify with to deduce which party makes most sense for them to identify with. The connections developed from being part of such groups can also allow people to acquire significant information about politics, which most often serves to reinforce group identifications with parties. For example, when a labor union member goes to a union meeting, leaders tell members who their political friends and enemies are. When union members socialize with other members of the group, shared views are likely to be reinforced rather than challenged. Similarly, when someone regularly attends an Evangelical Christian church, it brings that person together with people who are sympathetic to the Republican party and the policies it supports. Because church is a source for social opportunities outside church, those who are, for example, opposed to abortion rights will, on average, find themselves sharing a meal or an evening with others who share their opinions. Put another way, informal encounters with people connected with the church will often have a reinforcing effect on political opinions.

Although stable influences like parental partisanship and social group identification are clearly important, there have been too many shifts in party identification over the last forty years to think that they are the only important forces. Scholars have shown that early political experiences affect party identification as well. Figure 7.1 helps make the point.

In the 1950s, when academic political surveys first became available, Democrats outnumbered Republicans by about 20 percentage points. This was in large measure because of the Great Depression of the 1930s. People who grew up in its shadow, which was blamed on Republican president Herbert Hoover and the Republican majorities in Congress that presided over the collapse, tended to be less Republican than the population as a whole. Since Franklin Roosevelt and a series of Democratic Congresses were credited with lifting the

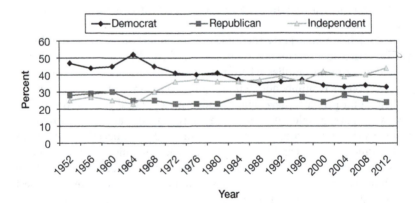

Figure 7.1 The Distribution of Party Identification in the Electorate, 1952–2012.

country out of the Depression, the Democrats developed a huge identification advantage that was still obvious in 1952.

Note, however, that the Democrats' identification advantage narrowed dramatically in the 1980s. In fact, if one examines only voters, the difference in party identification then was even narrower than what appears in the figure. The reason for the change is that those who came of age politically during what many perceived as Democratic president Jimmy Carter's failures in the late 1970s identified with the Democrats much less than the population as a whole. Instead this cohort was more likely to adopt the Republican label, due in large part to Republican Ronald Reagan's economic and foreign policy successes in the eight years after the Carter presidency. In that sense, to predict people's party identification, it is helpful to know when they were young.

That young people in the 1980s identified more as Republicans may seem strange given that young people today tend to identify more as Democrats. The story today fits the popular belief that young people are always liberals and Democrats and older people always conservatives and Republicans. In fact, young people do not always identify disproportionately with the more liberal party. Rather, young people today are more likely to be Democrats than Republicans because of the Great Recession that took hold late in George W. Bush's presidency combined with an unpopular war in Iraq, which was especially unpopular among young people, that Republicans initiated.

In fact, some scholars have argued that people's party identification is nowhere near as stable as the Michigan scholars originally argued in *The American Voter*. For example, Morris Fiorina argued that party identification was not an intense psychological attachment but rather a running tally of recent political outcomes.[5] If people perceived that the economy was getting better under a Republican president, then they shifted their party identification toward the Republicans. If they perceived the economy was getting worse under a Republican president, they shifted their party identification in a Democratic direction. In a similar vein, Charles Franklin and John Jackson argued that people's vote choices affected their party identification, in addition to party identification affecting their vote choices.[6] So, someone who might have identified himself as an independent going into an election might start to identify himself as a Republican if he really liked the Republican presidential candidate. Surely most young people today know people who did not seem particularly interested in politics before 2008 but came to identify as Democrats because of their positive feelings about Barack Obama.

The parental and group influence models make partisanship seem almost like a mindless decision guided by forces beyond people's control. Other research suggests a more rational basis for choosing a party. One stream of this research emphasizes issues. It suggests that people might be inclined to follow their parents and group identifications initially, but other things can override their importance. For example, someone who grew up in a Republican household but developed an intense pro-choice position on abortion may shift to the

Democratic Party or become an independent because they realize the party of their parents does not suit their preferences on an issue that is important to them. Similarly a person who grew up in a Democratic household might come to realize that his values are driven more by liberty (which Republicans tend to emphasize) than equality (which Democrats tend to emphasize). It would be rational, then, for this person to change his party identification. Such issue-based party updating is most likely to take place from a person's 20s through early 30s.

A person's personal circumstances could also change. For example, an irreligious Democrat might come to identify with a conservative church later in her life. This new religious identification might cause a turn in a Republican direction. Or, a person who grew up in a lower social class might move up the economic ladder at some point. This might encourage the person to move away from the Democratic party, the traditional champion of the working class, to the Republican party. A movement such as this is particularly likely to occur in the South today.[7]

It is also possible for the social group identifications of the parties to change, which would lead people to change their party identification from what their parents and the groups they grew up with encouraged. Since the states of the former Confederacy regularly vote for Republicans for president and Congress today, it is easy to forget that the Republican party—the party of Lincoln—barely existed in the region until the 1960s. Those who identified strongly as "southerners" seventy-five years ago would have connected themselves to the Democratic party because there was no group at the time more loyal to the Democratic party. Today, those who strongly identify as "southerners" would be apt to connect themselves to the Republican party, as that party has evolved to dominate the states of the former Confederacy. As a result, young southern whites are much more likely than their parents to identify with the Republican party.[8]

Although party is not immutable and these critiques have been very thoughtful over the years, the fact remains that party identification is stable for most people. Moreover, it appears that it has become even more stable recently. In analyzing data collected in the 1950s and 1970s, Morris Fiorina showed that about 15 percent of Americans either 1) changed their identification from one party to the other, 2) changed to being an independent, or 3) changed from being an independent over the course of only two short years. This was evidence he used to argue against the Michigan Model. His results were based on panel data, which is data from the same individuals collected at several different points in time. The American National Election Study's most recent panel survey occurred from 2000–2004. In it, changes in party identification were much less common than in Fiorina's day. In fact, only about 10 percent of Americans moved between party categories between 2002 and 2004, far fewer than what Fiorina found in the 1970s. And only 5 percent of panel respondents switched from identifying with one party in 2002 to the other in 2004. This suggests that party identification might be an even more important concept to understand now than it was when the authors of *The American Voter* identified it fifty years ago.

What Party Affects

For most people, party identification provides the most useful shortcut, or heuristic, for understanding a complicated political world. People have neither the time nor the desire to learn everything they should know about politics; party identification helps them navigate a complicated and often confusing political world with less than perfect information about all its nuances. The best way to evaluate the importance of party identification is to consider the way the authors of *The American Voter* thought of it, as a "perceptual screen." All incoming information about politics that people receive passes through the screen. As a result, Democrats will tend to take away certain bits of information from a given news report, conversation, or political advertisement while Republicans might take away different bits of information from the same piece of news.

John Zaller makes the most complete statement about the importance of party identification in processing political information.[9] He advances his RAS model, which stands for Receive, Accept, and Sample. People first *Receive* information, whether from the news media, a friend, or some personal experience. Some people, of course, take in more information than others because they care more about politics. The key point is that no one bothers to evaluate all information about anything because there is simply too much of it, so shortcuts are necessary.

Next, people decide whether to *Accept* the information that they just received. This is where a person's party identification plays the most critical role. When information runs counter to their partisan predispositions, people are more likely to reject it than accept it. For example, a Democrat who hears that Barack Obama is really a Muslim is much more likely than a Republican to reject such information than accept it. Similarly, when information is presented by a person from the party opposite the person receiving it, that person will be more likely to reject the information than if it came from someone with a shared party affiliation. In short, Democrats will be more likely than Republicans to reject information heard on Fox News and Republicans will be more likely than Democrats to reject information heard on MSNBC. In the end, the fact that people use their partisanship as perceptual filters means that the information they have in their memories will be biased by their party affiliation.

What information people accept and reject has important implications for the last stage in Zaller's model. When ordinary people are asked about their opinions in a survey, they *Sample* from all the pieces of information that have remained in their memories about a particular subject. This is important because their partisanship has caused them to reject information that ran counter to their partisanship and to accept information that was consistent with it. As a result, Democrats will, when asked about politics, tend to express pro-Democratic positions on the issues and Republicans will tend to express pro-Republican positions. This is even true of issues in which people really have no idea where they stand.

It is worth exploring just how powerful this partisan filter can be, especially in the present day where partisanship seems to play an increasingly outsized role. In his treatment of the polarizing presidency of George W. Bush, Gary Jacobson shows that Republicans and Democrats developed much different beliefs about factual information. For example, even though Saddam Hussein was not involved in the September 11 terrorist attacks, 44 percent of Republicans thought he was as late as October 2005. This is likely because Bush administration officials found that support for invading Iraq, a policy they pursued, increased when they connected Hussein and 9/11 indirectly. Importantly, partisanship profoundly affected whether or not people believed the Hussein connection, with only 25 percent of Democrats expressing belief.[10] It is not just Republicans who are prone to misperceiving the political world. Larry Bartels showed that Democrats were much more likely to think that inflation and unemployment had gotten worse when Republican Ronald Reagan was president even though both had gotten much better under Reagan.[11] Republicans, on the other hand, tended to get these questions right. One set of partisans filtered out the correct information because it ran counter to their view of Reagan while the other set of partisans embraced it.

Although sometimes Democrats and Republicans disagree about objective facts, it is even more common for them to adopt differing interpretations of facts they agree on. Consider the absence of weapons of mass destruction found in Iraq after the U.S. invasion. Initially, surveys showed that Republicans were more likely than Democrats to say that such weapons had, in fact, been found.[12] Later, however, Republicans became as likely as Democrats to allow that they had not been found. That is not to say Democrats and Republicans understood the situation the same way at that point. Instead, Brian Gaines and a group of his colleagues found that partisans interpreted the facts differently depending on their party identification.[13] Democrats concluded the weapons never existed. Republicans, on the other hand, interpreted their absence to mean that they had been moved out of Iraq before the U.S.-led invasion.

Not surprisingly, partisanship has an enormous impact on how well people think specific politicians are doing their jobs. In fact, since the scientific use of public opinion polling got its start in the 1930s, Republicans and Democrats in the electorate had never perceived a president's job performance more differently than they did George W. Bush's. According to a poll by *USA Today*–Gallup taken as Bush left office in January 2009, 78 percent of Republicans approved of his job performance compared with only 6 percent of Democrats, a 72 percentage point difference. The only leader who has generated a split as large as Bush is, perhaps not surprisingly, Barack Obama. In polls from Gallup leading up to the 2014 midterm elections, it was common to find nearly

80 percent of Democrats registering approval while fewer than 10 percent of Republicans did. These numbers are the mirror image of those for Bush in the last years of his presidency.

In addition to acting as a perceptual screen, party can help people make sense of the complicated nuances of politics. Since many know little about the political world, they can use their attachment to a party to decide where they stand on issues or how they should identify themselves ideologically. A surprisingly large percentage of Americans do not understand the words "liberal" and "conservative." In fact when asked to place themselves on a scale anchored at one end by "extremely liberal" and at the other by "extremely conservative," with moderate or middle of the road halfway between the poles, fully 20 percent of people fail to even place themselves. It is likely that a large chunk of those who do place themselves on ideology scales have a very incomplete understanding of the terms. Yet Americans are pretty good at knowing what goes with what. Based on data from the 2008 National Election Study, for example, only 3 percent of Republicans classified themselves as liberal, while fully 74 percent identified themselves as conservative (the other 23 percent either identified themselves as moderates or said they did not know).

Party also predicts a range of issue preferences. Democrats are much more likely than Republicans to take the liberal position on the degree to which government ought to provide aid to minority groups, provide Americans with a guaranteed job and standard of living, take a more active role in the health insurance system, be pro-choice on abortion and in favor of more rights for gays and lesbians. Indeed, Alan Abramowitz and Kyle Saunders show that over the last three decades party identifiers have become much better at matching their parties with their issue preferences.[14] The reason is that the Democrats and Republicans who represent us rarely profess a policy preference that runs counter to that of their party. Whereas many conservative Democrats and liberal Republicans once served in Congress, almost none exist today. As a result, partisans in the public are much less likely to depart from the party orthodoxy than they were 30 or 40 years ago.

It is important to note, too, that people are much more likely to use their party identification to inform their issue preferences rather than the other way around.[15] That is, most people do not decide first that they are pro-life on abortion, favor lower taxes on the wealthy, and want fewer government programs for the poor and, as a result, choose to be Republicans. Rather, most identify with a party first and then choose their issue preferences accordingly. Sometimes issues cause people to update their party identification. But, for that to happen, it requires that people care a lot about the issue, and know where the parties stand on it to bring about such a change in party.[16] This is passion and information that a lot of Americans simply do not have.

In sum, party identification affects an impressive array of things. When there is a Republican president, Democratic partisans always view the economy as worse than their Republican counterparts do, and vice versa. In evaluating the personal characteristics of political candidates, Republican partisans always rate the competence, character, and attractiveness of Republican candidates more favorably than do Democrats, and vice versa. Moreover, attitudes that were once somewhat immune to party differences, such as support for foreign wars and immigration now show massive differences by party, indicating that partisanship in the electorate is stronger than in decades past.[17] In short, party identification structures the political world of partisans more thoroughly than any other attitude or set of attitudes.

The choice that scholars have most often focused on in assessing the central importance of party identification is the voting decision. This was the end point in *The American Voter*'s famous "funnel of causality," for which party identification acted as the perceptual filter at the beginning of the process. Party identification profoundly affects the choices people make. For instance, in the 2012 presidential election, exit polls revealed that over 92 percent of self-identified Democrats voted for Barack Obama and 93 percent of Republicans voted for Mitt Romney. Although the effect of party identification is somewhat weaker in structuring vote choice for other federal and state level offices, it is still very strong and growing increasingly so at least as it relates to congressional voting.[18]

Are Ordinary Americans Polarized?

While scholars expressed concern about party weakness in the 1950s, they are now concerned that parties are too polarized. By polarization, people mean that Democrats and Republicans are so far apart on the issues and their outlook on the world that they cannot agree on much of anything or find compromises when compromises are necessary and possible. In that sense, polarization has a negative connotation, suggesting that parties have exactly the opposite problem from before. Some fear that they have such a strong influence on both office-holders and voters that it is as though they are wearing blinders and are thus incapable of perceiving relevant conditions and political arguments on the basis of reality.

Little doubt remains that political elites—partisans who serve in government and in party organizations—are polarized today. A host of scholars over the last several decades have identified marked increases in party line voting in both the House and Senate.[19] Figure 7.2 depicts the ideology of members who served in the 112th Congress (2011–2012) using a measure developed by Keith Poole and Howard Rosenthal called DW-NOMINATE scores. It uses the voting records of members of Congress to tap their ideology. Note that only a small handful of members grade out as moderates and the major parties have no members who would be better ideological fits in the other party. Data like these are often used to argue that Congress is polarized by party, although there is some question whether the polarization is really ideological.[20]

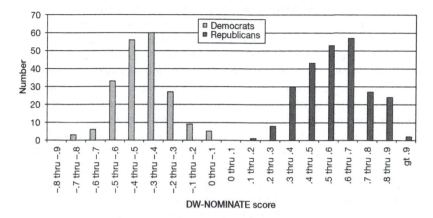

Figure 7.2 Ideology of Members of House of Representatives, 112th Congress, DW-NOMINATE Scores.

It remains unresolved whether ordinary people are polarized in their political outlooks. Whereas politics is a life and death struggle for party activists and representatives, it is simply not that important to most ordinary Americans. Can people be polarized about something that they have only a passing interest in?

Those who argue that the electorate is polarized usually point to recent election results as evidence. As I noted above, it is quite remarkable how loyal people are to their party's presidential candidate. In fact, partisans are now more loyal to both their party's presidential and congressional candidates than at any time for which we have survey data.[21] Moreover, the Electoral College map has been very resistant to change lately. Concerns about polarization picked up steam after the 2004 election when 47 of the 50 states voted the same way that they did in the 2000 election, with only New Mexico, Iowa, and New Hampshire switching sides. In fact, fully 40 states have voted for the same party's presidential candidate in every election between 2000 and 2012. This is true despite the fact that there have been Republican incumbents, Democratic incumbents, no incumbents, white candidates, black candidates, male candidates, and female (Vice Presidential) candidates. Nothing seems to disrupt the general behavior of most states.

Although true, states do not vote. People do. And Morris Fiorina argues that people aren't polarized. They only appear to be polarized because their choices are so extreme these days. A moderate electorate does not have the opportunity to appear particularly moderate when its members have to choose between liberal and conservative candidates like Barack Obama and Mitt Romney.[22] And even when candidates with a reputation for moderation run, as was the case with John McCain in 2008, they tend to run as more ideologically extreme than perhaps they really are in an effort to secure their party's nomination. Fiorina brings to bear an impressive amount of evidence to suggest that (1) people in Republican red states are not much different in their political thinking from people living in Democratic blue states; (2) Democrats and Republicans are somewhat more divided than they used to be, but the differences are not huge; (3) attitudes toward abortion, supposedly one of the most polarizing issues, have remained fairly constant and are not particularly extreme; and (4) Americans are decreasingly hostile toward homosexuality, which suggests moderation rather than polarization on another hot button social issue.

In that sense, Fiorina argues that the political world is *closely* divided rather than *deeply* divided. The percentage of Republican and Democratic voters tends to be almost equal in most elections, so, to Fiorina, it is little wonder that elections are generally close. But being closely divided does not mean that people are deeply divided on the issues or ideologically. Even on the most contentious issues, like abortion, Fiorina suggests the electorate is centrist, looking for common ground between the polarized choices that the parties provide ordinary people.

Polarization or Sorting?

If one is looking for a picture of the electorate like the one above of Congress, with Republican and Democratic preferences clustering at opposite poles, little evidence of polarization exists. Consider the NES's ideological self-placement question. The survey asks people to place themselves on a seven point scale from extremely liberal to extremely conservative with moderate, middle of the road at the midpoint. About fifty percent of Americans either call themselves moderate or are unable to place themselves on the scale. Figure 7.3 shows

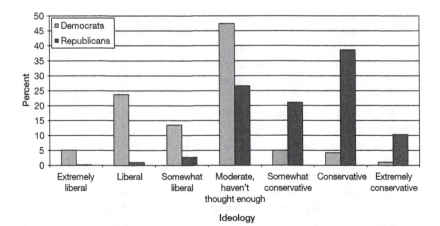

Figure 7.3 Ideological Self Placement by Party Identification, Leaners Not Treated as Partisans 2012.

responses in 2012 broken down by party. The most common response among Democrats is "moderate" or "haven't thought enough about it." In fact, fewer than 45 percent of Democrats label themselves as liberals of any sort. Republicans embrace the conservative label more easily than Democrats do the liberal label. Still, better than a quarter of Republicans consider themselves moderate or say they haven't thought enough about ideological labels to have an opinion.

It would be easy to conclude from these results that the American public is not polarized. Perhaps, though, this definition of polarization is too limited to apply to ordinary people. In surveys, many like the safety of the midpoint because moderation carries a positive connotation and, if people are not sure, the middle is an attractive place to choose. In fact, a relatively small percentage of Americans have the cognitive ability and the political certainty to choose responses toward the poles. Even during the Civil War, surely the most polarized time in the nation's history, many southerners sympathized with the north and many northerners sympathized with the south. Indeed, Dahl notes that less than a year before secession, "abolitionist" was not a word used by ordinary citizens, yet this was a polarized time.[23]

Scholars who argue that there is polarization in the electorate think about what polarization means differently from Fiorina. For them, the most important feature is that the distance between average Republicans and Democrats has increased even if their opinions are not getting more extreme.[24] How can this be? People are "sorting" themselves more "correctly," matching their party and issue preferences more often. They are better able to do this now than before because of the polarization that has occurred among political elites.[25] It is easy to tell where congressional Republicans and Democrats stand, making it easier for ordinary Republicans and Democrats to parrot these positions. This process decreases the heterogeneity within the parties, because there are now fewer conservative Democrats and liberal Republicans. It also increases the average distance between them.[26]

With sorting, differences between partisans in the electorate can increase, even if the public remains relatively moderate as Fiorina argues is the case. For example, opinions about abortion might not have become more extreme, but the average Democrat and Republican could be farther apart if formerly Democratic pro-lifers changed their party affiliation, realizing their old party was not an appropriate home (and vice versa). This is the process by which Democratic partisans have become more homogeneously liberal and Republican partisans more homogeneously conservative, creating a larger average difference between the two groups. Sorting of this type has definitely occurred. For example, the distance between where the average Democrat and Republican would place themselves on the ideology scale described above has nearly tripled between 1972, the first year the ANES asked its 7-point ideology scale question, and 2012.

In addition, Americans are better sorted by party now on things that might cause people to feel like the political system is polarized.[27] If Republicans and Democrats are increasingly far apart on values—and they are—it might be what contributes to the widespread sense that the differences between the parties feel irreconcilable. Since 1986, the American National Election Study has asked several questions to measure what it terms "moral traditionalism." Respondents are asked to agree or disagree with several statements, including "the newer lifestyles are contributing to the breakdown of our society," "the country would have many fewer problems if there were more emphasis on traditional family ties," and "the world is always changing and we should adjust our view of moral behavior to those changes." The items are designed to provide a fundamental understanding of how the world works, whether people are "orthodox" or "relativistic."

Figure 7.4 shows how wide the gap between partisans has grown since the 1980s. In 1986, the first year the items were asked, the average difference was a minuscule 4 percentage points. By the mid-1990s, the difference had increased into the double digits. In 2004, the year Bush faced Kerry in the presidential election, the difference had increased to nearly 20 points, and, in 2012, the difference had reached its maximum.

The figure also shows the parties are further apart on another deeply felt value, namely racial resentment. Developed by Donald Kinder and David Sears and extended by Kinder and Lynn Sanders to tap symbolic racism, the concept has replaced measures of overt racism from years past.[28] The difference between the average Republican and average Democrat in racial resentment was less than 10 percentage points in 1988, and it increased very gradually through the late twentieth century. The difference then surged to about 17 percentage points in

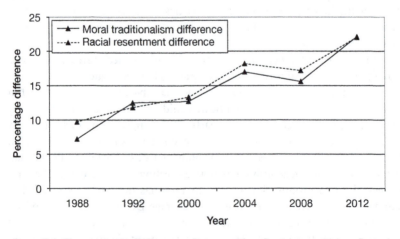

Figure 7.4 Changes in the Differences Between Mass Partisans on Values Batteries, 1988–2012.

2004 and 22 points in 2012. Race is what Edward Carmines and James Stimson term an "easy issue," one that is experienced more in their guts than their brains.[29] Differences in racial attitudes might also cause Americans to feel like the parties are polarized as well.

What Has Caused the Sorting?

The most likely reason that the public has gotten better at matching their party and their issue preferences is because elites are now polarized. The data provide strong evidence. Figure 7.5 tracks the average distance between the parties in Congress in the session before survey data about ordinary Americans was gathered and the average distance between Republicans and Democrats on the NES's ideology question. The correlation over the years 1972–2012 is .92. If I examine only presidential election years, when Americans are paying closer attention, the correlation is even higher.

In addition, some argue that hot button issues like morality and race have become more prominent lately. Although the popular conception is that issues like these are designed to fire up a party's base, D. Sunshine Hillygus and Todd Shields also show that they are used to win over what they call cross-pressured voters.[30] These are people who do not agree with their party on certain issues. This is more likely to happen on hot button issues. Specifically, there is a relatively high proportion of pro-school prayer Democrats, pro-choice Republicans, and anti-gay marriage Democrats. These issues excite the party base, but it is also an effective strategy for attracting a fair number of cross-pressured voters at the same time.

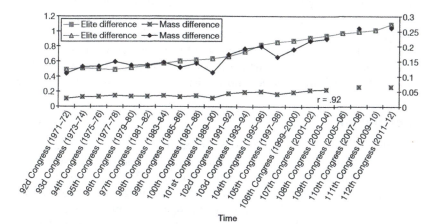

Figure 7.5 Mean Ideological Distance Between Congressional and Mass Partisans, DW-NOMINATE Scores and NES Ideological Self-Placement, 1971–2012.

Changes in the mass media might also provide an engine for party sorting. Thomas Patterson argues the media today are more adversarial and interpretive in their reporting than they were in the 1950s and 1960s.[31] Such changing conventions could encourage people to think more negatively about those in the other party because journalists are more likely to suggest nefarious motives to politicians. In addition, cable news is now full of ideological programming rather than the straight news of decades past. Fox News features its unabashed conservative voices while MSNBC provides their liberal counterparts. The format of these shows, and many other cable news offerings before them, facilitates party sorting in the electorate. Most often they invite guests from the far left of the Democratic party and the far right of the Republican party and let them have at it. Diana Mutz and Byron Reeves argue that such reporting, along with the close up camera angles employed on these shows, violates social norms of civility and proximity, causing people to ignore counter arguments, thereby intensifying their own opinions.[32]

Before blaming cable news as the main villain, however, keep in mind that fewer people watch these shows than might be popularly believed. Markus Prior notes that less than 5 million people tune in for even the highest rated cable news shows whereas popular non-news shows garner an audience of more than 20 million on a weekly basis.[33] It is also important to remember that most cable news viewers are probably pretty well sorted to begin with. Figures like Sean Hannity and Rachel Maddow probably do more to reinforce already strong feelings, rather than creating them.

Talk radio and the Internet blogosphere also probably contribute to the sense that the differences between Democrats and Republicans are irreconcilable. Conservatives who want the conservative spin on the day's events can listen to Rush Limbaugh or peruse the Drudge Report on line, while liberals might log onto Daily Kos, Huffington Post, or Talking Points Memo for their preferred spin. Both types of consumers will hear only their party's side of things, decreasing the number of counter arguments that they might be exposed to. This is in stark contrast to the 1960s and 1970s, when everyone got their TV news from one of three major networks and people read newspapers that adhered to roughly the same news norms that favored objectivity over ideology.

Conclusion

Whether or not the electorate is polarized, it is still the case that party identification is the most important political attitude. Knowing a person's party identification provides more information than any other single source about a person's political behaviors, positions on issues, or feelings about groups. Political commentators often suggest that people start with preferences about political issues, weigh the parties' positions on these issues carefully, and decide whether they are Democrats or Republicans. Decades worth of research suggests the process does not usually work this way because most Americans do not follow politics particularly closely. Instead people usually develop their partisanship first and match it with where office holders and other elites in their parties stand on the issues.[34] In that sense, people use their party identification as a shortcut, or heuristic, to help inform their own opinions. More generally, party identification provides a guide to how people process information, make decisions, and come to conclusions. Indeed making sense of politics for many, perhaps most, people would be all but impossible if not for the identification that they develop with one of the major political parties.

Although scholars still have not resolved the question of polarization in the electorate, perhaps the best way to make sense of the debate is in the following manner. Partisans are not, nor will they likely ever be, polar opposites. There is no doubt that they are more divided about things that people care about deeply. Things like morality, race, and maintaining safety and security are all things about which people have strong feelings. With the parties very deeply divided along these specific lines, the intensity generated by politics is stronger now than before. As evidence, partisans' feelings about the opposite party have grown intensely negative of late.[35] This "affective polarization," or polarization of feelings is clearly intense. Shanto Iyengar and his co-authors show in a 2010 survey that nearly half of Republicans and a third of Democrats would not be particularly happy if their children married someone who identified with the opposite political party.[36]

Certain things are easier to disagree about civilly—such as how high taxes ought to be or how much money we ought to spend on education. Other things are harder, such as when fundamental conceptions of right and wrong enter the fray. We are experiencing more of the latter today than politics typically once offered up. And, given that political parties are structuring this conflict, they are now even more relevant to us than they have been in many decades.

It also might be worth noting that differences between Republicans and Democrats today extend well beyond politics. Consider sports. You will find significantly more Republicans among professional football, college football, and especially NASCAR fans. Democrats like certain sports more than Republicans, particularly soccer and a range of sports played by women.[37] The same is true of television shows. Republicans are significantly more likely than Democrats to prefer reality shows like *Survivor* and *Amazing Race*. Democrats are more likely than Republicans to like critically acclaimed shows about quirky people like *Mad Men, Dexter*, and *30 Rock*.[38]

That said, it is important to keep in mind that many Americans still call themselves moderate or are non-ideological and most at least say they do not identify strongly with either party. That appears to make a difference. If all voters were seriously polarized into one camp or another, rapid turns in party electoral fortunes would be unlikely. But this has been happening over and over of late. In 2004, Republicans won a decisive victory with George Bush reelected and Republicans maintaining congressional majorities. In 2006 and 2008, Democrats won big victories, first taking back control of the House and Senate and then the presidency. Then, in 2010, voters handed control of the House back to the Republicans in the biggest seat swing since the 1940s. Although voters returned Barack Obama to the White House in 2012, they handed Republicans a sweeping 9-seat Senate pickup in 2014, giving them solid majorities in both houses of Congress. It is surely true that a substantial percentage of Americans could not conceive of voting for candidates of the party they do not identify with. But there are enough swing voters who are not so tightly tied to a party to cause these kinds of changes.

Consider what might happen if a self-professed moderate, with a strong record of governance either in politics, the military, or business, not to mention a willingness to spend a few hundred million dollars, decided to run in the next election as a third party presidential candidate. Let's further assume that the major parties continued their trend of nominating a liberal Democrat and a conservative Republican. The evidence seems to suggest that someone like Colin Powell or Bill Gates might do quite well with the American voter simply by virtue of not being perceived as a partisan. In that sense, while partisanship is increasingly strong for some people, there are enough for whom it is not that the present trend toward polarization in Washington could be a liability to the future success of the parties.

Notes

1. David S. Broder, *The Party's Over: The Failure of Politics in America* (New York: Harper and Row, 1972).
2. Angus Campbell, Philip Converse, Warren Miller, and Donald Stokes, *The American Voter* (New York: Wiley, 1960).
3. M. Kent Jennings and Richard G. Niemi, "The Transmission of Political Values from Parent to Child," *American Political Science Review* 62 (March 1968): 169–184.
4. Donald Green, Bradley Palmquist, and Eric Schickler, *Partisan Hearts and Minds: Political Parties and the Social Identities of Voters* (New Haven, Conn.: Yale University Press, 2002).
5. Morris P. Fiorina, *Retrospective Voting in American National Elections* (New Haven, Conn.: Yale University Press, 1981).
6. Charles H. Franklin and John E. Jackson, "The Dynamics of Party Identification," *American Political Science Review* 85 (December 1983): 957–973.
7. Andrew Gelman, *Red State, Blue State, Rich State, Poor State: Why Americans Vote the Way They Do* (Princeton, N.J.: Princeton University Press, 2008).
8. Green, Palmquist, and Schickler, *Partisan Hearts and Minds.*
9. John Zaller, *The Nature and Origins of Mass Opinion* (New York: Cambridge University Press, 1992).
10. Gary C. Jacobson, *A Divider, Not a Uniter: George W. Bush and the American People* (New York: Pearson Longman, 2007).
11. Larry M. Bartels, "Beyond the Running Tally: Partisan Bias in Political Perceptions," *Political Behavior* 24 (2002): 117–150.
12. Jacobson, *A Divider, Not a Uniter.*
13. Brian J. Gaines, James H. Kuklinski, Paul J. Quirk, Buddy Peyton, and Jay Verkuilen, "Interpreting Iraq: Partisanship and the Meaning of Facts," *Journal of Politics* 69 (2007): 957–974.

14. Alan Abramowitz and Kyle Saunders, "Is Polarization a Myth?" *Journal of Politics* 70 (2008): 542–555.
15. Thomas M. Carsey and Geoffrey C. Layman, "Changing Sides or Changing Minds? Party Identification and Policy Preferences in the American Electorate Party Identification and Policy Preferences in the American Electorate," *American Journal of Political Science* 50 (2006): 464–477.
16. Thomas M. Carsey and Geoffrey C. Layman, "Changing Sides or Changing Minds?"
17. Jacobson, A Divider Not a Uniter; Adam J. Berinsky, *In Time of War: Understanding American Public Opinion from World War II to Iraq* (Chicago: University of Chicago Press, 2009).
18. Larry M. Bartels, "Partisanship and Voting Behavior, 1952–1996," *American Journal of Political Science* 44 (January 2000): 35–50.
19. Joseph A. Schlesinger, "The New American Political Party," *American Political Science Review* 79 (1985): 1152–1169; David W. Rohde, *Parties and Leaders in the Postreform House* (Chicago: University of Chicago Press, 1991); Keith T. Poole and Howard Rosenthal, "The Polarization of American Politics," *Journal of Politics* 46 (1984): 1061–1079.
20. Frances E. Lee, *Beyond Ideology: Politics, Principles, and Partisanship in the U.S. Senate* (Chicago: University of Chicago Press, 2009).
21. Bartels, "Partisanship and Voting Behavior."
22. Morris Fiorina with Samuel J. Abrams, and Jeremy C. Pope, *Culture War? The Myth of Polarized America, 1st Edition* (New York: Pearson Longman, 2004).
23. Robert A. Dahl, *Democracy in the United States: Promise and Performance*, 3rd Edition (New York: Rand McNally, 1976), pp. 420–433.
24. Abramowitz and Saunders, "Is Polarization a Myth?"
25. Marc J. Hetherington, "Resurgent Mass Partisanship: The Role of Elite Polarization," *American Political Science Review* 95 (2001): 619–631.
26. Matthew Levendusky, *The Partisan Sort: How Liberals Became Democrats and Conservatives Became Republicans* (Chicago: University of Chicago Press, 2009).
27. Marc J. Hetherington and Jonathan Weiler, *Authoritarianism and Polarization in American Politics* (New York: Cambridge University Press, 2009).
28. Donald R. Kinder and David O. Sears, "Prejudice and Politics: Symbolic Racism versus Racial Threats to the Good Life," *Journal of Personality and Social Psychology* 40 (1981): 414–431; Donald R. Kinder and Lynn M. Sanders, *Divided By Color: Racial Politics and Democratic Ideals* (Chicago: University of Chicago Press, 1996).
29. Edward Carmines and James Stimson, *Issue Evolution* (Princeton, N.J.: Princeton University Press, 1989).
30. D. Sunshine Hillygus and Todd Shields, *The Persuadable Voter: Strategic Candidates and Wedge Issues in Presidential Campaigns* (Princeton, N.J.: Princeton University Press, 2008).
31. Thomas Patterson, *Out of Order* (New York: Knopf, 1993).
32. Diana C. Mutz and Byron Reeves, "The New Videomalaise: Effects of Televised Incivility on Political Trust," *American Political Science Review* 99 (2005): 1–15.
33. Markus Prior, *Post-Broadcast Democracy: How Media Choice Increases Inequality in Political Involvement and Polarizes Elections* (New York: Cambridge University Press, 2007).
34. Campbell, Converse, Miller, and Stokes, *The American Voter.*
35. Marc J. Hetherington and Thomas J. Rudolph, *Why Washington Won't Work: Polarization, Political Trust, and the Governing Crisis* (Chicago: University of Chicago Press, 2015).

36. Shanto G. Iyengar, G. Sood, and Y. Lelkes, "Affect, Not Ideology: A Social Identity Perspective on Polarization," *Public Opinion Quarterly* 76 (2012): 405–431.
37. These data were drawn from an NMRPP analysis of Scarborough USA+ surveys from August 2008 and September 2009.
38. James Hibberd, "'The Reign of Right-Wing Primetime." Accessed at http://www.hollywoodreporter.com/blogs/live-feed/right-wing-tv-43558, December 17, 2010.

Chapter 8

Personality and Public Opinion

Jeffery J. Mondak and Matthew V. Hibbing[1]

Public opinion has many facets. Because of this, scholars who seek to understand public opinion approach the topic from multiple directions and perspectives. The contributions in this volume demonstrate this point well. Public opinion is discussed in these chapters in terms of meaning, measurement, subgroup differences, media effects, partisanship and ideology, political campaigns, and public policy. One persistent question faced by students of public opinion is why people differ in their views. In attempting to answer this question, one might consider the influences of immediate factors such as the statements of public officials and the corresponding content of media coverage. Analysts also might consider more long-term influences such as the impact on public opinion of a person's core values and basic political orientations. The position we advocate is that any full account of why people's opinions vary requires that we search broadly, and especially that we consider both immediate and long-term factors.

In this chapter, we address one of the longest of long-term influences, people's personalities.[2] The discussion builds from the two-part premise that people differ with respect to fundamental psychological structures, and that these differences are consequential for what we think and how we act, including how we engage the political world. If our premise is correct, it would follow that we could better our understanding of public opinion by taking personality into account. Toward this end, the purpose of this chapter is to discuss how and why personality might matter for public opinion, and to provide examples of the sorts of effects personality might produce.

A link between personality and public opinion may not seem as obvious as possible differences in opinion among men and women, Democrats and Republicans, or Americans and Canadians. Recognizing this, our first task in this chapter is to develop, step by step, the case for why we advocate attention to personality. We do so by explaining what personality is, how and why people's personalities differ, and what researchers in psychology and in other fields have found regarding the consequences of personality for various facets of human behavior. After developing the rationale for how and why personality may matter for public opinion, we present evidence regarding examples of such effects. Drawing primarily on data from a survey conducted in the United States in 2010, with supplemental data from two additional surveys conducted in 2012, two types of influences are considered. First, we show that basic differences in people's personalities correspond with differences in a fundamental political orientation, ideology. Second, we test whether personality also matters for public opinion on a salient issue in contemporary American politics, same-sex marriage. Together, these examples demonstrate the basic point that personality traits influence people's opinions. We end our discussion by considering what this lesson implies regarding the nature of public opinion itself, along with what it means regarding other factors commonly thought to influence mass opinion.

Why Personality?

Personality may be of relevance for public opinion, but we first must understand what personality is before we seek to establish evidence of its influence. Psychologists have constructed many definitions of personality, and controversy continues among psychologists as to just what personality is. Fortunately, consensus does exist regarding the basic characteristics of personality. By reviewing the key characteristics of personality emphasized in trait research, we can develop a functional understanding of personality. This understanding, in turn, can inform the effort to link personality and public opinion.

The chief reason personality defies simple definition is that our personalities are not directly observable. Physical traits such as height, weight, and hair color can be defined and recorded in concrete terms, but greater ambiguity surrounds our psychological characteristics. With respect to personality, what psychologists have concluded is that people have persistent psychological tendencies. For example, some people are worriers, some are willing to try anything, and some are sticklers about keeping everything neat, tidy, and in its place. These consistent characteristics, or traits, are the outward signs pointing to the existence of a broader internal psychological structure—that is, of personality. Thus, we can define personality as being a multifaceted and enduring psychological structure that influences patterns in behavior.

A few aspects of this definition should be highlighted. First, personalities are thought to be multifaceted. In our own research, we focus mostly on personality traits. Personality traits capture many important psychological differences across individuals. As a result, a large-scale, multifaceted depiction of personality trait structure encompasses much of what we mean by personality. However, most psychologists contend that personality also includes components beyond traits, such as values, beliefs, and motives. Again, some disagreement continues among scholars as to the precise components that make up our personalities. In our view, such disagreement is inevitable because the central phenomenon in question, personality, cannot be observed or measured in any direct, objective manner. Fortunately, these lingering debates should not hamper the effort to study personality and public opinion provided that we focus on personality traits, which most contemporary scholars agree are central to personality.

A second noteworthy aspect of our definition is that personality is assumed to be an *enduring* psychological structure. What we mean by this is that personalities are relatively stable over time. They do not change from day to day, and they do not even change much from year to year. This feature helps establish why personality is important. There would not be much point in studying the possible effects of personality on behavior if personality itself lacked an enduring character. Psychologists measure the stability of personality by gathering data from the same people at multiple points in time, and then seeing whether a given individual's personality was similar each time it was measured. For the personality traits we study in our research, psychologists estimate stability levels averaging 0.94 (where 1.0 is perfect stability) with trait measures obtained in six-year intervals.[3]

The last feature of our definition that warrants emphasis is that personality is thought to influence patterns in behavior. For present purposes, this includes the opinions that people form and express. Personality can be thought of as establishing a person's central tendency. For example, if one individual scores high on the personality trait of extraversion and another person scores low on this trait, our general expectation would be that, over time and across various situations, the first individual would behave in a more outgoing and sociable manner than the second.[4] In other words, personality produces a similarity in behavior across circumstances. Importantly, this does not imply that a person's behavior will always be identical. Instead, people adapt their actions on a situational basis. In a given situation, it is safe to predict that the extravert will be more outgoing than the introvert. However, extraverts themselves can be expected to be more outgoing on a cruise ship than at a memorial service—and so can introverts. What this implies is that progress toward a full understanding of human behavior requires that we take into account features of the individual (such as personality), features of the situation (such as whether it is a holiday cruise or a funeral service), and person–situation interactions.

The discussion thus far has outlined what we mean by personality, and it has begun to suggest why personality may be important for public opinion. These are important steps, but further refinement is needed. Most critically, we require a means to represent some of the key facets of personality in concrete, measurable form. Rather than attempt to capture all aspects of personality, we will focus on several important personality traits. Until the late 1980s, the dominant approach in research on personality and politics was for researchers to focus on the one or two personality traits that appeared to be of most direct relevance to the aspect of politics being studied. Some research of this sort continues today. As examples, we will provide brief reviews of research on the authoritarian personality and on need for cognition. The alternative to focusing on one or two traits is for researchers to attempt to represent personality more broadly. In the past decade, research on personality and politics has come to embrace this approach. Since the late 1980s psychologists have highlighted what have come to be known as the "Big Five" personality trait dimensions.

The "Big Five" (sometimes also called the "Five Factor") research perspective has gained the most prominent position in contemporary research on personality. Although it was some time before this approach began to influence research in political science, we will demonstrate that it is now the case that most applied research on personality and political behavior follows this course.

Theoretical Approaches to Personality and Politics

Prior to the ascendance of the Big Five, scholars had examined dozens, and even hundreds, of different personality traits. While a comprehensive review of these traits would fill its own book, we will focus on two examples of personality constructs that have been employed in research on political behavior over the years: authoritarianism and need for cognition.

Research on authoritarianism dates back to the aftermath of the Second World War, when scholars became interested in trying to understand what kind of person was susceptible to the appeals of fascism.[5] *The Authoritarian Personality*, a controversial book published in 1950 by Theodor Adorno and colleagues, attempted to measure authoritarian tendencies in the mass public using a battery of questions called the "F-scale." This work has been heavily criticized on both theoretical and empirical grounds over the years. Personality psychologists questioned the Freudian principles at the heart of the theory and public opinion scholars expressed major concerns about the construction of the F-scale. However, Adorno and company deserve credit for their early recognition that people's personalities could influence their political behavior.

Despite the early criticism, the concept of an authoritarian personality has continued to play a central role in research on personality and mass politics. Over the past sixty years, scholars have revised and refined Adorno's early ideas and corrected several of the F-scale's empirical limitations. Canadian social psychologist Bob Altemeyer has been at the forefront of much of this research. Altemeyer's research focuses on what he calls "right wing authoritarianism" (RWA), and he has developed the "R-scale" to measure this construct. Using the R-scale, Altemeyer and others have examined empirical links between authoritarianism and a host of different political phenomena. Among many findings, it has been shown that authoritarian individuals tend to be more conservative and less politically tolerant.[6]

Even with Altemeyer's improved measure, the study of authoritarianism has remained controversial. One point of contention is whether authoritarianism is a personality trait at all, or whether it is instead an interrelated set of values rooted in deeper traits (including perhaps the Big Five). Important subsequent work on authoritarianism has concluded that authoritarian tendencies are stable and longstanding, but the way authoritarianism manifests is often conditioned by the situational context.[7] A second concern is that traditional measures of authoritarianism are often dangerously similar to the political attitudes and behaviors that authoritarianism purports to explain. For example, consider the empirical relationship between authoritarianism and conservative political views. On its face, this could be seen as evidence that authoritarianism plays a causal role in shaping issue positions, but consider the following item used to measure authoritarianism, on which respondents are asked the extent to which they agree that "God's laws about abortion, pornography and marriage must be strictly followed before it is too late, and those who break them must be strongly punished." In another context, that could be a question used to determine how socially conservative a person is. If we use the same items to measure authoritarianism and conservatism, then the relationship is circular and theoretically indeterminate.

Over the last few years, scholars of authoritarianism have wrestled with this issue and devised novel measures to remove this sort of tautology between authoritarianism and political attitudes. The most prominent measurement alternative asks respondents about the values they hold on raising children.[8] Authoritarians value discipline and obedience in their children, compared to non-authoritarians who might value independence and creativity more highly. By asking about child-rearing, scholars are able to identify authoritarians without explicit reference to politics or policy. In this way, authoritarianism research is moving closer to work on the Big Five in focusing on non-political indicators of personality.

Another branch of research on personality and politics that predates the Big Five instead approaches matters from an information-processing perspective. Over the last thirty years or so, research in cognitive psychology has coalesced behind the idea that a dual-process model best accounts for how humans think and reason. There are several different dual-processing theories,[9] but the basic idea is shared across all of them. Because our world is so complex, it is simply impossible for us to attend to all of the information that we encounter. This leads us to process most environmental stimuli in a heuristic fashion without much (or any) conscious thought. Information processed in this way (System 1) is handled unconsciously based on existing habits. On the other hand, we can devote conscious thought to some tasks (System 2), but there simply isn't the time or the capacity for us to carefully attend to everything. To understand how this works, think about how you get dressed in the morning. You probably make a conscious decision about what to wear (the blue shirt or the green shirt?), but it is unlikely that you devote much conscious effort to the process of putting that shirt on. Instead of consciously and deliberately thinking "I must slide the shirt over my head and then lift my arm and bend my elbow to the appropriate angle to slide it through the sleeve," you simply put on the shirt. Our minds are able to process a remarkable variety of complex tasks without consciously thinking about them, but there are also times when we need to exert conscious control (e.g. when we do something for the first time). This is all well and good, but what does any of it have to do with personality and politics? Well, despite the fact that we all employ System 1 and System 2 processing at times, there is considerable individual variation in how and when we will utilize different modes of processing. *Need for cognition* is a personality measure that taps into differences in how much people engage in System 2 processing. Some people enjoy thinking about and solving complex problems. They like to do puzzles and feel a strong need to keep their minds occupied. These individuals are high in need for cognition. On the other side of the spectrum there are individuals who prefer mindless tasks and who are easily frustrated by complication and nuance. Need for cognition has been linked to a host of political behaviors, including information acquisition via news media, political interest, and political activism.[10]

The Value of the Big Five Approach

Work on authoritarianism has a very different starting point from the work on need for cognition, but both research programs have been extremely valuable in advancing our understanding of how personality influences politics. Both research streams were in the vanguard in acknowledging that political behavior is a subset of more general human behavior, and thus likely to be influenced by general orientations like personality traits. However, both research streams also suffer from the same weakness: they focus on a single aspect of personality in isolation from the larger picture. While this kind of "one at a time" approach can be fruitful, it also has important limitations. One of the most troubling is that the study of numerous individual traits in isolation has inhibited the accumulation of knowledge on how personality traits influence politics. If every scholar is using her own preferred scale, it becomes difficult for subsequent research to build on what came before. Scholars using one personality construct could find themselves reinventing the wheel because they are not familiar with another stream of research using a related personality construct. The Big Five approach offers us a way out of this predicament. It provides us with a way to capture most of the meaningful variation in personality in a parsimonious fashion, thus helping to ensure that we are seeing the full picture.

The Big Five personality trait dimensions are openness to experience, conscientiousness, extraversion, agreeableness, and emotional stability. Although the earliest research on this framework traces to the 1950s and 1960s,[11] it was not until twenty years later that the use of five-factor approaches became common in research on trait psychology. Thanks largely to the pioneering efforts of psychologists Lewis Goldberg, Paul Costa, and Robert McCrae,[12] hundreds of studies on the Big Five now are being reported each year. Gosling and his colleagues have noted that the five-factor approach "has become the most widely used and extensively researched model of personality."[13]

The long, slow development of the Big Five allowed personality psychologists to be sure that what they were measuring was meaningful and comprehensive. What researchers eventually discovered was that the Big Five trait structure is seemingly universal in the sense that these same five trait dimensions are important aspects of people's personalities in nations and cultures all over the world.[14] This universality is important because it means that the many studies on the Big Five combine to provide a cumulative, well-integrated understanding of psychological differences. In addition to this cross-cultural breadth, five-factor models also enjoy breadth in terms of their representation of personality at the level of the individual. Although there is more to personality than the Big Five, these trait dimensions collectively capture the bulk of trait structure. This means that Big Five frameworks are especially useful for applied studies on the effects of personality, including for studies about personality and politics.

Applied research on the Big Five requires data on people's personality traits. Fortunately, we all tend to be relatively good judges of our own personalities.[15] Because of this, self-report data are common in research on personality. A study's participants are asked to rate themselves on various matters, with the resulting data then being used by the researcher to construct measures of particular personality traits. Research exploring the properties of the personality traits themselves will often draw on very large data sets, with from ten to fifty or more questions asked of participants for each trait dimension. In applied research, use of such exhaustive measures rarely is possible. For example, if a half-hour telephone or Internet survey about politics includes around one hundred questions, only a small portion of those could be devoted to measuring personality. Recognizing this, several teams of researchers have worked to develop brief measures of the Big Five, measures that can provide functional representations of personality trait structure with a total of only five to ten survey questions.[16] Recent research on personality and politics has made use of such brief measures, and the tests we report below are based on data using Gosling et al.'s 10-item personality measure, as well as a closely-related modified version.

Thus far, we have examined at length the rationales for why it may be that personality matters for public opinion, but we have not yet recounted what sorts of effects have been identified in past studies. Research we ourselves have conducted, along with research by several other teams of scholars, has shown that the Big Five personality traits do influence mass opinion. Our next step is to review what some of these studies have found. Later, we will introduce new data as a means to provide examples of a few key personality effects.

Personality, Ideology, and Opinion

Empirical studies regarding the effects of personality on political behavior cover considerable ground. Here, we will limit discussion in two manners. First, although personality traits may influence numerous facets of political behavior, we will devote the greatest attention to public opinion, while making only passing reference to research exploring the effects of personality on matters such as political information and political participation. Second, most of our discussion is limited to applications involving the Big Five trait taxonomy. Political scientists studied personality and politics prior to the emergence of five-factor models and some scholars today employ alternate frameworks, but these studies will receive minimal attention here. The important point to keep in mind is that "personality and political behavior" is a much broader topic than "the Big Five and public opinion."

Our own research on political applications of the Big Five began in 1997, and we have been gathering personality data on surveys since 1998. A team of researchers at Yale University headed by Alan Gerber and Gregory Huber then produced a series of studies that complement ours, using data from a series of surveys starting in 2006. Numerous other scholars subsequently have followed suit. Our own contributions include an article that provides a general overview of applications of the Big Five to public opinion, political information and other aspects of mass politics,[17] a much more extensive outline of our research agenda,[18] two examinations of effects of the Big Five on civic engagement and political participation,[19] and more specific treatments concerning the impact of the Big Five on patterns in social and political conversations,[20] jury service,[21] the political attitudes and behaviors of state legislators,[22] and the relationship between state-level aggregate measures of personality and state political culture.[23] Gerber and his colleagues have studied subgroup differences in Big Five effects on political behavior,[24] the specific impact of personality on participation,[25] political information,[26] and political discussion.[27]

Although the Big Five traits often are described in collective form, it is important to keep in mind that the taxonomy includes five distinct trait dimensions, each with its own behavioral correlates. All of the traits have been found to be related to multiple aspects of political behavior, but significant effects in the political domain are more common for openness, conscientiousness, and extraversion than for agreeableness and emotional stability. Further, extraversion most often predicts social forms of civic engagement such as participating in political discussion and attending meetings and rallies, whereas effects on political attitudes are less common. Hence, when applied to the study of public opinion, openness to experience and conscientiousness are the Big Five traits that generally should be expected to be of the greatest relevance.

People high in openness to experience exhibit imagination, curiosity, and analytical skill, and they seek information and engagement of all sorts. As the term "openness to experience" implies, these individuals are willing to try new things and to encounter new ideas. Conscientiousness includes a sense of dependability often represented in Big Five measures with reference to terms such as "reliable" and "organized." Conscientiousness also includes a volitional component captured by terms such as "hardworking" and "persevering." People scoring high in conscientiousness tend to be cautious and risk-averse.

Research on personality and public opinion has identified effects of the Big Five on ideology, values, and issue opinions. When scholars have examined the influence of the Big Five on political ideology they consistently have found effects for openness to experience and conscientiousness, along with occasional more modest effects for agreeableness and emotional stability.[28] Openness is positively associated with political liberalism (and thus negatively associated with conservatism), meaning that people who score high in openness to experience have a greater likelihood of being liberal than of being conservative.[29] This relationship makes sense when we consider the nature of liberal ideology. A key part of political liberalism is the interest in new solutions to existing political problems and the willingness to embrace societal change.

The other consistent finding in studies regarding the Big Five and ideology has been a positive relationship between conscientiousness and political conservatism. Many of the same studies that identified links between openness and liberalism have found parallel effects of conscientiousness on self-identification as a conservative. This relationship, like the openness–liberal link, enjoys strong intuitive appeal. Political conservatives are cautious in policy making and reluctant to alter the status quo, and many conservatives value personal responsibility and tradition. These preferences are the hallmarks of individuals psychologically inclined toward conscientiousness.

Consistent effects of openness and conscientiousness have been identified in many studies involving the mass public, and these same relationships have been found with data from elected officials—members of the state legislatures in Arizona, Connecticut, and Maine.[30] A last point about the Big Five and ideology is that agreeableness and emotional stability have emerged in some studies as predictors of ideology. Although more modest than the effects for openness and conscientiousness, the evidence suggests that agreeableness corresponds with a tendency toward ideological liberalism and emotional stability predicts conservatism.

Elsewhere in this volume, the importance of people's values (Federico), including religious beliefs (Campbell and Layman), is noted. Personality also may be important in this area. Openness and conscientiousness have both been found to be related to people's core values. For example, in one of our works, conscientiousness produced very strong positive effects on moral traditionalism and moral judgment, and openness yielded equally strong negative effects.[31] Caprara et al. find similar results with respect to two other core values, universalism and security.[32] In that study, the authors posit that the pathway linking the Big Five and ideology runs through values. That is, openness and conscientiousness shape views regarding universalism and security, which, in turn, influence ideology.

Beyond ideology and values, effects of the Big Five also have been found on people's specific policy judgments. To a large degree, such effects reflect the impact of personality on ideology. However, in many cases personality has been found to be influential even when controlling for ideology.[33] We present an example of such a test below by exploring whether, controlling for ideology, the Big Five traits affect opinion on same-sex marriage. To our knowledge, possible relationships between the Big Five traits and attitudes toward same-sex marriage have not been studied directly, although several findings are informative. Riemann et al. administered a survey of political attitudes to a sample of German citizens.[34] Their measure of general conservatism included attitudes toward same-sex marriage, and significant relationships were found for openness and agreeableness, with both shown to be positively associated with liberal attitudes. Cullen et al. included a measure of openness in their study of the correlates of homophobia.[35] Using a sample of university students they found that openness was negatively related to homophobia, meaning that individuals with low scores on openness were more likely to be homophobic. Similarly, McCrae et al. found that low scores on openness were associated with attitudes which stigmatized people with HIV/AIDS in both the United States and Russia.[36] Finally, Costa et al. found that higher scores on openness were associated with liberal sex attitudes.[37]

Thus far, we have discussed at some length the rationale for why personality should be expected to influence public opinion, along with what sorts of effects have been seen in prior research. This material has provided important background, but the most tangible way to demonstrate the personality–opinion link is to introduce direct evidence. Toward this end, our final substantive task is to report data from recent surveys. With past research to guide us, our expectation is that personality traits—especially openness to experience and conscientiousness—should emerge as determinants of both political ideology and respondents' policy stances.

Exploring the Personality–Opinion Connection

The initial data we will examine are from a national Internet survey conducted in March, 2010.[38] The survey's 1,500 respondents answered numerous questions about politics, and also a 10-item Big Five personality battery. Our interest is in whether values on the Big Five measures correspond with respondents' political views. Specifically, we will assess the possible effects of the Big Five trait dimensions on ideology and attitudes toward same-sex marriage. When analyzing relationships among variables using survey data, it is useful, if possible, to repeat the tests with measures from additional data sets because finding similar effects in new tests increases our confidence in the findings. Toward this end, we will replicate our key tests with data from two 2012 surveys, those conducted as part of the American National Election Studies (ANES) and the Cooperative Congressional Election Study (CCES).

On the 2010 survey, ideological orientation is measured with data from an item on which respondents were asked to place themselves on a 10-point scale on which 1 was labeled "liberal" and 10 was labeled "conservative." Both 2012 surveys employ seven-point measures of ideology (1 = strongly liberal, to 7 = strongly conservative).

Using the 2010 survey, we measure attitudes toward same-sex marriage with data from a question that asked "How strongly do you approve or disapprove that same-sex couples can have the right to marry?" A 10-point scale is used, with endpoints labeled "strongly disapprove" (1) and "strongly approve" (10).

All 1,500 respondents answered this question. Opinion was fairly evenly divided, with 53.5 percent of respondents expressing disapproval of same-sex marriage, and 46.5 percent indicating approval. The scale has a mean value of 5.27. On the ANES, a three-point ordinal measure is used; 1 = There should be no legal recognition of a gay or lesbian couple's relationship, 2 = Gay and lesbian couples should be allowed to form civil unions but not legally marry, 3 = Gay and lesbian couples should be allowed to legally marry. A dichotomous measure is used on the CCES, where respondents were asked "Do you favor or oppose gay marriage": 1 = favor, 0 = oppose.

The Big Five personality traits are measured on the 2010 survey using data from 10 items, two for each trait dimension. The questions were adapted from Gosling et al.'s "ten-item personality inventory," or TIPI, whereas the actual TIPI was used on the 2012 ANES and a 20-item battery was included on the 2012 CCES. In AmericasBarometer pilot tests conducted before our full surveys were administered throughout the Americas, we used the actual TIPI items. Especially outside of the United States, many of the respondents on the AmericasBarometer surveys have very low levels of education, and thus it is important that survey questions be tested carefully to make sure that respondents understand what they mean. In our pilot tests, many respondents struggled with some of the words on the TIPI, such as "extraverted," "reserved," and "conventional." With the help of feedback from interviewers, we were able to develop a revised set of personality questions that was better understood by respondents.[39] As on the TIPI, respondents were asked to use a seven-point scale to indicate the extent to which they agreed or disagreed that a series of statements applied to them. A value of 1 means "strongly disagree" and a value of 7 means "strongly agree." For each trait, one item is worded positively and one is worded negatively. In Table 8.1, we list the Big Five trait dimensions, the survey items used to measure them on the 2010 survey, and also our central expectations regarding possible effects of personality on ideology and on attitudes regarding same-sex marriage. Although different items are used to measure the Big Five on the two 2012 surveys, we have the same expectations regarding effects on ideology and opinion on same-sex marriage.

On all three surveys, the final personality scales are constructed by reversing the items that are worded negatively so that high scores indicate possession of the trait in question, adding the items pertaining to each trait, and then recoding the final measures so that they range from 0 to 1. The 0–1 scales will be used as independent variables in statistical models to see if variation in people's personality traits predicts variation in ideology and opinion regarding same-sex marriage. The statistical models enable us to assess the possible effects of the Big Five traits while also accounting for the possible influences of other factors.[40]

We begin our analyses by testing the possible effects of personality on ideology, with statistical estimates for this model reported in Table 8.2. With the exception of a measure of whether CCES respondents are Hispanic, all four demographic variables produced statistically significant results in all three surveys. Specifically, female respondents are, on average, somewhat more liberal than respondents who are male; African Americans and Hispanics are more liberal than respondents who are white; and older respondents are more conservative, as a whole, than are younger respondents.

Table 8.1 The Big Five and Public Opinion: Traits, Measures, and Expectations.

Trait dimension	Survey measures	Expected relationship with ideology	Expected relationship with opinion regarding same-sex marriage
Openness to experience	Open to new experiences and intellectual (5); uncreative and unimaginative (10, R)	High openness corresponds strongly with ideological liberalism	High openness corresponds with approval of same-sex couples having the right to marry
Conscientious-ness	Dependable and self-disciplined (3); disorganized and careless (8, R)	High conscientious-ness corresponds strongly with ideological conservatism	High conscientious-ness corresponds with disapproval of same-sex couples having the right to marry
Extraversion	Sociable and active (1); quiet and shy (6, R)		
Agreeableness	Critical and quarrelsome (2, R); generous and warm (7)	High agreeableness may correspond weakly with ideological liberalism	High agreeableness may correspond weakly with approval of same-sex couples having the right to marry
Emotional Stability	Anxious and easily upset (4, R); calm and emotionally stable (9)	High emotional stability may correspond weakly with ideological conservatism	High emotional stability may correspond weakly with disapproval of same-sex couples having the right to marry

Note: Entries in the second column are the question wording used on the 2010 Americas Barometer, which used a modified version of the TIPI. On the 2012 ANES survey, the actual TIPI was used, whereas a 20-item measure was used on the CCES. On the AmericasBarometer, survey measures were asked following this prompt: "Here are a series of personality traits that may or may not apply to you. Using the 1–7 ladder, where 1 means 'strongly disagree' and 7 means 'strongly agree,' please tell me the number that indicates the extent to which you agree or disagree with that statement. You should rate the extent to which the pair of traits applies to you, even if one characteristic applies more strongly than the other. You see yourself as a _____ person." Numbers in parentheses following the items indicate the order in which they were asked. An "R" within the parentheses means that values on this item were reversed in the final scale.

Table 8.2 Personality and Ideology.

	2010 Americas Barometer	2012 CCES	2012 ANES
Constant	4.77 (0.40)	4.10 (0.41)	0.60 (0.22)
Female	–0.55*** (0.14)	–0.29** (0.12)	–0.31*** (0.08)
African-American	–0.79*** (0.22)	–0.66*** (0.19)	–1.16*** (0.11)
Hispanic	–0.47** (0.21)	–0.23 (0.22)	–0.62*** (0.11)
Age	0.02*** (0.00)	0.02*** (0.00)	0.07*** (0.01)
Openness to experience	–2.17*** (0.35)	–2.38*** (0.36)	–2.87*** (0.23)
Conscientiousness	1.88*** (0.35)	1.18** (0.43)	1.69*** (0.23)
Extraversion	0.29 (0.31)	–0.17 (0.30)	0.23 (0.19)
Agreeableness	0.46 (0.39)	0.03 (0.34)	–0.43 (0.24)
Emotional stability	0.62* (0.34)	0.59* (0.34)	0.60** (0.22)
R^2	0.09	0.08	0.08
Number of cases	1493	879	4679

Note: Cell entries are OLS regression coefficients with standard errors in parentheses. The dependent variable is a 10-point (column one) or 7-point (columns two and three) measure of ideological self-placement, coded liberal (1) to conservative (highest value).
*** $p < .001$; ** $p < .05$; * $p < .10$.

Source: U.S. component of the 2010 AmericasBarometer (first column); 2012 Cooperative Congressional Election Study (second column); 2012 American National Election Study (third column).

Among the personality variables, the results are very much in line with the findings reported in past studies. To help illustrate the impact of personality, statistically significant personality effects found in analyses using data from the 2010 AmericasBarometer are summarized in Figure 8.1.[41] First, openness to experience is strongly negatively related to being conservative. On all three surveys, the estimate, or regression coefficient, for this trait is between –2 and –3. This means that as openness shifts in value from 0 to 1, the ideology of the respondent is predicted to move over two points toward the liberal end of the ideology measure.

As expected, conscientiousness emerges as a significant predictor of ideological conservatism. The coefficients for this trait all are positive, producing effects in the opposite direction of those for openness to experience. The second section of Figure 8.1 displays this effect for the AmericasBarometer. The results for openness and conscientiousness are substantively quite sizeable. For example, on all three surveys both are considerably larger in magnitude than the largest demographic effects, those for being African American. The influences of openness and conscientiousness on ideology are especially pronounced when the two traits are viewed in tandem. An AmericasBarometer respondent who is high in conscientiousness and low in openness is predicted to have an ideology value a full four points to the right of an individual with the opposite personality profile.

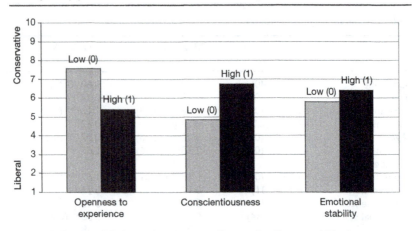

Figure 8.1 Estimated Relationships between Personality Traits and Ideology
(source: Table 8.2, column one).

Among the other three Big Five traits, extraversion is rarely found to be
linked to ideology, whereas agreeableness and emotional stability sometimes
produce modest effects. Present results match well to this pattern. The
regression coefficients for extraversion and agreeableness are small and
statistically insignificant. Emotional stability proves to be related to ideology
on all three surveys, but, as seen in Figure 8.1, the effect is much smaller than
those for openness and conscientiousness. Overall, the Big Five traits clearly do
matter for ideology, but, as expected, the five trait dimensions do not perform
comparably. Openness to experience is strongly associated with ideological
liberalism, conscientiousness is strongly associated with conservatism,
emotional stability modestly predicts conservatism, and agreeableness and
extraversion are unrelated to ideology.

These results show that personality influences one of people's most
fundamental political orientations, but are there also effects on opinions about
contemporary issues? Turning first to same-sex marriage, the general pattern
of results (summarized in Table 8.3) is highly similar to what we saw above for
ideology. First, women and younger people are more approving of same-sex
couples having the right to marry than are men and older people. However, unlike
with ideology, there are no differences in opinion associated with variation in
race and ethnicity. Second, openness to experience and conscientiousness once
again produce mostly strong effects, and emotional stability again exerts a
modest but statistically discernible influence in two of the three data sets.

The magnitude of the openness and conscientiousness effects warrants
emphasis. As Figure 8.2 reveals, on the AmericasBarometer, both traits are
estimated to produce greater than three-point swings on the 1–10 opinion
scale. The strongest impact emerges when we consider the joint influence of
openness and conscientiousness. An average respondent is estimated to have
a score of 8.43 on the same-sex marriage item if the person is high in openness

Table 8.3 Personality and Approval of Same-Sex Marriage.

	2010 Americas Barometer	2012 CCES	2012 ANES
Constant (columns one, two); Cut-point #1 (column three)	7.88 (0.55)	0.04 (0.49)	−1.35 (0.16)
Cut-point #2 (column three)			0.15 (0.16)
Female	0.73*** (0.20)	0.25 (0.15)	0.23*** (0.05)
African-American	−0.26 (0.31)	−0.32 (0.23)	−0.43*** (0.07)
Hispanic	−0.41 (0.29)	0.19 (0.27)	−0.14* (0.07)
Age	−0.05*** (0.01)	−0.02*** (0.00)	−0.09*** (0.01)
Openness to experience	3.28*** (0.48)	2.96*** (0.46)	1.68*** (0.15)
Conscientiousness	−3.10*** (0.48)	−0.11 (0.52)	−0.56*** (0.15)
Extraversion	0.05 (0.43)	−0.39 (0.37)	−0.27** (0.13)
Agreeableness	−0.63 (0.53)	−0.02 (0.41)	0.02 (0.16)
Emotional stability	−0.79* (0.48)	−1.04** (0.41)	−0.18 (0.14)
R^2 (column one); pseudo R^2 (columns two and three)	0.13	0.07	0.03
Number of cases	1499	922	5332

Note: Cell entries are OLS regression coefficients (column one), binomial logistic regression coefficients (column two), and ordered logistic regression coefficients (column three), with standard errors in parentheses.
*** $p < .001$; ** $p<.05$; * $p < .10$.

Source: U.S. component of the 2010 AmericasBarometer (first column); 2012 Cooperative Congressional Election Study (second column); 2012 American National Election Study (third column).

to experience and low in conscientiousness, versus a score of 2.05 if he has the opposite profile in terms of these two traits. This suggests that, to a substantial extent, opinion on same-sex marriage is shaped by people's core psychological differences.

Our initial account of opinion on same-sex marriage suffers from an important limitation in that it examines the possible effects of personality traits and of demographic attributes, but it omits basic political orientations such as ideology. Public debate over same-sex marriage has transpired largely along ideological lines, with many liberals expressing support of same-sex couples having the right to marry, and many conservatives expressing opposition. The same three personality traits that matter for opinion on same-sex marriage also matter for ideology. This raises the possibility that there is no direct relationship between personality and opinion in this case. Instead, it may be that personality shapes ideology, which, in turn, influences opinion on the issue of same-sex marriage. In other words, the effects of personality on opinion may be indirect rather than direct, with those effects operating through ideology.

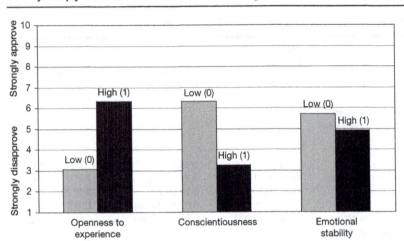

Figure 8.2 Estimated Relationships between Personality Traits and Approval of Same-Sex Couples Having the Right to Marry (source: Table 8.3, column one).

We believe that it is important to understand not only whether personality matters for public opinion, but also how, and through what channels, any influences of personality operate. Thus, we must try to sort out the relationships among personality, ideology, and opinion. One way to shed some light on this matter is to add ideology as a predictor of same-sex marriage.[42] If, as should be expected, ideology is related to opinion in this case, that would signal an indirect effect of personality. If inclusion of ideology causes the statistical estimates for the personality variables to weaken and slip to statistical insignificance, this would suggest that personality exerts *only* an indirect influence on opinion about same-sex marriage. Conversely, if ideology generates a significant effect and the personality variables also continue to produce strong influences, this would mean that personality affects opinion regarding same-sex marriage both indirectly (by shaping ideology) and directly, over and above the effect of ideology.

What happens when we incorporate ideology into our understanding of attitudes towards same-sex marriage? First, we find that ideology produces quite large effects. On the AmericasBarometer, for example, values on ideology range from 1 to 10, meaning that the –0.81 coefficient yields a predicted score on the same-sex marriage item that shifts by 7.29 points across the ideology scale. The important lesson with respect to personality is that part of the influence of the Big Five on opinion apparently is indirect, with this influence operating through ideology. As to the trait variables, the estimate for emotional stability is small and statistically insignificant. Therefore, it appears that the impact of this trait dimension on opinion is only indirect. In contrast, the estimates for openness to experience remain statistically significant in all three models, as does the conscientiousness effect with data from the 2010 survey. The new estimates for these variables are smaller than those seen in our initial

Table 8.4 Direct and Indirect Links between Personality and Approval of Same-Sex Marriage.

	2010 Americas Barometer	2012 CCES	2012 ANES
Constant (columns one, two); Cut-point #1 (column three)	11.77 (0.47)	3.66 (0.66)	−4.29 (0.21)
Cut-point #2 (column three)			−2.46 (0.20)
Female	0.27 (0.16)	0.10 (0.18)	0.12* (0.06)
African-American	−0.90*** (0.25)	−1.03*** (0.29)	−0.87*** (0.09)
Hispanic	−0.79** (0.24)	0.05 (0.33)	−0.40*** (0.08)
Age	−0.03*** (0.00)	−0.02*** (0.01)	−0.08*** (0.01)
Openness to experience	1.52*** (0.40)	2.26*** (0.57)	1.04*** (0.17)
Conscientiousness	−1.60*** (0.40)	0.74 (0.66)	−0.22 (0.18)
Extraversion	0.29 (0.35)	−0.83* (0.47)	−0.25 (0.14)
Agreeableness	−0.26 (0.44)	0.01 (0.53)	−0.05 (0.18)
Emotional stability	−0.31 (0.39)	−0.58 (0.51)	−0.08 (0.16)
Ideology	−0.81*** (0.03)	−0.88*** (0.06)	−0.36*** (0.01)
R^2 (column one); pseudo R^2 (columns two and three)	0.42	0.32	0.13
Number of cases	1499	868	4651

Note: Cell entries are OLS regression coefficients (column one), binomial logistic regression coefficients (column two), and ordered logistic regression coefficients (column three), with standard errors in parentheses.
*** $p < .001$; ** $p < .05$; * $p < .10$.

Source: U.S. component of the 2010 AmericasBarometer (first column); 2012 Cooperative Congressional Election Study (second column); 2012 American National Election Study (third column).

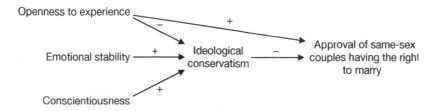

Figure 8.3 Direct and Indirect Effects of Personality Traits on Approval of Same-Sex Couples Having the Right to Marry.

analysis, before we added ideology to our account. At least for openness, it seems that this trait produces both direct and indirect effects on opinion about same-sex marriage. Part of the effect operates indirectly via ideology, but the remainder of the openness effect is independent of ideology (full results are summarized in Table 8.4).

We summarize the collective lessons from our empirical tests in Figure 8.3. First, arrows lead from each of the three personality traits to ideology. Specifically, openness is negatively associated with ideological conservatism, whereas conscientiousness and emotional stability are linked positively to conservatism. Second, conservatism is negatively associated with approval of same-sex couples having the right to marry. Third, openness produces a direct effect, over and above the impact operating via ideology, on opinion about same-sex marriage. This exercise serves to demonstrate that personality traits are important determinants of at least one facet of public opinion, and also that the effects of personality on opinion operate partly in conjunction with people's fundamental political orientations. By conducting analyses with data from three surveys, we have seen that highly similar results are obtained in two different years, and when somewhat different approaches are used to measure personality, ideology, and opinion about same-sex marriage. Together, the initial test and the two replications bring heightened confidence that personality is related to both people's core political dispositions and to public opinion.

Conclusions

The purpose of this chapter has been to discuss the effects of people's personality traits on public opinion. Toward that end, we sought in the first portion of the chapter to explain the rationale for how and why personality and public opinion may be linked, and to review recent scholarship that speaks to such a connection. In the second section of the chapter, we presented a few illustrative tests. Those exercises yielded evidence that people's personality traits influence political ideology, and also that personality produces both direct and indirect effects on public opinion regarding a salient topic in contemporary politics, the right of same-sex couples to be married.

Although our immediate objective has been to discuss the possible relationship between personality and public opinion, two broader concerns have motivated this effort. First, taking personality seriously requires one to take long-term influences seriously. A central theme in this chapter, and in our own research agenda, is that much of the political behavior we observe on a day-to-day basis arises partly as the consequence of long-term forces. In contrast with more immediate influences, such as exposure to information during the course of a political campaign, long-term forces trace back many years. Second, in studying the impact of personality and other long-term influences, we believe it is important to keep the big picture in sight. Many factors of various forms affect patterns in political behavior. Public opinion is not the exclusive product of personality traits any more than it is the exclusive product of what people see on the news. We will make the most progress toward understanding the bases of public opinion if we recognize that multiple influences are at work, and if we seek to discover how these influences combine.

In just the past few years, there has been a tremendous revitalization in research on personality and politics. As research in this area continues, students of public opinion will have to think carefully about what these developments imply regarding matters such as why people hold different views and what prospects exist for people with divergent opinions to engage in civil, constructive discourse about political affairs. The tests presented in this chapter are good cases in point. Personality and other long-term influences do not determine public opinion, and the effects of these influences are not such that opinion is set in stone. Nonetheless, personality effects are deep-seated. The strong impact of personality on people's political views therefore likely helps to explain some of the fundamental divisions seen today, divisions such as those between liberals and conservatives, and between proponents and opponents of same-sex marriage. These examples are of sufficient importance to demonstrate that research on personality constitutes a significant new direction in the study of public opinion.

Notes

1. This chapter was supported by a grant from the National Science Foundation (Award 0962153), which funded acquisition of some of the data reported in this chapter, data gathered as part of the United States component of the 2010 AmericasBarometer survey. The authors thank Raman Deol for research assistance on this chapter, and Damarys Canache and Mitchell Seligson for their contributions to this project.
2. For more on the influence of enduring individual differences, see F. J. Gonzalez, K. B. Smith, and J. R. Hibbing, "No Longer 'Beyond Our Scope:' The Biological and Non-Conscious Underpinnings of Public Opinion," this volume.
3. P. T. Costa and R. R. McCrae, "Personality in Adulthood: A Six-Year Longitudinal Study of Self-Reports and Spouse Ratings on the NEO Personality Inventory," *Journal of Personality and Social Psychology* 36)2015): 331–40.
4. For evidence that the effects of personality traits on political attitudes and behaviors exhibit consistency over time, see A. J. Bloeser, D. Canache, D. Mitchell, J. J. Mondak, and E. R. Poore, "The Temporal Consistency of Personality Effects: Evidence from the British Household Panel Survey," *Political Psychology* 35 (2014): in press.
5. For more on authoritarianism, see C. M. Federico, "The Structure, Foundations, and Expression of Ideology," this volume.
6. See for example J. L. Sullivan, G. E. Marcus, S. Feldman, and J. E. Piereson, "The Sources of Political Tolerance: A Multivariate Analysis," *American Political Science Review* 75 (1981): 92–106; and B. Altemeyer, *The Authoritarian Spector* (New York: Cambridge, 1996).
7. K. Stenner, *The Authoritarian Dynamic* (New York: Cambridge, 2005).
8. M. J. Hetherington, and J. D. Weiler, *Authoritarianism and Polarization in American Politics* (New York: Cambridge, 2009).
9. See, for example R. E. Petty, and J. T. Cacioppo, *Communication and Persuasion: Central and Peripheral Routes to Attitude Change* (New York: Springer-Verlag, 1986); and S. Chaiken, "Heuristic versus Systematic Information Processing and the use of Source versus Message Cues in Persuasion," *Journal of Personality and Social Psychology* 39 (1980): 752–766.

10. See, for example, G. Y. Bizer, J. A. Krosnick, A. L. Holbrook, S. C. Wheeler, D. D. Rucker, and R. E. Petty, "The Impact of Personality on Cognitive, Behavioral, and Affective Political Processes: The Effects of Need to Evaluate," *Journal of Personality* 72 (2004): 995–1027, and M. B. Condra, "The Link between Need for Cognition and Political Interest, Involvement, and Media Usage," *Psychology: A Journal of Human Behavior* 29 (1992): 13–18.

11. See, for example, E. C. Tupes and R. E. Christal, *Recurrent Personality Factors Based on Trait Ratings* (Lackland Air Force Base, TX: U.S. Air Force, 1961); and E. C. Tupes and R. E. Christal, *Stability of Personality Trait Rating Factors Obtained under Diverse Conditions* (Lackland Air Force Base, TX: U.S. Air Force, 1958).

12. See, for example, L. R. Goldberg, "An Alternative 'Description of Personality': The Big-Five Factor Structure," *Journal of Personality and Social Psychology* 59 (1990): 1216–1229; L. R. Goldberg, "The Development of Markers for the Big-Five Factor Structure," *Psychological Assessment* 4 (1992): 26–42; Costa and McCrae, "Personality in Adulthood,"; R. R. McCrae and P. T. Costa, "The Five-Factor Theory of Personality," in *Handbook of Personality: Theory and Research*, ed. O. P. John, R. W. Robins, and L. A. Pervin (New York: Guilford, 2008); and R. R. McCrae and P. T. Costa, *Personality in Adulthood: A Five-Factor Theory* (New York: Guilford, 2003).

13. S. D. Gosling, P. J. Rentfrow, and W. B. Swann, "A Very Brief Measure of the Big-Five Personality Domains," *Journal of Research in Personality* 37 (2003): 506.

14. McCrae and Costa, *Personality in Adulthood.*

15. A key way psychologists test the utility of self-report personality data is to gather personality descriptions about these individuals from other people who know them well so that self reports and other-person reports can be compared. High correlations between self reports and other-person reports consistently are recorded when such tests are conducted, which suggests that we see ourselves much as others see us.

16. See, for example, Gosling, Rentfrow, and Swann, "A Very Brief Measure,"; and S. A. Woods and S. E. Hampson, "Measuring the Big Five with Single Items Using a Bipolar Response Scale," *European Journal of Personality* 19 (2005): 373–390.

17. J. J. Mondak and K. D. Halperin, "A Framework for the Study of Personality and Political Behavior," *British Journal of Political Science* 38 (2008): 335–362.

18. J. J. Mondak, *Personality and the Foundations of Political Behavior* (New York: Cambridge, 2010).

19. J. J. Mondak, D. Canache, M. A. Seligson, and M. V. Hibbing, "The Participatory Personality: Evidence from Latin America," *British Journal of Political Science* 41 (2011): 211–21; and J. J. Mondak, M. V. Hibbing, D. Canache, M. A. Seligson, and M. R. Anderson, "Personality and Civic Engagement: An Integrative Framework for the Study of Trait Effects on Political Behavior," *American Political Science Review* 104 (2010): 85–110.

20. M. V. Hibbing, M. Ritchie, and M. R. Anderson, "Personality and Political Discussion," *Political Behavior* 33 (2011): 601–624.

21. A. J. Bloeser, C. McCurley, and J. J. Mondak, "Jury Service as Civic Engagement: Determinants of Jury Summons Compliance," *American Politics Research* 40 (2012): 179–204.

22. B. J. Dietrich, S. Lasley, J. J. Mondak, M. L. Remmel, and J. Turner, "Personality and Legislative Politics: The Big Five Trait Dimensions among US State Legislators," *Political Psychology* 33 (2012): 195–210.

23. J. J. Mondak and D. Canache, "Personality and Political Culture in the American States," *Political Research Quarterly* 67 (2014): 26–41.

24. A. S. Gerber, G. A. Huber, D. Doherty, C. M. Dowling, "Personality and Political Attitudes: Relationships across Issue Domains and Political Contexts," *American Political Science Review* 104 (2010): 111–133.

25. A. S. Gerber, G. A. Huber, D. Doherty, C. M. Dowling, C. Raso, and S. E. Ha, "Personality Traits and Participation in Political Processes," *Journal of Politics* 73 (2011): 692–706.

26. A. S. Gerber, G. A Huber, D. Doherty, and C. M. Dowling, "Personality Traits and the Consumption of Political Information," *American Politics Research* 39 (2011): 32–84.

27. A. S. Gerber, G. A. Huber, D. Doherty, and C. M. Dowling, "Disagreement and the Avoidance of Political Discussion: Aggregate Relationships and Differences across Personality Traits," *American Journal of Political Science* 56 (2012): 849–874.

28. See Federico, this volume.

29. See, for example, D. R. Carney, J. T. Jost, S. D. Gosling, and J. Potter, "The Secret Lives of Liberals and Conservatives: Personality Profiles, Interaction Styles, and the Things They Leave Behind," *Political Psychology* 29 (2008): 807–840; R. Riemann, C. Grubich, S. Hempel, S. Mergl, and M. Richter, "Personality and Attitudes towards Current Political Topics," *Personality and Individual Differences* 15 (1993): 313–321; Gerber et al. "Personality and Political Attitudes"; Mondak *Personality and the Foundations of Political Behavior*; Mondak and Halperin "A Framework for the Study of Personality and Political Behavior."

30. Dietrich et al. "Personality and Legislative Politics."

31. Mondak *Personality and the Foundations of Political Behavior*.

32. G. Caprara, M. Vecchione, and S. H. Schwartz, "Meditational Role of Values in Linking Personality Traits to Political Orientation," *Asian Journal of Social Psychology* 12 (2009): 82–94.

33. See, for example, Mondak, *Personality and the Foundations of Political Behavior*, 135–139.

34. Riemann et al., "Personality and Attitudes towards Current Political Topics."

35. J. M. Cullen, L. W. Wright, and M. Alessandri, "The Personality Variable Openness to Experience as it Relates to Homophobia," *Journal of Homosexuality* 42 (2002): 119–134.

36. R. R. McCrae, P. T. Costa, Jr., T. A. Martin, V. E. Oryol, I. G. Senin, and C. O'Cleirigh, "Personality Correlates of HIV Stigmatization in Russia and the United States," *Journal of Research in Personality* 41 (2007): 190–196.

37. P. T. Costa, Jr., P. J. Fagan, R. L. Piedmont, Y. Ponticas, and T. N. Wise, "The Five-Factor Model of Personality and Sexual Functioning in Outpatient Men and Women," *Psychiatric Medicine* 10 (1992): 199–215.

38. The survey was administered between March 17 and March 29, 2010. It is the U.S. portion of the 2010 AmericasBarometer project. Other surveys were administered as part of this project in an additional two dozen nations in the Americas. In most nations, face-to-face interviews were conducted.

39. The original TIPI has a readability score of 41.7, and a readability level (the expected number of years of education needed to understand a passage) of 9.2. Our revised measure has a readability score of 50.4 and a readability level of 8.4. The survey was, of course, translated into several languages in order to be administered in nations throughout the Americas.

40. In addition to the Big Five variables, the statistical models we estimate include four control variables: the respondent's sex (1 if female, 0 if male), whether the respondent is an African-American (1 if yes, 0 if no), whether the respondent is Hispanic (1 if yes, 0 if no), and the respondent's age.

41. All estimates are calculated for a hypothetical respondent who is a white male, age 40, and who has average values on the other personality traits.

42. Similar tests using data from a 2006 survey are reported in Mondak, *Personality and the Foundations of Political Behavior* 137–139, with focus on opinion regarding the PATRIOT Act, the Iraq War, abortion, tax cuts, and illegal immigration.

Chapter 9

No Longer "Beyond our Scope"

The Biological and Non-Conscious Underpinnings of Public Opinion

*Frank J. Gonzalez, Kevin B. Smith,
and John R. Hibbing*

Take a minute to think about your views on some prominent issues in contemporary American politics—healthcare, military intervention in the Middle East, affirmative action, or capital punishment, just to name a few. Whatever your views on these hotly contested issues, why do you suppose you have the attitudes that you do? As you have seen in the other chapters of this volume, scholars of public opinion typically attempt to answer questions like this by recruiting appropriate samples of the population and then preparing and administering carefully worded survey items that require respondents to "self-report" their attitudes, experiences, and inferences. For example, a survey respondent might report that he or she supports capital punishment and came to this opinion because of an influential parent or clergyperson.

Surveys are a powerful and tremendously valuable method of ascertaining the public's opinions as well as the reasons particular opinions are held. We find surveys essential in our own research. Still, surveys have an obvious, inherent, unavoidable limitation: they are only as good as the ability of respondents to self-report accurately. If respondents prevaricate, forget, or simply do not have access to the information being requested, the answers they provide as well as any subsequent analyses of those answers will be incomplete and misleading. As many students of public opinion have noted, survey responses are often distorted due to the fear of displaying socially unacceptable views, the desire to give the false impression that one cares deeply about politics, or the compulsion to give an answer other than "I don't know".[1]

For quite some time, survey researchers made two assumptions regarding these potential problems. First, that it is impossible or at least unrealistic to secure information based on something other than self-report; and second, that although self-reports might miss a little—perhaps a few people claim to vote regularly, to hold racially sensitive attitudes, or to know why they hold the attitudes they do when in truth they do not—they are largely accurate. As it turns out, both assumptions are incorrect. It is now possible and realistic to tap into aspects of the public's political mood that do not reside in conscious awareness and mounting empirical research demonstrates that conscious, "self-reportable" attitudes and inferences are only a small part of the picture. Who we are politically is shaped by forces of which we are unaware. Because of these forces, we are often blind to the sources of our attitudes and unaware of certain attitudes altogether. Our political opinions, therefore, consist of elements that we are not able to report to ourselves let alone to others.

This book is entitled "New Directions in Public Opinion" and one important new direction involves employing techniques capable of tapping those elements of public opinion that cannot be solicited by surveys. In this chapter, we address biological conditions that quite often do not enter conscious awareness but still have clear relevance for public opinion. It is our belief that collecting biological information alongside traditional survey self-reports makes possible a more complete picture of public opinion. We focus here on five general aspects of biology: genetics, electrodermal response, endocrines, directed attention, and neuroscience. Before turning to a discussion of these five areas and their relevance to public opinion, we set the stage by describing the importance of non-conscious information processing and by explaining the nature of biology as it pertains to politics.

It's Not Up to You; It's Up to Your Brain: Unconscious Processes and Decision-Making

Consider all of the information that you are processing right now—everything you are seeing, tasting, smelling, feeling, and hearing. Next, consider that only a small percentage of the information that the brain processes actually reaches conscious awareness.[2] In other words, most of the information obtained influences the mind and body in ways of which the individual being influenced is unaware. To make matters worse, humans are programmed to believe that their conscious awareness is the only game in town and that if we do not consciously know about something then that something could not be important. Psychologist Stephen Pinker refers to this feature of the human brain as the "baloney generator."[3]

Neuroscientist David Eagleman explains that at any given moment, the "self" exists in multitudes—various subsystems of the brain work rigorously to move the body toward action—but that people interpret their actions as products of a singular, conscious self.[4] The statement, "I just had a great idea," is more accurately worded, "a set of processes in my brain, most of which I was unaware of, just led me to this idea." As touched upon in the previous chapter, some use the metaphors of "System 1" thinking and "System 2" thinking to distinguish between thinking that is fast, emotional, and based on intuition (System 1) and thinking that is slow, deliberate, and based on logic (System 2).[5] One crucial aspect of this framework is that the two systems often run together—System 2 can shape System 1 and most System 2 thinking originates in System 1—but people typically minimize or deny the role of System 1 processes and then use System 2 to construct rationalizations for whatever decision was made.

One clear example of the "post hoc" rationalization of the conscious mind occurs in patients with anosognosia (denial of paralysis). Certain recently paralyzed individuals reject the notion that they are indeed unable to move—sometimes claiming they don't feel like moving and other times even experiencing the illusion of limb movement.[6] Neuroscientist Vilayanur S. Ramachandran points out that these individuals truly believe they are not paralyzed and he goes on to demonstrate that by stimulating the part of the brain associated with interpreting physical sensation these patients can be made to "remember" that they are paralyzed.[7] Particular parts of the brain construct stories that may or may not be true but that maintain consistency, and for individuals with anosognosia, the most efficient way to accomplish this feat is to fabricate a reality in which they can still move. Individuals with anosognosia are far from the only people to believe this kind of blatantly false rationalization. Most individuals believe that their attitudes toward issues such as universal healthcare or gun regulation must be products of deliberate, System 2 thinking rather than the evolutionarily-based instincts found in System 1. In truth, such notions are more wishful thinking than empirical reality and non-conscious System 1 processes heavily influence even political and moral judgments.

Seemingly irrelevant contextual factors have been found to alter politically relevant opinions and actions. For example, individuals placed in messy, foul-smelling rooms render sterner moral judgments than those in neat, clean environments.[8] When people are reminded of diseases they are more likely to oppose gay marriage.[9] People placed in a hot room are more likely to believe in global warming than those in rooms of normal temperature.[10] Individuals whose polling place is in a school rather than a church are more likely to vote for proposals to fund public education.[11] As a final example, it is even the case that when judges have not had a break in several hours they dole out harsher sentences than they do when they have just had refreshments.[12] The interesting aspect of all these situations is that the people involved vigorously deny that factors such as the cleanliness of the room or the nature of the voting place altered their decisions on such weighty matters in any way, shape, or form. For most, this assumption is wrong—their baloney generators are hard at work.

Milton Lodge and Charles Taber have done much to explicate the importance of non-conscious processes in the formation of political attitudes. They propose that all salient political thoughts and actions consist of both affective and cognitive components.[13] Political opinions, they argue, arise from interactions between people's automatic, non-conscious responses to political objects and their deliberate, conscious thoughts that develop in reaction to their automatic responses to the object. Lodge and Taber emphasize the primacy, or dominance, of affect over cognition, showing in various experiments that a) emotional stimuli shown subliminally (i.e., faster than can be consciously perceived) influence political attitudes, b) affect is contagious—in that emotional primes that are unrelated to the political object, when shown subliminally, can influence political attitudes, c) feelings toward one political object can easily transfer to related political objects even without any conscious association between the two, and d) the non-conscious, automatic feelings that people have toward political objects lead people to seek out information that reaffirms their preexisting feelings and beliefs while ignoring information contrary to their preexisting feelings and beliefs. The ongoing research by Lodge and Taber indicates that political attitudes and beliefs, despite traditionally being thought of as consciously-formed, deliberate, and even logical, are far from immune to the uncontrolled, automatic processes at work outside of consciousness.

Integrating the Biological and the Political

If some of the factors that shape people's political opinions are hidden from conscious awareness, how is it possible to learn about these factors? As it turns out, these forces are evident—albeit imperfectly—in various indicators of people's biological states. The biological body responds even when the conscious mind is unaware that it has responded. By measuring these biological forces, researchers can acquire information on the non-conscious features of public opinion. Biology, however, as it pertains to social and political behavior, is often misunderstood; therefore, before describing individual biological measures, we explain the manner in which biology and politics connect.

Human beings are organic, carbon-based organisms that constantly adjust to the environment. Differences between people in the biological traits they have inherited, as well as in the biological traits that have been shaped by their environment, structure the manner in which people respond to various stimuli. As a result of differences in biological predispositions and differences in politically relevant life experiences, individuals form their own political attitudes and behavioral patterns. This all sounds far too abstract so we now make it more concrete with a figure and further explanation.

The accompanying figure contains two panels that are designed to show the central differences between traditional, conscious and situationally-determined views of public opinion (the top panel) and biologically informed, non-consciously predisposed conceptions of public opinion (the bottom panel). In both panels, the human condition is represented by a rectangle, with time represented over the course of the life span from left to right. In the top panel, the politically relevant part of the human condition consists entirely of those life events that have been incorporated into conscious awareness. This is a "thin" conception of the human condition in that to understand people's politics all that needs to be known is their early (e.g., parental socialization) and later (e.g., a news program on the pros and cons of the Affordable Care Act) politically relevant life events and experiences, perhaps along with their general life situation (gender, age, education, income, etc.). As such, whenever new life events come along (the arrows at the bottom), they quite directly translate into political beliefs and actions (the top arrows). Nothing that is not conscious or not overtly political "gets in the way" of this translation. In this traditional view, the human mind and body are treated as parts of a largely uninteresting black box and there is no necessity to peer inside at the biological, cognitive, and deep psychological features of that box.

Contrast the traditional model in the upper panel with the lower panel, representing our preferred, biologically informed model. In the lower panel,

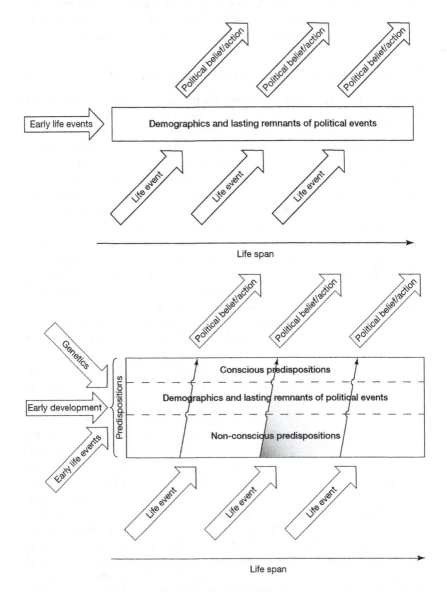

Figure 9.1 Upper Panel: Traditional View of Public Opinion. Lower Panel: Biologically Informed View of Public Opinion.

the box representing individual humans is now much thicker, consisting of non-conscious as well as conscious factors and also consisting of forces that are neither overtly political nor sociodemographic (e.g., personality traits and genetically influenced characteristics). In this model, each individual's set of predispositions serves as a unique prism that bends life events in a certain fashion. The very same life event will be experienced by different people in quite different ways and will, as a result, translate into distinct political beliefs and actions. Predispositions can be changed by life experiences (as indicated by the altered shading subsequent to the middle life event) but change is difficult because biological predispositions, while not "determined" by genetics, have by definition become physiologically instantiated and are therefore resistant to short-term alterations. Predispositions are not immutable but they are inertial. As a result, it is rare—though certainly not unheard of—for people over age 30 to alter fundamentally and permanently their political worldview.[14]

Note that nature versus nurture is not the issue here. Biology is much more than genetics, and no geneticist believes that genes work in isolation from the environment. Like all organisms, humans are built to respond to environmental stimuli. In fact, when humans are placed in situations where they receive minimal environmental input (known as sensory deprivation) highly abnormal responses are noted because processing environmental inputs is what humans do.[15] In other words, biology plays an important role in forming public opinion. We now go into more detail on five aspects of biologically-based and politically relevant predispositions, beginning with genetics.

Genetics and Politics

Biology may be about much more than genetics but the potential role of genetic variation in explaining the different political opinions individuals hold seems to be the element of biology and politics that most entrances and, we have found, occasionally enrages people. To many observers, it seems far-fetched that political opinions could be anything other than learned. How could an opinion be encoded in the biological material that is passed from parent to offspring? Still, the range of traits capable of being transmitted to offspring biologically should not be underestimated. Attitudes, predispositions, and opinions can be passed along from one generation to the next without any learning. This is known as heritability. The question becomes whether heritability is evident in humans for political opinions. The methodologies employed for heritability studies in animals like mice (e.g., selective breeding) are, for good reason, unavailable for studying humans, and so researchers must turn to naturally occurring experiments. Three possibilities have been explored: adoption studies, naturally occurring genetic variation between siblings, and twin studies.

The logic behind adoption studies is straightforward. Children who have been raised by parents who provided their genetic heritage cannot reveal much about the role of socialization versus genetics because these forces cannot be pulled apart. But when, because of an adoption, the offspring is reared by parents who did not provide the child's genetic material it becomes possible to partition influence. A recent study employing adoption data from a large registry in Sweden showed that, even controlling for the influence of the adoptive parents, the political orientations of the biological parents were relevant to the offspring (despite the fact that in most of these cases, the offspring ceased having contact with the birth parents at the age of just a few months and sometimes only a few weeks). The political orientations of the adoptive parents mattered too, of course, but the results of adoption studies, in indicating the relevance of birth parents, make it clear that learning is not the entire story even in the area of politics.[16]

A more complicated procedure also indicates that political views are heritable. On average, any two full sibling pairs share 50 percent of their genetic heritage; but this is just an average and it turns out some full siblings share as much as 62 percent of their genetic heritage and some as little as 38 percent. Scholars have reasoned that if a trait (height, for example) is heritable, sibling pairs closer to the 62 percent figure should be more similar on that trait than sibling pairs closer to the 38 percent figure. This turned out to be the case for height, and when these procedures were applied to political opinions, a significant degree of heritability is again found.[17]

The most common technique for assessing political heritability in humans involves twins. What renders this technique capable of assessing heritability is the fact that there are two very different types of twin pairs. Monozygotic (MZ, sometimes called identical) twins form in a single zygote and later split to form two embryos, and thus share nearly 100 percent of their genetic material. Dizygotic (DZ, sometime called fraternal) twins form from separate zygotes and share, on average and just like any other non-MZ full-sibling pair, 50 percent of their genetic material. The logic behind twin studies is that if a trait is heritable, it should be shared more often by MZ than DZ twins. The methodological techniques used in these analyses all essentially compare the degree to which MZ twins' political attitudes are correlated to the degree to which DZ twins' political attitudes are correlated. With this information, it is possible to parse out variability in a given trait (in this case, political attitudes) into 1) variability due to genetic heritability, 2) variability due to the common environment between twins, and 3) variability left unexplained by the model. In the end, these techniques yield estimates of the proportion of the trait that is explained by each of these three sources of variability. So, for example, a heritability estimate of .30 would suggest that 30 percent of the variation in that trait can be attributed to genetic inheritance.[18]

Numerous studies have employed twins to estimate the heritability of political opinions and tendencies,[19] and the consistent finding is that MZ twins are more politically similar than DZ twins, with heritability estimates roughly in the range of .25 to .45 (the remainder—somewhere between .55 and .75— would be attributable to environmental factors or simply unexplained). The conclusion of twin studies is that views on specific political issues, general political ideology, and tendencies to participate in politics are all heritable to a point and therefore are not entirely socialized.

These findings are believable in that other characteristics, such as personality traits and cognitive tendencies, generate similar estimates of heritability. Still, they have generated substantial controversy. Some critics raise a simple concern: might it be possible that MZ twins not only are more similar genetically but also are treated more similarly and, if they are treated more similarly, might it not be the case that this more similar treatment is the reason for the greater similarity of MZ twins relative to DZ twins?[20] This reflects a concern over what is referred to in genetics as the Equal Environments Assumption (EEA).

Numerous researchers have attempted to assess whether or not a more similar environment is the sole reason for the greater similarity of MZ twins on a variety of traits—i.e., whether or not the EEA holds—and most of them conclude that heritability is in fact important. For example, heritability estimates are similar for twins raised together and twins raised apart, and personality and cognitive differences between MZ and DZ twins persist even among twins whose zygosity has been miscategorized at birth (some parents think their twins are MZs when they are really DZs). Further, MZ twins' greater contact with one another can be the cause rather than the result of environmental similarities (e.g., if both are musically gifted from birth it is likely that they will both spend time around music and musicians), and similarity between MZ twins actually increases as they get older and continue living apart, thereby experiencing less common environments.[21] One study even showed that DZ twins in extremely similar environments are still much less politically similar as adults than MZ twins who were in very different environments.[22] Any way you cut it, genetics appears to play a role in shaping political views. Some researchers are even taking the next step and attempting to identify the specific genes that may account for these relationships.[23]

As stressed above, however, genetics is only one of the elements shaping the biological predispositions that convert individuals' life events into their political beliefs and actions (see Figure 9.1). Besides genetic analyses, most of the pertinent techniques for gauging biological processes involve aspects of human physiology. Since physiology is not something typically covered in courses on public opinion, we offer a few background comments before discussing several specific physiological measures.

Physiology is a broad concept that spans any physical and/or chemical processes occurring in the body. Conscious movements such as lifting a book, reaching out to open a door, or delivering a roundhouse kick all involve physiological processes—but so do non-conscious activities such as digestion and regulation of body temperature. Thinking, daydreaming, and imagining also rely on physiological processes, as do social interactions. Suppose someone cuts you off on the road without using a turn signal. Your reaction probably will not be based on thought alone—perhaps your heart races, your palms sweat. These particular physiological processes are relatively noticeable but with the appropriate equipment it is possible to measure the most subtle non-conscious physiological changes that can shape people's political opinions and behaviors. We will describe four such techniques.

Electrodermal Activity and Politics

The human nervous system consists of several parts. Here, our focus is on the sympathetic nervous system (SNS), also called the "fight or flight" system. The job of the SNS is to mobilize energy-expending reactions in response to threat, stress, or arousal. So when people encounter something threatening, exciting, or generally arousing, the sympathetic nervous system prepares the body for action by increasing blood movement toward relevant muscles, boosting heart and breathing rates, and opening sweat glands, to mention only a few of many changes. By measuring activity in these systems when the body is exposed to certain stimuli, researchers can identify the degree to which a given individual is physiologically responsive to these stimuli.

The most accepted and widely used measure of sympathetic nervous system activation is known as electrodermal activity (EDA). One of the most widely known effects of increases in sympathetic nervous system activity is perspiration. This is what allows us to measure EDA. Sweat glands can be thought of as tiny straws that draw moisture to the surface of the skin and as sweat is mostly water, and as more of those straws open and fill with sweat, the electrical resistance of the skin falls. The basic principle at work here is the same as putting a hair dryer in a bath tub. The hair dryer will not conduct an electrical current across the tub when it's empty, but fill it with water and get ready for a shock. Taking EDA measurements involves nothing quite so dramatic. The most common approach is to put two sensors on a subject's palm or fingers and pass a very small electrical current between those two sensors in order to measure how electrical conductance rises or falls in response to various stimuli. That rise or fall in conductance properties measures increases and decreases in SNS activation, thus allowing investigators to capture the extent to which individuals vary in their physiological responses. For decades, EDA has been employed to measure emotional arousal of which subjects may not be consciously aware.

When shown pictures of undesirable images such as a dangerous animal, a house on fire, or a person with a mouthful or worms, some individuals experience a major elevation in their electrodermal activity but others register barely any change. If the model pictured in Panel B of Figure 9.1 is correct, these different physiological predispositions could help to shape each individual's thoughts and actions—even as they pertain to politics. Evidence suggests this is in fact the case. People who tend to have the greatest physiological responses to negative situations in the environment tend to be the same ones who are the most eager to support public policies designed to mitigate perceived threats—

policies such as increased defense spending, harsh punishment for criminals, and restrictions on immigration.[24]

Diana Mutz and Byron Reeves offer another and quite different demonstration of the value of measuring electrodermal activity. They presented participants with videos of political exchanges that were either civil or not civil. In a clear demonstration that politics and physiology are closely related, the average electrodermal activity of those viewing the uncivil exchange was significantly higher than those viewing the civil exchange.[25] Viewing these two studies in tandem, the evidence suggests that baseline physiological predispositions affect political opinions but also that physiological characteristics can be altered, if only temporarily, by the nature of political events such as whether they are civil or not. Examining physiological processes such as electrodermal activity makes it possible to see a side of public opinion that is distinct from that revealed in self-reports and can even alter theoretical understandings of public opinion.[26] But electrodermal activity is only one small aspect of human physiology.

Endocrines and Politics

Another approach to assessing an individual's physiological predispositions and responses involves measuring levels of various chemical substances found in the body. These substances include compounds known as endocrines, hormones, and neurotransmitters, and several of them can be ascertained by careful analysis of saliva samples. All individuals have baseline levels of these substances but variation in levels occurs from person to person and from situation to situation. Some levels change markedly with the time of day; others spike under certain situations, such as stress. In the brain, levels rise and fall in response to environmental stimuli and trigger communication across neurons that ultimately results in thoughts, feelings, and behaviors. These chemical substances have been shown to have significant impacts on social behaviors such as love, hate, aggression, hunger, sexual arousal, metabolism, and, as illustrated in the example below, politics.[27]

Various behaviors closely tied to politics have been shown to be associated with naturally occurring chemical substances, including oxytocin, which is associated with trust and ethnocentrism (the tendency to perceive one's own ethnic or cultural group as central and superior to other groups),[28] and cortisol, which is associated with stress.[29] Another hormone often associated with politics is testosterone. Testosterone is a type of steroid hormone called an androgen that has been implicated in a variety of social behaviors, including aggression,[30] sexual behavior,[31] and social hierarchy.[32] Further, during intergroup competition, testosterone levels rise among winners and fall among losers.[33] In a somewhat parallel fashion, the authors of a study on the 2008 Presidential election, in which Democrat Barack Obama defeated Republican John McCain, showed that upon learning that Barack Obama had won, the testosterone levels of Democrats did not change but the testosterone levels of Republicans decreased significantly,[34] almost as if their status in the social hierarchy had been diminished. In this and countless other ways, variations in the chemical soup present in people's interstitial fluids and circulatory system capture aspects of their predispositions as well as their responses to political situations and stimuli that cannot be known if the focus is solely on survey self-reports.

Directed Attention and Politics

The influence of physiological processes on political opinions and behaviors can be studied without collecting saliva samples or using sensors to measure electrodermal activity. Another way is to analyze the movements of bodily features such as muscles and eyes. Electromyography (EMG) is a procedure by which sensors are able to detect electrical signals produced by muscle movements, even when those muscle movements are so slight they are not visible to the naked eye. EMG is commonly used to measure the activation of facial muscles that are associated with particular emotional states.

Even when frowns or smiles are not actually visible, the muscles that make those facial expressions may still activate. Facial expressions "leak" emotional states, and some of that leak can be picked up by EMG, even if someone is consciously putting on their best poker face or experiencing an emotional reaction that they are not consciously aware of. By placing sensors on particular facial muscles, researchers can measure how people affectively react to various stimuli. How might this help us measure public opinion? As an example, consider a controversial issue like affirmative action. There is a lively debate over whether opposition to affirmative action policies is rooted in racial attitudes or in genuine, principled opposition to public policies that assist people on the basis of race.[35]

Complicating resolution to this debate is the fact that racial attitudes are typically measured using standard survey batteries. As it has become increasingly unacceptable to openly express racial bias, responses to survey questions often reflect perceptions of what is socially acceptable rather than true racial attitudes.[36] Aside from conscious misrepresentation, there is also considerable evidence suggesting that individuals have implicit racial attitudes that are unlikely to be picked up even when people genuinely believe they are reporting their attitudes accurately.[37] EMG offers a useful solution to this difficult measurement problem. EMG activity in response to racial stimuli has been shown to predict attitudes and behaviors on racial policies.[38] People may be able to mask true racial attitudes when responding to survey questions; it is much more difficult to mask involuntary affective responses "leaking" from the face.

Another information-laden physical movement involves the eyes. Machines called eyetrackers are now available to record and quantify all aspects of eye movement. When something in the external environment warrants attention, people are likely to focus on it quickly and to dwell on it for some time. Psychologists have demonstrated that on average people tend to direct their attention to aspects of the environment that are negative,[39] novel[40] or vivid.[41] However, people vary widely in the extent to which they attend to particular types of stimuli.

With regard to political opinions, it seems likely that individuals who devote a great deal of attention to negative situations will be more likely to prefer public policies that might be thought to assist in protecting against those negative situations. To be more specific, it could be hypothesized that those attending to the negative would prefer safe, orderly, and uncontaminated environments and that they, therefore, would support policies that promote traditional lifestyles and a strong defense both against out-groups and in-group norm violators. On the other hand, those who devote significant attentional resources to positive aspects of the environment are likely to prefer a society in which new experiences, change, and openness are embraced.

Empirical research has largely confirmed these expectations. Michael Dodd and colleagues showed participants four images at a time on a screen—some positive and some negative. Participants were fitted with an eyetracker to detect which of the images participants were attending to. The results showed that, though negative images were given more attention than positive images across virtually all participants (thus confirming an overall negativity bias), the degree of negativity bias for those favoring policies directed at security and tradition (sometimes called social conservatives) was much greater than it was for those supporting policies consistent with social liberalism.[42]

The implications of these findings for students of public opinion, particularly when combined with the findings regarding individual variations in electrodermal response, are substantial. Physiological predispositions to respond and attend to certain aspects of the environment construct people's understanding of the world in which they live. Those responding and attending more to negative aspects of the environment in some respects experience a different world than those responding and attending more to positive aspects of the environment. In this vein, differences between liberals and conservatives are less the product of irrational fear, naiveté, or willful ignorance, and more the product of seeing and experiencing the world differently—tuning in to different but equally real (to them) aspects of the environment. One ideology is not necessarily better than the other because each makes sense given differing physiological predispositions.[43]

Modern techniques, however, make it possible to go beyond external indicators of physiology all the way into the internal operations of the brain. Neuroscience affords the opportunity to alter significantly the study of public opinion, allowing researchers to record not just what people self-report but also what is going on inside their heads.

Neuroscience and Politics

The control center of the physiological and psychological processes discussed to this point is a 3-pound, 6-inch long hunk of meat called the brain, which also happens to be one of the most complex structures in the known universe. Consistent with the "thin" conception of human variation, the traditional view was that environmental inputs and situations were the key so peering inside the brain was unnecessary—a useful belief since for most of human existence it has been impossible to view the inner workings of the brain. Relatively recent developments in technology, however, make it possible to catch a glimpse of the extremely complex processes occurring in the brain. Despite being a relatively new field, neuroscience has shed light on many processes in the brain—several of which are relevant to political attitudes and behaviors.

The ability to obtain quantitative measurements of brain activity are due mainly to advances in technology. The most discussed method for studying brain processes is functional Magnetic Resonance Imaging (fMRI). Because activity in specific regions of the brain is accompanied by increases in oxygenated blood and because oxygenated blood contains iron, an fMRI, which is essentially an extremely powerful magnet, can pick up on changes in brain activation across regions.[44] Various other methods can be used to peer inside the brain and have yielded valuable insights,[45] but fMRIs are the most commonly used in studies of social behavior, so we discuss how they have begun to be applied to understand the undergirding of political opinions.

Perhaps a good place to start is with the question: does brain activity differ between Democrats and Republicans? Schreiber and colleagues conducted a study suggesting the answer is "yes." In the study, individuals known to be either Republicans or Democrats were placed in an fMRI and asked to partake in a simple, risk-taking task. Among Republicans, the results showed that decision-making during the task was associated with heightened amygdala activation, perhaps suggesting externally-oriented evaluations of risk, but among Democrats decision-making was associated with heightened insula activation, which the authors interpret as suggesting internally-oriented evaluations of risk. In other words, when faced with a risky decision, Republicans may tend to see the risk in terms of external threats and consequences, while Democrats may tend to see the risk in terms of the negative internal feelings associated with the decision.[46]

This is not the place to discuss the functions of the regions of the brain just mentioned—besides, each brain region engages in multiple activities. What these studies do show is that merely by observing differences from person to person in brain activation patterns or structure, it is possible to make reasonably accurate predictions regarding the political opinions of the owners of the brain in question. The fact that such predictions are possible solely on the basis of observations of the inside of the brain when not engaged in overtly political tasks is further indication that political opinions are connected to biological characteristics.

Concerns with Employing Biology to Understand Public Opinion

Many students of public opinion harbor understandable reservations about according biology a greater role in the study of public opinion. In closing, we briefly address four of the most common reservations. The first centers on the belief that this new direction implies that political opinions are predetermined by biology and are therefore impervious to persuasion and new information. The key response to this reservation, which cannot be overemphasized, is that being biologically *predisposed* is not the same thing as being biologically *predetermined*. Genetics and other biological forces nudge some people one way or another but these forces hardly determine from birth whether every individual is going to be a raging liberal or a diehard conservative. Rather, political persuasion can be effective but individuals with clear biological predispositions will find it more difficult to budge from their established belief set. The real world, with its surplus of ideologically rigid individuals, seems consistent with this tenet of biology and politics.

The second common reservation stems from the belief that politics is too rich, idiosyncratic, and culturally variable to be explained by relatively universal biological variables. It is true that specific political issues come and go and that terms such as "liberal" and "conservative" mean different things at different times and in different cultures, but these evolving labels and "issues-of-the-day" can be seen as manifestations of bedrock dilemmas of politics which must be resolved in any human society and social group. These dilemmas include the structure of leadership and hierarchy, the distribution of resources, security from out-group threats, treatment of in-group norm violators, and attitudes toward traditional approaches as opposed to new lifestyles. The previous chapter explained various personality factors that are associated with these sorts of bedrock dilemmas. It is the enduring nature and stability of these bedrock dilemmas (rather than specific issues) that ensures that biological predispositions, in the same vein as stable personality factors, have the potential to shape public opinion. As Ralph Waldo Emerson put it, "the two parties which divide the state, the party of conservatism and that of innovation . . . have disputed possession of the world ever since it was made."[47]

The third reservation is perhaps the most serious and involves the potential normative implications of recognizing biology's role in politics. Some fear that this recognition could lead to intolerance (or worse). They point to the fact that Hitler and the Nazis believed that biology shaped people's behaviors and attitudes and believed that those whose behaviors and attitudes were deemed undesirable should be removed. In point of fact, recognizing that biological differences at the individual (not group) level shape behaviors and attitudes has typically led to significantly *more* tolerance. Hitler's notion that all members of any large ethnic group (Jews or so-called Aryans) have essentially identical behaviorally relevant biological traits is wildly inaccurate. We now know that within-group variation far exceeds across-group variation. Today, the ability of a biologically-informed understanding of social traits to *increase* tolerance is especially evident with regard to sexual orientation, where those who believe it to be environmentally determined are significantly less tolerant than those who believe it to be biologically influenced. Acknowledging a role for biology in political opinions is more likely to lead to greater tolerance of those with whom we disagree politically. After all, if a portion of people's political views is rooted in their biological predispositions, it becomes more difficult to view political opponents with deep hostility.

The fourth and final reservation concerning this new direction for public opinion research shifts from the normative to the practical. Some students of public opinion worry that employing biological techniques will be too difficult and expensive, and will require acquisition of too many additional skill sets. To this we only say that costs of the necessary equipment are coming down quickly, access is becoming easier, and that becoming conversant with new techniques is exciting and rewarding. Doing so opens doors to interdisciplinary collaboration with scholars from various fields. These multidisciplinary teams are increasingly the norm in other sciences and should become so in the social sciences as well. Besides, if the only justification for doing things the way they have always been done is that it is cheap and does not require learning new things, perhaps the justification is not all that compelling.

Conclusion

The "new direction" in the study of public opinion that we have outlined in this chapter does not entail dropping survey-based methods in order to move entirely toward biology-based methods. Incorporating biology into the study of public opinion should serve as a complement to survey self-reports but it is an important complement since the belief that everything relevant to people's political opinions takes place in the realm of conscious thought is simply untenable in the modern era. In truth, students of public opinion have long recognized this fact. In his pivotal book, John Zaller mentions that "the sources of variability in individuals' political predispositions," some of which are dependent on "inherited and acquired personality factors," are "beyond the scope of this book."[48] It can now be said that these predispositions are no longer "beyond our scope." All that is required is the willingness to travel in a new direction.

Notes

1. Phillip E. Converse, "The Nature of Belief Systems in Mass Publics," in *Ideology and Discontent*, ed. D. E. Apter (New York: Free Press, 1964), pp. 206–261.
2. David Eagleman, *Incognito: The Secret Lives of the Brain* (New York: Pantheon Books, 2011).
3. Steven Pinker, *The Blank Slate: The Modern Denial of Human Nature* (New York: Penguin, 2002).

4. Eagleman, *Incognito: The Secret Lives of the Brain*.
5. Daniel Kahneman, *Thinking, Fast and Slow* (New York, NY: Farrar, Straus, and Giroux, 2011).
6. A. Fotopoulou, "Illusions and Delusions in Anosognosia for Hemiplegia: From Motor Predictions to Prior Beliefs," *Brain* 135, no. 5 (2012): 1344–1346.
7. Vilayanur S. Ramachandran, "Anosognosia in Parietal Lobe Syndrome," *Consciousness and Cognition* 4, no. 1 (1995): 22–51.
8. S. Schnall, J. Haidt, G. L. Clore, and A. H. Jordan, "Disgust as Embodied Moral Judgment," *Personality and Social Psychology Bulletin* 34, no. 8 (2008): 1096–1109.
9. J. Faulkner, M. Schaller, J. H. Park, and L. A. Duncan, "Evolved Disease-Avoidance Mechanisms and Contemporary Xenophobic Attitudes," *Group Processes & Intergroup Relations* 7, no. 4 (2004): 333–353.
10. Jane L. Risen and Clayton R. Critcher, "Visceral Fit: While in a Visceral State, Associated States of the World Seem More Likely," *Journal of Personality and Social Psychology* 100, no. 5 (2011): 777–793.
11. Jonah Berger, Marc Meredith, and S. Christian Wheeler, "Contextual Priming: Where People Vote Affects How They Vote," *Proceedings of the National Academy of Sciences* 105, no. 26 (2008): 8846–8849.
12. S. Danziger, J. Levav, and L. Avnaim-Pesso, "Extraneous Factors in Judicial Decisions," *Proceedings of the National Academy of Sciences* 108, no. 17 (2011): 6889–6892.
13. Milton Lodge and Charles S. Taber, *The Rationalizing Voter* (Cambridge: Cambridge University Press, 2013).
14. David O. Sears and Carolyn L. Funk, "Evidence of the Long-Term Persistence of Adults' Political Predispositions," *The Journal of Politics* 61, no. 1 (1999): 1–28.
15. H. Neville, and D. Bavelier, "Human Brain Plasticity: Evidence from Sensory Deprivation and Altered Language Experience," in *Plasticity in the Adult Brain: From Genes to Neurotherapy*, ed. M. A. Hofman, G. J. Boer, A. J. G. D. Holtmaat, E. J. W. Van Someren, J. Verhaagen, and D. F. Swaab, vol. 138 (Amsterdam, The Netherlands: Elsevier Science B. V., 2002), p. 177–188.
16. David Cesarini, Magnus Johannesson, and Sven Oskarsson, "Pre-Birth Factors, Post-Birth Factors, and Voting: Evidence from Swedish Adoption Data," *American Political Science Review* 108, no. 1 (2014): 71–87.
17. Peter M. Visscher, Sarah E. Medland, Manuel A. R. Ferreira, Katherine I. Morley, Gu Zhu, Belinda K. Cornes, Grant W. Montgomery, and Nicholas G. Martin, "Assumption-Free Estimation of Heritability from Genome-Wide Identity-by-Descent Sharing between Full Siblings," *PLOS Genetics* 2, no. 3 (2006): E41.
18. David M. Evans, N.A. Gillespie, and N.G. Martin, "Biometrical Genetics," *Biological Psychology* 61, no. 1 (2002): 33–51.
19. John R. Alford, Carolyn L. Funk, and John R. Hibbing, "Are Political Orientations Genetically Transmitted?" *American Political Science Review* 99, no. 2 (2005): 153–67; N. G. Martin, L. J. Eaves, A. C. Heath, R. Jardine, L. M. Feingold, and H. J. Eysenck, "Transmission of Social Attitudes," *Proceedings of the National Academy of Sciences* 83, no. 12 (1986): 4364–368.
20. Evan Charney, "Genes and Ideologies," *Perspectives on Politics* 6, no. 2 (2008): 299–319.
21. John R. Alford, Carolyn L. Funk, and John R. Hibbing, "Beyond Liberals and Conservatives to Political Genotypes and Phenotypes," *Perspectives on Politics* 6, no. 2 (2008): 321–328; James H. Fowler, Laura A. Baker, and Christopher T. Dawes, "Genetic Variation in Political Participation," *American Political Science Review* 102, no. 2 (2008): 233–248; Peter K. Hatemi, John R. Hibbing, Sarah E. Medland,

Matthew C. Keller, John R. Alford, Kevin B. Smith, Nicholas G. Martin, and Lindon J. Eaves, "Not by Twins Alone: Using the Extended Family Design to Investigate Genetic Influence on Political Beliefs," *American Journal of Political Science* 54, no. 3 (2010): 798–814; Sarah E. Medland, and Peter K. Hatemi, "Political Science, Biometric Theory, and Twin Studies: A Methodological Introduction," *Political Analysis* 17, no. 2 (2009): 191–214.

22. Kevin B. Smith, John R. Alford, Peter K. Hatemi, Lindon J. Eaves, Carolyn Funk, and John R. Hibbing, "Biology, Ideology, and Epistemology: How Do We Know Political Attitudes Are Inherited and Why Should We Care?" *American Journal of Political Science* 56, no. 1 (2011): 17–33.

23. James H. Fowler and Christopher T. Dawes, "Two Genes Predict Voter Turnout," *The Journal of Politics* 70, no. 3 (2008): 579–94; Peter K. Hatemi, Nathan A. Gillespie, Lindon J. Eaves, Brion S. Maher, Bradley T. Webb, Andrew C. Heath, Sarah E. Medland, David C. Smyth, Harry N. Beeby, Scott D. Gordon, Grant W. Montgomery, Ghu Zhu, Enda M. Byrne, and Nicholas G. Martin, "A Genome-Wide Analysis of Liberal and Conservative Political Attitudes," *The Journal of Politics* 73, no. 1 (2011): 271–285; Jaime Settle, Christopher T. Dawes, Nicholas A. Christakis, and James H. Fowler, "Friendships Moderate an Association Between a Dopamine Gene Variant and Political Ideology," *The Journal of Politics* 72, no. 4 (2010): 1189–1198.

24. Douglas R. Oxley, Kevin B. Smith, John R. Alford, Matthew V. Hibbing, Jennifer L. Miller, Mario Scalora, Peter K. Hatemi, and John R. Hibbing, "Political Attitudes Vary with Physiological Traits," *Science* 321, no. 5896 (2008): 1667–1670.

25. Diana C. Mutz, and Byron Reeves, "The New Videomalaise: Effects of Televised Incivility on Political Trust," *American Political Science Review* 99, no. 1 (2005): 1–15.

26. Kevin B. Smith, Douglas R. Oxley, Matthew V. Hibbing, John R. Alford, and John R. Hibbing, "Linking Genetics and Political Attitudes: Reconceptualizing Political Ideology," *Political Psychology* 32, no. 3 (2011): 369–397.

27. Rose McDermott, "Hormones and Politics," in *Man Is by Nature a Political Animal: Evolution, Biology, and Politics*, ed. Peter K. Hatemi and Rose McDermott (Chicago: University of Chicago Press, 2011), pp. 247–260.

28. C. K. W. De Dreu, L. L. Greer, G. A. Van Kleef, S. Shalvi, and M. J. J. Handgraaf, "Oxytocin Promotes Human Ethnocentrism," *Proceedings of the National Academy of Sciences* 108, no. 4 (2011): 1262–1266; Michael Kosfeld, Markus Heinrichs, Paul J. Zak, Urs Fischbacher, and Ernst Fehr, "Oxytocin Increases Trust in Humans," *Nature* 435, no. 7042 (2005): 673–676.

29. Jeffrey A. French, Kevin B. Smith, John R. Alford, Adam Guck, Andrew K. Birnie, and John R. Hibbing, "Cortisol and Politics: Variance in Voting Behavior Is Predicted by Baseline Cortisol Levels," *Physiology and Behavior* 133, no. 22 (2014): 61–67; Steven J. Stanton, Kevin S. Labar, Ekjyot K. Saini, Cynthia M. Kuhn, and Jacinta C. Beehner, "Stressful Politics: Voters' Cortisol Responses to the Outcome of the 2008 United States Presidential Election," *Psychoneuroendocrinology* 35, no. 5 (2010): 768–774; Israel Waismel-Manor, Gal Ifergane, and Hagit Cohen, "When Endocrinology and Democracy Collide: Emotions, Cortisol and Voting at National Elections," *European Neuropsychopharmacology* 21, no. 11 (2011): 789–795.

30. John Archer, "Testosterone and Human Aggression: An Evaluation of the Challenge Hypothesis," *Neuroscience and Biobehavioral Reviews* 30, no. 3 (2006): 319–345.

31. Aaron W. Lukaszewski, and James R. Roney, "Estimated Hormones Predict Women's Mate Preferences for Dominant Personality Traits," *Personality and Individual Differences* 47, no. 3 (2009): 191–196.

32. Theodore D. Kemper, *Social Structure and Testosterone: Explorations of the Socio-bio-social Chain* (New Brunswick: Rutgers University Press, 1990).

33. Michael Elias, "Serum Cortisol, Testosterone, and Testosterone-binding Globulin Responses to Competitive Fighting in Human Males," *Aggressive Behavior* 7, no. 3 (1981): 215–224; Allan Mazur, and Alan Booth, "Testosterone and Dominance in Men," *Behavioral and Brain Sciences* 21, no. 3 (1998): 353–363.

34. Coren L. Apicella, and David Cesarini, "Testosterone and the Biology of Politics: Experimental Evidence from the 2008 Presidential Election," in *Man Is by Nature a Political Animal: Evolution, Biology, and Politics*, ed. Peter K. Hatemi and Rose McDermott (Chicago: University of Chicago Press, 2011), pp. 261–272.

35. Donald Kinder and Tali Mendelberg, "Individualism Reconsidered: Principles and Prejudice in Contemporary American Opinion," in *Racialized Politics: The Debate about Racism in America*, ed. David O. Sears, James Sidanius, and Lawrence Bobo (Chicago: University of Chicago Press, 2000), pp. 44–74; James Sidanius, Felicia Pratto, and Lawrence Bobo, "Racism, Conservatism, Affirmative Action, and Intellectual Sophistication: A Matter of Principled Conservatism or Group Dominance?" *Journal of Personality and Social Psychology* 70, no. 3 (1996): 476–490; Paul M. Sniderman, and Edward G. Carmines, *Reaching Beyond Race* (Cambridge, MA.: Harvard University Press, 1997).

36. Samuel L. Gaertner, and John F. Dovidio, *Reducing Intergroup Bias: The Common Ingroup Identity Model* (Philadelphia, PA: Psychology Press, 2000); Stanley Feldman and Leonie Huddy, "Racial Resentment and White Opposition to Race-Conscious Programs: Principles or Prejudice?" *American Journal of Political Science* 49, no. 1 (2005): 168–183.

37. Anthony G. Greenwald, Debbie E. Mcghee, and Jordan L. K. Schwartz, "Measuring Individual Differences in Implicit Cognition: The Implicit Association Test," *Journal of Personality and Social Psychology* 74, no. 6 (1998): 1464–1480.

38. Michael Dambrun, Gerard Despres, and Serge Guimond, "On the Multifaceted Nature of Prejudice: Psychophysiological Responses to Ingroup and Outgroup Ethnic Stimuli," *Current Research in Social Psychology* 8 (2003): 187–206; E. J. Vanman, J. L. Saltz, L. R. Nathan, and J. A. Warren, "Racial Discrimination by Low-Prejudiced Whites: Facial Movements as Implicit Measures of Attitudes Related to Behavior," *Psychological Science* 15, no. 11 (2004): 711–714.

39. Rachel L. Bannerman, Maarten Milders, and Arash Sahraie, "Attentional Bias to Brief Threat-related Faces Revealed by Saccadic Eye Movements," *Emotion* 10, no. 5 (2010): 733–738.

40. Leslie Zebrowitz Mcarthur and David L. Post, "Figural Emphasis and Person Perception," *Journal of Experimental Social Psychology* 13, no. 6 (1977): 520–535.

41. Michael Lynn, Sharon Shavitt, and Thomas Ostrom, "Effects of Pictures on the Organization and Recall of Social Information," *Journal of Personality and Social Psychology* 49, no. 5 (1985): 1160–1168.

42. Michael D. Dodd, Amanda Balzer, Carly M. Jacobs, Michael W. Gruszczynski, Kevin B. Smith, and John R. Hibbing, "The Political Left Rolls with the Good and the Political Right Confronts the Bad: Connecting Physiology and Cognition to Preferences," *Philosophical Transactions of the Royal Society B: Biological Sciences* 367, no. 1589 (2012): 640–649.

43. John R. Hibbing, Kevin B. Smith, and John R. Alford, *Predisposed: Liberals, Conservatives, and the Biology of Political Differences* (New York, NY: Routledge, 2014).

44. Karl Friston, "Causal Modelling and Brain Connectivity in Functional Magnetic Resonance Imaging," *PLoS Biology* 7, no. 2 (2009): e1000033.

45. David M. Amodio, John T. Jost, Sarah L. Master, and Cindy M. Yee, "Neurocognitive Correlates of Liberalism and Conservatism," *Nature Neuroscience* 10, no. 10 (2007): 1246–1247; John T. Jost and David M. Amodio, "Political Ideology as Motivated Social Cognition: Behavioral and Neuroscientific Evidence," *Motivation and Emotion* 36, no. 1 (2011): 55–64; Ryota Kanai, Tom Feilden, Colin Firth, and Geraint Rees, "Political Orientations Are Correlated with Brain Structure in Young Adults," *Current Biology* 21, no. 8 (2011): 677–680; for a review see Darren Schreiber, "From SCAN to Neuropolitics," in *Man Is by Nature a Political Animal: Evolution, Biology, and Politics*, ed. Peter K. Hatemi and Rose McDermott (Chicago: University of Chicago Press, 2011), pp. 273–299.

46. Darren Schreiber, Greg Fonzo, Alan N. Simmons, Christopher T. Dawes, Taru Flagan, James H. Fowler, and Martin P. Paulus, "Red Brain, Blue Brain: Evaluative Processes Differ in Democrats and Republicans," *PLoS ONE* 8, no. 2 (2013): E52970.

47. Ralph Waldo Emerson, *The Complete Works of Ralph Waldo Emerson: Comprising His Essays, Lectures, Poems, and Orations* (London: Bell & Daldy, 1866).

48. John Zaller, *The Nature and Origins of Mass Opinion* (England: Cambridge University Press, 1992), p. 23; also see David C. Barker and James D. Tinnick, "Competing Visions of Parental Roles and Ideological Constraint," *American Political Science Review* 100, no. 2 (2006): 249–263; Marc J. Hetherington and Jonathan Daniel Weiler, *Authoritarianism and Polarization in American Politics* (New York: Cambridge University Press, 2009).

Chapter 10

The Emotional Foundations of Democratic Citizenship

Ted Brader and Carly Wayne

In a democracy, the people rule. Citizens exercise power over government by choosing leaders in elections and, on some occasions, expressing their preferences on matters of policy directly. The quality of democracy therefore depends not only on how well leaders and political institutions respond to the needs and desires of the people, but also how effectively citizens participate in the process of self-government. A growing body of evidence testifies to the important role emotions play in shaping the ability and motivation of citizens to take part in politics. Fear, anger, enthusiasm, and other emotions affect public opinion by altering whether and how citizens pay attention, learn, think through their decisions, and act on their opinions. This chapter surveys this new evidence on the emotional foundations of democratic citizenship.

Emotions and the Performance of Democratic Citizenship

What does democracy require of citizens? The ideal citizen has been variously envisioned as some combination of vigilant, active, independent, open-minded, informed, thoughtful, tolerant, loyal, and courageous.[1] A substantial portion of public opinion scholarship over the past seventy years has focused, implicitly or explicitly, on how well citizens live up to these expectations. The conclusions have been decidedly mixed, with enough evidence to sustain the views of both optimists and pessimists. The tone on balance tips toward the negative, ranging from alarm and disappointment, on one side, to contentment (things are "good enough") on the other side.

We see such mixed results across many aspects of democratic citizenship. Americans pay only scattered attention to politics, though they occasionally become much more engaged for a limited time or on a particular issue. Their knowledge about public affairs is spotty at best, but many seem capable of learning what they need to know under the right conditions. Opinions on political candidates and policy matters typically exhibit an extraordinary—to some observers, a disturbing—level of loyalty to one's social group, nationality, and especially political party. Yet this loyalty is tempered by some measure of responsiveness to changing circumstances, for example, when governance is lackluster or cherished policies are threatened. Where participation is concerned, some Americans are habitually active while others appear withdrawn from politics entirely, but these general tendencies obscure tremendous fluctuations in participation over time and across situations. All of these conclusions apply not just to Americans, but also to citizens of many democracies around the world.

Scholars have not simply rested on the conclusion that the democratic glass is either half full or half empty. They have sought to identify features of both individuals and the political environment that help explain the better and worse in citizen performance. But we still know relatively little about the motivations that cause a person to react differently across situations or different people to respond differently to the same situation. Emotions turn out to be key motivational forces, capable of (re-)directing human decision making and behavior. Until recently, however, emotions received scant attention from public opinion scholars. But the past fifteen years have witnessed a surge in research suggesting that emotions are indeed a potent force guiding both the formation of opinions and decisions to take political action. This chapter highlights some of what we've learned about the role of emotions in politics.

What Are Emotions?

What we call emotions are, in fact, a complex "syndrome" of reactions to our circumstances that include electrochemical processes in the brain, changes in autonomic and motor systems (e.g., breathing, heart rate, muscle tension, facial expressions), and behavioral impulses. In our everyday lives, we know emotions primarily by our experience of the feeling states that accompany them—our awareness of what it *feels like* to be angry, overjoyed, sad, or frightened—even though emotions occur all of the time without rising to the level of consciousness. In this chapter, we discuss the political implications of a number of discrete emotional reactions such as anger, enthusiasm, fear, pride, shame, guilt, and disgust.

So what is the function of emotions? What purpose do they serve? Emotions are motivational impulses. Our brains monitor the world around us for changes that have relevance for our goals and well-being.[2] These changes in the environment become signals—"appraisals" of our circumstances—that trigger an emotional reaction, reflected in a distinct pattern of changes in our thinking and behavior. Scholars believe emotions evolved as a way to allow reasonably efficient, differentiated responses to the sorts of situations humans (and many other animals) tend to encounter repeatedly. Thus, emotions enable us to adapt our thinking and bodies rapidly to meet the needs of particular situations.

Consider examples for three emotions. When we make progress toward our goals, we feel enthusiastic and energized to keep doing what we've been doing. When something appears that threatens our well-being, we feel afraid, become more alert and focused on the danger, and shift from reliable habits to active reconsideration of our options. When someone puts obstacles between us and something we want (and feel entitled to), we feel angry and are emboldened to challenge and even punish those who stand in our way. Table 10.1 summarizes key appraisals that give rise to these and other emotions as well as some of the patterns of thinking and behavior ("action tendencies") motivated by the emotions.

These three emotions, perhaps because they are such common parts of our experiences, have been studied the most, including by scholars of public opinion. The present chapter, therefore, also focuses heavily on these emotions. These are not, however, the only emotions likely to hold relevance for public opinion: others are sadness, shame, guilt, pride, and disgust. Sadness, for example, stems from our failure to achieve goals and especially the loss of something (or someone) valued. It often causes us to withdraw and spend more time reflecting on the details of a situation. Disgust is a reaction to the presence of noxious conditions (e.g., rotting food, bodily excretions) and seems to have evolved to include both physical and moral impurities. It generates a strong desire to

Table 10.1 Some Appraisals and Action Tendencies of Common Emotions.

Emotion	Appraisals	Action tendencies
Enthusiasm	progress toward goals expectations for reward met/exceeded	continue pursuing goals less effortful thinking greater confidence
Fear/anxiety	threat to well-being uncertainty about outcomes	escape/prevent danger attention on potential danger more effortful thinking avoid risks more open to compromise
Anger	obstacles blocking goals undeserved harm inflicted by others	overcome/remove obstacle punish offender less effortful thinking take risks less open to compromise
Sadness	failure to achieve goals loss of something valued	withdraw more effortful thinking
Disgust	noxious contaminant physical/moral impurity	expel contaminant avoid contact harsh moral judgments
Pride	succeed by own effort/skill meet/exceed social standards	expressive displays maintain/enforce standards
Shame	fail to meet social standards	hide (self/failure) maintain/enforce standards
Guilt	recognize own action as wrong	repair harm done by action

purge the offending substance and thereby purify one's environment. Pride and shame are social emotions that arise when we contemplate how others judge us and how well we live up to the standards of our community. Both emotions motivate us to conform better to the expectations of our group, though pride makes us want to put ourselves on display, while shame makes us want to hide ourselves (or our actions) away. Guilt is also a social emotion that stems from the recognition that our actions are morally wrong (e.g., we hurt others who did not deserve it); it differs from shame principally in that our actions, not ourselves, are deemed to be bad and we are motivated to make amends by repairing the harm that we've done. The rest of the chapter considers what this relatively young, promising area of research has uncovered about the influence of emotions on public opinion and democratic citizenship.

Vigilance and (Selective) Learning about Politics

Emotions help explain why the public pays attention to some issues and events more than others. Because emotions arise from circumstances that are relevant to people, just about any emotion may predict *interest* in a subject. But we expect fear or anxiety to trigger greater attentiveness beyond what routinely interests a person, because it signals the need to deal with a potential threat to the person's safety or well-being.[3] Moreover, fear does not just make a person more attentive in general, but directs attention selectively toward the threat and ways of removing it. This heightened attention, in turn, creates conditions favorable for increased learning by citizens.

The Influence of Emotions on Political Attention and Engagement

Citizens pay more attention to politics during election campaigns, though their attention waxes and wanes from one election to the next and even over the course of a single campaign. Emotions contribute to some of these short-term fluctuations. Drawing heavily on data from the American National Election Studies surveys, Marcus and colleagues have conducted extensive research into the impact of emotions on electoral behavior.[4] Even controlling for long-term levels of engagement with politics, when citizens feel enthusiasm or anxiety (fear) about candidates, they report greater interest in the campaign, care more deeply about the election outcome, and spend more time watching and reading the news.[5] A more nuanced picture of the short-term effects of these emotions emerges from "panel" surveys in which individuals are re-interviewed at multiple points during the campaign. Such surveys can help researchers isolate *changes* in emotions, opinions, and behavior. In this case, the researchers found that enthusiasm produced short-term boosts in citizens' levels of interest and caring, while anxiety provoked greater attention to almost all sources of campaign news coverage.[6]

Other studies also support the notion that negative emotions have a positive impact on interest and attention to politics. Anxiety, for example, awakens greater interest in election campaigns particularly among citizens high in political efficacy—that is, those who feel competent to participate in politics.[7] This mirrors decades of research on the effectiveness of fear appeals in public health and safety campaigns (e.g., targeting seat belt usage, smoking cessation, dental hygiene), showing that fear appeals are more effective when people perceive the recommended actions as likely to work and themselves as capable of carrying out the recommendations.[8] In a study conducted during the build-up to the 2003 Iraq War, Americans who felt anxiety and anger toward terrorists and Saddam Hussein spent more time thinking about the war, talking about the war, and consuming national news.[9] The impact of anxiety on thinking and talking, however, was much larger than the impact of anger.

In a departure from the results discussed so far, a study of the 1996 presidential election found that citizens who felt hopeful about the candidates were more likely to watch TV coverage of the summer party conventions and the fall campaign.[10] The researchers distinguished hope from enthusiasm, as well as from anxiety and anger, in their analyses. Although self-reported feelings of hope and enthusiasm are often so highly correlated as to be statistically indistinguishable, appraisal theories of emotion emphasize their conceptual distinctiveness: hope is oriented toward future and uncertain outcomes, something it shares with fear.[11]

What is the source of these feelings? The emotions driving interest and attention in the preceding studies presumably are responses to events, messages, and other features of the political world, most of which citizens encounter through mass media. Scholars have made use of experiments to learn more about how such mass-mediated communications trigger emotions and in turn shape public opinion. For example, two companion experiments carried out during a gubernatorial primary election examined how political ads use imagery and music to trigger emotions and thereby influence viewers.[12] Ads eliciting enthusiasm stoked viewer interest in the campaign, increasing expressed levels of interest by over 12 percentage points after exposure to a single ad embedded in a news program.[13] Ads eliciting fear or anxiety increased the desire to contact campaigns for more information and to watch political news. As Figure 10.1 shows, fear cues caused the percentage of citizens wanting to contact campaigns to rise from 3 percent to 17 percent and the percentage wishing to watch more political news from 41 percent to 60 percent.[14] Enthusiasm-inducing images and music did spark interest in the news, but had no effect on the desire to contact campaigns. Thus, the impact of emotional advertising appeals parallels the effects of feelings toward candidates as uncovered in survey studies: enthusiasm boosts general interest, while fear principally stimulates attention to sources of new information.[15]

It is well documented that news coverage affects which social problems and policy issues the public sees as most important.[16] The roots of this "agenda

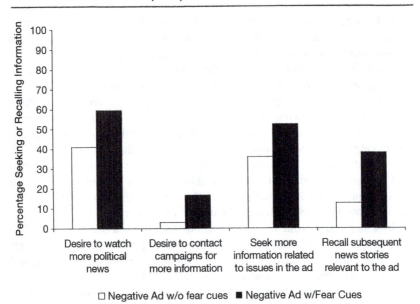

Figure 10.1 Fear Cues in Political Advertising Trigger Greater Attention and Information Seeking for Relevant Information.

setting" effect are often thought to lie in the way news stories make some issues more cognitively accessible (i.e., more readily called to mind) than other issues.[17] Although beliefs about issue importance are not precisely the same as *individual attentiveness*, they are about what issues should receive *public attention*. Recent research suggests that emotions play a key part in the agenda setting effect. Specifically, news stories alter perceptions of issue importance by either arousing or abating negative emotions, depending on whether the issue is portrayed as getting worse or better, respectively.[18] The experimental evidence confirms that, to change perceptions of importance, it is not enough for new stories to make the issue more accessible in the minds of the audience, they must also influence emotions. Fear and sadness in particular—as opposed to anger or any of several positive emotions—mediate these shifts in public priorities.

The Influence of Emotions on Political Information Seeking

Emotions influence not only citizens' attention and desire for information, but also their actual information seeking behavior. In the advertising study mentioned earlier, viewers exposed to fear-eliciting campaign ads more closely scrutinized and recalled information from subsequent news stories.[19] After watching the news broadcast in which the ad appeared, subjects had an opportunity to list as many topics from the news program as they could recall. Fear cues seemed to improve subjects' recall, specifically of topics that aired after the political ad and that were related to the themes contained in the ad. This suggests that fear cues caused subjects to keep their eyes out for relevant information even after the ad was finished; indeed, as Figure 10.1 indicates, recall of subsequent relevant news stories jumped from 13 percent to 38 percent when fearful images and music were present in the ad. In contrast, enthusiasm cues produced a 15 percentage point drop in the recall of those same news stories. Similarly, in a different experimental study, anxiety aroused by news stories about immigration caused citizens to request additional information from the government and advocacy groups.[20]

Researchers have turned recently to examining how people search for information on the Internet. One such study finds that campaign-related (and experimentally-induced) fear consistently makes voters more inclined to pay attention to the candidates and debates, but that enthusiasm and anger also increase those inclinations at least some of the time.[21] When actual information seeking is monitored, however, anger causes voters to spend *less time* searching candidate websites and *less time* on each page clicked. In contrast to this, anxiety provoked by threatening election news stories causes voters to seek out a broader range of information by visiting more unique web pages.

Fear therefore seems to play a strong role in motivating citizens to actively seek out more information. This inquisitiveness appears to be both broad and yet still selective or targeted in particular ways. Scholars have long argued that people have a tendency to engage in selective exposure to information that confirms their existing point of view and, while this tendency does not always prevail, in politics partisans often exhibit this sort of biased information search.[22] Studies, however, suggest that anxiety can disrupt this tendency while anger may reinforce it. Researchers compared the online behavior of individuals who got angry or anxious in response to threatening news stories about campus affirmative action policies.[23] Anxious citizens sought out more information that was challenging to their own views, but those who were angry avoided web pages that challenged their position. Another study found that anxiety made citizens more likely to visit an opposing candidate's website and indeed to visit the sites of both candidates in an election.[24] Anxiety generated such a balanced search, however, only when people were aware the information might be useful in the future (e.g., in defending their views to others).

While anxiety tends to broaden the focus of citizens' attention in terms of agreement with a person's political views, it also narrows the focus of their attention to information relevant to the potential threat. In experimental studies, fear ads prompted viewers to request more information about the campaign and about the threatening issues raised in the ad.[25] After viewing both news and ads, subjects were invited to list issues they would like to hear more about from journalists and politicians. When subjects saw a relatively unemotional ad, nearly 36 percent of them listed issues that had been raised in the political ads. This number jumped to over 52 percent among those who saw the identical ad messages except with fearful imagery and music (see Figure 10.1).

Enthusiasm-eliciting cues however had no discernible impact on these topical "wish lists." Similarly, fear appeals increased the desire for political news, *as opposed to other news content*, and focused viewers' attention on subsequent news stories that were relevant to the issues raised in the ad, *but not on irrelevant news stories*.[26] Other studies confirm this narrowing effect of fear and its potential for creating a vicious cycle in which fear drives citizens to consume information that further stokes those fears, rather than toward information that might reassure them. For example, fears about increasing immigration caused citizens to request information from government and anti-immigrant organizations, more so than from pro-immigrant or academic sources.[27] And, in a separate experimental study, anxious citizens were more likely to read online news stories about immigration, especially negative stories, than about other topics.[28] They also better remembered threatening news stories and agreed more with the arguments in those stories.

The Influence of Emotions on Political Learning

Does all of this increased interest, attention, and information seeking affect what citizens learn about candidates and issues? Few studies to date examine the ultimate impact of emotions on political learning. Evidence suggests that fear can precipitate increases in citizen knowledge during elections. Citizens who are particularly anxious possess more information about the candidates and know better their relative policy positions.[29] In addition, over the course of a campaign, anxious citizens' knowledge of candidate positions improves much faster than that of either enthusiastic or unemotional citizens.[30] Emotional appeals in political advertising do not universally enhance candidate name recognition, but when fear appeals target a viewer's preferred candidate, that viewer has an easier time recalling the names of both candidates.[31] Similarly, when threatening campaign information induces anxiety, as opposed to other emotions (i.e., anger, enthusiasm, disgust), citizens not only read a broader array of candidate web pages, they also demonstrate greater learning from these stories on a follow-up quiz.[32]

Some studies, however, arrive at more mixed conclusions about the relationship between anxiety and learning. One such study tracks subjects through a simulated, interactive campaign on computers. Anxious voters better learned their preferred candidate's policy views under highly threatening conditions (when subjects encountered lots of unexpected information), but this learning did not extend to learning *other* candidates' positions.[33] Other scholars have warned that anxiety and stress can impair learning even as those emotions cause people to devote more attention to what worries them.[34] Consistent with this, in surveys conducted between 2001 and 2003, researchers found that anxiety about terrorism, Saddam Hussein, and a possible war in Iraq led Americans to spend more time thinking about Iraq, yet worsened their knowledge of basic facts about the country.[35] Such discrepancies suggest we should be cautious about assuming that fear-driven increases in attention and information seeking will lead automatically to gains in relevant public knowledge.

Summary: Emotions, Attention, and Learning

Emotions influence the political engagement and attentiveness of citizens. Fear in particular powerfully shapes whether and when citizens adopt a more vigilant posture. Fear redirects the focus of citizens' attention as well as their beliefs about which issues merit public attention more generally. Fear motivates citizens to seek out new information from a broader, more balanced array of political viewpoints, yet focused more narrowly on potential threats. This targeted vigilance can be beneficial, helping people to learn information that is useful in reassessing, reducing, or escaping a potential threat. But it can also produce distortions in public attention and knowledge, to the extent citizens focus *too much* on threatening issues and neglect non-threatening information that might ease their anxieties. Similarly, fear-induced vigilance will not always give rise to better informed citizens, especially if citizens are routinely exposed to information that is unhelpful, error-filled, or misleading.

Rigidity versus Responsiveness in Opinion Formation

In addition to influencing attention and learning, emotions affect the way people make decisions and form opinions. Moreover, they do so in at least two ways. They can directly influence citizens' evaluations, with positive feelings leading to more positive judgments and negative feelings to negative judgments. Emotions can also influence opinions in a second, more indirect manner, by changing the *way* that citizens arrive at their views. Because these indirect effects are less obvious and speak to deeper questions of how people make up their minds, we devote special attention to them in this chapter.

The Direct Influence of Emotions on Opinions

Let us begin by briefly considering the direct impact of emotions on public opinion. That emotions exert such influence is not surprising since opinions usually involve "affect"—that is, liking or disliking, and affect of this sort is an emotional phenomenon much the same as the discrete emotions (fear, enthusiasm, etc.) we've been discussing. If a person makes you feel angry, afraid, sad, or disgusted, you will be inclined not to like that person as much. If a group or a policy makes you feel proud, hopeful, and enthusiastic, then you will be more apt to like it. Many studies, including some of the earliest research on emotions and public opinion, indeed find that emotions have a strong impact on evaluations of government and political leaders, over and above any influence of cognitive beliefs or judgments.[36] For example, feelings of enthusiasm about a presidential candidate or even about the policies he champions feed directly into greater support and likelihood of voting for the candidate.[37] Citizens also draw, consciously or not, on their emotions about the country when expressing opinions: people who experience positive feelings about the United States express more trust in other people, more trust in the government, and more support for policies like the North American Free Trade Agreement.[38] Even when unrelated events put people in a good or bad mood (e.g., the smell of freshly baked cookies, a sunny day), these feelings can cause more positive or negative evaluations of candidates, as long as the individual does not reflect on the true source of her feelings.[39]

The Influence of Emotions on Opinion Formation and Decision Making

Emotions also influence public opinion indirectly, altering the process by which citizens make decisions. People don't invest equal effort in making every decision. Sometimes they think through an issue carefully, taking the time and effort to sift through the available information and weigh arguments for or against each option. Other times they make a quick judgment based on simple cues or decision rules, such as a voter who decides just to mark the ballot for any candidates who are women or for all Republicans. The first mode of decision making is called "systematic," "central," or "effortful" processing; the second is called "heuristic" or "peripheral" processing.[40] There is mounting evidence that a person's emotional state affects whether she engages in more or less effortful thinking and therefore what sorts of considerations play a role in decision making. Fear and sadness, for example, both appear to trigger more effortful thinking, while enthusiasm and anger encourage more peripheral or habitual thought processes.

Fear breaks citizens out of their habitual modes of thinking and gets them to reconsider their choices in light of the situation. As a result, it opens the door to persuasion. Fear does not guarantee a change of mind, but does prompt "second thoughts" about the decision. A number of studies find evidence consistent with these expectations. In elections over the past thirty years, voters anxious about presidential candidates have been less likely to rely on partisan loyalties or ideological affinities, but more apt to make decisions on the basis of assessments of candidates' issue positions and leadership qualities.[41] Similarly, fear elicited by campaign ads causes voters to place greater weight on the advertising message; fearful ads are thus more persuasive.[42] Voters fearful about the threat of terrorism cast votes less according to partisanship and more according to evaluations of candidates' leadership qualities.[43]

Such findings are not confined to electoral settings, rather they extend to multiple domains of public opinion. For example, Americans anxious about the 1991 Gulf War were more likely to change their political judgments in light of their assessment of how well the war had gone.[44] Thus, *to the extent they felt anxiety*, Americans were more likely to set aside preconceptions and update their opinions about whether the U.S. did "the right thing" by going to war and, further, to update their support for President George H. W. Bush more generally, based on the outcome of the war. Under more controlled experimental conditions, researchers found that, as Republicans grew more anxious, they shed their party loyalties to express greater approval of the Democratic President Bill Clinton, even though the anxiety was induced subliminally with apolitical images (e.g., snakes, skulls).[45] Anxiety also influences political tolerance judgments: anxious citizens were found to be more responsive to persuasive pro- or anti-free speech arguments they had recently read.[46] These examples illustrate anxiety's role in loosening the hold of predispositions, while facilitating the incorporation of new information and changes of opinion.

These sorts of indirect effects on opinion formation, however, are not confined to anxiety. Enthusiasm elicited by campaign ads, in contrast to fear, causes voters to place extra emphasis on their initial candidate preferences and to express greater certainty about their choice.[47] Figure 10.2 illustrates the contrasting ways these two emotions affect the role of political predispositions in voter decision making.[48] In experimental research on emotional advertising appeals, many subjects expressed a clear fondness for one candidate over the other when they began the study.[49] When asked near the end of the study which way they planned to vote, their original loyalties or "predispositions" predicted

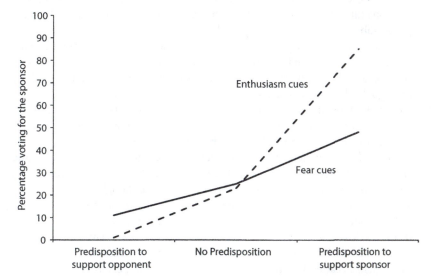

Figure 10.2 Fear Cues in Political Advertising Weaken the Impact of Predispositions on Voting Decisions, While Enthusiasm Cues Strengthen the Impact of Predispositions.

quite well their final voting decision. However, the strength of this relationship between predispositions and voting choice depended dramatically on which emotions, if any, had been elicited in the meantime by the political ad they saw. The correspondence between predispositions and voting decision is much stronger following exposure to enthusiasm appeals, and notably weaker following exposure to fear appeals.

We encounter a similar pattern in a study of how the framing of policy options affects preferences for risky policies. It is well-established that people are more willing to undertake risks when information is framed in terms of potential losses, while they prefer less risky options when information is framed in terms of gains.[50] But responsiveness to these frames turns out to depend on an individual's emotional state.[51] Whereas anxiety increases responsiveness to the framing of options, both enthusiasm and anger decrease responsiveness. Another study contrasts the effects of anger and sadness on opinion formation.[52] Sadness led citizens to engage in more effortful thinking when asked whether people should receive public welfare assistance, while angry citizens did not engage in more effortful thinking. This resulted in divergent preferences, with sad citizens favoring more public assistance and angry citizens favoring less.

Summary: Emotions on Opinion Formation

Emotions exert considerable influence over the opinions of citizens. In some cases, this impact is simple and direct. People who are in a bad mood or experiencing negative emotions such as anger, fear, or sadness, express more negative opinions (at times, regardless of whether their emotional state is at all related to the substance of the opinion), and people experiencing positive emotions express more positive opinions. But the impact of emotions goes deeper, to the very process of opinion formation. Some emotions, like fear and sadness, cause citizens to reconsider their political predispositions, expend more effort thinking through the decision, and display greater responsiveness to new information and the details of the situation. Other emotions, like enthusiasm and anger, reinforce the automatic tendency of citizens to spend little time reflecting on their opinions and to stick more closely to their political habits and loyalties.

Does this mean fear and sadness improve democratic citizenship, and anger and enthusiasm diminish it? Perhaps. Certainly many would consider it a good thing if public opinion were based on a more thoughtful review of the available information and arguments. But fear and sadness do not guarantee well-reasoned decisions or good outcomes. Indeed, as we have seen, detachment from political habits and a focus on details can render citizens more susceptible to persuasive advertising and framing effects, thus making political manipulation easier. Emotions clearly affect how people perform their functions as democratic citizens, but the normative desirability of the outcomes depends on more than the emotion or the thought process it provokes.

Turning Opinions into Political Action

Emotions motivate action and push it in particular directions. This doesn't mean people reflexively act on the emotional impulse, merely that action is more likely because the impulse exists. Emotions often elevate levels of physiological arousal and thus physically prepare people to take actions, though there are also emotional states that reduce arousal and the inclination to act (e.g., sadness, serenity). Emotions also motivate people to act in ways that are specific to a particular emotion, what psychologists call the "action tendencies" of the emotion in question.[53] For example, anger creates an impulse to confront and fight, fear an impulse to escape, and disgust an impulse to avoid and purge (see Table 10.1).

In considering the political consequences of these action tendencies, it is useful to remember that democratic politics is primarily a realm of collective action. Citizens do not often take direct action to deal with political issues. They instead express preferences over (a) policy actions to be taken on their behalf by the government, (b) the selection of leaders entrusted to take these actions, and (c) policy actions determined directly from a collective voting process (e.g., ballot initiatives). Most forms of democratic political action thus occur through fairly institutionalized channels: voting, working on a campaign, donating money, contacting government officials. As a result, we expect emotions to affect overall levels of political participation, spurring citizens to greater political involvement or prompting them to withdraw from politics, commensurate with their level of physical arousal. However, direct personal action to satisfy more specific emotional impulses (to flee, fight, hide, help, etc.) is likely to be limited in the political realm by the lack of opportunities for meaningful actions of this sort. Nonetheless, these impulses may affect citizens' *preferences for collective policy actions*; the impulse to fight, for example, may lead to greater support for aggressive policies. We therefore expect emotions to affect public opinion in distinct ways that reflect the action tendencies of the emotion in question.

The Influence of Emotions on Levels of Political Participation

Not surprisingly, "high arousal" emotions tend to be associated with more political action. This general relationship between emotions and participation has illuminated both persistent differences among individuals and short-term reactions to specific situations. Recall that people respond emotionally when circumstances hold relevance for them or, in other words, when they care about what is happening. Some scholars, therefore, look to see if individuals report ever having emotional reactions—positive or negative—to a particular issue, as a technique for measuring those individuals' level of *conviction*.[54] Citizens who report stronger feelings about policies indeed are more likely to take political action, above and beyond any intellectual investment reflected by their knowledge of the issue.

Other scholars are concerned with the participatory impact of short-term emotional reactions that can, from time to time, flare up and fade away for anyone regardless of a person's long-term interest in policies or politics. Both citizens who feel enthusiastic about presidential candidates and those who feel anxious are more likely to participate in election campaigns beyond simply voting.[55] Similarly, campaign ads that elicit enthusiasm and fear both increase the desire to volunteer and to vote during elections.[56] Such effects occur outside of elections as well: for example, anxiety triggered by news stories on immigration provokes more Americans to contact their members of Congress to advocate for reducing the number of immigrants to the U.S.[57] One recent study compares the impact of three emotions—fear, anger, and enthusiasm—on political participation and notes important distinctions among them.[58] Fear has the most variable effects; in some cases it motivates voters, but other times has no effect or even suppresses their participation levels. Anger, in contrast, has an especially powerful impact on political mobilization, but its impact depends more heavily on the person possessing the sorts of resources (e.g., education, income, social ties, experience) that enable participation.[59] Absent such resources, citizens are less likely to act on their anger in politically consequential ways.

Data from the 2008 presidential election in the U.S. provide an example of the direct and distinctive impact of emotions on political participation. In a national survey (conducted with Nicholas Valentino), we asked Americans how they felt about the way things were going in the country. Given the unpopularity of the incumbent president and the onset of a global financial crisis, most Americans felt a good deal more fear and anger than enthusiasm in the fall of 2008. We also asked during the campaign how likely they were to contact a government official and, right after the election, how often they had engaged in a range of different political activities.

Table 10.2 shows how enthusiasm, fear, and anger about the way things were going in the country affected the propensity to participate in these various ways, controlling for many other attributes known to predict participation.[60] Anger had the clearest, most consistent, and most powerful impact on political participation in 2008, exerting a strong positive effect for eight of the ten activities. In most cases, people who were extremely angry scored somewhere between 10 to 25 percentage points higher on the frequency-of-participation scale. The impact of enthusiasm was considerably spottier: it was positively related to several forms of participation, though the evidence was not always reliable enough to give us full confidence that these were genuine effects (in statistical parlance, they did not quite reach accepted levels of "statistical significance"). The results for fear, in contrast, point rather consistently in a negative direction, though these too fall shy of significance in all but one case.

Table 10.2 The Impact of Emotions on Political Participation in the 2008 Election.

Political participation	Emotional reactions to the way things are going in the country		
	Enthusiasm	Fear	Anger
Vote	–4%	–6%	–2%
Contact government officials	+2%	–23%**	+24%**
Discuss politics w/friends & family	+11%	0%	+17%*
Argue about politics	–2%	–4%	+22%*
Take part in a protest	0%	–5%	+7%*
Attend political events for a candidate	–7%	–3%	0%
Display a campaign sign	+11%	–8%	+18%*
Volunteer for a campaign	–6%	–11%	+12%*
Donate money to a candidate or party	+8%	–5%	+14%*
Sign a petition	+10%	–10%	+16%*

Note: The table shows the estimated effect of each emotion on various forms of political participation, expressed as a percentage point difference in the overall participation scale between those experiencing no emotion and those experiencing intense emotion (i.e., "not at all angry" vs. "extremely angry"). Participation questions asked respondents, whether they voted, as well as how likely they were to contact government officials or how often they had engaged in any of the other activities on a four, five, or eight point scale. Analyses are based on ordinary least squares regression and included statistical controls for gender, age, education, income, race, church attendance, residency, strength of partisanship, internal political efficacy, general interest in politics, and political knowledge (N = 460 to 568). Data are from a representative national survey carried out in the U.S. during the 2008 presidential election. Asterisks indicate levels of statistical significance: ** $p < .01$, * $p < .05$.

Although the pattern of results shown in Table 10.2 illustrates fairly well the relative contributions of these emotions to political participation,[61] it is important to reiterate that other data have revealed more positive participatory effects of fear and especially enthusiasm in some cases.[62] Studies uncovering positive effects for fear and enthusiasm have tended to investigate emotions that are closely tied to specific candidates and issues, as opposed to the sort of broad emotions about the state of the country we solicited in the 2008 survey.[63] Indeed, we can see evidence for such broader effects by turning to data on the 2012 presidential election from the American National Election Studies. This survey asked citizens about their emotions toward the candidates and whether they had recently undertaken a variety of political actions.

Table 10.3 shows the average impact of Americans' overall emotional reactions toward the Democratic and Republican candidates in 2012 (Barack Obama and Mitt Romney) across a range of political actions.[64] Note first that, when considering emotions toward candidates, the size of the effects tends to be as large or larger than observed in the 2008 study, effects are more universally positive, and effects are more broadly distributed across the three emotions. This is consistent with the fact that emotions measured in the 2012 study are even more closely related to the participatory behavior. Similarly, in keeping with

Table 10.3 The Impact of Emotions on Political Participation in the 2012 Election.

Political participation	Emotional reactions to the major party presidential candidates		
	Enthusiasm	Fear	Anger
Vote	+21%***	+6%	+4%
Contact government officials	+2%	+14%***	+22%***
Discuss politics w/friends & family	+18%***	+25%***	+24%***
Take part in a protest	+1%	+5%**	+4%*
Attend political events for a candidate	+9%***	+7%**	+3%
Display a campaign sign	+15%***	+9%**	+9%**
Volunteer for a campaign	+4%*	+4%**	+5%**
Donate money to a candidate or party	+5%	+9%**	+11%***
Sign a petition	+5%	+4%	+19%***

Note: The table shows the estimated effect of each emotion on political participation, expressed as a percentage point difference in the overall participation scale between those experiencing no emotion and those experiencing intense emotion (e.g., no anger toward either candidate vs. maximal anger toward both candidates). Participation questions asked respondents whether they had engaged in any of these activities. Analyses are based on ordinary least squares regression and included statistical controls for gender, age, education, income, race, church attendance, strength of partisanship, internal political efficacy, general interest in politics, and political knowledge (N = 5,059 to 5,078). Data are from the 2012 American National Election Studies Time Series survey. Asterisks indicate levels of statistical significance: *** $p < .001$, ** $p < .01$, * $p < .05$.

prior research, we observe positive effects of emotions on voting and a particularly strong impact of enthusiasm on the decision to vote.[65] Beyond voting, enthusiasm toward the candidates seems to predict appropriately expressive behavior such as attending campaign rallies and posting or wearing campaign signs. At the same time, both fear and anger are more likely (than enthusiasm) to be associated with actions that express grievances (i.e., protesting, signing petitions, contacting officials) and donating money to political candidates or parties. All three of these high arousal emotions predict a greater likelihood of talking about politics with friends and of volunteering for campaigns.

The Influence of Emotions on the Proclivity for Specific Types of Action

Emotions don't just impel us to do "more" or "less," they also trigger the desire to act in some fairly specific ways. When afraid, people don't feel an impulse to do just anything, but specifically to hide, flee, or otherwise protect themselves from harm. In contrast, angry people feel inclined to confront and punish. But, where politics is concerned, citizens typically act through a limited set of institutional channels to influence the direction of government, while government itself takes direct action to address problems and pursue collective goals.

Thus, the distinctive action tendencies of fear, anger, enthusiasm, and other emotions may not be visible in standard forms of political participation like voting as much as in preferences for what policies the government should pursue. Voting looks the same regardless of whether a voter is in the mood to protect, punish, help, or celebrate. Those motives may be readily distinguishable, however, in a voter's policy priorities and positions, such as through preferences for heightened security, harsher criminal penalties, more aid to the poor, or simply maintaining the status quo.

Emotions indeed seem to influence the policy opinions of citizens in a way that parallels the immediate "action tendencies" generated by the emotional state. Anger and fear, for example, have opposite implications for risk-taking. In the face of terrorism threats, fear decreases the willingness of citizens to engage in risky personal activities *and* the willingness to support policy actions that might put more Americans at risk.[66] Anger, meanwhile, increases support for taking both personal and policy risks. Faced with a public health threat, like the outbreak of a deadly disease, angry citizens prefer policy options that carry a risk of bigger losses or bigger gains over policy options with equivalent but more certain (known) outcomes.[67] But fearful citizens prefer certain results to actions that take a chance on bigger gains and bigger losses.

We can observe these distinct effects of fear and anger on risk preferences in the survey data from the 2008 election mentioned earlier. In light of the incipient economic meltdown and deep dissatisfaction about the direction of the country in the fall of 2008, we asked respondents their views on "the best way to deal with times of crisis and hardship": do they prefer "taking bold action to solve a crisis more quickly, even if it comes with a risk of making our problems worse" or, instead, "acting with caution and avoiding big risks, even if it will likely take much longer to solve the crisis"? Figure 10.3 plots the relationship between preferences for bold, risky action and levels of fear and anger, controlling for other attributes that may affect risk preferences. As fear became more intense, Americans shied away from a risky approach to crisis. Anger had the opposite effect, making Americans more likely to endorse risky action. Levels of enthusiasm (not shown in the figure) had no effect on risk preferences.

Anger and fear also diverge by pushing citizens toward aggressive or defensive actions, respectively. This is again visible in responses to terrorism. When angry, Americans are more willing to expand U.S. military efforts in the war on terror within and beyond Afghanistan; when afraid, Americans more strongly prefer to deport Arab Americans, Muslims, or first-generation immigrants.[68] Similar tendencies appear for other issues. In the face of a viral pandemic threatening public health, angry citizens are more apt to write letters urging prosecution of anyone found responsible, as well as to support official investigations and punishment of those at fault.[69] In this same situation, fear makes citizens more likely to undertake a variety of protective behaviors (e.g., learning more about the illness, telling friends and family about the danger,

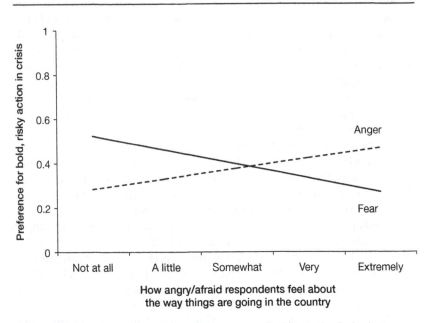

Figure 10.3 Anger Increases and Fear Decreases the Preference for Risky Action.

washing hands). Fear does not generate greater interest in prosecutions or punishments, but it does strengthen the preference for government oversight and regulation aimed at preventing future outbreaks. Finally, citizens anxious about affirmative action show greater willingness to consider compromises, while citizens angry about the policy are less willing to compromise.[70]

Summary: Emotions and Political Action

Emotions prepare and push people to act. Many citizens hold opinions about political candidates and policy issues, but only sometimes do they act on these opinions. Emotional reactions often provide citizens with the motivation to turn opinions into political action. This is especially true for high arousal emotions like fear, anger, and enthusiasm; anger in particular is a powerful resource for political mobilization. Although more participation typically is regarded as desirable, the consequences of emotional arousal are not simply a matter of participating more or less. In addition to the implications for attention and thoughtfulness already discussed, emotions have action tendencies that impel citizens in specific directions. These tendencies are manifest in both personal behavior and public opinion about collective policy actions. Fear motivates citizens to reduce risks, protect against harm, and consider compromises. In contrast, anger gives rise to behavior and opinions that are risky, aggressive, punitive, and uncompromising.

Group-Based Emotions and Intergroup Conflict

Until this point, our discussion has focused on emotions primarily as experienced by isolated individuals. Groups and intergroup conflict, however, are central features of politics, and emotions are no less central to this domain of public opinion. When people identify as members of a social group, that group becomes an extension of their self-identity and self-worth. As a result, the social group acquires deep emotional significance for an individual, and events affecting the group can cause strong emotional reactions.[71] Thus, for example, "wars, terrorist attacks, or natural disasters that affect a country as a whole generate feelings of sadness, anger, and fear among those who identify with the country even if they themselves or their families and friends are not directly affected."[72] The strength of these group-based emotions depends, in part, on the relative level of identification with the group.[73]

Because of the role of social identity in fomenting intragroup and intergroup emotions, emotions can be a powerful mover of opinion and action in contexts of intergroup conflict. Take national identity as an example. In times of war or in the aftermath of an attack (e.g., the September 11 terrorist attacks on the U.S.), the collective sense of identification with the nation is often enhanced, leading to stronger in-group identification and therefore stronger emotional responses to events affecting the in-group. Indeed, "modern nation-states serve as vehicles of political emotion," and strong national identity can magnify the influence of intergroup emotions on political attitudes.[74]

Efforts to resolve problems of discriminatory behavior and intergroup violence must take account of group-based emotions and their role in spurring and perpetuating conflict between groups irrespective of any material basis for such conflict (e.g., competition over scarce resources).[75] This has long been treated as a problem of ethnocentrism and prejudice; that is, group identifiers tend to see the in-group as superior to out-groups (*ethnocentrism*), and tend to feel and think positive things about the in-group, while automatically feeling and thinking negative things about the out-group (*prejudice*).[76] More recently, however, scholars have argued for the importance of going beyond prejudice to recognize that people experience a wide array of group-based emotions, which arise under distinct circumstances and have distinct implications for public opinion and behavior (such as those discussed earlier in this chapter).[77] In other words, members of a particular group may feel anger toward one out-group, fear a second out-group, pity a third, and feel admiration for a fourth, with corresponding differences in the policies that will be supported towards each out-group.[78] For example, researchers contend that contemporary racial hostility of white Americans toward blacks is linked to anger rather than fear or other emotions,[79] while another line of studies links opposition to gays and gay rights to feelings of disgust.[80] In the international realm, feelings of humiliation arise when members of one group feel their status or dignity has been harmed by the actions of another group, often fueling negative attitudes toward the offending group and even motivating political violence.[81]

On the other hand, emotions can also be central to mitigating or resolving group conflict. Fostering a more inclusive social identity and "intergroup empathy" can reduce negative attitudes toward the out-group, even when groups are in direct competition with one another.[82] Collective guilt is a prime example of an intergroup emotion that can help "repair" relations between groups. Guilt arises when people perceive that actions under their own control or the control of their group have illegitimately harmed others.[83] It motivates introspection and more positive attitudes toward an out-group. Collective guilt also alters policy preferences by motivating individuals to restore justice and make reparations to the harmed group.[84] Like other group-based emotions, the experience of collective guilt depends on the strength of one's identity with the harm-causing group; but, unlike other emotions, high group identity tends to *decrease* feelings of collective guilt.[85] This is because strong identifiers are especially motivated to view their group positively. Thus, collective guilt is relatively rare, as people develop psychological mechanisms to justify harms committed by the in-group against out-groups (e.g., dehumanization of the out-group and emphasis on personal or in-group victimization).[86]

Conclusion

In sum, emotions serve as guides that adapt thinking and behavior to meet certain situational needs. They direct attention and learning selectively. They modulate how actively and broadly citizens think through the matter at hand. They prepare and motivate citizens to take appropriate actions, including no action at all.

Researchers have especially learned a good deal about the political implications of three commonplace emotions: enthusiasm, fear, and anger. Enthusiasm arises when things are going well, when people are achieving or exceeding their goals. It causes citizens to take a greater interest in politics, adhere to partisan or other political loyalties, feel more confident in their views, and participate more in campaigns and elections. Because it encourages more participation that hews more closely to partisan lines, the feel-good emotion of enthusiasm can ironically be the source of more intense political polarization.

Fear is a response to circumstances that are threatening or where the potential for danger is unknown. It causes citizens to pay greater attention to what is happening (especially as relates to possible danger), seek out more information, reconsider their options in light of available information, avoid risky courses of action, and prefer public policies focused on prevention and protection. As a result, fear may lead to an increase in learning, persuasion, and compromise.

Anger is triggered when someone intentionally threatens or stands in the way of a person's goals, especially if the situation is seen as unfair and controllable. It causes citizens to stick with their convictions, eschew compromise, spend less time thinking things through, embrace risks more readily, and prefer aggressive and punitive public policies. Anger is a consistently powerful source of political mobilization, motivating people to act on their opinions, particularly to the extent citizens feel they have the ability and resources to contribute effectively.

People of course experience many feelings beyond these three best understood emotions. Scholars are beginning to explore the implications of other emotions for public opinion and politics. For example, sadness, not unlike fear, prompts people to expend more effort on thinking through decisions. When sadness is elicited, citizens are therefore more likely to pay attention to the details of a situation and, as a result, take account of those situational details in deciding whether the government should provide welfare assistance to individuals.[87] Disgust triggers an inclination to purify one's environment. Accordingly, it seems to give rise to harsher moral judgments and moral conservatism such as disapproval of gays.[88] Pride and shame are "social emotions" that people experience when they realize that others may judge them as exemplifying or falling short of, respectively, the standards and values expected by their community or group. As a result, both emotions motivate citizens to adopt or apply more faithfully the values of their group.[89] While shame prompts a desire to hide one's transgressions, pride triggers a desire to display one's behavior and group membership proudly.[90]

Although emotions often arise unbidden and automatically in response to events, new research is demonstrating the ways in which people can try to manage and redirect their feelings. Specifically, work on *emotional regulation* argues that, by reappraising a situation (i.e., evaluating it from a different perspective), people can change their emotional state and, with it, their political attitudes and behavior.[91] This may be particularly helpful in countering undesirable effects of emotions like anger, fear, and hatred, during intractable conflicts (e.g., the Israeli–Palestinian conflict), or in neutralizing the spontaneous disgust reactions some people feel when encountering things they perceive as impure (e.g., open wounds and unsanitary conditions during humanitarian or military crises, "strange" eating and drinking practices of other cultures, sexual practices perceived as "deviant"). Nonetheless, this sort of emotional regulation requires individuals to be trained in specific techniques and motivated to "correct" their behavior.[92]

Emotions, specifically their role in opinion formation and political behavior, can help us to understand more fully the vicissitudes of democratic citizenship. But they typically can't tell us whether a person is a good or bad citizen, nor whether people on average are better or worse citizens than we expected. Emotions are neither good nor bad in themselves, but simply useful for human reasoning and action. Moreover, though they collectively and individually serve useful functions, this does not mean emotions improve decisions and actions in every instance. They can distract attention needlessly, disrupt learning, give rise to wrong or bad decisions, and motivate harmful behaviors. As public opinion scholars and political observers begin to appreciate more and more the critical role emotions play, it is important to become neither overly sanguine nor overly discouraging about their implications for democratic citizenship.

Notes

1. Charles Bens, "What Does It Mean to Be a Good Citizen?" *National Civic Review* 90 (2001): 193–197; Michael Delli Carpini and Scott Keeter, *What Americans Know about Politics and Why It Matters* (New Haven: Yale University Press, 1996); Will Kymlicka and Wayne Norman, "The Return of the Citizen," in *Democracy*, ed. Ricardo Blaug and John Schwarzmantel (New York: Columbia University Press, 2001), 220–227; Michael Schudson, *The Good Citizen: A History of American Civic Life* (New York: Free Press, 1998); and Michael Walzer, *What It Means to Be an American* (New York: Marsilio, 1992).
2. For example, see Richard S. Lazarus, *Emotion and Adaptation* (New York: Oxford University Press, 1991).
3. The terms fear and anxiety are often (but not always) used interchangeably in the scientific research on emotion, an approach we adopt here. For example, see Michael Davis, "The Role of the Amygdala in Fear and Anxiety," *Annual Review of Neuroscience* 15 (1992): 353–375; and Leonie Huddy, Stanley Feldman, Theresa Capelos, and Colin Provost, "The Consequences of Terrorism: Disentangling the Effects of Personal and National Threat," *Political Psychology* 23 (2002): 485–509. Both emotions are associated with increased sensitivity to potential threat and the perception that the individual or group has low relative power to change the situation.
4. George E. Marcus, W. Russell Neuman, and Michael MacKuen, *Affective Intelligence and Political Judgment* (Chicago: University of Chicago Press, 2000).
5. Ibid., 85–87.
6. Ibid., 91–92.
7. Thomas Rudolph, Amy Gangl, and Dan Stevens, "The Effects of Efficacy and Emotions on Campaign Involvement," *Journal of Politics* 62 (2000): 1189–1197.
8. Kim Witte and Mike Allen, "A Meta-Analysis of Fear Appeals: Implications for Effective Public Health Campaigns," *Health Education Research* 27 (2000): 591–615.
9. Leonie Huddy, Stanley Feldman, and Erin Cassese, "On the Distinct Political Effects of Anxiety and Anger," in *The Affect Effect*, ed. W. Russell Neuman, George Marcus, Ann Crigler, and Michael MacKuen (Chicago: University of Chicago Press, 2007), 202–230.
10. Marion Just, Ann Crigler, and Todd Belt, "Don't Give Up Hope: Emotions, Candidate Appraisals, and Votes," in *The Affect Effect*, ed. W. Russell Neuman, George Marcus, Ann Crigler, and Michael MacKuen (Chicago: University of Chicago Press, 2007), pp. 231–259.
11. Cf. Donald Kinder, "Reason and Emotion in American Political Life," in *Beliefs, Reasoning, and Decision Making*, ed. Roger Schank and Ellen Langer (Hillsdale, NJ: Lawrence Erlbaum, 1994), pp. 277–314; and Lazarus, *Emotion and Adaptation*.
12. Ted Brader, *Campaigning for Hearts and Minds* (Chicago: University of Chicago Press, 2006).
13. Emotions often last for relatively short periods of time, unless they continue to be aroused by new or ongoing circumstances. There has been little research to date into the persistence of political emotions or their effects over time. Regardless of how long the emotions themselves last, some effects might be expected to fade with the emotion (e.g., effects on attention or inclinations to act in a certain way) and others to last beyond the life of the emotion (e.g., effects on thought processes that lead to lasting changes in opinions or knowledge).

14. For more details on the design of the study and analyses, see Ted Brader, "Striking a Responsive Chord: How Political Ads Motivate and Persuade Voters by Appealing to Emotions," *American Journal of Political Science* 49 (2005): 388–405; and Brader, *Campaigning for Hearts and Minds*.
15. Marcus, Neuman, and MacKuen, *Affective Intelligence and Political Judgment*.
16. Maxwell McCombs, Maxwell, *Setting the Agenda: The Mass Media and Public Opinion* (Cambridge: Polity, 2004).
17. Shanto Iyengar and Donald Kinder, *News That Matters* (Chicago: University of Chicago Press, 1987).
18. Joanne Miller, "Examining the Mediators of Agenda Setting: A New Experimental Paradigm Reveals the Role of Emotions," *Political Psychology* 28 (2007): 689–717.
19. Brader, *Campaigning for Hearts and Minds*.
20. Ted Brader, Nicholas A. Valentino, and Elizabeth Suhay, "What Triggers Public Opposition to Immigration? Anxiety, Group Cues, and Immigration Threat," *American Journal of Political Science* 52 (2008): 959–978.
21. Nicholas Valentino, Vincent Hutchings, Antoine Banks, and Anne Davis, "Is a Worried Citizen a Good Citizen? Emotions, Political Information Seeking, and Learning via the Internet," *Political Psychology* 29 (2008): 247–273.
22. Shanto Iyengar, Kyu S. Hahn, Jon A. Krosnick, and John Walker, "Selective Exposure to Campaign Communication: The Role of Anticipated Agreement and Issue Public Membership," *Journal of Politics* 70 (2008): 186–200; and Natalie Jomini Stroud, "Media Use and Political Predispositions: Revisiting the Concept of Selective Exposure," *Political Behavior* 30 (2008): 341–366.
23. Michael MacKuen, Jennifer Wolak, Luke Keele, and George Marcus, "Civic Engagements: Resolute Partisanship or Reflective Deliberation," *American Journal of Political Science* 54 (2010): 440–458.
24. Nicholas Valentino, Antoine Banks, Vincent Hutchings, and Anne Davis, "Selective Exposure in the Internet Age: The Interaction Between Anxiety and Information Utility," *Political Psychology* 30 (2009): 591–613.
25. Brader, "Striking a Responsive Chord."
26. Brader, *Campaigning for Hearts and Minds*, 134–139.
27. Brader, Valentino, and Suhay, "What Triggers Public Opposition to Immigration?"
28. Shana Kushner Gadarian and Bethany Albertson, "Anxiety, Information, and Political Information," *Political Psychology* 35 (2014): 133–164; see also Bethany Albertson and Shana Kushner Gadarian, *Anxious Politics: Democratic Citizenship in a Threatening World* (New York: Cambridge University Press, 2015).
29. Marcus, Neuman, and MacKuen, *Affective Intelligence and Political Judgment*, 87–89.
30. Ibid., 93.
31. Brader, *Campaigning for Hearts and Minds*, 135.
32. Valentino et al., "Is a Worried Citizen a Good Citizen?"
33. David Redlawsk, Andrew Civettini, and Richard Lau, "Affective Intelligence and Voting," in *The Affect Effect*, ed. W. Russell Neuman, George Marcus, Ann Crigler, and Michael MacKuen (Chicago: University of Chicago Press, 2007), pp. 152–179.
34. Stanley Feldman and Leonie Huddy, "The Paradoxical Effects of Anxiety on Political Learning" (unpublished manuscript, Stony Brook University, n.d.).
35. It remains unclear whether the discrepancy between these and other findings is due to the nature of the threat (e.g., fears about life and death), to anxiety shifting attention to other information in the environment at the expense of these sorts of factual details, or some other reason.
36. Robert Abelson, Donald Kinder, Mark Peters, and Susan Fiske, "Affective and Semantic Components in Political Personal Perception," *Journal of Personality and*

Social Psychology 42 (1982): 619–630; Pamela Conover and Stanley Feldman, "Emotional Reactions to the Economy," *American Journal of Political Science* 30 (1986): 30–78; Kimberly Gross, "Framing Persuasive Appeals: Episodic and Thematic Framing, Emotional Response, and Policy Opinion," *Political Psychology* 29 (2008): 169–192; Kimberly Gross, Paul Brewer, and Sean Aday, "Confidence in Government and Emotional Responses to Terrorism After September 11, 2001," *American Politics Research* 37 (2009): 107–128; Just, Crigler, and Belt, "Don't Give Up Hope"; and Kinder, "Reason and Emotion in American Political Life."

37. Marcus, Neuman, and MacKuen, *Affective Intelligence and Political Judgment*.
38. Wendy M. Rahn, Brian Kroeger, and Cynthia M. Kite, "A Framework for the Study of Public Mood," *Political Psychology* 17 (1996): 29–58; and Wendy M. Rahn, "Affect as Information: The Role of Public Mood in Political Reasoning," in *Elements of Reason*, ed. Arthur Lupia, Mathew McCubbins, and Samuel Popkin (New York: Cambridge University Press, 2000), pp. 135–150.
39. Linda Isbell and Victor Ottati, "The Emotional Voter," in *The Social Psychology of Politics*, ed. Victor Ottati, Scott Tindale, et al. (New York: Kluwer, 2002), pp. 55–74.
40. Alice H. Eagly and Shelly Chaiken, "Attitude Structure and Function," in *Handbook of Social Psychology*, ed. Daniel Gilbert, Susan Fiske, and Gardner Lindzey, 4th ed., vol. 2 (Boston: McGraw-Hill, 1998), pp. 269–322.
41. Marcus, Neuman, and MacKuen, *Affective Intelligence and Political Judgment*. Ladd and Lenz raise reasonable concerns that the emotions voters express toward candidates in surveys may partially or wholly be a consequence—rather than a cause—of the voting decision those voters have made. See Jonathan Ladd and Gabriel Lenz, "Reassessing the Role of Anxiety in Vote Choice," *Political Psychology* 29 (2008): 275–296; and cf. George Marcus, Michael MacKuen, and W. Russell Neuman, "Parsimony and Complexity: Developing and Testing Theories of Affective Intelligence," *Political Psychology* (2011). Fortunately, evidence on the indirect effects of emotions on opinion formation is now available from a diverse array of studies, some of which use methodological and measurement strategies where such concerns of reverse causation are minimized or eliminated. See Ted Brader, "The Political Relevance of Emotions: 'Reassessing' Revisited," *Political Psychology* (2011). Nonetheless, Ladd and Lenz's warning is an important reminder about interpreting and designing future studies.
42. Brader, *Campaigning for Hearts and Minds*.
43. Jennifer Merolla and Elizabeth Zechmeister, *Democracy at Risk: How Terrorist Threats Affect the Public* (Chicago: University of Chicago Press, 2009).
44. Donald Kinder and Lisa D'Ambrosio, "War, Emotion, and Public Opinion" (unpublished manuscript, University of Michigan, Ann Arbor, 2000); see also Marcus, Neuman, and MacKuen, *Affective Intelligence and Political Judgment*.
45. Baldwin M. Way and Roger D. Masters, "Political Attitudes: Interactions of Cognition and Affect," *Motivation and Emotion* 20 (1996): 205–236.
46. George Marcus, John Sullivan, Elizabeth Theiss-Morse, and Daniel Stevens, "The Emotional Foundation of Political Cognition," *Political Psychology* 26 (2005): 949–963.
47. Brader, *Campaigning for Hearts and Minds*.
48. For more details regarding the design of the study and these findings see Brader, *Campaigning for Hearts and Minds*, especially tables 5.1 and B.3.
49. Brader, *Campaigning for Hearts and Minds*.
50. Daniel T. Kahneman and Amos Tversky, "Choices, Values, and Frames," *American Psychologist* 39 (1984): 341–350.

51. James Druckman and Rose McDermott, "Emotion and the Framing of Risky Choice," *Political Behavior* 30 (2008): 297–321.
52. Deboral Small and Jennifer Lerner, "Emotional Policy: Personal Sadness and Anger Shape Judgments About a Welfare Case," *Political Psychology* 29 (2008): 149–168.
53. Lazarus, *Emotion and Adaptation*.
54. Nancy Burns and Donald Kinder, "Conviction and Its Consequences" (unpublished manuscript, University of Michigan, Ann Arbor, 2003); and Kinder, "Reason and Emotion in American Political Life."
55. Marcus, Neuman, and MacKuen, *Affective Intelligence and Political Judgment*.
56. Brader, *Campaigning for Hearts and Minds*.
57. Brader, Valentino, and Suhay, "What Triggers Public Opposition to Immigration?"
58. Nicholas Valentino, Ted Brader, Eric Groenendyk, Krysha Gregorowicz, and Vincent Hutchings, "Election Night's Alright for Fighting: The Role of Emotions in Political Participation," *Journal of Politics* 73 (2011): 156–170.
59. Nicholas Valentino, Krysha Gregorowicz, and Eric Groenendyk, "Efficacy, Emotions and the Habit of Participation," *Political Behavior* 31 (2009): 307–330.
60. For more details on the data and more extensive analyses of the impact of emotions on political participation, see Valentino et al., "Election Night's Alright for Fighting."
61. Cf. Valentino et al., "Election Night's Alright for Fighting."
62. Brader, *Campaigning for Hearts and Minds*; Brader, Valentino, and Suhay, "What Triggers Public Opposition to Immigration?"; and Marcus, Neuman, and MacKuen, *Affective Intelligence and Political Judgment*.
63. Note also that statistical controls include respondents' general interest in politics, which is not only a powerful predictor of participation, but also an outcome that previous experimental research demonstrates can be *influenced by* emotions. See Brader, *Campaigning for Hearts and Minds*. Thus, to the extent emotions are elevating the public's interest in politics and thereby encouraging more participation, Table 10.2 is likely to underestimate the impact of the emotions on participation.
64. For this analysis, we combine emotional responses to the two candidates. While we expect anger toward Obama and anger toward Romney to have very different effects on which candidate a person prefers, we expect them to have quite similar effects on motivating individuals to vote and get involved in politics. Thus, it makes sense to look at the overall level of each emotion when predicting citizens' motivation to take political action.
65. See Brader, *Campaigning for Hearts and Minds*; and Brader, "Striking a Responsible Chord."
66. Huddy, Feldman, and Cassese, "On the Distinct Political Effects of Anxiety and Anger"; and Jennifer Lerner, Roxana Gonzalez, Deborah Small, and Baruch Fischhoff, "Effects of Fear and Anger on Perceived Risks of Terrorism: A National Field Experiment," *Psychological Science* 14 (2003): 144–150.
67. Druckman and McDermott, "Emotion and the Framing of Risky Choice."
68. Linda Skitka, Christopher Bauman, Nicholas Aramovich, and G. Scott Morgan, "Confrontational and Preventative Policy Responses to Terrorism: Anger Wants a Fight and Fear Wants 'Them' to Go Away," *Basic and Applied Social Psychology* 28 (2006): 375–84; and cf. Leonie Huddy, Stanley Feldman, Charles Taber, and Gallya Lahav, "Threat, Anxiety, and Support for Antiterrorism Policies," *American Journal of Political Science* 4 (2005): 593–608.
69. Ted Brader, Eric Groenendyk, and Nicholas Valentino, "Fight or Flight? When Political Threats Arouse Public Anger or Fear" (unpublished manuscript, University of Michigan, 2010).
70. MacKuen et al., "Civic Engagements."

71. Diane Mackie, Thierry Devos and Eliot Smith, "Intergroup Emotions: Explaining Offensive Action Tendencies in an Intergroup Context," *Journal of Personality and Social Psychology* 79(4) (2000): 602–616.

72. Eliot Smith, Charles Seger, and Diane Mackie, "Can Emotions Be Truly Group Level? Evidence Regarding Four Conceptual Criteria," *Journal of Personality and Social Psychology* 93(3) (2007): 431–46 (p. 431). Importantly, group emotions are often distinct from individual emotions. For example, an individual can feel happy in their own life (about their achievements, family, etc.) but feel despair about the future of their social group (i.e. that their nation is heading down a wrong path, their religion is disappearing, etc.).

73. Vincent Yzerbyt, Muriel Dumont, Daniel Wibgoldus, and Ernestine Gordijn, "I Feel For Us: The Impact of Categorization and Identification on Emotions and Action Tendencies," *British Journal of Social Psychology* 42(4) (2003): 533–549.

74. Mabel Berezin, "Emotions and Political Identity: Mobilizing Affection towards a Polity," in *Passionate Politics: Emotions and Social Movements*, ed. J. Polletta (University of Chicago Press: Chicago, 2001), pp. 83–98.

75. Henry Tajfel and John Turner, "An Integrative Theory of Intergroup Conflict," in *The Social Psychology of Intergroup Relations*, eds William G. Austin, Stephen Worchel (California: Brooks/Cole Publishing Company, 1979), pp. 33–47.

76. Previous research has even found that individuals attribute higher-level 'secondary' emotions (e.g., admiration, nostalgia, sympathy) only to their in-group and not to out-group members. See Jacques-Philippe Leyens, Paula Paladino, Ramon Rodriguez-Torres, Jeroen Vaes, Stephanie Demoulin, and Armando Rodriguez Perez, "The Emotional Side of Prejudice: The Attributions of Secondary Emotions to Ingroups and Outgroups," *Personality and Social Psychology Review* 4(2) (2000): 186–197.

77. Smith et al., "Can Emotions Be Truly Group Level?"

78. Catherine A. Cottrell and Steven L. Neuberg, "Emotional Reactions to Different Groups: A Sociofunctional Threat-Based Approach to 'Prejudice,'" *Journal of Personality and Social Psychology* 88 (2005): 770–789; Catherine A. Cottrell, David A. R. Richards, and Austin Lee Nichols, "Predicting Policy Attitudes from General Prejudice versus Specific Intergroup Emotions," *Journal of Experimental Social Psychology* 46 (2010): 247–254.

79. Antoine J. Banks, *Anger and Racial Politics: The Emotional Foundation of Racial Attitudes in America* (New York: Cambridge University Press, 2014).

80. Yoel Inbar, David A. Pizarro, Joshua Knobe, and Paul Bloom, "Disgust Sensitivity Predicts Intuitive Disapproval of Gays," *Emotion* 9 (2009): 435–439; Yoel Inbar, David Pizarro, and Paul Bloom, "Disgusting Smells Cause Decreased Liking of Gay Men," *Emotion* 12 (2012): 23–27; Matthew Feiber, Olga Antonenko, Robb Willer, E. J. Horberg, and Oliver P. John, "Gut Check: Reappraisal of Disgust Helps Explain Liberal-Conservative Differences on Issues of Purity," *Emotion* 14 (2014): 513–521.

81. Khaled Fattah and K. Fierke, "A Clash of Emotions: The Politics of Humiliation and Political Violence in the Middle East," *European Journal of International Relations* 15(1) (2009): 67–93.

82. Cigdem Sirin, Jose Villarobos, and Nicholas Valentino, "Group Empathy Theory: Explaining Racial and Ethnic Gaps in Reactions to Terrorism and Immigration Threat" (unpublished).

83. K. Kugler, and W. H. Jones, "On conceptualizing and assessing guilt," *Journal of Personality and Social Psychology* 62 (1992): 318–327.

84. M. T. Schmitt, N. R. Branscombe, and J. W. Brehm, "Gender Inequality and the Intensity of Men's Collective Guilt," in N. R. Branscombe and B. Doosje (eds),

Collective Guilt: International Perspectives (New York: Cambridge University Press, 2003), pp. 75–94.

85. N. R. Branscombe, "A Social Psychological Process Perspective on Collective Guilt," in N. R. Branscombe and B. Doosje (eds), *Collective Guilt: International Perspectives* (New York: Cambridge University Press), pp. 320–334.

86. A. Bandura, B. Underwood, and M. E. Fromson, "Disinhibition of Aggression through Diffusion of Responsibility and Dehumanization of Victims," *Journal of Personality and Social Psychology* 9 (1975): 253–269; M. Hewstone, E. Cairns, A. Voci, F. McLernon, U. Neins, and M. Noor (2004), "Intergroup Forgiveness and Guilt in Northern Ireland," in N. R. Branscombe and B. Doosje (eds), *Collective Guilt: International Perspectives* (New York: Cambridge University Press), pp. 193–215; A. Balint (2003), "We are not Guilty: Alleviation of Group-Based Guilt in Readers' Letters to Gideon Levi's 'Twilight Time' Column," unpublished manuscript, Tel-Aviv University.

87. Small and Lerner, "Emotional Policy."

88. Yoel Inbar, David A. Pizarro, and Paul Bloom, "Conservatives Are More Easily Disgusted than Liberals," *Cognition and Emotion* 23 (2009): 714–25; and Simone Schnall, Jonathan Haidt, Gerald L. Clore, and Alexander H. Jordan, "Disgust as Embodied Moral Judgment," *Personality and Social Psychology Bulletin* 34 (2008): 1096–1109.

89. Elizabeth A. Suhay, "Group Influence and American Ideals: How Social Identity and Emotion Shape Our Political Values and Attitudes" (PhD diss., University of Michigan, 2008); cf. Alan S. Gerber, Donald P. Green, and Christopher W. Larimer, "An Experiment Testing the Relative Effectiveness of Encouraging Voter Participation by Inducing Feelings of Pride or Shame," *Political Behavior* 32 (2010): 409–422; and Stephen Knack and Martha Kropf, "For Shame! The Effect of Community Cooperative Context on the Probability of Voting," *Political Psychology* 19 (1998): 585–600.

90. Bryce Corrigan and Ted Brader, "Campaign Advertising: Reassessing the Impact of Campaign Ads on Political Behavior," in *New Directions in Campaigns and Elections*, ed. Stephen Medvic (New York: Routledge, 2011).

91. Eran Halperin, Keren Sharvit and James Gross, "Emotion and Emotion Regulations in Intergroup Conflict—An Appraisal Based Framework," in *Intergroup Conflicts and their Resolution: Social Psychological Perspective*, ed. Daniel Bar-Tal (New York: Psychology Press, 2008).

92. Eran Halperin, Roni Porat, Maya Tamir and James Gross, "Can Emotion Regulation Change Political Attitudes in Intractable Conflicts? From the Laboratory to the Field," *Psychological Science* 24(1) (2013): 106–111.

A Jump to the Right, A Step to the Left

Religion and Public Opinion

David E. Campbell, Geoffrey C. Layman, and John C. Green

On June 16, 2010, the Southern Baptist Convention (SBC) passed a resolution denouncing the massive oil spill in the Gulf of Mexico. The resolution called on the government "to act determinatively and with undeterred resolve to end this crisis; to fortify our coastal defenses; to ensure full corporate accountability for damages, clean-up and restoration; to ensure that government and private industry are not again caught without planning for such possibilities; and to promote future energy policies based on prudence, conservation, accountability, and safety." The SBC resolutions committee chairman told reporters, "There is no Pharaoh-like dominion over the Earth . . . there is a Christ-like stewardship of the Earth."[1]

Why was the largest evangelical Protestant denomination in the United States endorsing a liberal position on the environment—and justifying it on biblical grounds? Aren't evangelicals all extremely conservative and Republican?

As suggested by this one example, there is no iron law that links religion to the political right. It is true that on some issues many evangelicals, and religious Americans more generally, are highly conservative. But this is not true for all issues, nor for Americans of all religions. Neither has it been true over the nation's history. While, today, religion is most commonly associated with conservative positions like opposition to abortion and gay marriage, this has not always been so. In the past, abolitionism, pacifism, and calls for the radical redistribution of wealth have all emanated from the pulpits of America's churches, synagogues, and other places of worship. And even in today's political environment, there are religious leaders trying to nudge their flocks to the left rather than the right. This is most obviously the case in Black Protestant churches and Jewish synagogues—where there is a long tradition of political liberalism—but other religious voices advocate environmentalism, opposition to the death penalty, and amnesty for illegal immigrants. For example, Jim Wallis is an articulate, forceful voice for progressive causes—and a devout evangelical Protestant. Wallis speaks of how he holds his political views because of his evangelical beliefs, not in spite of them.[2] When put in that context, a pro-environmental resolution by the Southern Baptists should not be so surprising.

This chapter digs deep into the connections between public opinion and religion, to go beyond a simplistic description of religion-as-right-wing. We will show evidence that, on some issues, religion can also move opinions to the left. More broadly, our point is simply that the connections between religion and public opinion are more complex than commonly realized.

What Do We Mean By Religion?

Studying religion's impact on public opinion is complicated by the fact that religion is multidimensional. Scholars of religion often refer to the three "B's": belonging, behaving, and believing. These include the religious community or tradition to which someone belongs, the frequency of religious behavior (attendance at worship services, private prayer), and one's specific religious beliefs (Is there life after death? Should scripture be taken literally?). But even these three dimensions do not exhaust the many facets of religion, and therefore the ways that it might affect public opinion.

Given this complexity in the analysis of religion, a good place to start is with religious belonging—specifically, the *religious tradition* to which someone belongs. Social scientists have classified the myriad religions, and denominations within those religions, into a manageable set of religious families, or traditions. These include evangelical and mainline Protestants—the former being more theologically conservative than the latter. Owing to the unique history of the Black Church in America, Black Protestants are considered distinct—agreeing with white evangelicals on many doctrines, but diverging in other important ways (e.g. their emphasis on liberation theology). Other religious traditions include Catholics, Jews, and Mormons. There are still more traditions, including Muslims, Buddhists, Sikhs and the like, but they are generally in such small numbers that most surveys of the national population have too few cases for reliable analysis. As the United States becomes more religiously diverse and these religious groups grow in numbers, scholars will be wise to learn more about the public opinion of members of these small-but-growing religions.

It is also important to pause and note that in speaking about how religion affects public opinion, we are implicitly acknowledging that public opinion can also be affected by the absence of religion in someone's worldview. While the United States remains a highly religious nation—especially when compared to other industrialized democracies—recent years have seen an increase in the percentage of Americans who report having no religious affiliation. Up until the late 1980s, roughly 7 percent of the population told pollsters they had no religion. By the mid-2000s that had more than doubled to 15 percent—and up to 25 percent among people under age thirty. Many of these "religious nones"[3] appear to be disassociated from organized religion but not from religious beliefs per se, as large numbers of them believe in God. One theory explaining the rise of the nones is that they are the product of a political environment where religion is intimately connected to politics, and to conservative politics at that.

They believe that identifying with a religion implies that they are sympathetic to the Religious Right; thus, they choose to identify as a none. Whatever the explanation for their growth, roughly a third of the nones are what Putnam and Campbell label "liminals"—half in a religion and half out—as they flit back and forth from reporting a religious affiliation to identifying as a none.[4] Also found among the ranks of the nones, though, is a group of ardent secularists. They are more than passively "non religious"; they have affirmatively rejected any religious influence on their lives. As their ranks grow, public opinion scholars will need to remember that studying "religion" also means studying the absence of, or even outright rejection of, religion. This chapter will take a step in that direction by examining how voters who have both high and low levels of personal religiosity react to religious cues by political candidates. Future research will profit from employing measures that differentiate between liminal, passive, and committed secularists.

Why Religion Might, or Might Not, Affect Public Opinion

However, we are getting ahead of ourselves. To discuss *how* religion affects public opinion presupposes that it does, indeed, have such an effect. Not everyone agrees. Below we lay out the arguments for both points of view.

Why Religion Might Matter

Perhaps the primary reason why we might expect religion to shape public opinion is simply that religion is a source of values and beliefs. What other institution regularly offers instruction explicitly designed to inculcate a particular worldview, and has extensive terminology and symbology to do so? Religions are in the business of indoctrination. It seems reasonable to expect that at least some of those religious doctrines would have political relevance.

Previous research has provided evidence that various aspects of religion can have an effect on public opinion. The clearest evidence is that higher religiosity—no matter how measured—corresponds to conservative opinions on issues that relate to sex and the family, specifically abortion and gay marriage.[5] The fact that religious people have conservative opinions on issues related to sexuality is not new. For as far back as we have data, this has been the case.[6] However, the political salience of these issues is relatively new. In the current political environment, these issues are the glue uniting the "coalition of the religious" that votes predominantly Republican. Prior to the mid-1980s— when the Religious Right emerged in American politics—these issues had little political relevance and, consequently, religion had little to do with how Americans voted.

There have also been a few studies that examine how religion affects opinion in domains other than social issues. For example, Barker and Carman provide a detailed analysis of how religious doctrine affects economic attitudes. Drawing on Max Weber's seminal *Spirit of Capitalism*, they find evidence that the beliefs of theologically-conservative Protestants lead to economically conservative opinions.[7] Similarly, Wilson shows that economic attitudes have historically differed by religious tradition.[8] In an intriguing study, Guth et al. find a belief that the "end times" are coming soon correlates with opposition to environmentalism. According to this apocalyptic worldview, not only does the imminent end of the world make efforts toward environmental protection futile, environmental problems are themselves a sign that Christ will soon return (a doctrine known as "dispensationalism" or "pre-millennialism").[9] In a study of religion and opinion on international affairs, Barker et al. find that a belief in the authority of the Bible leads to greater support for a militaristic foreign policy, especially military support for Israel.[10] Guth also highlights how religious beliefs correspond to support for an aggressively interventionist foreign policy—again, with conservative beliefs corresponding to conservative political opinions.[11]

Layman and Green offer an explanation for why religion matters most for attitudes on social issues, and less so for issues like the economy and foreign policy.[12] They use Converse's famous distinction between various "sources of constraint" in public opinion to argue that the relationship between religious orientations and policy attitudes is likely to be strongest and most consistent across religious contexts when there is a logical connection between religious values and issue positions. For example, someone who views the Bible as the authoritative Word of God might be expected to oppose gay marriage. When the logic of how religious values relate to policy positions is less clear, the sources of constraint linking religion and issue attitudes have to be either individuals' psychological orientations or their social experiences—making the relevance of religion for these policy attitudes weaker overall and stronger in some religious groups than in others. Consider tax policy. It is not obvious what a belief in authoritative scripture means for one's opinion regarding the capital gains tax. Supporting this argument, Layman and Green find that religious commitment and the orthodoxy of religious beliefs are strongly related to conservative attitudes on moral and cultural issues such as abortion and gay rights across all of the major religious traditions. However, the effect of religious orientations on positions regarding social welfare, defense, and environmental attitudes is generally weaker and far more pronounced for evangelical Protestants than for mainline Protestants and Catholics. Consistent with Layman and Green, Putnam and Campbell show that, when controlling for other factors affecting public opinion, religious and secular Americans have sharply different opinions on abortion and gay marriage—with opposition to both concentrated among the highly religious. However, religious and secular Americans' opinions differ only modestly on social welfare, foreign aid, foreign policy, and civil liberties. They also find that, within the general population, religion has no connection to attitudes on immigration and the death penalty—two of the issues that we will examine in more detail below.[13]

The challenge in making sense out of this research literature is that scholars often conceptualize and thus measure "religion" in different ways. Some studies look at belonging, others examine behaving, and others focus on believing. Even when two studies are looking at the same dimension of religion, their precise measures often differ. Nonetheless, this small literature has, collectively, begun to make the case that religion does have a causal effect on political attitudes.

Why Religion Might Not Matter

That case, though, is not yet closed. For all the reasons that the various dimensions of religion might affect public opinion, there are also plausible reasons to suspect that they do not actually have any effect. For example, while there is no doubt that religions are in the belief business, it is not always clear how a given religious belief translates into public policy. Virtually all religions speak of concern for the poor; but does that mean a believer should support a generous welfare state or favor private charities as a means to provide assistance to the disadvantaged?

Even when religious leaders do make explicit the connection between a religious belief and a political view, there is no guarantee that the "people in the pews" will adopt that political attitude. American Catholics are an excellent example. In spite of the Roman Catholic Church's longstanding opposition to abortion, a majority of Catholics nonetheless support a woman's right to choose an abortion in at least some circumstances. An even greater majority of Catholics support the death penalty, again in spite of the Church's teachings otherwise.

Even when the political beliefs held by members of a religious group correlate with the teachings within a religion, it is still not the "smoking gun" to establish a truly causal relationship. The fluid nature of American religion means that where and how one worships is typically a matter of individual choice. This is why in the U.S. religion is often referred to as a preference rather than an ascribed characteristic. People frequently switch religions and, even more frequently, move from one congregation to another. Roughly a third of all Americans switch religious traditions over the course of their lifetimes, including switching to "no religion"; half have shopped for a new congregation.[14] With all of this fluidity, Americans sort themselves into like-minded religious groups— including when it comes to politics. Thus, for some people, it may not be that religion influences someone's political attitudes so much as those political attitudes influence someone's choice of religion. Or, as noted in the above discussion of the rise of the religious nones, a negative reaction to the mixture of religion and politics can lead people to disavow a religious identity at all. Similarly, politics can also influence religious behavior such that, over time, conservatives become more fervent and liberals less so. In other words, Americans are sorting themselves into "camps" defined both by their religion and their politics—religious conservatives in one and secular liberals in another.

Religion and Party Identification: The Indirect Effect Hypothesis

In between the contrasting arguments that religion either does, or does not, shape public opinion is still another possibility. It could be that religion affects public opinion through its impact on party identification. Party identification, in turn, shapes political attitudes. Call this the "indirect effect" hypothesis. It would still mean that religion matters, but is one step removed from having a direct effect on voters' opinions. Or, it could be that religion has a direct effect on some attitudes toward issues, and an indirect effect—through party identification—on others.

Religion, or more accurately "religious traditionalism," has become a major predictor of partisanship over roughly the last three decades. A number of studies have shown that, beginning in the 1980s and then accelerating through the 1990s, a so-called "God gap" has opened up in American politics, whereby highly religious voters are more likely to identify as Republicans than Democrats. Some have described this change as a "culture war" that divides the electorate between religiously orthodox and religiously progressive voters. Using more temperate language, Green refers to this change as the "old religion gap" between religious denominations—e.g., Catholic vs. Protestant—being replaced by a new "religion gap." This new gap is defined not by one's denomination, but instead one's level of religious devotion.[15]

One important reason for this shift has been the parties' differing positions on cultural issues like homosexual rights and—especially—abortion, which as noted above, are the two issues that have the strongest correlation with religiosity. But in addition to the issues emphasized by candidates, the God gap has resulted from the religious "brand label" adopted by many Republican candidates. For at least a generation, Republicans running for office have been more likely to describe themselves in religious terms than their Democratic opponents. A particularly memorable example arose in the 2004 presidential election, when the Republican National Committee sent many thousands of glossy fliers to Ohio voters, complete with prominent images of churches and statements that the Republicans are the party "defending traditional marriage."[16]

We need not rely on anecdotal examples to see how religion has infused the Republican Party's brand. When we examine systematic data, the Republican Party is more likely to be associated with religion than is the Democratic Party. For example, when compared to the Democrats, more Americans say that the Republicans are friendly to religion.[17] Another piece of evidence comes from the groups that voters associate with each of the parties. When we asked voters to list the groups that came to mind when they thought of either party, the only group of people who came out ahead of various religious groups was "conservatives"—a group that, for many readers, is probably synonymous with Republicans (although in the not-so-distant past, there really was such a thing as a liberal Republican, and even today there are still a few conservative Democrats left). In sharp contrast, religious groups provide an infinitesimal share of the groups associated with the Democratic Party.[18] The Democrats' brand appears to be undergoing a shift. While voters see the Republicans as friendly to religion, they have not generally viewed the Democrats as hostile to religion.[19] However, this might be starting to change, as the percentage of Americans who say the Democrats are friendly to religion has been dropping steadily, from 42 percent in 2003 to 29 percent in 2014, while the percentage saying that the Democrats are unfriendly toward religion has risen from 12 percent in 2003 to 25 percent in 2014.[20] This perception is no doubt due to incidents like the controversy stirred by the initial omission of a reference to God in the 2012 Democratic Party platform; because of the controversy, God was inserted into the platform—a reminder both that America is a highly religious nation, and that many Americans expect religion and politics to go hand in hand.[21] (The 2012 Republican platform mentions God at least 10 times.) Perhaps not surprisingly, the Republicans' religious brand label has meant that it is increasingly the home of religiously devout voters. Nonetheless, we should not forget the notable exception of African Americans, who as a group are highly religious but also predominantly Democratic (a hint that religion does not always move people rightward).

Thus far, we have proposed three alternatives for the potential influence of religion and public opinion. Perhaps it has no effect, in which case there is no point in studying religion and public opinion any further. Or, maybe religion has an indirect effect, by influencing partisanship which, in turn, affects public opinion. If so, future research could be limited to understanding how religion affects party identification. Alternatively, there could be a direct, causal link between religion and public opinion, which would justify the further study of how, when, and why it has an effect.

Does Religious Always Mean Conservative?

Today, religion is routinely equated with political conservatism. But this has not always been the case. American history is replete with political mobilizers who have drawn on religion to inspire support for their cause. Some are easily categorized as conservatives, others as liberals, while still others do not map neatly onto a one-dimensional ideological map. Today, conservative opponents of abortion and gay marriage often use religiously-grounded arguments. While these issues are, in historical terms, relatively new on the political agenda, the religious inflection of political rhetoric is not new at all. The American Revolution itself had religious underpinnings. Later on, abolitionism and, later still, the civil rights movement both had religious roots. Prohibition had a religious inflection, as did anti-communism in the Cold War. But so did opposition to the Vietnam War, and to war in general. In presidential politics, William Jennings Bryan—three-time Democratic nominee for the presidency— passionately defended the economic interests of laborers and farmers with fiery religious talk in the late nineteenth and early twentieth centuries. In perhaps the most famous speech ever delivered at a political convention, Bryan declared that the economic system of his day would "crucify mankind upon a cross of gold." Just to make his meaning clear, he then stood with his arms outstretched as though hanging on a cross.[22] More recently, while running for president in 1976 Jimmy Carter declared himself to be "born again," while—in probably the most cited example of presidential God talk—presidential candidate George W. Bush described "Christ" as his favorite political philosopher because "he changed my heart." Barack Obama is also no stranger to religious language; as a presidential candidate he spoke often of his conversion to Christianity.[23]

The fact that so many political candidates and activists use religious language suggests that religion can shape public opinion. These examples are hardly an exhaustive list of how religion has been woven into our national politics. Yet because they are all over the political map, collectively they suggest that the religious framing of issues has not historically been limited to one side of the political spectrum.

Unfortunately, however, the scholarship on religion and public opinion might also lead you to the conclusion that religion nearly always pulls attitudes rightward. Since virtually all empirical research on religion and political attitudes has come during the era of the God gap, the great majority of it has focused on how religion and conservative ideology/Republican partisanship go together. Similarly, you may recall that the above examples of how religion affects attitudes on the environment, economic policy, and foreign policy all show how various religious beliefs drive conservative opinions. One intriguing exception is found in Barker et al.'s research on religion and militarism in foreign policy. They actually find that greater religious devotion leads to a liberal perspective on foreign policy—once they subtract out the influence of exposure to the Religious Right (what they refer to as "Christian culture").

When we direct our attention from political rhetoric to the substance of religious teachings, we see further reason to think that religion can buttress liberal, as well as conservative, attitudes. Many religions have doctrines that unambiguously align with the political left. In fact, there are notable examples of religious traditions whose adherents are predominantly political liberals rather than conservatives. Jews are one, while Black Protestants are another.

Even religious traditions that are not known as bastions of liberal politics can have left-leaning teachings. Among Protestants there is a long tradition of the "social gospel," a belief that churches should be involved in eradicating poverty. In recent years, some evangelical pastors have publicly called for anti-poverty legislation, aid to Africa to fight AIDS, and greater environmental regulation. Do these appeals work? As evidence that they do, or at least that they *can*, Djupe and Gwiasda[24] find that evangelicals—known for their political conservatism—become more liberal on environmental policy when they learn of a fellow evangelical having a religious "conversion experience" about the danger of global warming.

Catholicism also espouses teachings that align with the political left. Many Catholic theologians speak of a "preferential option for the poor"—which often translates into support for a generous welfare state. As we noted earlier, Catholic teaching also opposes the death penalty. While, as also noted, most Catholics actually favor capital punishment, this fact does not necessarily mean that the Church's teachings fall on deaf ears. Below we will test whether devout Catholics are more likely to oppose the death penalty than less-committed Catholics— which would suggest that they are absorbing their Church's teachings after all.

Even religious traditions known for their political conservatism occasionally take policy stands on the left. Consider, for example, the Church of Jesus Christ of Latter-day Saints, or the Mormon Church. Mormons are arguably the most politically conservative religious group in the country; certainly, they are the most heavily Republican. Typically, when the Mormon Church has been involved in politics it has been on the conservative side of social issues. Most recently, the Mormon Church has been a leading opponent of gay marriage. Indeed, in 2008 the Mormon Church took a high-profile position in support of California's Proposition 8, a state constitutional amendment to ban gay marriage. On immigration, though, Mormons are not nearly as conservative as on other issues. Immigration is an issue on which Mormon leaders have cut against the grain and sent signals favoring a liberal position, thus providing an important test for the influence of religion over political ideology. In the predominantly Mormon state of Utah, support for a bill that was punitive toward illegal immigrants (it would have denied them in-state tuition at Utah colleges) dropped over 20 points once a prominent Mormon leader spoke publicly of the need for compassion toward immigrants, and another signed a statement opposing the bill. As shown below, Mormons are also the religious group least likely to think that there should be a decrease in the percentage of "immigrants from foreign countries who are permitted to come to the United States to live."

In sum, while there is generally a correlation between religiosity and political conservatism, both historical and contemporary evidence indicates that religion has often been used in defense of positions on the ideological left rather than the right. However, it remains an open question whether, *in the current religious and political environment*, religion can actually move political attitudes to the left.

The Verdict

Having laid out the reasons why religion might—and might not—influence public opinion and, if so, why it might not always move attitudes rightward, we turn to some evidence to try and answer these questions.

We begin by comparing the attitudes of people in America's major religious traditions, including "none of the above." In addition to the nones, these include Catholics, mainline Protestants, evangelical Protestants, Black Protestants, Jews, and Mormons.[25] The data we use comes from the Faith Matters survey, a nationally-representative survey of 3,100 respondents.[26] Our comparisons are made by estimating a statistical model that holds constant an array of demographic factors that could both affect political attitudes and are potentially confounded with membership in a given religious tradition, including living in the South, education, age, race (African American), ethnicity (Hispanic), marital status, and gender. For example, the model controls for whether someone lives in the South because Southerners are most likely to be evangelicals and to have conservative moral and cultural attitudes. We want to ensure that any impact we attribute to being an evangelical is not actually because someone lives in the South.

Figures 11.1–11.4 include one more control variable that, given our above discussion, is especially critical: party identification. We have accounted for any differences in partisanship across these religious traditions. In doing so, we are testing what we labeled above the "indirect effect" hypothesis: that religion's impact on public opinion works through partisanship. If there are no differences across religious traditions once we account for their differing partisan allegiances, then we can conclude that the indirect effect hypothesis is correct. On the other hand, if differences across religious traditions survive even when accounting for their adherents' party identification, that is evidence for a direct effect of religion on political attitudes. (Although there could still be indirect effects; it would only mean that they are not the whole story.)[27]

We focus on four issues: abortion, the death penalty, environmental policy, and immigration. These four issues are all politically salient, and have a plausible connection to religious doctrines. Abortion and capital punishment are often discussed in religious terms, while the environment has increasingly been given a religious frame (e.g., "creation care"). As the immigration debate has heated up, many religious leaders have argued on behalf of compassion for undocumented workers over the strict enforcement of immigration laws.[28]

We calculate the mean opinion on each issue within each of America's major religious traditions, while also accounting for demographic and partisan differences across these groups. The results are displayed in Figures 11.1–11.4. The figures all display the percentage taking a conservative position on the issue in question: the percentage who are pro-life favor the death penalty, oppose more government spending on the environment, and favor reducing immigration. Figure 11.1, for example, displays the results for abortion. Specifically, the figure shows the percentage in each religious tradition who oppose abortion in all circumstances, or only approve of it in cases of rape, incest, and when the life of the mother is in jeopardy. As you can see, attitudes on abortion vary dramatically across religious traditions. Only 15 percent of Jews oppose abortion, compared to 62 percent of both evangelicals and Mormons.

Differences are far more muted on the death penalty, however. Capital punishment has majority support across all religious traditions, although support among Jews and Catholics is a little lower. On the environment, there

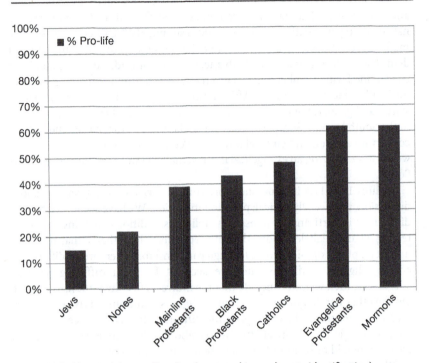

Figure 11.1 Abortion (controlling for demographics and party identification).

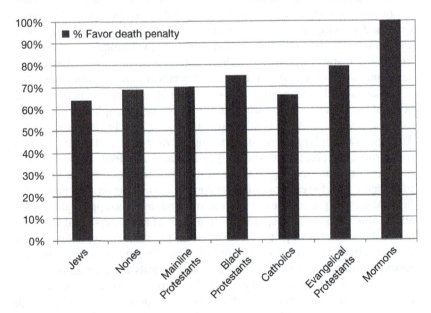

Figure 11.2 Death Penalty (controlling for demographics and party identification).

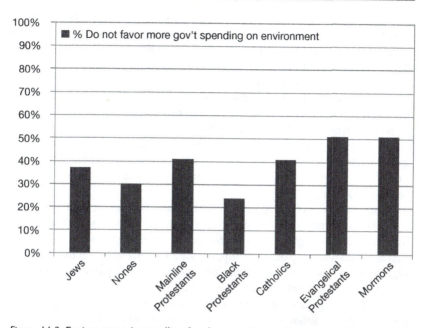

Figure 11.3 Environment (controlling for demographics and party identification).

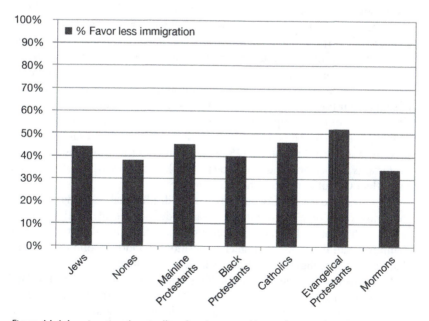

Figure 11.4 Immigration (controlling for demographics and party identification).

are again only modest differences, but this time because the conservative option is in the minority—except among evangelicals and Mormons, where opinion splits half-and-half. On this issue, Black Protestants are the most liberal, with nones and Jews right behind.

Immigration is another story all together. Opinion on immigration does not vary much across religious traditions. Nones and Black Protestants are among the most liberal, which is no surprise given their general liberal ideology. Only 38 percent of nones and 40 percent of Black Protestants favor less immigration, compared to 52 percent of evangelicals. As alluded to earlier, Mormons are the group whose attitudes on immigration cut against their general ideological profile. Only 34 percent of Mormons favor less immigration—the lowest of any religious tradition.

What do we learn from these comparisons across religious traditions? First, we see that differences in opinion survive even when accounting for the partisan make-up of each religious tradition. So, even though most Jews are Democrats, that alone does not explain their support for abortion rights. On the other side of that issue, evangelicals are heavily Republican, but their party affiliation does not completely account for their opposition to abortion.

Nor does religion's impact reduce to demography. Even when accounting for demographic differences across these groups, members of different religious traditions have widely varying opinions on some issues (most notably abortion). Nonetheless, the mere existence of these differences does not cinch the case that religion in and of itself shapes opinion. The very same results could follow from people sorting themselves into different religions on the basis of their political views, rather than the religions themselves influencing their politics.

Some of the specific differences we observe, however, suggest that perhaps the religions themselves influence opinion, rather than the other way around. Furthermore, they also provide some evidence that religion can move opinions to the left as well as the right. Catholics, for example, have a relatively low level of support for the death penalty, which is presumably because of the Catholic Church's opposition to capital punishment. While a majority of Catholics favor capital punishment (66 percent), that is quite a bit lower than evangelicals (79 percent) and Black Protestants (75 percent), and a little lower than mainline Protestants (70 percent) and nones (69 percent). Only Jews (64 percent) are less likely than Catholics to favor the death penalty.

A modestly lower level of support for the death penalty among Catholics than most other religious traditions is hardly definitive evidence that Church teachings have had a huge, or any, effect on Catholics' attitudes. It is no more definitive than the modestly higher opposition to abortion among Catholics than most other religious traditions. Still, it is suggestive.

More convincing evidence of religion's impact on political attitudes—and in a leftward direction—can be seen among Mormons. This highly conservative group nonetheless has the most liberal attitudes on immigration, an outcome that is difficult to explain solely on the basis of self-selection. It seems more plausible that Mormons' relatively liberal perspective on immigration is a result of their religion. However, scratching below the surface of that conclusion only underscores the complexity of understanding religion's impact on attitudes. Are Mormons liberal on immigration because they are members of a religious minority, and thus empathize with immigrants?[29] Is it because so many Mormons do missionary work in foreign countries, often in Latin America?[30] Is it because the LDS Church accommodates undocumented immigrants within its ranks?[31] Or, most likely, is it owing to some combination of these, and perhaps other, factors? These are the sorts of questions to which the public opinion literature has not yet provided definitive answers—whether for the specific case of Mormons, or for other religious traditions more generally.

Religiosity

Having seen some evidence of differences in public opinion across religious traditions, we turn next to a different aspect of religion: religious commitment, or religiosity. Think of religious tradition—Catholic, evangelical, etc.—as the "flavor" of one's religion, while religiosity is the intensity of that flavor. Our measure of religiosity is an index that includes six different measures of religious commitment: frequency of religious attendance, frequency of prayer, importance of religion in one's daily life, religion as a source of personal identity, being a strong believer in one's religion, and strength of belief in God. All of these go together, so that people who score high on one measure are likely to be high on another.

We examine how attitudes vary as religiosity increases in Figures 11.5–11.7. Each graph displays how attitudes in a given religious tradition change as religiosity moves from low to high, while also accounting for demographic characteristics.[32] For these figures, religiosity is divided into quintiles—that is, five equal-sized "bins" of religiosity. Each line in the graph represents a different issue: abortion, death penalty, environment, and immigration. We are only able to show results for the three largest religious traditions in the United States; evangelical Protestants, mainline Protestants, and Catholics. The other traditions have too few members, even in a large national survey, to produce reliable results in an analysis such as this.[33]

Across these three religious traditions, the results are strikingly similar. In each group, abortion has far and away the strongest relationship to religiosity—higher religiosity is associated with greater opposition to abortion. Among the two Protestant traditions, attitudes on the environment also shift rightward as religiosity increases; among Catholics, religiosity has no bearing on environmental attitudes. On immigration, there is essentially a flat line for all three traditions, meaning that opinion on immigration is unrelated to religiosity.

Opinion on the death penalty also shows a consistent pattern. Within each tradition, greater religiosity is associated with considerably less support for the death penalty. Majorities still support capital punishment, but the drop in

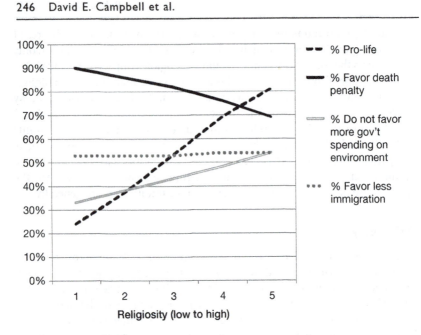

Figure 11.5 Evangelical Protestants.

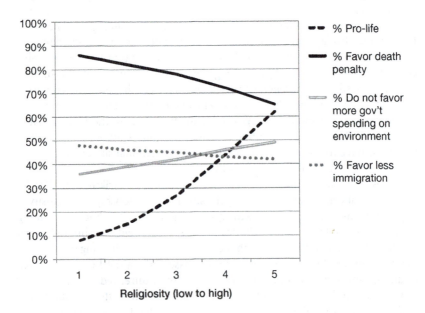

Figure 11.6 Mainline Protestants.

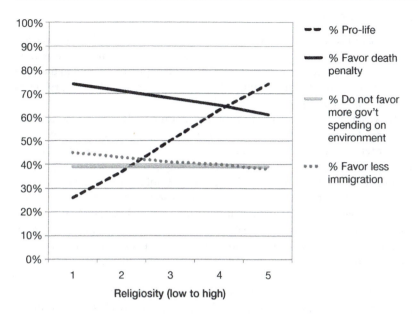

Figure 11.7 Catholics.

support as religiosity rises from the bottom to the top quintile is nonetheless considerable. In other words, higher religiosity correlates with a liberal position on capital punishment.[34]

What conclusions can be drawn from this analysis of religiosity's impact on attitudes? For one, religiosity generally has a consistent relationship with opinions across the three largest religious traditions in the United States. That consistency includes one case where there is no connection between religiosity and opinion (immigration), one where religiosity moves opinion rightward (abortion), and another where it moves to the left (death penalty).

In the fourth case, environmental policy, rising religiosity moves attitudes to the right among evangelical and mainline Protestants, but not among Catholics. This difference in environmental attitudes among Protestants and Catholics could be related to Protestant beliefs about the "end times." As has been noted already, previous research has shown that those who believe that the world will end soon, a belief more commonly held by Protestants than Catholics—and highly religious Protestants at that—are less likely to support pro-environmental policies.

In sum, we have seen evidence that even in a political climate where religion is generally associated with conservative politics, religion can also serve to push public opinion to the left. No iron law links religion and political conservatism.

Religious Framing

As we have already mentioned, determining a causal relationship between any aspect of religion and public opinion is elusive. Causal inference is most convincing with a randomized experiment, but that proves difficult in the study of religion. It would require randomly assigning people to different religions, or different levels of personal religiosity.

However, it *is* possible to use experimental methods to test how voters of differing degrees of religiosity react when an issue is framed in religious vs. secular terms. Can candidates succeed in using a religious frame, thus winning the support of highly religious voters? And can they do so without losing the support of low-religiosity voters? We can test voters' reactions to religious frames by presenting hypothetical candidates to voters, some of whom use religious language to explain their rationale for a certain issue position and some who instead offer a secular rationale. In conducting such an experiment, we are able to test our two central questions from a new perspective: does religious framing influence voters' opinion, and can that influence be in a liberal direction?

The design of the experiment is simple. Respondents were given descriptions of two candidates, and asked whether they would be more likely to vote for one or the other. Each candidate had a party label, and was identified as having taken a conservative or liberal position on global warming, the death penalty, or immigration. In the results we display below, we examine what happens when a Republican candidate takes the liberal position on each of these three issues, in contrast to a conservative Democratic opponent. Half of the time the Republican candidate uses a religious frame for his liberal position, and the other half he uses a secular frame. The experiment thus enables us to see whether a candidate can earn greater support for a liberal policy position by framing it in religious terms.[35] (For the wording used in the experiment, see the appendix to this chapter.)

In presenting the results, we divide respondents into three levels of religious commitment, as determined by an index similar to the one employed above.[36] This way, we can see how religious frames affect voters who have varying levels of personal religiosity.[37]

Figures 11.8–11.10 all have the same format. The darker bars show the percentage choosing the Republican candidate when he uses a secular frame; the lighter bars represent the Republican's support when using a religious frame. The difference between the bars, then, is the effect of a religious vs. a secular frame. For all three issues, we see that highly religious voters respond favorably to a religious frame, and thus are more likely to vote for the Republican candidate than when he uses a secular frame for the same issue position. For them, the religion effect is positive, statistically significant, and in a liberal direction.

Among voters with low religiosity, the story is more nuanced. On the environment, there is such a slight drop for the religious frame that it is

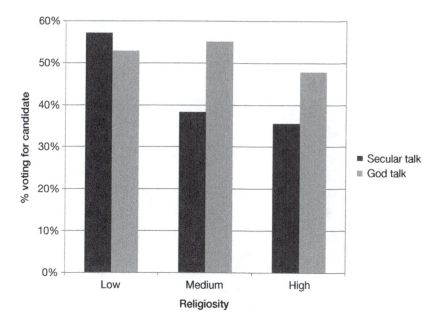

Figure 11.8 Secular Vs. Religious Frame for the Environment.

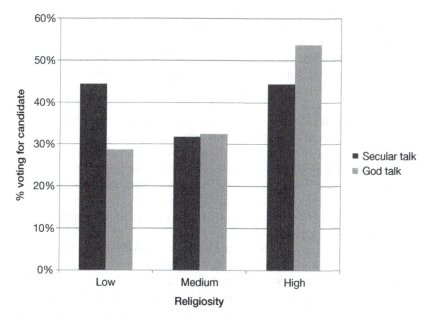

Figure 11.9 Secular Vs. Religious Frame for the Death Penalty.

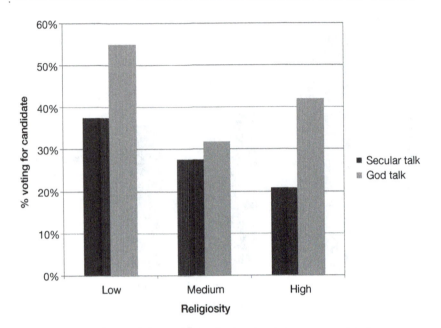

Figure 11.10 Secular Vs. Religious Frame for Immigration.

statistically meaningless. On the death penalty, there is a more substantial drop in support for a God-talking candidate (from 44 to 29 percent, which is statistically significant). However, when the issue is immigration, the God-talking candidate actually picks up support from low-religiosity voters.[38] This is the only issue for which God talk increases support across the religiosity spectrum. (Middle-religiosity voters increase their support, but the 4-point rise does not achieve statistical significance.)

The overall story is that religious framing of issues can affect how voters respond to a candidate. For high-religiosity voters, this effect is most pronounced for the environment and immigration. The weaker effect for the death penalty may be related to the fact that high-religiosity voters are actually less likely to support capital punishment than more secular voters. Consequently, a religious cue to justify opposition to it may only be reinforcing a previously-held opinion rather than successfully challenging voters' preconceptions.

Among low-religiosity voters, sometimes a religious frame decreases support for a liberal position (death penalty), sometimes it has no effect (environment), and sometimes it can increase support (immigration). The increased support for a liberal position on immigration is intriguing, as it suggests that even secular voters may be persuaded by a religious rationale for a controversial position.

Conclusion

The discussion of religion in contemporary politics typically assumes that religion equals conservatism, and support for the Republican Party in particular. That assumption is not wholly unwarranted, as more religious Americans are generally more likely to identify as Republicans than the less religious. Yet notwithstanding this general tendency, there are still important exceptions. Most notably, African Americans are simultaneously the most religious and the most Democratic group within the population. Historically, religion has also inspired many politically progressive causes. Even in today's political environment, religion is associated with liberal attitudes on at least one issue— the death penalty. Furthermore, our experimental evidence suggests that highly religious voters respond favorably to candidates who use religious frames for liberal positions on the environment, capital punishment, and immigration.

In showing that religion is not ineluctably associated with conservatism, our results also speak to the fundamental question of whether religion affects public opinion at all. Given that highly religious voters are *generally* conservative and Republican, to find a correlation between religion (and/or religiosity) and liberal attitudes strengthens the argument that it is religion driving opinion, and not opinion driving the choice of religion.

However, this chapter is merely a start to understanding the ways in which religion may—or may not—affect public opinion. Many more facets of religion in America are largely unexplored. Djupe and Gilbert, for example, stress the need for more attention to the political deliberation that takes place within congregations.[39] Other examples include the political implications of specific beliefs taught in various denominations, the growing ranks of the nones (who themselves are not monolithic), and the rising number of Americans who affiliate with Islam and other minority religions. But this list, too, is only a start, as there are myriad ways that the varied aspects of religion might move public opinion—both to the left and the right.

Appendix

Following are the questions used to gauge opinion on abortion, the death penalty, the environment, and immigration policy in the Faith Matters 2006 survey.

Abortion

Which one of these opinions best corresponds to your view?

1. By law, abortion should never be permitted;
2. The law should permit abortion only in cases of rape, incest, or when the woman's life is in danger;

3. The law should permit abortion for reasons other than rape, incest, or danger to the woman's life, but only after the need for the abortion has been clearly established; or
4. By law, a woman should always be able to obtain an abortion as a matter of personal choice.

(Respondents were randomly assigned to receive the options in this or the reverse order)

In the results shown, options 1 and 2 were combined into one pro-life category, and 3 and 4 into a pro-choice category.

Death Penalty

Do you favor or oppose the death penalty for persons convicted of murder?

1. Favor death penalty for persons convicted of murder.
2. Oppose death penalty for persons convicted of murder.

Environment

Next I am going to read you a list of federal programs. For each one, I would like you to tell me whether you would like to see spending increased, decreased or kept about the same. The (first/next) program is Environmental Protection. Would you like to see spending for this increased, decreased, or kept about the same?

1. Spending increased.
2. Decreased.
3. Kept about the same.

Immigration

Do you think the number of immigrants from foreign countries who are permitted to come to the United States to live should be increased a lot, increased a little, left the same as it is now, decreased a little or decreased a lot?

1. Increased a lot.
2. Increased a little.
3. Left the same as it is now.
4. Decreased a little.
5. Decreased a lot.

In the analysis, options 1–2 and 4–5 were each combined into one category, thus creating a tripartite variable. The results show the percentage who favor less immigration (options 4 and 5). Below are the frames used in the framing experiment in the 2008 Cooperative Campaign Analysis Project.

Environment

Please read the descriptions of the following two candidates for the U.S. Congress and tell us who you would be more likely to vote for.

Robert Williams is age 48, married, and has three children. A Republican, he has served three terms in his state legislature. When asked in a debate about his position on the need to reduce global warming, he responded with enthusiasm:

> "Protecting the environment must be our top priority. I am in favor of working to reduce global warming." <Secular>

Or

> "God has given us this earth, and we must protect it. The Bible says we are to care for God's creation." <Religious>

Michael Clark is age 51, married, and also has three children. A Democrat, he has served for six years on his local school board. When asked in a debate about his position on the need to reduce global warming, he responded with skepticism:

> "I am in favor of putting jobs first, and oppose any so-called environmental bill that would hurt our economy." <Secular>

Based on the above information, would you be more likely to vote for Robert Williams or Michael Clark?

The frames for the death penalty used the same biographical information for the two candidates but varied the issue frames, as below.

Death Penalty

When asked in a debate about his position on the death penalty, he indicated his opposition.

> "I am against the death penalty. It is too easy to convict the wrong person, as shown whenever DNA evidence frees an innocent man." <Secular>

Or

"Only God should decide who lives and who dies. The Bible says 'thou shalt not kill,' which means even those who have committed terrible crimes." <Religious>

When asked in a debate about his position on the death penalty, he indicated his support.

"I favor capital punishment for the most violent criminals. The death penalty is the right punishment for those found guilty of first-degree murder." <Secular>

The immigration experiment was conducted on a separate survey than the previous two and thus used different hypothetical candidates, as described below.

Immigration

Please read the descriptions of the following two candidates for the U.S. Senate and tell us who you would be more likely to vote for.

John Layman is a Democrat who wants to crack down on the problem of illegal immigration. He was recently quoted in the news as saying:

"We are a nation that respects the law. Illegal aliens should not be rewarded for breaking the law."

David Green is a Republican who favors immigration reform so that people who have entered the U.S. illegally can stay in the country legally. In a recent news article, he said the following:

"As a nation, we must show compassion to everyone. Undocumented workers in America should have a chance to become U.S. citizens." <Secular>

"Jesus taught that we must show compassion to everyone. These hard-working people should have a chance to become U.S. citizens." <Religious>

Notes

1. Bob Allen, "Southern Baptists Denounce Gulf Oil Spill, Divorce, Gay-Rights Proposals," *Associated Baptist Press*, June 16 2010.
2. Jim Wallis, *God's Politics: Why the Right Gets It Wrong and the Left Doesn't Get It* (New York: HarperCollins, 2005).
3. Throughout this chapter, we will use the short-hand term "nones" to describe those who report no religious affiliation. Within the sociology of religion it has been used

for decades and, more recently, has come into wider usage. See, for example, Joseph O. Baker and Buster G. Smith, "The Nones: Social Characteristics of the Religiously Unaffiliated," *Social Forces* 87, no. 3 (2009).

4. Robert D. Putnam and David E. Campbell, *American Grace: How Religion Divides and Unites Us* (New York: Simon and Schuster, 2010).

5. For a thorough discussion of religion and public opinion on social issues, see Ted G. Jelen, "Religion and American Public Opinion: Social Issues," in *The Oxford Handbook of Religion and American Politics*, ed. Corwin E. Smidt, Lyman A. Kellstedt, and James L. Guth (New York: Oxford University Press, 2009).

6. See Putnam and Campbell, *American Grace*, for evidence on this point.

7. David C. Barker and Christopher Jan Carman, "The Spirit of Capitalism? Religious Doctrine, Values, and Economic Attitude Constructs," *Political Behavior* 22, no. 1 (2000).

8. J. Matthew Wilson, "Religion and American Public Opinion: Economic Issues," in *The Oxford Handbook of Religion and American Politics*, ed. Corwin E. Smidt, Lyman A. Kellstedt, and James L. Guth (New York: Oxford University Press, 2009).

9. James L. Guth et al., "Faith and the Environment: Religious Beliefs and Attitudes on Environmental Policy," *American Journal of Political Science* 39, no. 2 (1995).

10. David C. Barker, Jon Hurwitz, and Traci L. Nelson, "Of Crusades and Culture Wars: 'Messianic' Militarism and Political Conflict in the United States," *Journal of Politics* 70, no. 2 (2008).

11. James L. Guth, "Religion and American Public Opinion: Foreign Policy," in *The Oxford Handbook of Religion and American Politics*, ed. Corwin E. Smidt, Lyman A. Kellstedt, and James L. Guth (New York: Oxford University Press, 2009).

12. Geoffrey C. Layman and John C. Green, "Wars and Rumours of Wars: The Contexts of Cultural Conflict in American Political Behavior," *British Journal of Political Science* 36 (2006).

13. Putnam and Campbell, *American Grace*.

14. For more on religious switching, see Putnam and Campbell, *American Grace*.

15. John C. Green, *The Faith Factor: How Religion Influences American Elections* (Westport, CT: Praeger, 2007).

16. David E. Campbell and J. Quin Monson, "The Case of Bush's Re-Election: Did Gay Marriage Do It?," in *A Matter of Faith: Religion in the 2004 Presidential Election*, ed. David E. Campbell (Washington, DC: Brookings Institution Press, 2007).

17. For recent trends in the religious "brand labels" of the parties, see "Public Sees Religion's Influence Waning," a report by the Pew Research Center: http://www.pewforum.org/2014/09/22/section-1-religion-in-public-life/# (accessed November 17, 2014).

18. David E. Campbell, John C. Green, and Geoffrey C. Layman, "The Party Faithful: Partisan Images, Candidate Religion, and the Electoral Impact of Party Identification," *American Journal of Political Science* (forthcoming).

19. In the 2007 Faith Matters survey, a majority of Americans said that the Democratic Party is "neutral toward religion." See Putnam and Campbell, *American Grace*, for more on how the public perceives the two parties' stance toward religion (pp. 400–401).

20. These numbers come from the Pew Research Center, for details consult http://www.pewforum.org/2014/09/22/section-1-religion-in-public-life/# (accessed November 17, 2014).

21. Timothy Noah, "Closing the God Gap," NewRepublic.com, September 6, 2012 (accessed June 26, 2014).

22. Michael Kazin, *A Godly Hero: The Life of William Jennings Bryan* (New York: Alfred A. Knopf, 2006).

23. Eamon Javers, "Obama Invokes Jesus More Than Bush," *Politico*, June 9, 2009.

24. Paul Djupe and Gregory W. Gwiasda, "Evangelizing the Environment: Decision Process Effects in Political Persuasion," *Journal for the Scientific Study of Religion* 49, no. 1 (2010).

25. The number of respondents in other religious traditions (e.g. Muslims, Hindus, etc.) is too small to conduct a reliable analysis, so they have been omitted.

26. The survey was conducted in the summer of 2006. For more details on Faith Matters, see Putnam and Campbell, *American Grace*.

27. More technically, these results have been generated from logistic or ordered logistic regression models. All control variables were set to their means.

28. See the appendix to the chapter for the exact wording of the questions.

29. Benjamin Knoll, "'And Who Is My Neighbor?' Religion and Immigration Policy Attitudes," *Journal for the Scientific Study of Religion* 48, no. 2 (2009).

30. David E. Campbell, Christopher Karpowitz, and J. Quin Monson, "A Politically Peculiar People: How Mormons Moved into and Then out of the Political Mainstream," (n.d.).

31. Daniel Gonzalez, "LDS Members Conflicted on Church's Illegal-Migrant Growth," *USA Today*, April 3 2009.

32. These models mirror those used to create Figures 11.1–11.4, except that each one is limited to a single religious tradition and Religiosity was included as an independent variable (along with all the same independent variables as before). The results are generated by holding each control variable at its mean value, and varying Religiosity.

33. The religious nones are actually a larger group than mainline Protestants, but it is nonsensical to examine the impact of religiosity on the attitudes of nones.

34. Even though they also analyze the Faith Matters data, these results for the death penalty are slightly different than those reported by Putnam and Campbell in *American Grace* for two reasons. First, Putnam and Campbell do not examine the impact of religiosity on attitudes toward the death penalty across religious traditions, but only for the population as a whole. Second, they do not control for party identification in their models.

35. These experiments were conducted as part of the 2008 Cooperative Campaign Analysis Project (CCAP), a large online panel survey that ran throughout 2008. CCAP was a collaborative effort by a consortium of universities; the surveys were administered by You Gov/Polimetrix to a sample of registered voters. The survey oversampled battleground states, such that voters in non-battleground and battleground states are represented in equal proportions. See Simon Jackman and Lynn Vavreck, "Primary Politics: Race, Gender, and Age in the 2008 Democratic Primary," *Journal of Elections, Public Opinion, and Policy* 20, no. 2 (2010). The experiments discussed in this chapter were administered in September (environment, death penalty) and October (immigration) of 2008. The average size for each cell of the experiment is roughly 200 cases.

36. The index has two components, religious attendance and the degree of guidance provided by religion. Frequency of attendance is measured with the following categories: never, less than once a year, once or twice a year, several times a year, once a month, two or three times a month, about once a week, once a week, more than once a week. Religious guidance has four categories: none, some, quite a bit, and a great deal. A principal factor of these items has an eigenvalue of 1.17.

37. Ideally, an experiment like this would also incorporate information about religious belonging. However, even with an experiment of this size, it still leaves too few members of any given religious tradition to conduct a reliable analysis. The general consistency in the relationship between religiosity and political attitudes shown in the previous section justifies our concentration on religiosity.

38. We do not have a ready explanation for why a God-talking liberal picks up support from low-religiosity voters, but one possibility may be that since the frame invokes compassion, it is more palatable to non-religious people than religious frames that appeal to authority. This is yet another example of where more research is needed to understand how religious language and framing is perceived within the population.

39. Paul Djupe and Christopher Gilbert, *The Political Influence of Churches* (New York: Cambridge University Press, 2009).

Part III

The Public and Society

Chapter 12

Campaigns and Elections

John Sides and Jake Haselswerdt

On the day of Barack Obama's victory in the 2012 presidential election, *Slate's* John Dickerson wrote:

> What was ratified on election night was the benefit of a permanent campaign and the talent of the Obama team . . . His campaign team was so formidable that it made up for all the inadequacies, vulnerabilities, and missteps (remember that first debate?) of a weak incumbent president in a sputtering economy.

This high praise was perhaps exceeded only after Obama's first victory, in 2008, when the *New York Times* said this: "The story of Mr. Obama's journey to the pinnacle of American politics is the story of a campaign that was, even in the view of many rivals, almost flawless." These sentiments—which implicitly attribute Obama's victory to his campaign—are commonplace in the news media. While the campaign is underway, media accounts similarly focus on every twist and turn, suggesting that all kinds of events matter—in 2012, anything from Mitt Romney's comments about the "47 percent" to Hurricane Sandy. The portrait that emerges is one of instability and unpredictability: with a blizzard of ads, money, spin, and counter-spin, we don't know what voters will do and so we don't know who will win.

And yet, by Labor Day weekend in both 2008 and 2012, many political scientists were able to forecast the winner of both elections—in some cases, within a couple of percentage points. The average of their predictions was almost exactly correct in 2008 and about one and a half points lower than Obama's actual vote share in 2012. How is it possible that elections are fairly predictable even amidst the apparent volatility of the campaign? And if elections are so predictable, how much does the campaign matter?

To tackle these questions, we first discuss what is lacking in news coverage: why the influence of campaigns might in fact be limited. We discuss how voters' choices depend in part on "the fundamentals," including longstanding political identities and larger political events and trends—all of which are largely outside of the control of campaigns and make both voters and elections predictable.

This presents a further puzzle: if the fundamentals matter so much, then why do the polls vary during the campaign? In fact, the ups and downs in the polls do suggest a role for the campaign. We then consider the circumstances in which campaigns can matter and three different ways that campaigns matter: changing voters' minds, changing the criteria they use in making decisions, and "getting out the vote" or encouraging them to participate on Election Day. Ultimately, political campaigns do play some role, although their contribution to the election's outcome may still be outweighed by events beyond the candidates' control.

The Predictability of Voters

Voters rarely approach a campaign as blank slates, devoid of ideas about politics or the candidates. In many elections, voters can draw on longstanding political identities to guide their choices, even without any detailed information about the candidates. Some relevant identities involve race, ethnicity, socioeconomic status, and religion. The power of race derives in part from the historical linkages between racial communities and political parties, linkages that are nurtured by the attention parties pay to the concerns of racial groups. For example, African Americans have a longstanding tie to the Democratic Party because it, more than the Republican Party, took up the cause of civil rights. Even 40 years after the Civil Rights Movement, the tie remains strong. It is nurtured by Democratic politicians, who pursue policies favored by most African Americans and who routinely engage in symbolic gestures, such as speaking before the NAACP or in predominantly black churches. It is also nurtured by African American leaders who provide important cues for their followers, suggesting explicitly or implicitly that Democratic candidates deserve support. Finally, it is nurtured by the simple fact that residential and other patterns of segregation ensure that African Americans associate mostly with each other, thereby making it less likely they will encounter opposite or alternative political views. For these and other reasons, the vast majority of African Americans—upwards of 90 percent in presidential elections—vote for Democratic candidates. One can easily tell a similar story about other groups—for example, white evangelical Christians, whose close ties to the Republican Party have arisen via a similar process. In all such cases, voters behave predictably based on social identities and their associated group interests, which limits the ability of the campaign to persuade them otherwise.

Voters are also predictable because of *party identification*, which was discussed in chapter 7. Party identification is a psychological tie to a political party, which means that voters think of themselves as members of a party and feel some affinity for it. It does not change for most people, despite dramatic political or personal events. In fact, some researchers have found party identification as stable as religious identification.[1] This is not to say that party identification never changes, but typically it changes only gradually.

The relevance of party identification to campaigns and elections is two-fold. First, party identification influences how we see the world and process new information. The biases it creates (see chapter 7) are very relevant to elections. For example, opposing groups of partisans watch the exact same candidates debate and most of them conclude that their candidate won. After the second presidential debate in 2012, a CNN poll found that 90 percent of Democrats believed that Obama won, 5 percent thought it was a tie, and 3 percent thought that Romney had won. Among Republicans, 54 percent thought that Romney had won, 32 percent thought it was a tie, and only 9 percent thought that Obama had won.

Second, party identification also influences how we make political choices, notably voting. Voters who identify with a party are very loyal to that party's candidates. Although voters sometimes "defect" and vote for a candidate of the opposite party—due to that candidate's appealing personality, a compelling policy issue, or the lack of a credible candidate in their own party—this is the exception rather than the rule. In fact, defections have become increasingly rare. Partisans have become more loyal to their parties, and fewer and fewer voters "split their tickets" by voting for candidates of different parties for different offices.

The true nature of contemporary party identification flies in the face of much conventional wisdom, which suggests that party identification has weakened as more and more voters have come to identify as "independent." Pundits routinely claim that independents are numerous—the "largest group in the electorate," "the vast middle ground where elections are won and lost in America," and "the fast-growing swath of voters."[2] It is true that the number of people who call themselves independent has grown to outnumber the fractions calling themselves Democrats or Republicans. But most of these independents profess that they "lean" toward one of the two major parties and, in elections, are just as likely to vote for that party as many who identify with that party in the first place.[3] Both facts were illustrated in 2012. In that year's American National Election Study, a large election survey carried out by political scientists, only 14 percent of the sample, and 9 percent of self-reported voters, identified as independent and did not indicate any leaning toward a political party. These "pure" independents were fairly evenly split between Obama and Romney (54–46 percent). However, independents who leaned Democratic were almost unanimously behind Obama: 91 percent reported voting for him. Independents who leaned Republican were as loyal to Romney: 91 percent voted for him as well.

The relevance of party identification for campaigns is obvious: no amount of clever advertising by one candidate will persuade many of those who identify with the opponent's party to change their minds. Campaigns often only reinforce party loyalty rather than encourage defections. This is the conclusion of many studies of American presidential elections stretching back to the 1940s.[4] And when campaigns do have an impact, it is often small. During the 2012 campaign, Obama's and Romney's poll numbers only ever changed by a few percentage points at most. Of course, in close elections, the decisions of less predictable and truly independent voters can be consequential. But media coverage—with its laser focus on these voters—understates how much of voting is a predictable expression of social and partisan identities.

The Predictability of Elections

When political scientists endeavor to predict presidential elections, they typically do so at least two months ahead of time, before the candidate debates and the vast majority of television advertising. The predictability of elections stems from how fundamental factors affect how we vote and, thus, who wins the election.

Two factors are most important, especially in presidential elections: the health of the economy, and whether the country is at war (particularly an unsuccessful war) or at peace.[5] Their importance seems sensible: prosperity and peace are foundational goals, without which it is difficult for government to accomplish other things. The reason both factors affect elections is because they underlie the public's evaluation of political figures. The public holds elected officials responsible for how well the economy is doing and whether the United States is at war (and, if so, whether it is winning). Presidents are held most responsible and, if the president is not running for reelection, then his party is held responsible. When the economy is doing well and the country is at peace, the incumbent president or his party will do better than when the economy is weak and war casualties are mounting. Voters behave "retrospectively"—looking backwards at the state of the country and evaluating incumbents accordingly.

Retrospective voting sounds sensible and fair, but in some ways it is not. For one, presidents have limited control over the economy and many events that take place during war, so they probably do not deserve much of the credit or blame that they receive. In fact, retrospective voting sometimes appears to depend on events that have nothing to do with politics at all, much less the actions of incumbent leaders. For example, incumbent leaders do better in elections held soon after the local college football team has won: a victory is worth about an extra 1 percent for the incumbent, and 2 percent if the team is a well-known powerhouse.[6] Second, the public's judgment about the economy is not necessarily sound. Voters can be more influenced by media reporting about the economy than the economy itself. This helps explain why, in 1992, Bill Clinton benefited from perceptions of a weak economy, even though the recession was over.[7] Moreover, voters' memories are short: they are much more influenced by change in the economy in the year before the presidential election, and tend to ignore the prior years.[8] A president who presides over three years of a bad economy and then one final year of growth may do better than a president who presides over three years of growth and one final year of recession.

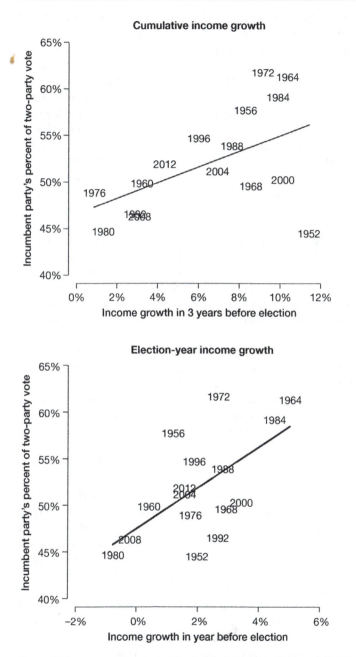

Figure 12.1 Income Growth and Presidential Election Outcomes, 1952–2012.

These points are illustrated in Figure 12. 1. Both graphs in this figure depict the relationship between economic growth, measured as change in real per capita disposable income, and presidential election outcomes, measured as the incumbent party's percentage of the major-party vote. The top graph relies on a measure of economic growth over the last three years of the president's term, assuming that his policies would not take effect until the second year of his term. As economic growth increases, so does the incumbent party's share of the vote. But in the bottom graph, which relies on a measure of economic growth only in the election year, the relationship between the economy and election outcomes is stronger: the line capturing the relationship tilts upward more steeply, and the election years are more closely clustered around the line. Presidential election outcomes depend more on recent economic trends than on the trend across a president's term.

Presidential elections are not the only contests where the fundamentals, particularly economic performance, loom large. Similar factors affect congressional, state and local elections as well. On their face, congressional elections might seem difficult to predict because states and House districts, not to mention congressional candidates, are so diverse. And it is certainly true that the unique circumstances within districts matter. However, congressional elections also depend on national trends. Just as voters punish the president for a weak economy, they also punish representatives from the president's party. In election years when the economy is weak and the president unpopular, the president's party can expect to lose seats in Congress.[9] The last two midterm elections, in 2010 and 2014, were no exception: the Democratic Party lost Senate and House seats in both years. The economy is also an important factor in state elections, particularly gubernatorial elections, though a state's particular economic circumstances may be more important than national trends in such elections.[10]

The predictability of elections limits how much campaign strategy can accomplish. No amount of campaigning will change the state of the economy or improve prospects in war. These fundamental factors may be out of the control of any leader. They are certainly out of the control of any challenger. Nonetheless, they strongly affect any candidate's chances of winning and may render campaign strategy irrelevant in some cases. If an incumbent president is running amidst a weak economy, even a brilliant campaign may not be enough. Similarly, strategic wizardry may be superfluous when conditions are favorable. Consider the 2008 election, conducted amidst a recession and financial crisis. Was Obama's victory, as the *New York Times* suggested, the story of a flawless campaign? Or would a mediocre campaign have had much the same result, so difficult was it for the Republican Party to hold onto the presidency as home foreclosures were increasing and banks were failing?

In addition to the fundamental forces of the economy and war, another factor can often overshadow even the best campaign: the presence of an incumbent running for reelection. There may be occasions when an incumbent is disadvantaged, such as during an economic crisis or a scandal, but in most cases incumbency is an asset. Even if things look bad for the incumbent's party, the incumbent will usually stand a better chance than a new candidate of the same party running in an open-seat race. This is because the incumbent is almost always better known than the challenger, and voters tend to favor more familiar candidates unless they strongly support the opposite party.

The size of the incumbency advantage varies with the visibility and nature of the office. In general, since higher offices attract more famous challengers, the incumbency advantage is reduced. Incumbent presidents definitely have an advantage; since the Second World War, seven of the ten presidents who ran for reelection won. But their advantage is not as great as that enjoyed by senators, who have been reelected at a rate of 75 percent or higher since 1982. Even incumbent senators' advantage pales in comparison to that of their House counterparts, at least 86 percent of whom have been reelected in every election since 1982. In fact, in five of these elections, 98 percent of House incumbents running for reelection have been reelected. Even in the 1994, 2006, and 2010 elections, in which new House majorities were swept into office in spectacular fashion, 90 percent, 94 percent, and 86 percent of incumbents still managed to win reelection, respectively.[11] The incumbency advantage is so strong in these elections that many potential challengers choose not to run rather than risk a defeat that could set back their political careers. This is why, in the 2010 general election, 27 House incumbents ran totally unopposed. In most elections, incumbents do face a challenger, but it is rarely the most qualified or well-known challenger possible; high-quality challengers are especially likely to bide their time and wait for open-seat races that they have a good chance of winning.[12]

The nature of the office also determines the size of the incumbency effect. Research has shown that incumbent members of Congress owe some of their advantage to constituent casework—essentially, favors that congressional staff do for constituents (e.g., helping to track down a Social Security check that was lost in the mail).[13] Members of Congress also enjoy the franking privilege, which allows them to send certain kinds of mail to their constituents without paying for postage, thereby increasing their name recognition. Furthermore, being a member of Congress is a full-time job with a generous salary (currently $174,000), allowing members to devote themselves completely to politics. Many legislators in the American states and around the world do not enjoy a large staff, free postage, or a full-time salary, and their incumbency advantage is therefore reduced. The more professionalized and "Congress-like" a state legislature becomes, the more reliably its incumbents are reelected.[14]

As we shall see, in the rare instances when incumbents are defeated, the challenger's campaign plays a crucial role. It is important to keep in mind, however, that these are in fact rare events. In many cases, the natural advantages of incumbency are too much for any campaign to overcome. This reality discourages many potential challengers from even trying.

When Campaigns Matter

Even though elections are often predictable, this does not mean the campaign is irrelevant. For example, even if a weak economy helped Obama in 2008, he was not always ahead in the polls during the campaign. After the Republican National Convention, McCain surged to the lead for a couple weeks, making Democrats very nervous. Such changes in fortune are not uncommon in elections. Romney appeared to surge in the polls after the first presidential debate in 2012. There were weeks and even months when John Kerry and Michael Dukakis seemed destined to become the next president. Clearly, events that happen during the campaign can matter over and above the fundamentals, which, while powerful, do not entirely explain election outcomes. In fact, as we discuss later, campaigns may help ensure that the fundamentals end up influencing the election's outcome by making voters think more about the economy. But this does not mean that every campaign event will matter. To unpack the effects of campaigns, it is helpful to think about when exactly campaigns matter. Two factors are paramount: the number of undecided voters and the balance of resources among the competing candidates.

Campaigns will have larger effects when there are more voters who have not made up their minds. Although most voters can draw on social and partisan identities to make decisions about candidates, there will still be some who are uncertain about or unfamiliar with the candidates. Whenever these voters are more numerous, the campaign has a greater potential to affect voters' decisions.

For example, undecided voters are typically more numerous earlier rather than later in the campaign. As the campaign goes on, the information that voters acquire via news and advertisements will typically lead them to a decision. This helps explain why presidential nomination conventions, which are usually held in July or August of the election year, tend to have larger effects than the candidate debates that are usually held in late September or October.[15] At the time of the conventions, some partisans may not fully support their party's nominee. The convention's hoopla helps solidify their support and perhaps also persuades some independent voters to support that candidate.[16] By the time the debates roll around, the pool of undecided voters has shrunk even further and, as noted earlier, voters who have made a decision will rarely change their minds after the debate because they tend to believe that their preferred candidate won.

Figure 12.2 presents the averages of the public polls for Obama and Romney, with demarcations for various events: the selection of Paul Ryan as Romney's running mate; the conventions; the attack on the American compound in Benghazi, Libya; the publication of Romney's comments about the "47 percent"; the candidate debates (presidential and vice-presidential); and Hurricane Sandy. The effects of the Democratic convention, although less so the Republican convention, are evident in late August and early September. And although the polls moved quite a bit after the first presidential debate, none of the other debates had much impact.

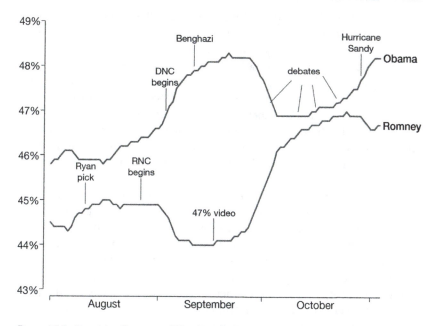

Figure 12.2 Campaign Events and Tracking Polls in the 2012 Presidential Campaign.

Undecided voters are also more numerous in elections other than presidential general elections. Compared to presidential primaries and congressional elections (especially open-seat races), presidential general elections tend to feature candidates who are relatively familiar and about whom voters have stronger opinions. Presidential primaries often feature a large and largely unknown pool of candidates, typically senators and governors who are familiar mostly in their home states and sometimes not even there. Moreover, voters cannot rely on party identification because all of the candidates are of the same party. This makes events during the primaries much more consequential, especially the outcomes of the earliest caucuses and primaries. In the 2012 Republican presidential primary, there were many important shifts in the polls as voters reacted to media coverage of the candidates.[17] These shifts in the polls were typically larger than the conventions or debates have created in general elections, at least in the era of public opinion polling.

Campaign activity in congressional elections also matters. Many of these races feature a relatively well-known incumbent and a lesser-known challenger. Both incumbent and challenger campaigns can matter. Typically, the more the candidate spends, the more votes they receive. But campaign spending matters more for challengers because so few voters know them. Over time, challengers with more money to spend become better known than poorer challengers;

voters are more able both to recall and to recognize their names, for example.[18] And this translates into a greater chance of winning. In congressional elections from 1972–2006, no challenger who raised less than $100,000 won. By contrast almost a third of those who raised at least $1 million won.[19]

Campaign spending is arguably even more vital for challengers in elections for state legislature, state supreme court, and city council.[20] In these elections, which attract relatively little media coverage, voters are not likely to see, hear, or read anything about challengers unless it comes from their campaigns. Thus, campaigns can be crucial to the outcomes of such elections, even if the dollar amounts spent on them are miniscule compared to what is spent in higher-profile races.

A second factor affecting the impact of a campaign is the balance of information coming from the opposing sides. The logic here is straightforward: when the opponents have roughly the same amount of money to spend, produce similar numbers of advertisements in important media markets, and receive equivalent amounts of positive and negative news coverage, it is difficult for either one of them to gain any advantage. The net outcome of all of this campaign activity will not favor either candidate, and the polls will not move much at all. This is one reason why the polls during presidential campaigns are so static. In 2012, Obama and Romney were relatively evenly matched in resources: Obama and his allies spent about $1.1 billion and Romney and his allies spent about $1.2 billion.

It is when disparities between the candidates emerge that campaign activity can benefit the advantaged candidate. Several examples will illustrate. First, incumbent members of Congress are reelected at high rates in part because of resource disparities: the vast majority of incumbents out-spend their challengers. Second, disparities can emerge in news coverage during presidential campaigns. During a nominating convention, the party holding the convention receives a sudden increase in positive news coverage that is not counterbalanced by positive coverage of the other side.[21] This disparity helps explain why conventions give parties a bump in the polls. Third, in presidential debates, one candidate occasionally out-performs the other enough that the polls move in the winner's favor. This is what appeared to happen after the first presidential debate in 2012, when Romney's performance was judged superior by many in the news media and by many voters as well. Fourth, even in presidential elections, disparities in television advertising can also emerge. In 2000, Bush outspent Gore in the battleground states late in the campaign, and the resulting advantage in advertising may have cost Gore four points of the vote—a large number in states where the outcome was so close (e.g., Florida).[22] In 2008 and 2012, advertising advantages also appeared to translate into votes.[23] But it was rare that either candidate had a large and durable enough advantage to affect the overall outcome of the election, suggesting how difficult it is to persuade voters in presidential elections.

How Campaigns Matter

If we want to know when and where political campaigns matter, the number of undecided voters and the balance of resources among the candidates are very helpful. The next question is *how* campaigns matter. Their effects on voters can take one of four basic forms: reinforcement, persuasion, priming, and mobilization. Each of these can contribute to the number of votes a candidate wins and thus to the election's outcome.

Reinforcement

Reinforcement occurs when campaigns solidify the preferences of voters. Some voters may have a natural tendency to vote for one party but still be uncertain how they will vote in some elections. Campaigns tend to bring these voters back into the partisan fold, leading them to a decision that is in line with their party identification.[24] Political operatives and commentators often call this activity "rallying the base," referring to the candidate's natural base of support. Reinforcement may be visible in polls, as voters move from the undecided column into a candidate's camp. For example, among Democrats who were undecided as of December 2011 but ended up voting in November 2012, 71 percent ended up supporting Obama. The majority of undecided Republicans (69 percent) ended up supporting Romney.[25]

Reinforcement may also be relatively invisible. For example, in 2012, an uncertain voter who identified as a Republican could have told a pollster that he supported Romney but have done so out of partisan habit rather than any real affinity for Romney. If the campaign reinforced this choice, however, then the voter's answer to the pollster would not change but the sentiments underlying this answer would change a great deal—from tentative support to genuine enthusiasm. This was evident in 2012: Romney's early supporters came to have a much more favorable view of him as the campaign progressed.[26] And even if not all reinforcement can be measured with polls, it is certainly consequential nonetheless. Candidates who cannot rally their own partisans will face especially long odds.

Persuasion

Persuasion is the most familiar campaign effect, and the one on which much popular commentary centers. It involves changing the attitudes of people, especially leading them to switch their support from one party to the other. In highly visible elections, such as presidential races, outright persuasion is not very common, thanks to the prevalence and power of the social and political identities discussed earlier. In 2012, among those who supported Obama in December 2011 and reported voting in the election itself, 95 percent voted for him. The same was true of Romney supporters, 92 percent of whom voted for him. But in less visible elections for state-wide or local offices, persuasion and thus defections are more common.[27]

How is it that campaigns come to persuade voters? One possibility has to do with policy issues. Voters whose views on policy are out of step with the party's platform (e.g., conservative Democrats or liberal Republicans) are more likely to defect to the opposing party's presidential candidate, especially if they live in a battleground state that is closely contested by the candidates.[28] This suggests that persuasion depends at least in part on the information that campaigns convey about where the parties and candidates stand.

Another possibility is that persuasion depends on candidates' personalities or physical attractiveness. Some studies do show that these factors can affect voters' decisions. In one experiment, people shown the faces of competing candidates for only one second picked the candidate who actually won the election about two-thirds of the time.[29] In another experiment, people were provided profiles of two opposing candidates. When an attractive picture of the first candidate was paired with an unattractive picture of the second, the attractive candidate did about 10 percent better than if their roles were reversed and the first candidate's picture was more unattractive.[30] Studies have also shown that candidates who are rated as physically attractive by third party observers tend to do better on Election Day.[31] Finally, campaigns can change perceptions of the candidates' attributes, for better or worse. In 2000, the news media's attention to exaggerated statements made by Al Gore led voters to perceive him as less honest.[32]

At the same time, other evidence suggests that personality and attractiveness may not matter all that much. For one, people's perceptions of personality—which candidate is more honest, a stronger leader, etc.—are strongly shaped by their party identification. It may be that voters' perceptions of the candidates essentially come *after* they have decided to support one of those candidates. Second, the apparent effect of attractiveness may be due to other factors entirely. Parties tend to run better-looking candidates in races they have a good chance of winning and uglier candidates in races they are unlikely to win—so the fact that better-looking candidates do better at the polls may have little to do with their looks.[33]

All in all, while persuasion of voters is certainly possible under the right circumstances, it is difficult for campaigns to achieve. Furthermore, attempts at persuading voters of the opposite party to defect may be costly. If a Democratic candidate broadcasts some of her more conservative positions in an attempt to persuade Republican voters, she may undermine attempts to reinforce support among her natural Democratic base. For these reasons, in many elections, persuasion is the least prominent of the campaign's effects.

Priming

Campaigns are not only about whom voters choose but *why* they choose them. Through the process of priming, campaigns can affect the criteria that voters use in making decisions. Candidates strive to make the election "about" the issues that favor them. They provide voters with information about those issues and ultimately help voters to link their own attitudes about those issues to their decisions at the ballot box.[34] The possibility of priming suggests how campaigns can matter even if elections are strongly affected by fundamental factors like the economy. The economy may not automatically be the most important criterion in voters' minds. The candidate who is advantaged by the state of the economy—the incumbent when the economy is strong, or the challenger when the economy is weak—will want to remind people about the economy and make it a more influential criterion. By contrast, the candidate disadvantaged by the economy will want to change the subject.

The importance of priming can be illustrated with the 2000 election. The essential puzzle in this election is why Gore did not win more of the popular vote, given how well the economy was doing at the time. In the bottom panel of Figure 12.1, the datapoint for the 2000 election is below the diagonal line, suggesting that Gore did not do as well as the state of the economy, which was growing robustly, would have predicted. One answer to the puzzle is that Gore simply failed to remind voters of the strong economy. He was, it seems, afraid to associate himself with the Clinton administration's record for fear that, as Clinton's vice president, he would be punished for Clinton's scandals. Thus, voters did not reward him for being part of an administration that presided over an economic expansion. Gore's strategy also contrasts sharply with Obama's in 2008, which entailed continual emphasis of the weak economy. A systematic study of presidential elections since 1952 shows the importance of priming: when candidates who benefit from the fundamentals emphasize them in their campaigns, they are more likely to win than candidates who, like Gore, focus on some other issue.[35]

Mobilization

A final way that campaigns matter involves mobilizing voters. This means helping them to register and get to the polls to vote. After all, it does not do a campaign much good if they persuade voters to support a candidate but those voters stay home on Election Day. Campaigns are increasingly interested in mobilization—sometimes referred to as get-out-the-vote (GOTV) or "the ground game," in contrast to the "air war" of campaign advertising. By using extensive databases of information about voters, candidates can better target those voters who are likely to support them.

How do we know that campaigns actually mobilize? A first piece of evidence: higher levels of campaign spending in gubernatorial and U.S. Senate races are associated with higher turnout, particularly in years with no presidential election on the ballot.[36] Second, careful experimental studies have randomly assigned households to receive non-partisan GOTV reminders during elections. These studies show that GOTV does stimulate turnout, although personal forms of contact, particularly in-person conversations, are more effective than impersonal forms such as mail or phone calls.[37] Other studies have found that campaign activity mobilizes partisans in particular: when Democrats outspend Republicans, for example, the proportion of Democrats among voters goes up.[38] In 2008 and 2012, Obama's extensive GOTV operation appears to have mattered: Obama did better in counties in which he had opened field offices.[39]

These campaign effects—reinforcement, persuasion, mobilization, or priming—may all affect individual voters. Arguably even more important, however, is whether or not campaigns actually affect the outcomes. In other words, do the individual voters affected by the campaign "add up" to a number that actually makes one candidate win and the other lose? In some cases, campaign activity produces effects large enough to decide the election. A presidential campaign that successfully responds to the fundamentals does six points better overall.[40] The votes attributed to Obama field offices may have been sufficient to win him several states in 2008, although perhaps only Florida in 2012.[41] Ultimately it is harder for campaigns to change an outcome than simply to affect some individual voters. After comparing early poll numbers to the actual outcome, political scientist James Campbell finds that only 5 of 14 presidential campaigns from 1948–2000 appear to have changed the outcome.[42]

Conclusion

The news cycle demands a constant stream of fresh stories, interpretations, and analysis, and so naturally, during election season, journalists and commentators feature the twists and turns of the campaign itself. The results may make for interesting news but they also tend to exaggerate what campaigns can accomplish. Moreover, commentators often focus on trivial moments of the campaign that are unlikely to affect anything, such as minor misstatements or "gaffes" by the candidates. Instead, it is more accurate to say that campaigns can have an impact only when certain conditions are met—a large number of undecided voters, resource disparities among candidates—and even then may not sway enough voters in a particular direction to affect the overall outcome. None of this means that campaigns are inconsequential, particularly in close races. Moreover, even their occasional impact may have big policy consequences, given the differences between what a Democratic and Republican president, governor, or congressional majority will typically do while in office. But it does mean that the furious efforts of candidates often accomplish less than they would like, and certainly less than pundits perceive.

In reality, many crucial determinants of electoral outcomes are outside of the control of candidates and campaigns. The best campaign advertising will not revive a flagging economy. The most dominant debate performance will probably fail to impress most viewers from the opposite party. The most charismatic challenger will probably lose to a strong incumbent. While these realities may make following elections less entertaining for journalists and other observers, they do point the way toward a richer understanding of what those elections are really about. Furthermore, they provide some reassurance for those concerned about American democracy in an age of media overload. While money and tactics can play a role under the right circumstances, American voters are far more than passive recipients of campaign advertising or media strategies.

Notes

1. Donald Green, Bradley Palmquist, and Eric Schickler, *Partisan Hearts and Minds* (New Haven: Yale University Press, 2002).
2. David Brooks, "What Independents Want," *New York Times*, November 5, 2009, accessed August 26, 2010, http://www.nytimes.com/2009/11/06/opinion/06brooks. html; Fareed Zakaria, "Obama Should Act More Like a President Than a Prime Minister," *Washington Post*, January 25, 2010, accessed August 26, 2010, http://www. washingtonpost.com/wp-dyn/content/article/2010/01/24/AR2010012402300.html? hpid=opinionsbox1; Matt Bai, "The Great Unalignment," *New York Times*, January 20, 2010, accessed August 26, 2010, http://www.nytimes.com/2010/01/24/magazine/ 24fob-wwln-t.html?ref=magazine
3. Bruce E. Keith, David B. Magleby, Candice J. Nelson, Elizabeth Orr, Mark C. Westlye, and Raymond E. Wolfinger, *The Myth of the Independent Voter* (Berkeley: University of California Press, 1992); John Sides, "Three Myths About Political Independents," *The Monkey Cage*, December 19, 2009, retrieved from http://www. themonkeycage.org/2009/12/three_myths_about_political_in.html
4. Paul F. Lazarsfeld, Bernard Berelson, and Hazel Gaudet, *The People's Choice: How the Voter Makes Up His Mind in a Presidential Campaign* (New York: Columbia University Press, 1948); Steven E. Finkel, "Reexamining the 'Minimal Effects' Model in Recent Presidential Campaigns," *Journal of Politics* 55 (1993): 1–31.
5. Douglas Hibbs, "Bread and Peace Voting in U.S. Presidential Elections," *Public Choice* 104 (2000): 149–180; John Zaller, "Monica Lewinsky's Contribution to Political Science," *PS: Political Science and Politics* 31 (1998): 182–189.
6. Andrew J. Healy, Neil Malhotra, and Cecilia Hyunjung Mo, "Irrelevant Events Affect Voters' Evaluations of Government Performance," *Proceedings of the National Academy of Sciences* 107 (2010): 12804–12809.
7. Marc Hetherington, "The Media's Effect on Voters' National Retrospective Economic Evaluations in 1992," *American Journal of Political Science* 40 (1996): 372–395.
8. Larry M. Bartels, *Unequal Democracy: The Political Economy of the New Gilded Age* (Princeton: Princeton University Press, 2008).
9. Gary Jacobson, *The Politics of Congressional Elections* (New York: Pearson Longman, 2009), 7th edition.
10. Lonna Rae Atkeson and Randall W. Partin, "Economic and Referendum Voting: A Comparison of Gubernatorial and Senatorial Elections," *American Political Science Review* 89 (1995): 99–107; Deborah A. Orth, "Accountability in a Federal System: The Governor, the President and Economic Expectations," *State Politics and Policy Quarterly* 1 (2001): 412–432.
11. "Reelection Rates Over the Years," Center for Responsive Politics, accessed August 30, 2010, http://www.opensecrets.org/bigpicture/reelect.php. The 2010 figures are from the authors' calculations.
12. Gary W. Cox and Jonathan N. Katz, "Why Did the Incumbency Advantage in U.S. House Elections Grow?" *American Journal of Political Science* 40 (1996): 478–497.

13. Bruce E. Cain, John A. Ferejohn, and Morris P. Fiorina, "The Constituency Service Basis of the Personal Vote for U.S. Representatives and British Members of Parliament," *American Political Science Review* 78 (1984): 110–125.

14. William D. Berry, Michael B. Berkman, and Stuart Schneiderman, "Legislative Professionalism and Incumbent Reelection: The Development of Institutional Boundaries," *American Political Science Review* 94 (2000): 859–874; John M. Carey, Richard G. Niemi, and Lynda W. Powell, "Incumbency and the Probability of Reelection in State Legislative Elections," *Journal of Politics* 62 (2000): 671–700.

15. James Stimson, *Tides of Consent: How Public Opinion Shapes American Politics* (New York: Cambridge University Press, 2004); Daron Shaw, "A Study of Presidential Campaign Event Effects from 1952 to 1992," *Journal of Politics* 61 (1999): 387–422; Robert Erikson and Christopher Wlezien, *The Timeline of Presidential Elections* (Chicago: Chicago University Press, 2012).

16. D. Sunshine Hillygus and Simon Jackman, "Voter Decision Making in Election 2000: Campaign Effects, Partisan Activation, and the Clinton Legacy," *American Journal of Political Science* 47 (2003): 583–596.

17. John Sides and Lynn Vavreck, *The Gamble: Choice and Chance in the 2012 Presidential Election* (Princeton: Princeton University Press, 2013).

18. Gary C. Jacobson, "Measuring Campaign Spending Effects in U.S. House Elections," in *Capturing Campaign Effects*, eds. Henry E. Brady and Richard Johnston (Ann Arbor: University of Michigan Press, 2006), 199–220; Laurel Elms and Paul M. Sniderman, "Informational Rhythms of Incumbent Dominated Congressional Elections," in *Capturing Campaign Effects*, eds. Brady and Johnston, pp. 221–241.

19. Jacobson, *Politics of Congressional Elections*, 46. Dollar amounts are in 2006 and thus adjusted for inflation.

20. Anthony Gierzynski and David Breaux, "Legislative Elections and the Importance of Money," *Legislative Studies Quarterly* 21 (1996): 337–357; Chris W. Bonneau, "The Effects of Campaign Spending in State Supreme Court Elections," *Political Research Quarterly* 60 (2007): 489–499; Timothy B. Krebs, "The Determinants of Candidates' Vote Share and the Advantages of Incumbency in City Council Elections," *American Journal of Political Science* 42 (1998): 921–935.

21. Holbrook, *Do Campaigns Matter?* (Thousand Oaks: Sage Publications, 1996); Richard Johnston, Michael G. Hagen, and Kathleen Hall Jamieson, *The 2000 Presidential Election and the Foundations of Party Politics* (New York: Cambridge University Press, 2004), 90.

22. Johnston, Hagen, and Jamieson, *2000 Presidential Election*, 85.

23. Michael M. Franz and Travis N. Ridout, "Political Advertising and Persuasion in the 2004 and 2008 Presidential Elections," *American Politics Research* 38 (2010): 303–329; Sides and Vavreck, *The Gamble*.

24. Lazarsfeld, Berelson, and Gaudet, *The People's Choice*.

25. Sides and Vavreck, *The Gamble*, p.185.

26. Sides and Vavreck, *The Gamble*, p. 213.

27. John Zaller, *The Nature and Origins of Mass Opinion* (New York: Cambridge University Press, 1992), Chapter 10.

28. D. Sunshine Hillygus and Todd G. Shields, *The Persuadable Voter* (Princeton: Princeton University Press, 2008).

29. Alexander Todorov, Anesu M. Mandisodza, Amir Goren, and Crystal C. Hall. "Inference of Competence from Faces Predict Election Outcomes," *Science* 308 (2005): 1623–1626.

30. Shawn W. Rosenberg and Patrick Cafferty, "The Image and the Vote: Manipulating Voters' Preferences," *Public Opinion Quarterly* 51, no. 1 (1987): 31–47.

31. Chappell Lawson, Gabriel S. Lenz, Andy Baker, and Michael Myers, "Looking Like a Winner: Candidate Appearance and Electoral Success in New Democracies," *World Politics* 62 (2010): 561–593.
32. Johnston, Hagen, and Jamieson, *2000 Presidential Election.*
33. Matthew D. Atkinson, Ryan D. Enos, and Seth J. Hill, "Candidate Faces and Election Outcomes: Is the Face-Vote Correlation Caused by Candidate Selection?" *Quarterly Journal of Political Science* 4 (2009): 229–249.
34. Andrew Gelman and Gary King, "Why Are Presidential Election Campaign Polls so Variable When Votes Are so Predictable?" *British Journal of Political Science* 23, no. 4 (1993): 409–451.
35. Lynn Vavreck, *The Message Matters: The Economy and Presidential Campaigns* (Princeton: Princeton University Press, 2009).
36. Robert A. Jackson, "Gubernatorial and Senatorial Campaign Mobilization of Voters," *Political Research Quarterly* 55 (2002): 825–844.
37. Alan S. Gerber and Donald P. Green, "The Effects of Canvassing, Telephone Calls, and Direct Mail on Voter Turnout: A Field Experiment," *American Political Science Review* 94 (2000): 653–663.
38. Thomas M. Holbrook and Scott D. McClurg, "The Mobilization of Core Supporters: Campaigns, Turnout, and Electoral Composition in United States Presidential Elections," *American Journal of Political Science* 49 (2005): 689–703; Eric McGhee and John Sides, "What Drives Partisan Turnout?" *Political Behavior* 32 (2011): 313–334.
39. Seth E. Masket, "Did Obama's Ground Game Matter? The Influence of Local Field Offices during the 2008 Presidential Election," *Public Opinion Quarterly* 73 (2009): 1023–1039; Sides and Vavreck, *The Gamble.*
40. Vavreck, *The Message Matters.*
41. Masket, "Obama's Ground Game"; Sides and Vavreck, *The Gamble*; Joshua Darr and Matthew Levendusky, "Relying on the Ground Game: The Placement and Effect of Campaign Field Offices," *American Politics Research* 42 (2014): 529–548.
42. James E. Campbell, "When Have Presidential Campaigns Decided Election Outcomes?" *American Politics Research* 29 (2001): 437–460.

Chapter 13

Ambivalence in American Public Opinion about Immigration

Deborah J. Schildkraut

Introduction

Since the 2010 Census was conducted, there has been a parade of headlines informing the American public of the great demographic changes underway in the United States population. Examples of such headlines include: "Most Children Younger than Age 1 Are Minorities,"[1] "Asians Fastest-Growing Race or Ethnic Group in 2012,"[2] "13% in U.S. Foreign-Born, a Level Last Seen in 1920,"[3] and "U.S. Will Have a Majority-Minority Population by 2043."[4] This growing diversity has largely been driven by immigration. Although immigration is certainly not a new phenomenon in the United States, changes in immigration policy in the 1960s spurred significant changes in immigration trends that have led to our current demographic makeup.

It should not be surprising that reports of such population changes can cause native-born, non-Hispanic white Americans (hereafter "whites") to feel a sense of anxiety, leading them to develop negative sentiments about today's immigrants and their immediate descendants and to press their elected officials to slow down the immigration flows. Yet most Americans also have a romantic attachment to the idea of immigration and view immigration as a central element of what being American is all about.[5] Immigrants are often viewed as the very embodiment of the American Dream: arriving with little, working hard, and providing a better life for their children, who grow up as Americans.

In this chapter, I explore public opinion about immigration from several angles. First, I provide a brief overview of modern immigration policy. Then, I discuss attitudes about immigration over time and note how political events and differences in question wording can affect public preferences. Next, I examine the ambivalence that Americans express toward immigrants, both celebrating their contributions to American society while also blaming them for the nation's problems. I also discuss how the large number of first generation immigrants currently in the country creates the impression that immigrants are failing to assimilate to American culture, which makes many Americans resentful. I then turn our attention to several factors that shape attitudes toward immigration. This section covers socio-demographic factors (such as one's race and partisan identification), as well as the roles of self-interest (such as one's occupation) and national interest (such as one's attitudes about American identity and culture). Finally, I consider the role that current debates about immigration play in electoral politics.

Brief History of Immigration Policy Since 1965

Strict limits on immigration were in place from the 1920s to the 1960s, thanks to the Johnson-Reed Act of 1924 (a.k.a. the National Origins Act). The policy favored immigrants coming from northern Europe over other parts of the world and ensured that the overall rate of immigration in those decades was low. Congress eliminated those quotas during the tumultuous years of the Civil Rights Movement. Upon signing the Immigration and Nationality Act of 1965 at the Statue of Liberty, President Lyndon Johnson decried the "harsh injustice" and "un-American" nature of the quotas and praised the new law for focusing immigration policy on the skills that immigrants possess and on reuniting families.[6] Prior to this policy, roughly 300,000 legal immigrants entered the country annually. Throughout the 1980s, approximately 575,000 legal immigrants arrived per year. Ever since 1989, the average has been closer to a million.[7] Today, the percentage of the population that is foreign born rivals the percentage from 100 years ago, as seen in Figure 13.1. The 1965 law also led to significant changes in the racial and ethnic makeup of immigrants. As Figure 13.2 demonstrates, the proportion of legal immigrants arriving from Europe in 1960 was 74.5 percent; in 2010, it was only 12 percent.[8]

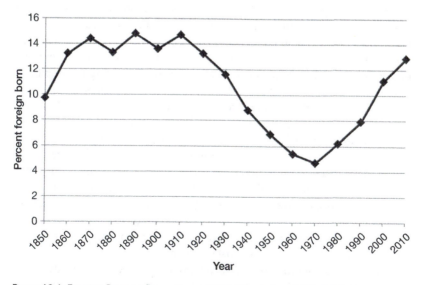

Figure 13.1 Foreign Born as Percentage of U.S. Population, 1850–2010 (source: Migration Policy Institute, http://www.migrationpolicy.org/programs/data-hub/us-immigration-trends).

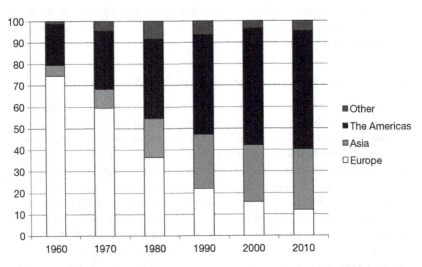

Figure 13.2 Immigrants in the United States by Region of Birth, 1960–2010 (source: Migration Policy Institute, http://www.migrationpolicy.org/programs/data-hub/us-immigration-trends).

In the years after 1965, attention turned to the phenomenon of illegal immigration. Although the concept of an "illegal immigrant" emerged back in the 1880s with the passage of the Chinese Exclusion Act (the first federal law to restrict immigration), it was not conceived as a political problem requiring legislative attention until the 1980s. At that time, an estimated 3 to 5 million undocumented immigrants were living in the country, and issues that arose from their presence, such as their effect on social and economic indicators, grew in significance. The first major legislation aimed at reducing the number of immigrants living in the country illegally was the 1986 Immigration Reform and Control Act (IRCA). Initial versions of the law would have allowed all unauthorized immigrants to obtain legal status, but the final version only permitted this so-called "amnesty" for immigrants who had been in the country prior to 1982, which left many immigrants unable to change their status. The law also included provisions related to border security and employer penalties for hiring unauthorized immigrants. Today, few consider the law to have been a success with respect to reducing illegal immigration. As we have seen, when the 1986 reform was enacted roughly 3 to 5 million unauthorized immigrants were living in the United States. Today, there are approximately 11.6 million, a figure that has been relatively constant since 2006.[9]

The 1990s saw additional noteworthy policies enacted by the federal government. They include both *immigration* policy (which addresses immigration flows) and *immigrant* policy (which addresses domestic issues that arise as a result of immigration). Operation Hold the Line and Operation Gatekeeper were implemented along the southern borders of Texas and California in 1993 and 1994, respectively. These operations involved a buildup of border agents, surveillance technology, and physical barriers. They were successful at diminishing the number of illegal crossings near El Paso and San Diego, but they did not diminish illegal crossings overall. Rather, immigrants opted for riskier paths through the rough terrain of the Arizona desert.

In 1996, Congress passed two important laws related to immigration: the Illegal Immigration Reform and Immigrant Responsibility Act (IIRIRA) and the Personal Responsibility and Work Opportunity Reconciliation Act (PRWORA). The former emphasized immigrant detention, deportation, and refugee processes, with a particular emphasis on creating a list of deportable offenses. The latter, in its amended form, prohibits legal immigrants from receiving most social welfare benefits, such as supplemental nutrition and Medicaid, until they have been in the country for at least five years.

Contemporary debates about immigration reform concentrate on the same themes that have characterized policy debates since the passage of IRCA, with a seemingly intractable emphasis on the need to figure out how to address the situation of unauthorized immigrants who are already here. Since 2005, Presidents George W. Bush and Barack Obama have tried to work with Congress to develop a set of comprehensive reforms to the nation's immigration policy, but their efforts have stalled in Congress time and again. Even though Bush was a Republican and Obama is a Democrat, they agreed that comprehensive immigration reform should provide an opportunity for undocumented immigrants to obtain legal status. Republicans in Congress, however, have largely opposed this approach. The inability of Democrats and Republicans in Congress to arrive at a compromise on this aspect of reform has sustained the ongoing impasse.

In addition to the question of illegal immigration, contemporary debates continue to include immigrant policy. These debates take place in state and local governments as well as in the U.S. Congress. Examples of such debates include whether immigrants should be eligible for social safety net services, whether to allow unauthorized immigrants to obtain driver's licenses, whether they should be allowed to pay in-state tuition at public universities, how to accommodate the needs of language minorities both in schools and at the voting booth, whether children who were brought to the country illegally by their parents (a.k.a. DREAMERS, after the proposed DREAM Act) should have an opportunity to become legal permanent residents and/or citizens, and whether local law enforcement agents should be able to inquire about one's immigrant status. Public discussions of these issues occur with regularity, and concern with how the American public would react to any policy changes is always front and center. As such, our attention now turns to the nature of public opinion about immigration.

Aggregate Trends in Public Opinion

Starting in 1965, Gallup polls have periodically asked Americans, "In your view, should immigration be kept at its present level, increased or decreased?" Responses to this question through 2014 appear in Figure 13.3. The time trend has several notable aspects. First, for nearly the entire time period, a plurality of Americans expressed a desire for decreasing immigration levels. Second, the highest level of restrictionist sentiment occurred in the early 1990s, years marked by economic recession and high-profile controversies over statewide responses to immigration, the most notable of which occurred in California. In 1994, California voters adopted Proposition 187, which barred undocumented immigrants from social services, including schools and non-emergency health care, though legal challenges prevented the law from being fully enacted.[10] The other high points in preferences for decreasing immigration levels occurred just after the domestic terrorist attacks on September 11, 2001 and during the Great Recession in 2009. Finally, it is important to note that the most recent data points in the figure are among the least restrictionist. Since 2003, the percentage preferring to increase immigration levels has been rising, and in 2012 and 2013, the percentage preferring to keep immigration levels the same was greater than the percentage preferring to decrease immigration levels.

National events, such as the performance of the nation's economy and terrorist attacks, seem to have a clear impact on aggregate opinions on immigration. As the nation's population has become more racially diverse, the composition of the respondents included in Gallup's polls has likely become more ethnically diverse as well, which could also be a factor contributing to the general rise in immigration-friendly responses, since whites tend to have more restrictionist preferences than nonwhites (see Figures 13.5 and 13.6, discussed below).

Despite the failure of reform efforts in Congress, public support for a path to citizenship has consistently been high. Since late 2007, polls conducted by CBS and the *New York Times* have asked respondents which policy option they prefer when it comes to "illegal immigrants working in the United States": allowing them to stay in their jobs and eventually apply for U.S. citizenship; allowing them to stay only as guest workers but not apply for citizenship; or requiring them to leave their jobs and the country.[11] Answers to this question over time are depicted in Figure 13.4. The question has been asked 16 times; in 15 of them, offering citizenship is the most popular option; in 7 of them (including all 4 instances in 2014), it is the majority preference. Together, the trends depicted in Figures 13.3 and 13.4 show that it would be a mistake to assume that the failure of lawmakers to enact immigration reform is mainly due to resistance among the American public as a whole. It would also be a mistake to assume that most Americans are reacting to the rise of immigration-driven diversity with nativism or xenophobia. If that were the case, the public would be becoming more supportive of restrictive policies, not less.

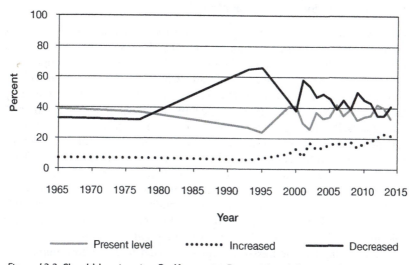

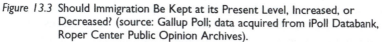

Figure 13.3 Should Immigration Be Kept at its Present Level, Increased, or Decreased? (source: Gallup Poll; data acquired from iPoll Databank, Roper Center Public Opinion Archives).

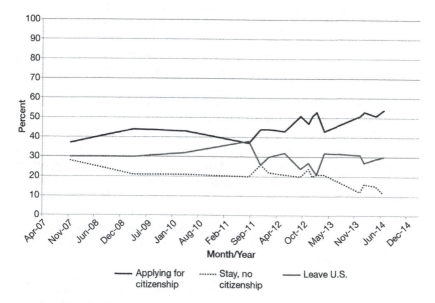

Figure 13.4 Public Opinion About a Path to Citizenship for Unauthorized Immigrants, 2007–2014 (source: CBS-New York Times polls; data acquired from iPoll Databank, Roper Center Public Opinion Archives).

An Immigrant by Any Other Name?

It is well known among public opinion scholars that the way in which issues are discussed (or *framed*) can sometimes alter the results of public opinion polls.[12] Do such effects emerge when the public is polled about immigration? To this point, I have described immigrants who are in the country illegally as "unauthorized" or "undocumented" immigrants, yet the question posed by CBS and the *New York Times* asks people for their views about "illegal" immigrants. Pro-immigration activists say the term "illegal immigrant" encourages people to dehumanize immigrants and view them as criminals, despite the fact that being in the country illegally is a civil, not a criminal, offense. They say "illegal" should only be used to describe an action, not a person.[13] If they are correct, then using the term "illegal immigrant" could exacerbate anti-immigrant preferences. This debate over terminology leads to a reasonable question: Would support for a path to citizenship and other immigrant-friendly reforms be higher if surveys did not label immigrants as illegal?

A few studies have addressed this question. They find that how immigrants and immigration are framed can affect public opinion, but it is not necessarily the term "illegal immigrant" that matters. One study of Iowa caucus-goers in 2008 found that using the term "illegal immigrant" instead of "undocumented immigrant" did not affect policy preferences, but using the term "Mexican immigrant" did, especially for Republicans.[14] This ethnic cue increased support for deporting immigrants and decreased support for a path to citizenship. A nationally representative study conducted prior to the 2008 election likewise concluded that using the term "illegal" instead of "undocumented" or "unauthorized" did not alter preferences.[15]

My own research on framing effects arrives at a similar conclusion. I collected all nationally representative public opinion survey questions on immigration policy from 2001 to 2008 that were available at the Roper Center's Public Opinion Archives and examined whether public preferences systematically varied based on the phrasing used in the question. I found that including the term "illegal" decreased support for immigrant-friendly policy options in only limited circumstances, such as when asking about whether there should be stiffer penalties for employers who hire unauthorized workers (support for penalties increased when "illegal immigrant" was used). The effects with respect to a path to citizenship and deportation were much weaker.[16] In sum, although framing effects have been demonstrated on many topics in public opinion research, the effects are limited with respect to whether immigrants are described as illegal or undocumented, an indication that people's views about this group are rather firmly established.

Their views about which policy approach is best, however, are less firmly established, as evidenced by the fact that changes in how the *policy* is described *can* move opinions. Notice that the CBS-*New York Times* poll asked if immigrants should be allowed to "eventually apply for U.S. citizenship." It did not ask whether unauthorized immigrants should be given "amnesty." As with the term "illegal immigrant," activists and politicians on both sides of this issue disagree over which phrasing to use. Here, question wording does matter. Public support for offering unauthorized immigrants a path to citizenship decreases when such a policy is called "amnesty."[17] It is important to note, however, that even when responding to questions that use the amnesty frame, the American public still tends to support offering citizenship relative to other options, albeit at a lower level.[18]

Ambivalent Attitudes about Immigrants

In addition to examining attitudes about immigration policy, scholars have also been interested in understanding attitudes about immigrants. These investigations reveal a sense of ambivalence and contradiction in how Americans as a whole think about immigrants. On the one hand, immigrants have been criticized for being lazy, but they have also been celebrated for being hardworking. They represent the country's legacy of providing opportunities for success and social mobility while also being chastised for allegedly taking unfair advantage of those opportunities without wanting to become "true" Americans. These contradictory sentiments are hardly new; they have characterized debates about immigrants throughout American history.[19]

The ambivalence over whether immigrants help or hurt the nation becomes evident when looking at surveys from the Pew Research Center conducted from 2011 to 2013. These surveys show that on the one hand 49 percent of Americans say that immigrants strengthen the country because of their hard work and talents, while 40 percent say immigrants are a burden because they take our jobs, housing, and healthcare. They also show that 35 percent of Americans say that immigrants have changed our society for the worse while 28 percent say they have changed it for the better.[20] Looking at surveys from other organizations tells a similar story: Americans overall are of two minds when it comes to assessing immigrants, and there is no consensus over whether they are a net benefit or a hindrance.

This ambivalence exists not just at the national level but at the individual level as well. I developed the concept of *immigrant resentment* to help characterize this ambivalence.[21] Americans hold a deep respect for the country's legacy of accepting immigrants from around the world and giving them an opportunity to start anew. Yet the high immigration rates of the past few decades have made it common for Americans to encounter immigrants in their daily lives. These encounters lead many Americans to think that assimilation to traditional American norms—such as learning English, striving for economic success through hard work, becoming an engaged member of one's community, and thinking of oneself first and foremost as an American—is not happening among today's immigrants. Such assimilation actually does happen, but it takes time.[22] Many Americans attribute the alleged failure of immigrants to "blend in" to the behavioral choices that immigrants themselves make. Doing so allows people to reconcile their genuine belief that immigration is a unique and valuable component of the country's identity with the discomfort that they feel when they think about contemporary cultural change. They can simultaneously take pride in the country's immigration legacy while harboring negative feelings toward today's immigrants.

I measured immigrant resentment by asking people the extent to which they agree or disagree with the following statements about immigrants: "Immigrants today take advantage of jobs and opportunities here without doing enough to give back to the community," "Immigrants should really know what's going on in the United States if they want to stay here, but a lot of them just don't want to be bothered," and "If immigrants only tried harder to fit in, then more Americans would accept their cultural differences."[23] These three questions all focus on the behavioral choices that people think immigrants make. By doing so, it allows respondents to simultaneously adhere to support for the concept of immigration and express displeasure with today's immigrants.

The results reveal that while not all Americans are resentful toward immigrants, many are. Forty-four percent of white Americans agree strongly or somewhat that immigrants take advantage of jobs without doing their part; 62 percent agree (strongly or somewhat) that immigrants don't want to learn about what's going on in the U.S.; and 53 percent agree (strongly or somewhat) that immigrants would be accepted more if only they tried harder to fit in. When these measures were combined into a scale running from 0 to 1, where 0 is the lowest level of immigrant resentment and 1 is the highest, the average score for white respondents was 0.53 (with a standard deviation of 0.28).

I then examined the individual-level factors that promote immigrant resentment. Republicans, people with lower household incomes, and people with lower levels of education were more likely to harbor immigrant resentment than their counterparts with higher incomes and educational levels or who were Democrats. People who said that whites are discriminated against in American society also had higher immigrant resentment scores, as did people who said that "true" Americans are Christian, born in the United States, have European ancestors, and think of themselves as American. In short, people's political orientations and ideas about what being American means were stronger predictors than economic factors of whether they resented immigrants for their apparent violations of American traditions and values.[24] Political orientations, cultural concerns and perceptions of immigrants tend to shape attitudes about immigration policy as well, more so than personal economic concerns, as we shall see in the next section.

Predictors of Immigration Policy Preferences

There is a tendency for general orientations toward American culture and politics to affect attitudes about immigration policy more than one's own economic condition. One's location in the racial hierarchy is also an important determinant of preferences. These tendencies are evident when we look at how people of different backgrounds responded to two questions about immigration policy in the 2012 American National Election Study (ANES). Figure 13.5 shows levels of support for a path to citizenship for unauthorized immigrants, and Figure 13.6 shows levels of support for policies that allow local law enforcement agents to check people's immigration status.[25] They show that whites are less likely than blacks and Hispanics to support a path to citizenship and more likely to support status checks by local law enforcement (though note that even a majority of whites favors a path to citizenship). Regarding party and ideology, Democrats and liberals exhibit more immigrant-friendly preferences than Republicans or conservatives. Responses vary much less when the sample is broken down by gender, education, and income.

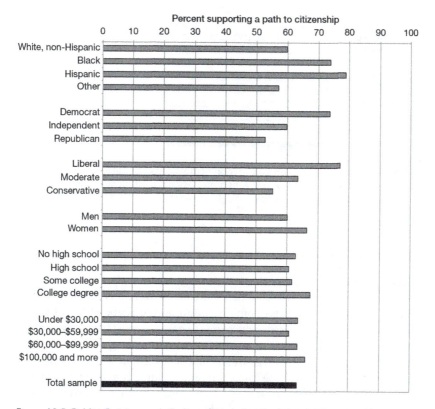

Figure 13.5 Public Opinion on a Path to Citizenship by Selected Demographic Groups, 2012 (source: American National Election Study, 2012, face-to-face and online samples; weighted results).

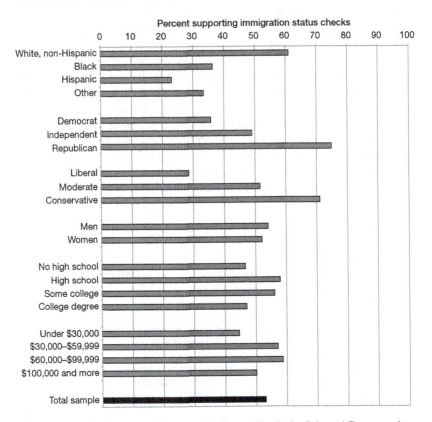

Figure 13.6 Public Opinion on Immigration Status Checks by Selected Demographic Groups, 2012 (source: American National Election Study, 2012, face-to-face and online samples; weighted results).

Self-Interest vs. National Interest

People are often thought of as rational beings whose main motivation is self-preservation of themselves and their families. As such, it is intuitive to think that one's own personal economic standing would shape attitudes toward immigration policy. A person who seems to have the most to lose by an influx of immigrant workers, perhaps someone who is unemployed, has a lower income, or has a lower level of education, might be more in favor of restrictionist policies than someone whose socioeconomic standing is more secure. Despite the intuitive appeal of this reasoning, a large volume of scholarship investigating the individual-level determinants of public opinion toward immigration policy finds that when self-interest is analyzed through such broad measures, it matters less than we might expect.[26]

Yet self-interest remains a compelling consideration, and in certain circumstances it can shape attitudes. Nteta, for instance, finds that whites who say they or a family member has lost a job specifically due to immigration have more restrictive preferences than other whites.[27] His study, as well as many others, also relies on education level as a proxy for socioeconomic status and finds that higher education levels tend to be associated with more welcoming immigration attitudes.[28] Other scholars have likewise found that direct threats to one's job posed by immigration can lead to restrictionist preferences. A study by Malhotra and colleagues, for instance, focused on the 25 American counties with the highest proportion of workers in the technology sector.[29] They found that in these counties, people with jobs in the tech sector were less likely than other people to support increasing the number of visas for high-skilled immigrant workers. Having a high-tech job, however, was *not* related to whether people thought the overall level of immigration from India should be decreased; the job sector effect was confined to the question of high-skilled visas. Scholarly debates about whether job sectors, labor market competition, and other individual economic concerns affect immigration attitudes remain ongoing.[30]

Although concerns about one's personal economic situation are, at best, erratic influences over attitudes about immigration policy, concerns about the impact of immigration on the nation's economy (a.k.a. *sociotropic* concerns) can matter more. Recall Figure 13.3, which indicated that restrictionist sentiment appears to rise during times of economic downturn. In one widely cited study, Citrin and colleagues demonstrated that negative assessments of the national economy during the previous year in terms of unemployment, inflation, and overall economic health led to greater support for restricting immigration.[31] Sociotropic concerns matter because people use their ideas about the national condition to help them figure out what to expect in their own lives.[32]

An even more important national-level factor that shapes how people feel about immigration pertains to American culture. The extent to which people define being American in cultural terms and how people think immigration affects American culture are consistently powerful influences on public opinion about immigration. While most Americans agree that in order to be considered a "true" American people need to believe in such bedrock principles as freedom, equality, and individualism, many Americans also think that "true" Americans are people who are Christian, were born in the United States, speak English, and have European ancestors. [33] When a person defines being American in terms of values and principles, she possesses a civic understanding of American identity; when she defines being American in terms of more ascriptive characteristics, such as birthplace, she has an ethnic understanding of American identity. Many Americans hold both civic and ethnic beliefs about what it means to be American.[34] Several studies have shown that people who define being American in ethnic terms are more likely than others to favor restricting immigration levels, denying public services to immigrants, and making English the official language of the country. The ways in which civic views of American identity affect immigration attitudes are more mixed, with some studies showing that they promote immigrant-friendly preferences, and others showing that they promote more hostile preferences.[35]

In addition to popular understandings of what being American means, how people think immigration might affect American culture also predicts immigration policy preferences. Perhaps not surprisingly, people who think that immigration threatens the American way of life and who think that the country's increasing numbers of Latinos and Asians have a negative impact on American society are more likely than others to support restrictive policies.[36] Higher levels of immigrant resentment are also associated with greater support for restricting immigration and denying government benefits to immigrants.[37] Recall that immigrant resentment is grounded in the belief that contemporary immigrants fail to emulate American cultural ideals, such as becoming engaged in their new communities and thinking of themselves as American.

Latino Immigration, Spanish, and Encounters With "The Other"

In addition to concerns about American culture and national economic conditions, research shows that how whites feel about Latinos in general is an important predictor of their attitudes about immigration policy. It is attitudes about Latinos, more so than attitudes about other ethnic groups, that fuel immigration policy preferences because of the extent to which today's immigrants hail from Latin America (recall Figure 13.2). An experiment by Brader and colleagues revealed that opposition to immigration was higher when the photo accompanying a news article about the costs of immigration depicted a Latino immigrant, compared to when the photo depicted an Anglo-European immigrant.[38] In later research, Brader and colleagues find that attitudes about Latinos drive immigration policy preferences more than attitudes about Asians.[39] They go on to argue that the link in America between immigration and Latin America has become so strong that when people hear the word "immigrant," an image of Latinos automatically comes to mind.[40] Whether that association continues to hold now that immigration from Asia outpaces immigration from Latin America remains to be seen.[41]

The growing share of Latino immigrants in the country has led scholars to identify two additional factors that can affect the immigration preferences of whites: the presence of the Spanish language, and the degree to which whites encounter immigrants, nonwhites, and language minorities in their surroundings (also see Czaja, Junn, and Mendelberg, this volume). Several experimental studies show that exposing people to Spanish can promote anti-immigration preferences.[42] At the same time, having close Latino friends leads whites to have more immigrant-friendly policy views.[43] The presence of Spanish is interpreted as a cultural threat, while having Latino friends provides direct information about the group, which then dispels stereotypes and promotes more favorable intergroup attitudes.

Scholars have also studied how the proportion of immigrants or ethnic minorities living in one's community affects immigration attitudes. The effects of local demographic context, however, are challenging to investigate, and results to date have been mixed. Some studies have found that diverse surroundings promote immigrant-friendly attitudes while others have found that such surroundings lead to greater anti-immigrant sentiments. Still other studies find that the effect of one's context depends on factors such as the ethnicity of the immigrants in question and the extent to which immigration is a prominent topic in national politics.[44]

Attitudes about Immigration among Nonwhites

It should be clear by now that most investigations into public opinion about immigration in the United States focus on the attitudes of native-born, non-Hispanic whites. That focus is understandable for multiple reasons. From a methodological standpoint, random samples of Americans (on which most public opinion studies rely) inevitably produce a set of respondents that mainly consists of native-born whites. From a theoretical standpoint, the way in which the cultural majority responds to rapid ethnic change is a profound question for any multiethnic self-governing society to consider. Understanding the conditions that generate greater or lesser degrees of tension among the host society is incredibly important. Finally, political scientists are also interested in the extent to which policymakers respond to the wishes of their constituents, and for a long time most lawmakers had voting constituencies that were mostly white. Yet, given current demographic trends, examining only non-Hispanic whites is no longer acceptable practice. Advances in survey sampling have also made it more feasible to collect data on enough minority respondents (and in enough non-English languages) to enable rigorous statistical analyses (see Czaja, Junn, and Mendelberg, this volume). As a result, recent studies have turned their attention to the views of nonwhites.

Not surprisingly, Latinos and Asian Americans tend to have less restrictive attitudes about immigration than whites.[45] Among Latinos and Asian Americans, however, there is variation in attitudes, and as with whites, this variation is best explained by factors related to group interest rather than personal economic interest. In particular, having a strong psychological connection to one's ethnic group matters. Latinos and Asian Americans who identify strongly with their ethnic group and who feel that their own wellbeing is connected to the status of the group as a whole hold less restrictive preferences than their counterparts who identify more weakly with their group.[46]

Another consistent influence on the immigration attitudes of Latinos and Asian Americans is acculturation. Latinos and Asian Americans who are first generation immigrants have less restrictive preferences on immigration policy than Latinos and Asian Americans who are the children or grandchildren of immigrants.[47] Similarly, Latinos who primarily speak Spanish have less restrictive preferences than Latinos who primarily speak English.[48]

On the question of the overall level of immigration, the attitudes of African Americans tend to be in between the attitudes of whites and Latinos. According to the 2012 American National Election Study, 48 percent of whites and 35 percent of blacks felt that the level of immigration should be decreased, compared to only 28 percent of Latinos. Figures 13.5 and 13.6 also show blacks taking a middle position between whites and Latinos when it comes to a path to citizenship and immigration status checks. Like whites, blacks' attitudes about immigration appear to be shaped by perceptions about the impact of immigrants on American society.[49] But, self-interest can also matter: Nteta finds that blacks who are working class (defined by not having a college degree) and who say that they or a family member lost out on a job because of immigration hold more restrictive preferences than middle class blacks.[50]

In a short period of time, research on nonwhite attitudes about immigration has led to a wide range of interesting and nuanced findings, but it has only begun to scratch the surface. Only in the past decade or so have political scientists had access to a variety of data that has enabled examinations of how nonwhites feel about immigration. Compared to the volume of research on the attitudes of whites, analyses that focus on nonwhites remain rudimentary. There has been scant attention, for instance, to national origin differences within ethnic groups, how local context affects the views of nonwhites, or the conditions that make economic concerns more or less salient to nonwhites in their assessments of immigrants and immigration.[51] It is an area, however, that is ripe for expansion. As the population continues to diversify and as access to more appropriate data sources continues to grow, studies of nonwhite attitudes toward immigration will broaden and deepen.

Immigration and Electoral Politics

Debates about immigration reform have taken a prominent place in political discourse since the early 2000s. Over this time, the Republican Party has taken a more restrictionist stance on immigration reform than the Democratic Party. Therefore, scholars have begun to consider whether partisan debates over immigration might affect partisan alignments and electoral outcomes. The answer so far is that they do. To put it simply, whites with negative views of Latinos and immigrants are more likely to be Republicans than other whites. The effect of attitudes about Latinos and immigrants on Republican identification holds even after controlling for a wide range of more traditional predictors of partisanship, including racial attitudes.[52] Additionally, whites with negative views about immigrants have been more likely to vote for Republican candidates for President and Congress, even after controlling for their partisan identification.[53] Since concerns about immigration have been on the rise in recent decades, the net result is that the Republican Party increasingly comprises whites, while the Democratic Party is increasingly nonwhite.

Partisan divisions on immigration appear to affect the partisanship and vote choice of Latinos and Asian Americans as well. Studies have found that the anti-immigration rhetoric that accompanied debates about Proposition 187 in California in 1994 had lasting effects on the Latinos in the state. Since 1994, the proportion of voters in California who are Latino has grown, as has their tendency to identify as Democrats and vote for Democratic candidates at all levels of government.[54]

Policy debates like those in California in 1994 create the impression that one party welcomes Latinos and Asian Americans while the other does not. More general feelings of welcome or exclusion (not explicitly tied to a particular party) can now have partisan effects as well. One interesting study of Asian Americans demonstrates this phenomenon. Kuo and colleagues recruited Asian Americans to participate in a study, and before having them fill out the survey, some were asked if they were American citizens.[55] This question was meant to remind participants that Asian Americans are often considered to be foreigners. Participants who were asked about their citizenship ended up evaluating the Democratic Party more favorably and the Republican Party less favorably, relative to participants who were not asked about their citizenship. The authors use this finding to argue that the growing tendency of Asian Americans across the country to vote for Democratic candidates is due in part to the differing stances each party has taken on immigration policy, stances that send a message about which party offers a more welcoming platform.

In sum, current debates about immigration reform appear to lead some whites to identify more with Republicans and some Latinos and Asians to identify more with Democrats (the impact of such debates among blacks has yet to be studied). While there is little reason to expect this trend to change direction in the short term, party operatives in both camps are surely interested in finding ways to appeal to voters on the other side. More specifically, making genuine progress on crafting successful immigration reform legislation could be a way for Republicans to turn the tide and gain more support among Latino and Asian American voters.

Conclusion

The Greek philosopher Heraclitus is attributed with saying that the only constant in life is change. The aphorism is apt with respect to public opinion about immigration policy in the United States. While it is true that there are some well-established findings across multiple studies (such as the power of cultural and economic concerns at the national level relative to self-interest), the political, economic, and demographic landscape of the country is always in flux. As policies, the stances of the parties, and the ethnic makeup of the population change, scholars face a constant challenge of finding generalizable insights into how all of these moving parts come together to influence attitudes about immigration policy and about immigrant policy.

What we know for sure is that public opinion about immigration is complex. It is a mistake, for instance, to assume that most whites in the United States are consistently anti-immigrant. There are conditions under which native-born, non-Hispanic whites become more supportive of immigration and immigrants, and there are conditions under which they become more restrictionist. Although gaps exist between whites and nonwhites, many whites today are fairly supportive of creating a path to citizenship for undocumented immigrants and have warm recollections of their own immigrant ancestors. At the same time, most whites also favor allowing local law enforcement officers to check on people's immigration status. Put simply, ambivalence abounds. National forces, including the health of the economy and the rhetoric of political leaders, local contexts, and ideas about what being American even means all help dictate the direction in which that ambivalence bends.

Notes

1. U.S. Census Bureau, 2012, "Most Children Younger than Age 1 are Minorities, Census Bureau Reports," accessed 2013, 01/03, http://www.census.gov/newsroom/releases/archives/population/cb12-90.html
2. U.S. Census Bureau, 2013, "Asians Fastest-Growing Race or Ethnic Group in 2012," accessed 2014, 3/17, https://www.census.gov/newsroom/releases/archives/population/cb13-112.html, Washington, D.C.
3. Rebecca Trounson, "13% in US Foreign-Born, a Level Last seen in 1920," May 11, 2012, *Los Angeles Times.*
4. Chris Wilson, 2012, "U.S. Will have A Majority-Minority Population by 2043, Census Predicts," accessed 2014, 3/17, http://news.yahoo.com/blogs/lookout/u-majority-minority-population-2043-census-predicts-164735561.html
5. Deborah J. Schildkraut, *Press One for English: Language Policy, Public Opinion, and American Identity* (Princeton, N.J.: Princeton University Press, 2005).
6. Lyndon Johnson, 1965, "Remarks at the Signing of the Immigration Bill," accessed 2014, 3/21, http://www.lbjlib.utexas.edu/johnson/archives.hom/speeches.hom/651003.asp
7. United States Department of Homeland Security, "Yearbook of Immigration Statistics: 2011" (Washington, D.C.: U.S. Department of Homeland Security, Office of Immigration Statistics, 2012).
8. Migration Policy Institute, 2014, "U.S. Immigration Trends," accessed 2014, 3/21, http://migrationpolicy.org/programs/data-hub/us-immigration-trends#history
9. Michael Hoefer, Nancy Rytina and Bryan Baker, "Estimates of the Unauthorized Immigrant Population Residing in the United States: January 2011" (Washington, D.C.: Department of Homeland Security, Office of Immigration Statistics, 2012).
10. Philip Martin, "Proposition 187 in California," *International Migration Review* 29(1, Special Issue: Diversity and Comparability: International Migrants in Host Countries on Four Continents) (1995): 255–263.
11. In 2014, CBS and the *New York Times* changed the wording of this question by replacing "working" with "living." The current wording is: "Which comes closest

to your view about illegal immigrants who are living in the U.S.? They should be allowed to stay in the U.S. and eventually apply for citizenship. They should be allowed to stay in the U.S. legally, but not be allowed to apply for citizenship. They should be required to leave the U.S." Wording and data were acquired from the iPoll Databank, Roper Center Public Opinion Archives.

12. Dennis Chong and James N. Druckman, "Framing Theory," *Annual Review of Political Science* 10(1) (2007): 103–126; also see Hillygus, this volume.

13. Charles Garcia, 2012, "Why 'Illegal Immigrant' is a Slur," accessed 2014, 3/24, http://www.cnn.com/2012/07/05/opinion/garcia-illegal-immigrants/. Media outlets have taken different approaches in determining whether to allow their journalists to use the term "illegal immigrant." See Haughney, "The Times Shifts on 'Illegal Immigrant,' but Doesn't Ban the Use," April 23, 2013, *New York Times*.

14. Benjamin Knoll, David Redlawsk, and Howard Sanborn, "Framing Labels and Immigration Policy Attitudes in the Iowa Caucuses: 'Trying to Out-Tancredo Tancredo'," *Political Behavior* 33(3) (2011): 433–454.

15. Jennifer L. Merolla, S. Karthick Ramakrishnan, and Chris Haynes, "'Illegal,' 'Undocumented,' Or 'Unauthorized': Equivalency Frames, Issue Frames, and Public Opinion on Immigration," *Perspectives on Politics* 11(3) (2013): 789–807.

16. Deborah J. Schildkraut, "Amnesty, Guest Workers, Fences! Oh My! Public Opinion about 'Comprehensive Immigration Reform'," in *Immigration and Public Opinion in Liberal Democracies*, Gary Freeman, Randall Hansen, and David L. Leal, eds (New York: Routledge, 2013), pp. 207–231.

17. Jennifer L. Merolla, S. Karthick Ramakrishnan, and Chris Haynes, "'Illegal,' 'Undocumented,' Or 'Unauthorized': Equivalency Frames, Issue Frames, and Public Opinion on Immigration."

18. Deborah J. Schildkraut, "Amnesty, Guest Workers, Fences! Oh My! Public Opinion about 'Comprehensive Immigration Reform.'" It is unclear the extent to which survey respondents know what is meant by "amnesty." The fact that support declines when the term is used suggests that they interpret it as unfairly letting immigrants off the hook for entering the country illegally. Further investigation of what Americans think when they hear this frame is needed.

19. Dorothy Roberts, "Who may Give Birth to Citizens? Reproduction, Eugenics, and Immigration," in *Immigrants Out! The New Nativism and the Anti-Immigrant Impulse in the United States*, Juan Perea, ed. (New York: New York University Press, 1997), pp. 205–219; Desmond King, *Making Americans: Immigration, Race, and the Origins of the Diverse Democracy* (Cambridge, Mass.: Harvard University Press, 2000); Desmond King, *The Liberty of Strangers: Making the American Nation* (Oxford: Oxford University Press, 2005).

20. All Pew data were found at the iPoll Databank, Roper Center Public Opinion Archives.

21. Deborah J. Schildkraut, *Americanism in the Twenty-First Century: Public Opinion in the Age of Immigration* (New York: Cambridge University Press, 2011).

22. Richard D. Alba and Victor Nee, *Remaking the American Mainstream: Assimilation and Contemporary Immigration* (Cambridge, Mass.: Harvard University Press, 2003); Jack Citrin, Amy Lerman, Michael Murakami, and Kathryn Pearson, "Testing Huntington: Is Hispanic Immigration a Threat to American Identity?" *Perspectives on Politics* 5(1) (2007): 31–48.

23. Deborah J. Schildkraut, *Americanism in the Twenty-First Century: Public Opinion in the Age of Immigration*.

24. Ibid.

25. The question wording for the item in Figure 13.5 is, "Which comes closest to your view about what government policy should be toward unauthorized immigrants now living in the United States? Make all unauthorized immigrants felons and send them back to their home country. Have a guest worker program that allows unauthorized immigrants to remain in the United States in order to work, but only for a limited amount of time. Allow unauthorized immigrants to remain in the United States and eventually qualify for U.S. citizenship, but only if they meet certain requirements like paying back taxes and fines, learning English, and passing background checks. Allow unauthorized immigrants to remain in the United States and eventually qualify for U.S. citizenship, without penalties." Responses to the last two options are combined and displayed in Figure 13.5. The question wording for the item in Figure 13.6 is, "Some states have passed a law that will require state and local police to determine the immigration status of a person if they find that there is a reasonable suspicion he or she is an undocumented immigrant. Those found to be in the U.S. without permission will have broken state law. From what you have heard, do you favor, oppose, or neither favor nor oppose these immigration laws?" Data were accessed at http://electionstudies.org/

26. E.g., Thomas J. Espenshade and Katherine Hempstead, "Contemporary American Attitudes Toward U.S. Immigration," *International Migration Review* 30(2) (1996): 535–570; M. V. Hood III and Irwin L. Morris,"?Amigo O Enemigo? Context, Attitudes, and Anglo Public Opinion Toward Immigration," *Social Science Quarterly* 78(2) (1997): 309–323; Jack Citrin, Donald P. Green, Christopher Muste, and Cara Wong, "Public Opinion Toward Immigration Reform: The Role of Economic Motivations," *Journal of Politics* 59(3) (1997): 858–881; Peter Burns and James Gimpel, "Economic Insecurity, Prejudicial Stereotypes, and Public Opinion on Immigration Policy," *Political Science Quarterly* 115(2) (2000): 201–225; Deborah J. Schildkraut, *Press One for English: Language Policy, Public Opinion, and American Identity*; Jens Hainmueller and Daniel J. Hopkins, "Public Attitudes Toward Immigration," *Annual Review of Political Science* 17 (2014); Jens Hainmueller and Daniel J. Hopkins, "The Hidden American Immigration Consensus: A Conjoint Analysis of Attitudes Toward Immigrants," *American Journal of Political Science*, forthcoming.

27. Tatishe Nteta, "United We Stand? African Americans, Self Interest, and Immigration Reform," *American Politics Research* 41(1) (2013): 147–172.

28. Jack Citrin, Donald P. Green, Christopher Muste, and Cara Wong, "Public Opinion Toward Immigration Reform: The Role of Economic Motivations"; Peter Burns and James Gimpel, "Economic Insecurity, Prejudicial Stereotypes, and Public Opinion on Immigration Policy"; Deborah J. Schildkraut, "Press One for English: Language Policy, Public Opinion, and American Identity"; Jack Citrin and John Sides, "Immigration and the Imagined Community in Europe and the United States," *Political Studies* 5633–56 (2008); Deborah J. Schildkraut, *Americanism in the Twenty-First Century: Public Opinion in the Age of Immigration*.

29. Malhotra, Neil, Yotam Margalit, and Cecilia Hyunjung Mo "Economic Explanations for Opposition to Immigration: Distinguishing between Prevalence and Conditional Support," *American Journal of Political Science* 57(2) (2013): 391–410.

30. Kenneth Scheve and Matthew Slaughter, "Labor Market Competition and Individual Preferences Over Immigration Policy," 83(1) (2001): 133–145; Anna Maria Mayda, "Who is Against Immigration? A Cross-Country Investigation of Individual Attitudes Toward Immigrants," *Review of Economics and Statistics* 88(3) (2006): 510–530; Jens Hainmueller and Michael Hiscox, "Attitudes Toward Highly Skilled and Low-Skilled Immigration: Evidence from a Survey Experiment," *American*

Political Science Review 104(1) (2010): 61–84; Jens Hainmueller and Daniel J. Hopkins, "Public Attitudes Toward Immigration."

31. Jack Citrin, Donald P. Green, Christopher Muste, and Cara Wong, "Public Opinion Toward Immigration Reform: The Role of Economic Motivations"; also see Espenshade and Hempstead, 1996.

32. Donald R. Kinder and D. Roderick Kiewiet, "Sociotropic Politics: The American Case," *British Journal of Political Science* 11(2) (1981): 129–161.

33. Deborah J. Schildkraut, *Americanism in the Twenty-First Century: Public Opinion in the Age of Immigration*.

34. Deborah J. Schildkraut, *Press One for English: Language Policy, Public Opinion, and American Identity*; Elizabeth Theiss-Morse, *Who Counts as an American? The Boundaries of National Identity* (New York: Cambridge University Press, 2009).

35. Jack Citrin, Beth Reingold, and Donald P. Green, "American Identity and the Politics of Ethnic Change," *Journal of Politics* 52(4) (1990): 1124–1154; John Frendreis and Raymond Tatalovich, "Who Supports English-Only Language Laws? Evidence from the 1992 National Election Study," *Social Science Quarterly* 78(2) (1997): 354–368; Jack Citrin, Cara Wong, and Brian Duff, "The Meaning of American National Identity," in *Social Identity, Intergroup Conflict, and Conflict Resolution*, Richard Ashmore, Lee Jussim, and David Wilder, eds (New York: Oxford University Press, 2011), pp. 71–100; Deborah J. Schildkraut, *Press One for English: Language Policy, Public Opinion, and American Identity*; Jack Citrin and Matthew Wright, "Defining the Circle of We: American Identity and Immigration Policy," *The Forum* 7(3) (2009): 1–20; Cara Wong, *Boundaries of Obligation in American Politics: Geographic, National, and Racial Communities* (New York: Cambridge University Press, 2010); Deborah J. Schildkraut, *Americanism in the Twenty-First Century: Public Opinion in the Age of Immigration*.

36. Jack Citrin, Beth Reingold, and Donald P. Green, "American Identity and the Politics of Ethnic Change"; JackCitrin, Beth Reinhold, Evelyn Walters, and Donald P. Green, "The 'Official English' Movement and the Symbolic Politics of Language in the United States," *Western Political Quarterly* 43(3) (1990): 535; Thomas J. Espenshade and Katherine Hempstead, "Contemporary American Attitudes Toward U.S. Immigration"; Neil Malhotra, Yotam Margalit, and Cecilia Hyunjung Mo, "Economic Explanations for Opposition to Immigration: Distinguishing between Prevalence and Conditional Support."

37. Deborah J. Schildkraut, *Americanism in the Twenty-First Century: Public Opinion in the Age of Immigration*.

38. Ted Brader, Nicholas Valentino, and Elizabeth Suhay, "What Triggers Opposition to Immigration? Anxiety, Group Cues, and Immigration Threat," *American Journal of Political Science* 52(4) (2008): 959–978.

39. Nicholas Valentino, Ted Brader, and Ashley Jardina, "Immigration Opposition among U.S. Whites: General Ethnocentrism Or Media Priming of Attitudes about Latinos?" *Political Psychology* 34(2) (2013): 149–166.

40. Also see Zoltan Hajnal and Michael Rivera, forthcoming, "Immigration, Latinos, and White Partisan Politics: The New Democratic Defection," *American Journal of Political Science*.

41. U.S. Census Bureau, "Asians Fastest-Growing Race or Ethnic Group in 2012."

42. Benjamin Newman, Todd Hartman, and Charles Taber, "Foreign Language Exposure, Cultural Threat, and Opposition to Immigration," *Political Psychology* 33(5) (2012): 635–657; Daniel J. Hopkins, Van C. Tran, and Abigail Fisher Williamson, "See No Spanish: Language, Local Context, and Attitudes Toward Immigration," *Politics, Groups, and Identities* 2(1) (2014): 35–51; Daniel J. Hopkins,

"One Language, Two Meanings: Partisanship and Responses to Spanish," *Political Communication*, forthcoming.

43. Christopher Ellison, Heeju Shin, and David L. Leal, "The Contact Hypothesis and Attitudes Toward Latinos in the United States," *Social Science Quarterly* 92(4) (2011): 938–958.

44. M. V. Hood III and Irwin L. Morris, "?Amigo O Enemigo? Context, Attitudes, and Anglo Public Opinion Toward Immigration"; Andrea Louise Campbell, Cara Wong, and Jack Citrin, "'Racial Threat', Partisan Climate, and Direct Democracy: Contextual Effects in Three California Initiatives," *Political Behavior* 28(2) (2006): 129–150; Daniel J. Hopkins, "Politicized Places: Explaining Where and When Immigrants Provoke Local Opposition," *American Political Science Review* 104(1) (2010): 40–60; Deborah J. Schildkraut, *Americanism in the Twenty-First Century: Public Opinion in the Age of Immigration*.

45. Shaun Bowler and Gary M. Segura, *The Future is Ours: Minority Politics, Political Behavior, and the Multiracial Era of American Politics* (Thousand Oaks, CA: CQ Press, 2012); also see Figures 13.5 and 13.6.

46. Natalie Masuoka and Jane Junn, *The Politics of Belonging: Race, Public Opinion, and Immigration* (Chicago, IL: Chicago University Press, 2013).

47. M. V. III Hood, Irwin L. Morris, and Kurt A. Shirkey, "'!Quedate O Vente!': Uncovering the Determinants of Hispanic Public Opinion Toward Immigration," 50(3) (1997): 627–647; Regina Branton, "Latino Attitudes Toward Various Areas of Public Policy," *Political Research Quarterly* 60(2) (2007): 293–303; Mark Hugo Lopez, Paul Taylor, Cary Funk and Ana Gonzalez-Barrera, "On Immigration Policy, Deportation Relief seen as More Important than Citizenship: A Survey of Hispanics and Asian Americans," Pew Research Center, 2013, accessed May 1, 2014, http://www.pewhispanic.org/2013/12/19/on-immigration-policy-deportation-relief-seen-as-more-important-than-citizenship/

48. Regina Branton, "Latino Attitudes Toward Various Areas of Public Policy."

49. Shaun Bowler and Gary M. Segura, *The Future is Ours: Minority Politics, Political Behavior, and the Multiracial Era of American Politics*; Tatishe Nteta, "United we Stand? African Americans, Self Interest, and Immigration Reform."

50. Tatishe Nteta, "United We Stand? African Americans, Self Interest, and Immigration Reform."

51. For an exception, see Luis Fraga, John Garcia, Rodney E. Hero, Michael Jones-Correa, Valerie Martinez-Ebers, and Gary M. Segura, *Latinos in the New Millennium: An Almanac of Opinion, Behavior, and Policy Preferences* (New York: Cambridge University Press, 2012).

52. Zoltan Hajnal and Michael Rivera, "Immigration, Latinos, and White Partisan Politics: The New Democratic Defection."

53. Ibid.

54. Shaun Bowler, Stephen P. Nicholson, and Gary M. Segura, "Earthquakes and Aftershocks: Race, Direct Democracy, and Partisan Change," *American Journal of Political Science* 50(1) (2006): 146–159; David Damore and Adrian Pantoja, 2013, "Anti-Immigrant Politics and Lessons for the GOP from California," Latino Decisions, accessed May 15, 2014, http://www.latinodecisions.com/blog/2013/10/17/prop187effect/

55. Alexander Kuo, Neil Malhotra, and Cecilia Hyunjung Mo, n.d, "Why Do Asian Americans Identify as Democrats? Testing Theories of Social Exclusion and Intergroup Solidarity."

Chapter 14

Public Opinion and Reactionary Movements

From the Klan to the Tea Party

Matt A. Barreto and Christopher S. Parker

For the last five years the Tea Party has made a lot of noise. It helped the GOP regain the House in 2010. Further, from the debates over the debt ceiling to immigration reform, the Tea Party has forced the GOP to take very conservative positions and caused a rift in the Republican Party. The success of the Tea Party movement has roused media types and academics alike to better understand from whence it came. They wonder how and why it's come to dominate the political landscape. These are worthy, even necessary, questions. However, we believe that gaining traction on those questions requires placing the Tea Party in historical context because we don't believe the Tea Party is something new.

What, exactly, is a reactionary movement? According to sociologist Rory McVeigh, it's

> a social movement that acts on behalf of relatively advantaged groups with the goal of preserving, restoring, and expanding the rights and privileges of its members and constituents. These movements also attempt to deny similar rights and privileges to other groups in society . . . [something that] distinguishes right-wing movements from progressive movements.[1]

Who are the "advantaged groups" to which McVeigh refers? Historically, people that identify with reactionary movements tend to be overwhelmingly white, predominantly male, middle class, native born, Christian, and heterosexual. Taken together, this is the classical cultural and racial image of American identity.[2] Further, this stratum of the population is also more likely than other people to favor strong military presence, support more strict moral codes, back free market capitalism, reject government policies that give minorities a shot at equality, and prefer to maintain the advantaged status of native-born whites more than any other social group.[3] As middle class, white males with a stake in America—both cultural and economic—members and supporters of the Klan, John Birch Society, and the Tea Party committed (and commit) to fighting what they perceive(d) as tyrannical forces. Moreover, they defended freedom in the face of what they argued were unjust laws and court decisions, ones they cast as oppressive. Each, moreover, suggested that sometimes intolerance is necessary to protect liberty.[4]

Beginning with the Know-Nothing Party of the 1850s clear through the Tea Party of today, reactionary movements are motivated by a belief that America is in rapid decline, something that's associated with perceived social and cultural change.[5,6] Indeed, thanks to interpretive work relying on historical accounts, we have a firm grasp of the macro-historical forces that provoke the emergence of right-wing movements. At the individual level, however, beyond race, ethnicity, class, and religious orientation, we know relatively little about why people are drawn to right-wing movements. We know even less about whether or not supporting right-wing movements can explain social and political attitudes and preferences beyond the influence of other factors, including ideology, partisanship, and racial group membership.

In this chapter, we examine the attitudes, beliefs, and behavior of the reactionary right. By the time the present chapter closes, if we've done our job, the reader will emerge with a better understanding of what motivates the reactionary right, and how such motivations inform the policy preferences and behavior of its constituents. Right off the bat, however, we must be clear about the limits of our examination, the largest of which is its scope. Limits on the data restrict our substantive analysis of the reactionary right to a fifty-year span, from the 1960s through the Tea Party. However, we begin with an overview of reactionary thought.

Toward an Explanation of the Reactionary Right

So, what is the reactionary right? How, if at all, does it depart from the "establishment" right? The reactionary right is commensurate with what Seymour Martin Lipset and Earl Raab called "preservatism," or what Clinton Rossiter identified as "ultraconservatism."[7] Unlike establishment conservatism that tolerates change as a means of maintaining social, political, and economic stability, reactionary conservatives are willing to undermine stability in service to maintaining the social prestige associated with their stratum: white, male, middle class, relatively old, heterosexual, native-born Americans. Anytime the dominance of this stratum is jeopardized, as it is when threatened by rapid, large-scale social change, it provokes a "reaction" from the dominant group. This reaction includes violating the rule of law, something that establishment types as far back as John Adams would oppose.[8] Further, the "reaction" will, more often than not, include one or more scapegoats to which the group under siege ascribes an ongoing conspiracy.[9] In other words, the principal way in which the in-group explains their loss of relative prestige is by way of a concerted campaign of displacement directed by the out-group(s).

Many years ago, noted historian Richard Hofstadter offered a framework in which we may better understand the reactionary right. In his seminal essay, *The Paranoid Style in American Politics*, he argued that the far right wing practiced a style of politics consistent with paranoia. For him, there was no other way to explain the "heated exaggeration, suspiciousness, and the conspiratorial fantasy" associated with the Goldwater movement.[10] He is careful to distinguish paranoid politics, or the *paranoid style*, from the clinical version. However, he cites important similarities between political and clinical paranoia in that "both tend to be overheated, over-suspicious, overaggressive, grandiose, and apocalyptic in expression."[11] The key difference, as he sees it, is that the clinical paranoid perceives *himself* the object of the conspiracy. The paranoid politico, on the other hand, perceives the conspiracy to be

> directed against a nation, a culture, a way of life whose fate affects not himself but millions of others. . . . His sense that his political passions are unselfish and patriotic, in fact, goes far to intensify his feeling of righteousness and his moral indignation.[12]

Hofstadter also outlined a belief system on which the paranoid style rests: pseudo-conservatism. The pseudo-conservative is a person who is quick to use the *rhetoric* of conservatism, a belief system that prizes traditions and institutions and has an appreciation for the history of both. Yet, according to Hofstadter, the pseudo-conservative fails to behave like a conservative in that "in the name of upholding traditional American values and institutions and defending them against more or less fictitious dangers, consciously or unconsciously [he] aims at their abolition."[13] Furthermore, the pseudo-conservative "believes himself to be living in a world in which he is spied upon, plotted against, betrayed, and very likely destined for ruin."[14] This state of mind pushes him to attack a way of life and institutions he purports to revere, pressing his representatives to insist upon a rash of Constitutional amendments, including abolishing the income tax, cutting spending on welfare, and charging with treason people who try to weaken the government.

Hofstadter believed such a person is attempting to get a fix on his position in the rapidly changing social system in which members of this group believe their material and/or cultural status to be in decline. Moreover, as Hofstadter suggests, they no longer have something to which they may anchor their American identity. Indeed, the pseudo-conservative has lost his bearings amidst a raft of social changes, much as someone suffering from paranoid social cognition does upon induction into a new social order—be it at school, in a neighborhood, or a new job. In this environment, the pseudo-conservative in the paranoid style is simply trying to maintain their social status.

Consider the twentieth century. The Ku Klux Klan of the 1920s provides the first example. Founded in Stone Mountain, Georgia, in 1915, the second version of the "Invisible Empire" was truly a national movement, spreading beyond the South to the states of Washington, Oregon, New York, Indiana, and Michigan, to name but a few.[15] According to a well-researched documentary by the Public Broadcasting Station (PBS), by the mid-1920s, "national membership in this secret organization ranged from three million to as high as eight million Klansmen."[16] The modal Klan member was white (of course), male, middle class, heterosexual, and native born.

To maintain the dominance of the strata to which they belonged, the Klan stopped at almost nothing. Frequently, they relied upon violence to keep "uppity" blacks in their place, as well as Jews and Catholic immigrants. All of this is well known. What's not so well known is the fact that the Klan also used violence to police white men. White men who beat their wives, were chronic drunks, cheated on their spouse, among other things, were subject to beatings by Klansmen. In short, the Klan enforced the moral standards of the community. Regardless of the purpose for which it's used, extra-legal violence is, by definition, a violation of the rule of law.

Law and order, of course, is something by which conservatives typically swear. The fact that the Klan employed lynching and beatings as a means of maintaining social order isn't news. What is new, though, is the theoretical reason behind them doing so: to maintain the group's social prestige. It's abundantly clear now that the Klan perceived their way of life under siege. Blacks posed a threat socially, Jews economically, and Catholics politically. In other words, all three threatened the America with which Klan members identified: white, male, middle class, older, Christian, native born, and heterosexual. In the absence of the social-scientific methods and measures to which we now have access, it's difficult to say what, from an empirical perspective, drove people to identify with the Klan.

Social histories of the KKK suggest the complicity of racism and xenophobia, among other things, in the mobilization of the Klan. Unfortunately, we cannot adjudicate this issue for the Invisible Empire. However, if we're correct in that the KKK of the 1920s represents a pattern of social change followed by the formation of reactionary movements, we're confident that we can eventually assay the correlates of the reactionary right. We now turn to this task.

The Reactionary Right of the 1960s

Some 30 years after the Klan's renaissance another reactionary movement emerged. Retired candy manufacturer Robert Welch founded the John Birch Society (JBS). Founded in 1958, the organization was born of the anxiety associated with the perceived spread of communism at home and abroad: they believed the "American" way of life threatened by communist subversion.[17] During its heyday, the JBS enjoyed a membership that stood at eighty thousand, and six to eight million sympathizers, i.e., non-members who, nonetheless, identified with the organization.[18] By the mid-1960s, though, the movement spread beyond California and Arizona to the remainder of the country, represented by approximately five thousand local chapters.[19] Like the Klan, its members were firmly middle class. For instance, approximately 33 percent of them had completed college, with another 32 percent that had attended, though not completed, college. The numbers for the general public were 10 and 12 percent, respectively. Further, only 14 percent of Birchers belonged to the manual labor class versus 49 percent of the general public.[20]

Welch was a big believer in small government. This is no surprise given his business background. But it was his belief that the United States was being torn asunder by communism for which he was best known. He accused President Eisenhower of being in cahoots with the communists, and attempted to impeach Chief Justice Earl Warren for his support of civil rights for blacks. In fact, he suggested that the Civil Rights Movement was, among other things, a means by which communism might gain traction in the United States. Indeed, communism did a lot of heavy lifting for Birchers: anything they perceived as a deviation from the "American" way, they labeled "communist." This included racial and gender equality, what they believed was the cause of the moral "decay" of American society (e.g., homosexuality, pornography, and the absence of deference to authority), and rising crime rates.[21]

At this point, even the skeptical reader would have to concede the emergence of a strong, consistent pattern. However, as social scientists, we remain vulnerable on at least one count for our evidence rests, in the main, on interpretive claims. We have no way of identifying what really underpins identification with reactionary movements, much less assessing the political consequences associated with them. After accounting for education, age, and income does religion remain a factor? What about racism, nativism, or ideology? Do any of the latter group of possible determinants affect the likelihood of someone sympathizing with reactionary movements? Finally, does membership or identification with a reactionary movement influence individual-level attitudes, policy preferences and behavior, beyond competing, more established explanations?

To answer these questions we turn to a group known as the supporters of the late Arizona senator, and presidential candidate, Barry Goldwater. After losing a close election in 1960 when John F. Kennedy bested Richard M. Nixon, right-leaning factions of the GOP wished to run a "real" conservative instead of a "me too Democrat," a moniker akin to today's RINO: Republican In Name Only. In Goldwater, the GOP at last had a candidate who would completely dismantle the New Deal by shrinking government. On foreign policy, the senator promised to roll back the spread of communism instead of simply containing it as President Eisenhower had chosen to do. In 1964, Goldwater's fidelity to small government resulted in his failure to support the Civil Rights Act, a maneuver that won him support in the South. He had also won the support of Strom Thurmond, Goldwater's colleague from South Carolina, and the leader of the Dixiecrat revolt of 1948.

These are all important reasons why we have chosen to draw on Goldwater supporters as proxies for reactionary conservatism in the 1960s. But the most important—if not dispositive—factor for us is the fact that the JBS were the senator's most fervent supporters. In fact, some have even ventured that in the absence of the JBS (including JBS identifiers, i.e., non- members), Goldwater may have failed to secure his party's nomination.[22] Demographically, Goldwater supporters are very similar to the JBS's constituency: they're well educated, all white, older, predominantly male, and members of the white-collar crowd.[23]

Until now, our analysis has been limited by a lack of attitudinal data. Now, however, we can press forward and assay the individual-level underpinnings of reactionary movements, and the extent to which identification with these movements shapes attitudes, policy preferences, and behavior. We begin with the attitudes believed conducive to identification with the reactionary right. We turn to Christopher Towler's work on the reactionary right in the 1960s for the bulk of the following analysis.[24] He hypothesized that anxiety among the far right was building up surrounding the conspiracy theory that communists were infiltrating vast parts of America. Towler was right: as anxiety increased among people in the electorate, the probability of identifying with the reactionary right, indexed by support for Goldwater, increased by 33 percent. This effect is above and beyond that which he found for alternative explanations including racism, anti-communism, partisanship, and a preference for small government, each of which increased the likelihood of identifying with the reactionary right by 21 percent, 11 percent, 52 percent (Republican versus Democrat), and 11 percent, respectively.

Now that we've pinned down what promotes identification with the reactionary right, it's time for us to examine the consequences of attachment to the movement. We turn first to intergroup relations. Net of the effects of racism, anti-communism, partisanship, and ideology, support for Goldwater dampened the way people felt about blacks and Jews. Further, identification with the reactionary right was also associated with negative attitudes toward the NAACP and CORE, two prominent civil rights organizations. We see similar, but stronger results when the analysis moves to race-related policies in the 1960s.

Towler examines the ways in which reactionary conservatism informed the electorate's views concerning the government's role in school integration, whether or not busing was necessary, and the extent to which they supported integration of their neighborhoods. Conventional wisdom suggests that racism should provide most of the explanatory power we should find once we specify a model. Likewise, in the context of the 1960s, communism and racial equality were often linked in the minds of Goldwater supporters via their association with the JBS. Therefore, anti-communist attitudes must also be taken into account if the results on race-based policy preferences are to be taken seriously.

As it turns out, even after correcting for racism and anti-communism, Towler shows that reactionary conservatism continued to animate people's views on racial policy preferences in the 1960s. Net of the effects of racism and anti-communism, among other things, reactionary conservatism dampened support for government-backed school integration by 11 percent, and by 9 percent for busing. Yet, for neighborhood integration, the impact of reactionary conservatism dissolves. Given the size of the effect of racism, in which it reduced support for integration by 52 percent, reactionary conservatism appears bound up with the negative way in which many whites viewed blacks. This is no big surprise insofar as the prospect of one of "them" moving next door significantly decreases the social distance to which many whites had become accustomed.

Most would agree that the 1960s represents one of the most volatile periods in the relatively short existence of the United States. Many believed, with some justification, that the Soviet Union threatened American security interests. But there were others who subscribed to a way of thinking in which the communism threat—from without and within—was existential: it threatened the "American way" of life. Among the ways in which this menace became manifest is through the Civil Rights Movement. But as the analysis makes clear, reactionary conservatism—indexed by support for Goldwater—discriminates between the fear of a communist takeover and the anxiety related to the perception that social change, i.e., the Civil Rights Movement, was happening too fast. Needless to say, this is roughly the same scenario we observed with the Klan and the JBS.

Concern with change also had behavioral implications. Even upon correcting for the usual cast of characters that account for political engagement, reactionary conservatism remained an important predictor. This finding indicates that the negative affect associated with change successfully motivated mobilization.

The totality of the work we've reviewed so far suggests continuity on the reactionary right from the 1920s through the 1960s. We argued as much in our own work. But times have changed since then. After all, we now have a black president, same-sex rights are on the march, and the demographics of America are rapidly changing. Surely, there's no place for the reactionary right in America now, is there? Of course there is. The next section presents irrefutable evidence to that effect.

The Tea Party

Around 2009, shortly after President Obama's first inauguration, a group of loosely organized, highly motivated individuals, organizations, and political action committees coalesced to form what has come to be known as the Tea Party. In 2010 the Tea Party boasted major electoral wins in the U.S. House and Senate, defeating both incumbent Republican and Democratic lawmakers alike. These results should come as no great surprise, given the widespread support the movement enjoyed back in 2010. During its height in 2010, the Tea Party claimed a core membership of approximately 550,000 who have signed up to be members of at least one of the national Tea Party groups: 1776 Tea Party, ResistNet (Patriot Action network), Tea Party Express, Tea Party Nation, and Tea Party Patriots. Beyond this core group are two additional constituencies. One consists of the people who have attended at least one rally, donated, or purchased Tea Party literature: an estimated 3 million people.[25] Another layer consists of Tea Party sympathizers, people who approve of the Tea Party. According to data from a 2010 University of Washington study, 27 percent of the adult population, or 63 million Americans, strongly approve of the Tea Party.[26]

Given this level of support, what does the Tea Party want? From at least one account, the Tea Party believes in a reduced role for the federal government, more fiscal responsibility, lower taxes, a free market, and a commitment to states' rights.[27] Indeed, these are core conservative, even libertarian, principles, very much in keeping with traditional American political culture.[28] What's more, commitment to these values is widely considered patriotic. Yet, time after time, supporters of the Tea Party seem to be united by something *beyond* a belief in limited government. Specifically, Tea Party sympathizers appear united in their fervent disdain for President Barack Obama, and seem to be squarely opposed to any policies that might benefit minority groups.

In the preceding sections we sought to illustrate a pattern we associate with the rise of reactionary movements. From the Klan to the JBS, individuals appear to react to what they perceive as rapid social change in which the social prestige of "real Americans" is under siege. In this section, we take up the question of the Tea Party's emergence and common Tea Party attitudes in the age of Obama. We argue that the Tea Party represents a right-wing movement distinct from mainstream conservatism, which has reacted with great anxiety to the social and demographic changes in America over the past few decades. Through a comprehensive review of published data analysis we show that Tea Party sympathizers hold strong out-group resentment, in particular towards blacks, immigrants, and gays. Briefly, we then review public opinion data to determine if the findings can be generalized to the population of Tea Party sympathizers at large.

Contemporary observers and Tea Party events gesture towards concerns that transcend limited government and fiscal conservatism. For instance, the NAACP has charged the Tea Party with promoting racism, and Tea Party Express leader Mark Williams has been chastised by other Tea Party leaders for penning an overtly racist letter poking fun at the NAACP. Their activists were a driving force behind the Arizona state statute SB1070 (among other things, this bill proposed to empower local authorities to interrogate the immigration status of people who "looked like" immigrants), which many said would result in the targeting of Latinos for racial profiling. They may be best known for their many caricatures of President Obama, often depicting him as a primate, African "witch doctor," and modern-day Hitler, among other things. Consider, moreover, the constant references to President Obama as a socialist. In fact, a recent study issued by Democracy Corps reports that 90 percent of Tea Party supporters believe President Obama to be a socialist; as such, they view him as the "defining and motivating threat to the country and its well-being."[29] Perhaps the fact that the movement harbors members of white nationalist groups helps to explain the apparent intolerance of the movement.[30] However, beyond a perception of intolerance, we think there is something deeper in the emergence of the Tea Party that is more in line with studies of paranoia, conspiratorial beliefs, and out-group suspicion—in short, a right-wing reactionary movement.

A Changing America and the Emergence of the Tea Party

We have already mentioned what we believe triggered the emergence of the Tea Party: the election of the country's first black president. However, it was not just the election of Obama that triggered the Tea Party, but also the changing demographics and political debates in America over the past 40 years. In 1970, 83 percent of the U.S. population was white, non-Hispanic, and in 2010 63 percent was white—a 20 percentage point decline in one generation. Accompanying this change has been an increase in the black, Hispanic, and Asian populations in the United States and a vigorous debate about civil rights and immigration. Whether we're talking about blacks or immigrants, the Tea Party and its followers appear to reject the presence of racial "others."

Racial Resentment

For many, the election of the Nation's first African American President is evidence of the end of racism in America. Yet, the emergence of the Tea Party in the months following the inauguration of Barack Obama, and the propensity for racially charged antics exposed at many of the group's events and rallies, warrants a closer look at the immediacy of racism in America today. As research has shown, racism and racial resentment play an important role in determining not only support for Obama, but also support for black candidates in general.[31] The influence of modern-day racism is most known for its place in opposition towards affirmative action and other race-conscious programs.[32] The racism that commonly guides contemporary white attitudes has been coined *racial resentment* and relies upon anti-black affect, or a "pre-existing negative attitude toward blacks."[33] In other words, racial resentment is fueled by the gains and growing demands of black Americans,[34] a resentment that has a new level of fuel with the country led by an African American President for the first time in its history.

Old-fashioned racism, based on biological differences between blacks and whites, is no longer acceptable in society today and a new, subtler, racism works to predict attitudes and behaviors.[35] This new form of racism relies on stereotypes surrounding African Americans; stereotypes that put blacks in opposition to treasured American values such as hard work, honesty, and lawfulness.[36] In addition, ascribing these stereotypes to blacks allows for whites to continue justifying their privileged position in society.[37] The centrality of American values in racial resentment links American individualism to expressions of prejudice.[38] The attributes (or stereotypes) assigned to blacks— laziness, preference for welfare, predisposition to crime—place them in opposition to the values American society rests upon, isolating and alienating blacks from the ideals that go hand in hand with being a good citizen in America.

The timing behind the emergence of the Tea Party in American politics begs for a further examination of a group that is determined to "take back" their country and fight against a government absorbed by socialism. The Tea Party movement's emphasis on American values and individualism places many of their policy stances and positions in opposition to minority policies, such as an increase in social programs, including spending for the poor and health care reform. Also, the rhetoric of the Tea Party places its members in opposition to minority groups in America as well as the new leadership of the country.

The Tea Party's focus on individualism and American values alone is not enough to validate claims of racial resentment. In addition, accusations of racism within the Tea Party have existed since its beginning. A 2010 report by the Institute for Research and Education on Human Rights (IREHR) chronicles the involvement of white supremacy groups in the Tea Party since the movement's first events on April 15, 2009 and, if nothing more, speaks to the Tea Party's availability as a vehicle for white supremacist recruitment and thought. Other watchdog agencies, such as *teapartytracker.org*, have made it a point to highlight acts of racism and extremism within the Tea Party and at their rallies and events. Beyond the consistent chronicling of individual acts of racism and bigotry, much of the resentment in the Tea Party boiled over at the height of the health care debate. As congressmen and women came together to vote on the proposed health care bill in March of 2010, a Tea Party protest boiled over as racial epithets were launched at Rep. John Lewis, a Democrat from Georgia, and Rep. Emanuel Cleaver, a Democrat from Missouri, was spat upon while trying to make it through the crowd at Capitol Hill.[39, 40]

These instances, among others, led to the denunciation of racism and bigotry in the Tea Party movement on a national stage. Although making it clear that the NAACP was not condemning the entire Tea Party as racist, the following reaction from one of the movement's prominent leaders brought racial resentment to the forefront. Mark Williams, a leader of the Tea Party at the time, released a satirical commentary in response to the NAACP resolution. The response was a letter to President Lincoln from "colored people" and insinuated not only ignorance on the part of blacks in America, but also reinforced many of the stereotypes central to racial resentment such as blacks are lazy, lacking a work ethic.

Even as the evidence consistently finds the Tea Party rampant with racial resentment and extremism, the movement's members argue that they are following their conservative principles centered on small government and limited spending—stances that do not favor minorities or people of color by their political nature. This position, though, is not new as ideological conservatism is often invoked as a means of avoiding accusations of racism.[41]

Scholars have worked hard to separate the influence of conservative principles from racial resentment. Whites' disapproval of affirmative action and social welfare programs has been justified through a violation of norms central to conservative principles, such as hard work and self-reliance. The *group dominance approach* stands in opposition to principled conservatism, explaining that groups will use ideology and political symbols to "legitimize" each group's claims over resources.[42] Furthermore, scholars have shown that racism not only works in conjunction with the individual values associated with principled conservatism—Kinder and Mendelberg tell us that individualism becomes part of racism—but racism goes beyond conservative individualism to predict negative attitudes towards race-conscious policy and politicians of color.[43] When specifically examining negative attitudes towards President Obama, racism plays a major role regardless of ideological preference.[44] The recent emergence of the Tea Party allows for a closer examination of the racial attitudes held by this unique group of Americans, emphasizing the principles of individualism over all else. Beyond anti-black racial resentment, much is made today of anti-immigrant beliefs as the next frontier in racial attitudes. Certainly as a policy issue, immigration became a major topic during the Obama years, and while the Tea Party *claimed* to be mostly concerned with taxes and spending, it also staked out a very clear position on immigration.

Anti-Immigrant Attitudes

Statements about immigration from Tea Party politicians and groups largely portrayed immigration as a threat to Americans or American culture. One glaring example of this is Sharon Angle's 2010 campaign ad "Best Friend," which features a voice-over that ominously states, "Illegals sneaking across our borders putting Americans' jobs and safety at risk," while showing video of dark-skinned actors sneaking around a chain link fence.[45] Angle was a darling of the Tea Party movement in Nevada and attacked Harry Reid on immigration in both the "Best Friend" ad as well as a second ad called "At Your Expense," which charged that Reid supported special college tuition rates for undocumented immigrants, which would be paid for by Nevada taxpayers.[46] Both ads juxtaposed the dark-skinned actors portraying illegal immigrants with white Americans working or with their families on the same screen. The implicit racism in Angle's ad was reminiscent of the now notorious "White Hands" ad of Jesse Helms and the "Willie Horton" campaign ad run by George W. Bush in 1988.

Sharon Angle was not the only Tea Party candidate who tried to use the threat of Latino immigration to capture votes in the 2010 election. In Arizona, J. D. Hayworth, John McCain's Republican primary challenger, similarly made immigration one of the central planks of his campaign. Hayworth had actually written a whole book on the subject of undocumented immigration in 2005 called *Whatever It Takes*, in which he argued in favor of increased immigration enforcement and notes that while immigration is clearly good for the country, the proportion of immigrants coming from Mexico is too high because it could lead to America becoming a bicultural nation. In Hayworth's own words, "Bicultural societies are among the least stable in the world."[47] Hayworth was a strong supporter of Arizona's SB1070 but believed that even more steps had to be taken against undocumented immigrants, stating at a 2010 rally in Mesa,

Arizona, that, "There is a whole new term: birth tourism. In the jet age there are people who time their gestation period so they give birth on American soil."[48] To prevent this, Hayworth argued that the state of Arizona should stop birthright citizenship, a view echoed by Russell Pearce, a state senator from Arizona and the architect of SB1070.

Tea Party organizations also sought to portray immigration as a threat to America in the lead up to the 2010 general election. The Tea Party Nation emailed its roughly 35,000 members in August and asked them to post stories highlighting the victimization of Americans by illegal immigrants. The group specifically asked for stories about undocumented immigrants taking the jobs of members, committing crimes, or undermining business by providing cheap labor to competitors.[49] The Americans for Legal Immigration PAC (ALIPAC) assisted two Tea Party groups, Voice of the People USA and Tea Party Patriots Live, in coordinating rallies in support of Arizona's SB1070. The ALIPAC mission statement points out that,

> Our state and federal budgets are being overwhelmed. Schools, hospitals, law enforcement, and public services are being strained while the taxpayers incur more costs and more debt. Our nation's very survival and identity are being threatened along with our national security.[50]

ALIPAC is supported by the Federation for American Immigration Reform (FAIR), a group designated a hate group by the Southern Poverty Law Center because of its links to white supremacist organizations.[51]

The Tea Party, while disavowing that its anti-immigrant rhetoric was based on racism, has continued to portray immigration in starkly threatening terms, which while not explicitly racist has strong undercurrents of implicit racism, with Sharon Angle's campaign videos being the most obvious example of this. A New York Times/CBS News poll released in August of 2010 unsurprisingly found that 82 percent of self-identified Tea Party supporters believed illegal immigration was a "serious problem."[52] Perceived threats from immigrant groups have been shown to be a powerful predictor for immigration restriction and anti-immigrant attitudes in the sociology, psychology, and political science literatures.

It's plain to see that the Tea Party and its followers are concerned with more than small government and fiscal responsibility. But why is this the case? What do blacks and immigrants have in common? Race. More specifically, the ways in which blacks and immigrants—especially the undocumented—represent a departure from the White Anglo-Saxon Protestant (WASP) representation of American culture with which America has come to be identified. "Real Americans," in other words, are neither black nor born elsewhere. As Parker and Barreto demonstrate to great effect, Tea Partiers are anxious that the America to which they've grown accustomed is under siege from non-WASP groups.[53] For this reason, Tea Partiers are loath to extend rights and benefits to these "others."

Looking Forward: Will the Tea Party Survive?

Five years into its political existence, many now wonder where the Tea Party is headed. Is it still influential after the 2012 election when Tea Partiers failed to help the GOP capture the White House? But failing to secure the Executive Branch of government, as the Tea Party has shown, isn't the end of the world. In fact, it's shown that holding half of the Legislative Branch suffices to arrest the change sought by the president and his party. Indeed, the 50 or so Republican members of the House aligned with the Tea Party in some way have managed to frustrate not only President Obama and his agenda, but also the conservative establishment.

Since 2010, pundits have declared the Tea Party dead at least eighteen times. Yet, its membership continues to climb. For instance, since 2010 the Institute for Research and Education on Human Rights (IREHR) reports that card-carrying members of the insurgent group increased from 185K to approximately 550K—a three-fold increase. The number of Tea Party sympathizers, however, has recently declined from a high of around 30 percent in 2010 to 20 percent as of the last quarter of 2013, during the federal government shutdown, though the most recent polling data suggests a slight uptick in 2014, with 24 percent now identifying themselves as supporters of the movement.[54] In raw numbers, assuming the movement never recovers its pre-shutdown popularity among sympathizers, it still means that 36 million Americans identify with the Tea Party.

If the level of Tea Party sympathizers is subject to periodic dips, the financial backing of the reactionary movement resembles the steady growth we see in the ranks of membership. As of February 2014, the *New York Times* reported that fundraising efforts of Tea Party affiliated organizations have outstripped those associated with establishment conservative groups by a three to one margin. During the early stages of the Tea Party insurgency, questions were asked about the authenticity of the movement insofar as the Koch brothers and other big money donors bank-rolled Tea Party organizations. As a result, some on the left derided the Tea Party as a movement funded by wealthy business interests, as opposed to the grassroots phenomenon many in the movement claimed it was.

If this represented even a sliver of truth in the early stages of the movement, the same cannot be said now. The Institution for Research on Education and Human Rights (IREHR) reports that 82 percent of individual donors' contributions to Tea Party organizations were limited to no more than $200. We see a similar pattern as it pertains to Superpacs, in which 97 percent of their receipts were confined to no more than $1K. If this information is even remotely accurate, and we believe it is, Tea Party fundraising is more democratic, buying itself a measure of independence from big money, special-interest patrons.

So, what keeps the Tea Party thriving? Why does it continue as a major force in American politics? To answer these questions, and many others, we conducted a national survey of 1,000 adults in December 2013. As a way of demonstrating that fear and anxiety is the driving force behind Tea Party intransigence, we contrast the attitudes and preferences of Tea Party conservatives with those of non-Tea Party conservatives. If Tea Party resistance is really about fidelity to conservative principles such as law and order, small government, and fiscal responsibility, we should observe no difference among conservatives. If, however, differences do emerge, we can attribute them to fear and anxiety.

As it turns out, the data suggests important fissures among conservatives. We begin with immigrants. Consider the following: forty percent of non-Tea Party conservatives believe that "restrictive immigration policies are based on racism," but only 18 percent of Tea Party conservatives agree. Perhaps this is why we see such a large gap among conservatives when it comes to supporting comprehensive immigration reform: eighty percent of mainstream conservatives want to see a comprehensive solution to immigration versus 60 percent of Tea Party conservatives. Again, if resistance were really about conservative principles—law and order, in the case of immigration—our findings would've revealed no differences between the rival conservative camps, but they did. Piecing together what's implied from the questions, this leads us to conclude that Tea Partiers, relative to establishment types, believe the current policies are adequate.

Another race-related issue encountered by the American public for which we gathered evidence is the controversial Supreme Court decision on the renewal of the Voting Rights Act (VRA). In June of 2013, in a 5–4 decision, the Court released several states with a record of violating the voting rights of blacks and other minorities from federal oversight in which the covered jurisdictions were required to clear any changes to their voting laws with the Department of Justice. This ruling cleared the way for states to effectively enact legislation that may have the effect—if not intent—of discriminating against some voters in ways that inhibit their ability to vote. An establishment conservative would object to the continuing necessity of the VRA's preclearance provision as a violation of state sovereignty. Indeed, this constituted a major part of the conservative majority's opinion. However, we have reason to believe that something beyond conservatism informs the Tea Party's opinion on the issue.

Our theory suggests that Tea Party conservatives' support for the ruling on the VRA has less to do with the federal government violating states' rights, and has more to do with the ways in which the ruling will ultimately impede the ability of people of color to vote. We examined our claim by asking people whether or not they believe discrimination remains a problem when it comes to voting rights. As it turns out, roughly 50 percent of establishment conservatives believe discrimination remains a problem versus just 37 percent of Tea Party conservatives. We acknowledge that the difference isn't especially striking: a mere 13 percentage points. The point, however, isn't the size of the difference. Rather, the point is that there's *any* difference at all.

Our assessment of the Tea Party suggests that reports of its death have been overblown. If the Tea Party were truly on its way out, would its membership continue increasing? Would its fundraising be so robust? Would it continue to enjoy such influence on the Republican Party? We don't think so. In addition to the organizational strength it continues to demonstrate, and the political clout it continues to wield, we have also documented the enduring cleavage that exists between establishment conservatives and reactionary conservatives. Our theory indicates establishment conservatives are committed to conventional conservative principles, whereas reactionary conservatives are motivated more by the fear and anxiety associated with the perception that "real" Americans are losing the country.

Having discussed the continuing strength of the Tea Party, and its animating forces in the present, we now take a moment to touch on the Tea Party's prospects in the near future. In 2016, the most likely scenario appears to be one in which a President Hillary Clinton takes the reins. As almost every pundit has noted, turnout patterns in presidential years are increasingly favorable to Democrats and Clinton is far and away the front runner on the left. If this comes to pass, Obama's departure from office won't necessarily lead to the Tea Party's disappearance. Just as the far right rejected feminism in the 1960s and 1970s, people who identify with the Tea Party are more likely to harbor anti-feminist tendencies. For this reason, we will likely witness continued Tea Party activity— recall protesters in 2008 who showed up at Clinton events with signs stating "Iron my shirt."[55] But even though Obama's rise helped mobilize the movement, its intensity will wane. The Tea Party's reaction to the first woman in the Oval Office will likely be muted compared to their reaction to the first black president. The movement saw—and continues to see—Obama as a vessel for the hitherto ignored claims for equality from marginalized groups. While not new, the push for equality by these groups appears to have gained currency on Obama's watch. The simultaneity, suddenness, and force with which marginalized groups have pressed their claims during the Obama presidency no doubt contributed to the fear, anxiety, and anger felt by Tea Partiers. But even if Clinton succeeds Obama, these issues will have already been on the radar for eight years. And since Tea Partiers have already been exposed to the new political playing field, we suspect their reaction to Clinton won't be as rabid if she chooses to continue the president's equality-based agenda. By this logic, only if a white male Democrat wins the White House in 2016 will the Tea Party movement go underground.

Conclusion

Our review of public opinion and right-wing movements is now complete. At least two things are very clear. First, from the Klan to the Tea Party, there's a certain segment of the country that remains anxious and angry when it perceives rapid social change: white, male, native born, middle class, Christian, and middle-aged folks. This is not to say that EVERY person in this group is reactionary. This is patently untrue. Instead, we invite you to think of it in the following way: someone from this group is more likely to harbor reactionary sentiments than, say, someone who is a black, female, working class, young, Jamaican immigrant. Second, reactionaries hold beliefs that lead to policy preferences different from both "liberals" and establishment conservatives. That their preferences depart from establishment conservatives belies reactionaries' claims that they're merely simple—if angry—conservatives.

Moving beyond sympathy for the Klan, for which we have no hard public opinion data, we see these themes play out in the 1960s, as well as the present moment. Similar to the ways in which the Tea Party and its supporters fail to embrace social change now, as it pertains to racial and sexual minorities,[56] the JBS and its supporters failed to embrace change if it involved racially progressive policies. In both cases, even after ideology is taken into account, our theory of reactionary conservatism remains a valid alternative explanation for what we (and Towler) observe. What this suggests is more than fifty years after the height of the Civil Rights Movement, the event that helped spawn the JBS, reactionary forces were once again mobilized to thwart change, in the guise of the Tea Party. The only difference this time is that a single—albeit powerful—person mobilized reactionary forces: the President of the United States.

The discerning reader may ask why it took the prospect of progress for an entire race to jumpstart a reactionary movement fifty years ago, but a single man is capable of doing so now. As we've discussed elsewhere, it's really quite simple. As the Commander-in-Chief, Chief Law Enforcement officer, head of government, etc., the President of the United States wields enormous power. However, perhaps more important, is what the office represents: the leader of the American people, the titular head of the country. For reactionary conservatives, this is simply too much to bear: a black man in the White House. It's an affront to their identity as Americans. For them, Barack Obama's "occupation" of the Oval Office symbolizes too much change. They believe the America in which they've grown up, the America to which they've become attached, is no more. In like fashion, the reactionaries believed the Civil Rights Movement would ultimately result in the undoing of the country.

Unfortunately, there's no end in sight for reactionary movements. One is always around the corner, waiting to issue a call to arms in response to what its adherents believe is too much change. In fact, research now underway with Parker and Towler reveals that reactionary conservatism is passed down from generation to generation. Even so, as the demographic segment from which reactionary conservatives are drawn—White Anglo-Saxon, Christian, heterosexual, and native born—diminishes, so too will their political influence. Of course, as their influence as "real Americans" continues to wane, the influence of marginalized groups such as racial and sexual minorities, as well as immigrants and women, will continue to rise. As the legendary crooner Sam Cooke said so eloquently: "A Change is Gonna Come." It's just a matter of time.

Notes

1. Rory McVeigh, *The Rise of the Ku Klux Klan: Right-Wing Movements and National Politics* (Minneapolis: University of Minnesota Press, 2009), pp. 32–33.

2. Thierry Devos and Mahzarin R. Banaji, "American = White?" *Journal of Personality and Social Psychology* 88, no. 3; Margot Canaday, *The Straight State* (Princeton:, Princeton University Press, 2009); and Rogers M. Smith, *Civic Ideals: Conflicting Visions of Citizenship in U.S. History* (New Haven: Yale University Press, 1997).

3. Sara Diamond, *Roads to Dominion: Right-Wing Movements and Political Power in the United States* (New York: Guilford Press, 1995).

4. J. Allen Broyles, *The John Birch Society: Anatomy of a Protest* (Boston: Beacon Press, 1966); Benjamin R. Epstein and Arnold Forster, *The Radical Right: Report in on the John Birch Society and Its Allies* (New York: Vintage Books, 1967); Nancy McClean, *Behind the Mask of Chivalry: The Making of the Second Ku Klux Klan* (New York: Oxford University Press, 1995); Christopher Parker and Matt Barreto, *Change They Can't Believe In: The Tea Party and Reactionary Politics in America* (Princeton: Princeton University Press, 2013); and Robert Welch, *The Blue Book of the John Birch Society* (self-published, 1961).

5. Parker and Barreto, *Change They Can't Believe In: The Tea Party and Reactionary Politics in America* (Princeton: Princeton University Press, 2013).

6. E. D. Knowles, B. S. Lowery, E. P. Shulman, and R. L. Schaumberg, Race, Ideology, and the Tea Party: A Longitudinal Study, PLoS ONE 8(6) (2013): e67110.doi:10.1371/journal.pone.0067110

7. Seymour Martin Lipset and Earl Raab, *The Politics of Unreason: Right-Wing Extremism in American Politics, 1790–1970* (New York: Harper and Row, 1970); Clinton Rossiter, *Conservatism in America* (Cambridge, MA: Harvard University Press, 1982).

8. Patrick Allitt, *The Conservatives: Ideas & and Personalities throughout American History* (New Haven: Yale University Press, 2009).

9. Lipset and Raab, *The Politics of Unreason: Right-Wing Extremism in American Politics, 1790–1970*; and Richard Hofstadter, *The Paranoid Style in American Politics* (New York: Vintage Books, 1965).

10. Hofstadter, *The Paranoid Style in American Politics*.

11. Ibid., p. 4.

12. Ibid., p. 4.

13. T. W. Adorno et al., *The Authoritarian Personality* (New York: Harper and Row, 1950), pp. 675–676.

14. Hofstadter, *The Paranoid Style in American Politics*, chapter 2.

15. Rory McVeigh, *The Rise of the Ku Klux Klan: Right-Wing Movements and National Politics*.

16. http://www.pbs.org/wgbh/americanexperience/features/general-article/flood-klan/

17. Sara Diamond, *Roads to Dominion: Right-Wing Movements and Political Power in the United States* (New York: Guilford Press, 1995); see also Parker and Barreto, *Change They Can't Believe In: The Tea Party and Reactionary Politics in America*.

18. Fred W. Grupp Jr., "The Political Perspectives of Birch Society Members," in *The American Right Wing: Readings in Political Behavior*, ed. Robert A. Schoenberger (New York: Holt, Rinehart and Winston, 1969).

19. Grupp, "The Political Perspectives of Birch Society Members," in *The American Right Wing: Readings in Political Behavior*, ed. Robert A. Schoenberger.

20. Grupp, "The Political Perspectives of Birch Society Members," in *The American Right Wing: Readings in Political Behavior*, ed. Robert A. Schoenberger.

21. Ira S. Rohter, "Social and Psychological Determinants of Radical Rightism," in Robert A. Schoenberger, ed., *The American Right Wing: Readings in American Political Behavior* (New York: Holt, Rinehart,and Winston, 1969).

22. Geoffrey Kabaservice, *Rule and Ruin: The Downfall of Moderation and the Destruction of the Republican Party; From Eisenhower to the Tea Party* (New York: Oxford University Press, 2012); and Rick Perlstein, *Before the Storm: Barry Goldwater and the Unmaking of the American Consensus* (New York: Hill and Wang, 2001).

23. James McEvoy III, *Radicals or Conservatives?: The Contemporary American Right* (Chicago: Rand, McNally & Company, 1971).

24. Christopher Towler, "Reactionary or Traditional Conservatism?: The Originsand Consequences of the Far Right Movement of the 1960s," Doctoral Dissertation (Seattle: University of Washington Political Science Department, 2014).

25. Data compiled by Devin Burghart, Institute for Research on Education & Human Rights.

26. 2010, Multi State Survey on Race and Politics (MSSRP).

27. http://www.teapartypatriots.org/mission.aspx

28. See among others, Mark A. Smith, *The Right Talk: How Conservatives Transformed the Great Society into the Economic Society* (Princeton, Princeton University Press, 2007); Clinton Rossiter, *Conservatism in America* (Cambridge, MA: Harvard University Press, 1982).

29. Stanley B. Greenberg, James Carville, Jim Gerstein, Peyton M. Craighill, and Kate Monninger, *Special Report on the Tea Party Movement: The Tea Party—An Ideological Republican Grass-Roots Movement—But Don't Mistake it for a Populist Rebellion*, Democracy Corps, July 19, 2010.

30. Devin Burghart and Leonard Zeskind, *Special Report to the NAACP on the Tea Party Movement: Tea Party Nation*, Institute for Research on Education & Human Rights, August 24, 2010.

31. Michael Tesler and David O. Sears, *Obama's Race: The 2008 Election and the Dream of a Post-Racial America* (Chicago: University of Chicago Press, 2010); Christopher S. Parker, Mark Q. Sawyer, and Christopher Towler, "A Black Man in the White House?: The Role of Racism and Patriotism in the 2008 Presidential Election," *Du Bois Review* 6(1) (2009): 193–217.

32. Lawrence D. Bobo, "Prejudice as Group Position: Microfoundations of a Sociological Approach to Racism and Race Relations," *Journal of Social Issues* 55(3): 445–472; Lawrence D. Bobo and James R. Kluegel, "Opposition to Race-Targeting: Self-Interest, Stratification, Ideology, or Racial Attitudes?" *American Sociological Review* 58 (August 1993): 443–464; Stanley Feldman and Leonie Huddy, "Racial Resentment and White Opposition to Race-Conscious Programs: Principles or Prejudice? "*American Journal of Political Science* 49 (1) (2005): 168–183.

33. Feldman and Huddy, p. 169.

34. Donald R. Kinder and Lynn M. Sanders, *Divided by Color: Racial Politics and Democratic Ideals* (Chicago: University of Chicago Press, 1996).

35. Parker et al.; David O. Sears and P. J. Henry, "The Origins of Symbolic Racism," *Journal of Personality and Social Psychology* 85(2): 259–275.

36. Kinder and Sanders, *Divided by Color: Racial Politics and Democratic Ideals*; David O. Sears, "Symbolic Politics: A Socio-Psychological Theory," in *Explorations in Political Psychology*, ed. Shanto Iyengar and William J. McGuire (Durham, NC: Duke University Press, 1993).

37. Lawrence D. Bobo and James R. Kluegel, "Status, Ideology, and Dimensions of Whites' Racial Beliefs and Attitudes: Progress and Stagnation," in Steven A. Tuch

and Jack K. Martin, eds., *Racial Attitudes in the 1990s: Continuity and Change* (Greenwood, CT: Praeger.Bobo, 1997), pp. 93–120.

38. Feldman and Huddy, 2005.
39. Scott Rasmussen and Douglas Schoen, *Mad as Hell: How the Tea Party Movement Is Fundamentally Remaking Our Two-Party System* (New York: HarperCollins, 2010).
40. Benjamin Todd Jealous, Foreword to *Tea Party Nationalism: A Critical Examination of the Tea Party Movement and the Size, Scope, and Focus of its National Factions*, Devin Burghart and Leonard Zeskind (Kansas City, MO: IREHR, 2010).
41. Paul M. Sniderman and Thomas Piazza, *The Scar of Race* (Cambridge: Harvard University Press, 1993).
42. Jim Sidanius and Felicia Pratto, *Social Dominance* (Cambridge: Harvard University Press, 1999).
43. Tesler and Sears, 2010; Donald R. Kinder, and Tali Mendelberg, "Individualism Reconsidered," in *Racialized Politics: The Debate about Racism in America*, ed., David O. Sears, Jim Sidanius, and Lawrence Bobo (Chicago: University of Chicago Press, 2000), pp. 44–74; Feldman and Huddy, 2005.
44. Parker et al., 2009.
45. http://www.youtube.com/watch?v=tb-zZM9-vB0&feature=channel
46. http://www.youtube.com/watch?v=uJC_RmcO7Ts&feature=channel
47. J. D. Hayworth, *Whatever It Takes: Illegal Immigration, Border Security, and the War on Terror* (Washington: Regnery Press, 2005), p. 30.
48. http://www.guardian.co.uk/world/2010/jul/25/jd-hayworth-arizona-immigration-anger
49. http://www.foxnews.com/politics/2010/08/03/tea-party-seeks-stories-horrors-illegal-immigration/
50. http://www.alipac.us/content-16.html
51. John Tomasic, "Tea Party groups rallying in support of Arizona immigration law," *Colorado Independent*, May 6, 2010; http://www.splcenter.org/get-informed/intelligence-report/browse-all-issues/2007/winter/the-teflon-nativists
52. http://www.nytimes.com/2010/04/20/us/20immig.html?_r=1
53. Parker and Barreto, 2013.
54. NBC News/Wall Street Journal monthly tracking poll, n=1000 each wave, http://pollingreport.com/politics.htm
55. James Joyner, January 8, 2008, "Hillary Clinton 'Iron my shirt' Stunt" Outside the Beltway, http://www.outsidethebeltway.com/hillary_clinton_iron_my_shirt_stunt/
56. Parker and Barreto, 2013, Chapter 4.

Chapter 15

Media, Public Opinion, and Presidential Leadership

Matthew A. Baum

On September 9, 2009, over 32 million Americans watched President Barack Obama deliver a prime time television address on healthcare reform to a joint session of Congress.[1] Twelve days later, Obama appeared on the *Late Show With David Letterman*. For Obama, the first sitting U.S. president to appear on a late-night entertainment-oriented talk show, this was the second such appearance. It capped an intensive personal media push by the president to promote healthcare reform, including interviews on five Sunday news shows the previous day (on ABC, NBC, CBS, CNN, and Univision). That same month, Obama's Internet team sent weekly—and sometimes twice-weekly—emails on healthcare to the roughly 13 million individuals in its famed email database.

Obama's media blitz was notable for the sheer number of public appeals, the diversity of outlets to which he carried his message, and the quite distinct tenor of the messages delivered across the differing outlets. In his nationally televised address, the president was, to paraphrase his predecessor, "a unifier, not a divider," offering a solemn appeal for national unity:

> In 1965, when some argued that Medicare represented a government takeover of health care, members of Congress—Democrats and Republicans—did not back down. They jointed together so that all of us could enter our golden years with some basic peace of mind . . . I still believe we can replace acrimony with civility.

In contrast, Obama's email appeals invited recipients to make donations, join discussion groups, participate in rallies, watch a video clip, visit his "Organizing for America" website, submit homemade videos, or call Congress to support the healthcare reform effort. They also issued partisan alerts, like: "Those who profit from the status quo—and those who put partisan advantage above all else—will fight us every inch of the way . . . The stakes are too high to let scare tactics cloud the debate . . . ".[2]

On *Letterman*, Obama lightened his tone, for instance quipping, in response to a question about racism in the anti-healthcare reform movement, "I think it is important to realize that I was actually black before the election." No mention of political parties or partisanship crossed the president's lips, except when he asserted that "it doesn't matter" if you are a Democrat or a Republican.

The liberal blogosphere dutifully replayed video highlights from all of Obama's appearances, thereby magnifying his message and delivering it directly to his base. For instance, on September 21, Huffingtonpost.com featured "Highlights from Obama's Sunday Show Blitz," inviting readers to "vote for the best clip." The next day the site featured video clips from Obama's *Letterman* appearance.

Taken together, this arguably represents an unprecedented presidential media blitz aimed at a single policy initiative. It raises the question of why President Obama pursued such a strategy, and why he spoke in such starkly differing manners across different media outlets. The answer is that a combination of fragmenting media and audiences, along with journalistic norms favoring critical coverage of the president, especially during unified government, has forced Obama to adopt a multi-tiered communication strategy aimed at reaching (and persuading), in the aggregate, an audience comparable in numbers and partisan diversity to those his predecessors from the 1960s to the 1980s largely took for granted virtually any time they appeared on national TV. The changing media landscape means the president must work harder to communicate with the public, and to be far more precise in tailoring his messages to particular sub-constituencies who might otherwise dismiss his message, or tune him out entirely.

In doing so, presidents have two primary leadership strategy alternatives, which Tim Groeling and I refer to as *Preaching to the Choir* and *Converting the Flock*.[3] The former consists of reaching out to their political base in order to excite core supporters so they will show up in large numbers on election day, as well as enthusiastically support their major policy initiatives. The latter entails reaching out beyond the base, in order to recruit additional supporters and thereby expand their support coalition. Neither strategy is new; presidents have long pursued both, varying their emphasis depending on which groups support or oppose a given policy. However, the ground underneath which presidents have stood while pursuing these strategies has shifted dramatically, thereby altering their relative costs, benefits, and efficacies.

The first decade of the twenty-first century has been characterized by an arguably unique historical circumstance in which three distinct types of media—each appealing to quite different audience types—coexist, cover news and politics, and compete for the attention of the American public. These are the traditional news media, dominated by the major broadcast networks and national newspapers, the "new media," most notably cable TV news and the Internet—ranging from blogs to social media to online versions of traditional news outlets—and the soft news media, consisting of daytime and late-night talk shows, as well as entertainment-oriented and tabloid news magazine outlets.[4] The audiences for these three media differ in important ways, with profound implications for their place in modern presidential communication strategies. I discuss each in turn, including their effects on public opinion.

Traditional News Media

For nearly four decades, the traditional news media—particularly network television—were the primary vehicle through which presidents communicated with the American people, and in so doing sought primarily to convert the flock. Network television was the informational commons, where a broad cross-section of Americans gathered to learn about the events of the day. When the president appeared on television, 50–60 million households routinely tuned in to hear what he had to say. No longer. Today, barely more than half as many Americans typically watch prime time presidential television appearances. The combined ratings for the evening newscasts of the "big three" broadcast networks (ABC, CBS, and NBC) have fallen from about 58 million in 1969 to 15.6 million in 2013.[5] According to a 2012 survey,[6] the percentage of Americans indicating that they regularly watch cable news now exceeds the percentage regularly watching network news (by 34 to 27 percent).

What little remains of the informational commons has itself become contested partisan territory, as the president's supporters are more and his opponents less likely to stay tuned when the president appears on TV. Figure 15.1 presents the trend, from 2002 to 2012, in partisan viewing of network news, based on self-reports in Pew Center surveys. According to these data, as recently as 2002, Republicans were 7 percentage points more likely than Democrats to describe themselves as regular viewers of network news (35 vs. 28 percent). By 2012 the self-described network audience was composed of over 50 percent more Democrats than Republicans (36 vs. 23 percent "regular" viewers). Interestingly, among Democrats this represents somewhat of a decline from 2008,

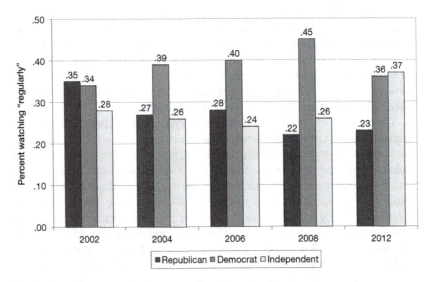

Figure 15.1 Partisan Trend in "Regular" Viewing of Network TV News.

mostly due to migration away from broadcast television and toward cable news (primarily MSNBC) and the Internet. These figures suggest that nationally televised presidential addresses are increasingly unlikely to reach the same cross-section of Americans as they did in earlier decades.

According to data reported by Kernell and Rice,[7] the partisan skew in audiences for presidential television addresses has also increased substantially over time. Across the 18 prime time presidential addresses they investigated between 1971 and 1995, the gap in audience between members of the president's party and opposition partisans averaged 2.6 percent. Between 1996 and 2007, the average partisan gap across the 14 appearances for which data were available increased more than fourfold, to 11.8 percent. In short, over time the audience for presidential addresses has increasingly come to be dominated by his fellow partisans.

Moreover, the news values of the traditional news media have made it a particularly difficult environment for presidential communications, particularly during the Bush II and Obama presidencies, the bulk of which took place during unified government. Elsewhere, Tim Groeling and I document the tremendous network news bias toward negative, hostile coverage of presidents and their policies.[8] We focused on a particularly hard case for locating such a pattern: foreign policy. To the extent politics do "stop at the water's edge," then we should have been *least* likely to find a predominance of partisan attacks on the president in foreign policy. We examined news coverage of 42 U.S. foreign policy crises between 1979 and 2003 and found that nearly 80 percent of all rhetoric from members of Congress (MCs) appearing on network evening newscasts within 61-day periods surrounding the events was critical of the president and his policies. While this skew was somewhat larger for domestic than foreign policy, it clearly emerged for both domestic and foreign policy issues. It was particularly severe during unified government, when criticism of the president by his fellow partisan MCs was both *novel*—since the members of the president's party usually support him—and *authoritative*—given the party's leadership role in Congress. The ratio was far more favorable to the president on network Sunday morning talk shows, where MCs could speak in a largely unfiltered format. This suggests a strong network negativity bias on the heavily edited network news.

The predominant *style* of news coverage of the president has also shifted, with the president's own words increasingly supplanted by the interpretations of journalists. The average presidential soundbite on the evening news—that is, a president speaking in his own words—declined from about 40 seconds in 1968[9] to 7.8 seconds in 2004. This means that journalists' relatively negative coverage of the president increasingly dominates news broadcasts.

Whereas network television once afforded presidents an ideal opportunity to communicate with a broad cross-section of the public, today whenever a president takes to the airwaves he must compete with myriad alternative media for the public's attention. Indeed, broadcast networks have grown increasingly hesitant to surrender their airwaves for presidential communication. According to one report, network executives lost roughly $30 million in advertising revenue in the first half of 2009 due to preemptions for Obama news conferences.[10] This concern, in turn, prompted one of the "big four" networks (Fox) to decline the president's request for airtime on April 29, 2009. Fox's decision prompted one network executive to comment:

> We will continue to make our decisions on White House requests on a case-by-case basis, but the Fox decision [to not broadcast Obama's 4/29/09 press conference] gives us cover to reject a request if we feel that there is no urgent breaking news that is going to be discussed.[11]

This combination of audiences smaller in size and narrower in breadth, along with generally skeptical treatment by reporters of nearly any presidential statement or policy proposal, means that traditional news outlets have lost much of their utility to presidents as vehicles for converting the flock.

New Media

The so-called new media, by which I refer primarily to cable news channels and the Internet, differ in important ways from their traditional media cousins. For instance, on cable television and in the Internet blogosphere, nearly all such outlets self-consciously seek to appeal to relatively narrow niches of the public. Rather than seeking to be all things to all people—as the major networks did during their heyday—cable news outlets and political blogs try to provide content that more closely fits the preferences of particular subgroups of the public. In news and politics, the primary dimension upon which they have differentiated themselves is ideology. For instance, in 2014 there are prominent cable news channels aimed primarily at liberals (MSNBC), conservatives (Fox), and moderates (CNN). On the Internet, the political blogosphere is dominated by ideologically narrow websites like Huffingtonpost.com on the left and Michellemalkin.com on the right.

Indeed, in news content analysis, Tim Groeling and I found substantial, and sometimes dramatic, differences in the ideological skew of news from left- and right-leaning Internet blogs, as well as on cable news outlets.[12] For instance, our data indicate that between 2004 and 2007 Fox News offered substantially less critical coverage of the Iraq war than CNN or the broadcast networks.

Consumers, in turn, are not passive recipients of whatever messages a given media outlet presents. Rather, they evaluate the credibility, and hence persuasiveness, of media messages in part by assessing the credibility of the messenger (the speaker) and the media outlet, as well as the costliness of the message. In a series of experiments,[13] Groeling and I found that typical individuals exposed to the identical praise or criticism of the president's handling of national security issues by MCs differed systematically in their assessments of the information's reliability, depending on the party of the speaker, the speaker's perceived incentives vis-à-vis the message (that is, whether praise or criticism of the president was, for that messenger, self-serving or costly), and the perceived ideological orientation of the media outlet. While media outlet reputations are perhaps most stark in the new media, increasing numbers of consumers—primarily, albeit not exclusively, Republicans and Independents—also view the *traditional* news media as ideologically biased (in a liberal direction), thereby allowing them to more easily discount information inconsistent with their prior beliefs.

As the range of options available to consumers seeking political information has expanded, making available media environments that closely match their personal political preferences, audiences have increasingly self-selected into ideologically friendly political news environments. For instance according to data from Scarborough research,[14] graphically illustrated in Figure 15.2, in 2000 the differentials between Republican and Democratic viewers of CNN, Fox, and MSNBC were 4, 8, and 2 percentage points, respectively. By 2009, these gaps had expanded to 30, 20, and 27 points, respectively, with Democrats all but abandoning Fox in favor of CNN and MSNBC and Republicans moving in the opposite direction.

As with cable news, some Internet consumers seek out news from across the ideological spectrum. Indeed, some evidence suggests they do so to a greater extent on the Internet than on cable.[15] While some additional research suggests that broad news gathering strategies are primarily limited to political

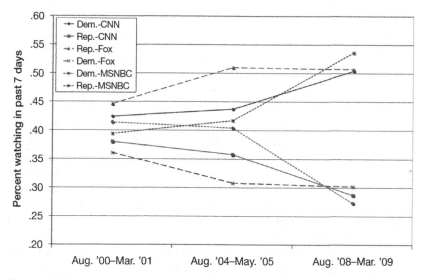

Figure 15.2 Trend in Partisan Viewing of CNN, Fox, and MSNBC (sources: Kernell and Rice (2010), Feltus (2009)).

sophisticates,[16] the Internet is nonetheless a particularly amenable environment for ideological self-selection. For instance, according to an April 2007 Nielsen report,[17] 77 percent of readers of the left-leaning HuffingtonPost.com blogsite were registered Democrats, compared to only 3.8 percent registered Republicans. Even to the extent that individuals expose themselves to news from multiple perspectives, they are still able to discount any information that challenges their preexisting beliefs if they view either the message or messenger as lacking credibility.

At first glance, the rise of social media might seem likely to upend this pattern, to at least some degree. After all, typical social networks on the most popular social media sites, like Twitter and Facebook, are not organized around political partisanship or ideology. In theory, Facebook might expose a typical user to a diverse range of political views, depending on the interests of members of their social network. To the extent a Facebook user chooses his or her "friends" significantly based upon non-political considerations, the resulting network ought to include at least some ideological diversity. In fact, survey data appear to support this conjecture. In a 2012 Pew Center survey, 73 percent of social network site (SNS) users whose friends post political content indicated that they "only sometimes" or "never" agree with their friends' political postings, compared to only 25 percent who "always" or "mostly" agree with their friends' political postings.

However, upon closer scrutiny, it is unclear whether or to what extent social media do actually change the dynamics of self-selection in the fragmented media marketplace. For instance, in the same survey, fully two-thirds of the aforementioned SNS users indicated that when they disagree with others' political posts, they ignore them. Moreover, on Twitter, political discourse appears to be disproportionately shaped by ideological extremes. For instance, one study found that members of Congress were more likely to adopt Twitter as they became increasingly ideologically extreme (to the left or right).[18] The same study also found that ideological extremists had more Twitter followers than their less-extreme counterparts. These findings suggest that social media are subject to the same sorts of niche appeals as other media, while the Pew survey results suggest that typical SNS users do not check their capacity to discount what they perceive as non-credible information at the social network site door. Rather, they appear to be employing the same credibility assessment strategies within social network sites as they do in the traditional news media.

The capacity of individuals to discriminate between credible and non-credible information, based on perceptions of shared political interests, makes the new media particularly ill-suited for converting the flock, yet ideally suited for preaching to the choir. By providing "red meat to the base," presidents can rally supporters to organize in their communities to support policy proposals, as well as to turn out at elections. More effective local organizing of core supporters can indirectly enhance presidents' capacities to convert the flock, by transforming their core supporters into messengers charged with reaching out beyond the base. Indeed, much of the aforementioned Obama email campaign was aimed at inspiring core supporters to become active advocates of his healthcare reform policy in their communities.

Soft News Media

Regular consumers of political blogs and cable news outlets continue to constitute a fairly small minority of the American public. Many millions of other Americans who eschew most traditional news outlets, at least most of the time, and who rarely if ever read political blogs or watch cable news channels, are nonetheless exposed to at least *some* political news via the so-called soft news media, including daytime and late-night talk shows, as well as entertainment-oriented news outlets and tabloids.

Sam Popkin describes politicians as "crowd-seeking missiles." It is thus unsurprising that they seek to exploit the opportunity afforded them by the soft news media to reach out beyond their bases. They do so with good reason. Soft news outlets attract large crowds; nearly 7.2 million Americans watched the president exchange one-liners with Letterman. This represents more than double the 3.1 million who tuned in to Obama's interview the day before on ABC's *This Week with George Stephanopoulos*.[19]

Letterman's audience also differs substantially from those of most traditional news outlets. For instance, compared to the typical audience for traditional news shows such as *This Week*, Letterman's audience is *less* politically engaged, *less* ideologically extreme and *less* partisan.[20] Consequently, a presidential appeal is *more* likely to persuade Letterman's viewers than the relatively more partisan and ideologically extreme audiences of typical traditional news venues.[21] This persuasion gap is even larger for (mostly partisan) political Internet blog readers relative to traditional news venues.[22]

Soft news interviews tend to present candidates in a more favorable light than traditional political interview shows. For example, commenting on 2008 Democratic presidential candidate John Edwards' appearances on Leno, one reporter observed, "John and Elizabeth Edwards got substantially gentler treatment from Leno on 'The Tonight Show' than they did from Katie Couric on '60 Minutes.'"[23] In short, appearances on daytime and late-night entertainment talk shows, or other soft news programs, afford politicians one of their best opportunities to reach a large group of potentially persuadable voters in a relatively sympathetic venue. A mounting body of research, in turn, indicates that exposure to soft news influences voter's political attentiveness,[24] knowledge[25] and attitudes,[26] and even their voting behavior.[27] In reviewing the literature on soft news, Baum and Jamison refer to these as the four Oprah Effects.[28] The soft news media thus arguably represent one of the *last*, and perhaps the *best*, opportunities for political leaders to convert the flock. Recognizing this, it is perhaps unsurprising to find more and more political candidates and elected officials reaching out to soft news venues.

That said, not all soft news is alike. Existing alongside the lighter fare offered by Letterman, Leno, Regis, and *The View*, among other daytime and late-night talk shows, is a parallel niche of political satire-oriented talk shows, like *The Daily Show with Jon Stewart* and the *Colbert Report*, which cater to more politically sophisticated and ideological viewers, and whose audiences tripled from 2001–2005.[29] These shows assume a substantial amount of political knowledge on the part of audience members in order to "get the joke." Consequently, they are far more amenable to preaching to the choir than converting the flock.

Back to the Future?

Though in some ways unique, the current period is by no means the first time in American politics that partisan media have strongly influenced public debate. Rather, viewed in a broader context, overwhelmingly nonpartisan journalism, as we saw in roughly the first four decades following the Second World War, appears to have been an historical anomaly.

To better understand the implications of our increasingly polarized information environment, it is helpful to consider the partisan press of the nineteenth and early twentieth centuries. In that era, citizens who wanted an accurate picture of the political landscape could read multiple newspapers with differing partisan loyalties in order to triangulate on the "truth."[30] Such a strategy could offset to some extent the potentially harmful effects of partisan-oriented media. Yet the question remains as to whether typical citizens in the contemporary period, faced with far more varied alternatives, are likely to embrace a triangulation approach to news consumption. The present differs from the past in numerous important respects, not least of which is the explosion in the twenty-first century of entertainment mass media and other competitors for scarce public attention.

While it may be the case that politically attentive Americans in the twenty-first century are proportionately similar in number to their counterparts in prior news eras, a far larger portion of the contemporary population enjoys and exercises the franchise than was the case in the eighteenth or nineteenth centuries. Moreover, the ability of party organizations to reliably direct the voting of their members has declined with the death of party machines and the waning influence of state party bosses. Consequently, the *breadth* of consensus necessary to forge a bipartisan accord is far greater in the twenty-first century, and modern communication and polling technology allows nervous politicians to sense precisely when that consensus is eroding. Of course, gaining consent first requires capturing public attention, and even politically attentive citizens are unlikely to be able to attend to all of the competing messages avilable in the modern media environment.

Not only is it possible to consume nearly limitless political news from virtually any ideological perspective, it is also possible to consume equally limitless soft news, or pure entertainment, while rarely if ever encountering politics.[31] This raises the opportunity costs for typical consumers of seeking out alternative political perspectives. Survey evidence suggests that substantial portions of the public also appear to lack the motive to do so. Not surprisingly, these same data indicate that as the strength of an individual's political ideology increases, so too does that individual's preference for news that reinforces her preexisting beliefs.[32]

If the era of three medias, and particularly its more polarizing elements, is characterized more by *reinforcement seeking* than by triangulation, forging and sustaining bipartisan consensus will likely prove a daunting and perhaps all but insurmountable task for future leaders. Evidence of this dilemma is abundant in public reactions to the 2003 U.S. invasion and subsequent occupation of Iraq, a conflict that produced the greatest partisan divide ever recorded in scientific polling, both in terms of support for a U.S. military conflict and in terms of overall presidential approval.[33] Scholars continue to debate the media's role in sharpening, if not altogether producing, the partisan gulf in evaluations of the president and the Iraq War.[34] Jacobson, for instance, speculates that a combination of differences in content and partisan self-selection into friendly news environments—such as Fox for Republicans and conservatives, PBS, MSNBC, and CNN for Democrats and liberals, and network news for independents and moderates—may have contributed to partisan differences in perceptions of the war and the president leading it.[35]

As the prior discussion attests, self-selection, a concept dating back to Campbell and colleagues' theory of minimalism, may well be sharpening partisan polarization, and this phenomenon seems likely to expand in the future.[36] However, there exists a second, perhaps complementary, culprit: ideologically driven credibility assessments. In other words, contemporary citizens possess, arguably to a greater extent than their predecessors, the means to engage in a multipronged dissonance-avoidance strategy. Selective exposure, or avoiding dissonant information altogether, presumably represents the first such prong. However, even when this first defense mechanism fails and individuals are exposed to ideologically hostile news, they increasingly possess the means—by assigning ideological reputations to individual sources and media outlets—to systematically discount it. In other words, consumers appear also to selectively accept or reject information to which they are exposed based on its perceived credibility.[37] Credibility assessments in turn depend on the perceived ideological leaning of the outlet presenting the information, as well as on the content of the information itself (e.g., its perceived costliness). The combined influence of selective exposure and acceptance appears, at least in the cases of Iraq and overall assessments of President Bush's job performance, to have contributed substantially to the historically unprecedented levels of partisan polarization in America during President Bush's second term.

Conclusion

The picture I have painted of the contemporary media landscape is in some respects overly stark. For one thing, there is certainly overlap between the three medias, both in terms of content and audience. Viewers of traditional news media, especially network news, are more left-leaning than in the past, while as noted, the fastest growing segment of the soft news media—satiric political news shows like *the Daily Show*—caters primarily to politically sophisticated ideologues. Some Democrats consume conservative media, while some Republicans consume liberal media. Though not primarily politically oriented, social network sites nonetheless do appear to expose users to varying degrees of ideologically diverse political information. All three medias, in turn, continue to afford presidents at least *some* capacity to both preach to the choir and convert the flock. Political messages frequently cross the boundaries of the three medias, as exemplified by the Obama media blitz described at the outset of this chapter. Hence, the media commons, and the common civic space for public affairs dialogue it created, has not entirely disappeared, nor has the capacity of presidents to use the media as a tool for building broader support constituencies via converting the flock.

That said, current trends toward ever more consumer self-selection and increasingly sophisticated information filtering and media targeting of consumer preferences all appear to portend a trend toward greater audience fragmentation and hence continued shrinking of the media commons. It seems inevitable that news providers will increasingly apply the same filtering technologies that allow media content distributors like Netflix and iTunes to determine the types of movies or music a customer is likely to prefer, and suggest to them precisely that, to news and public affairs content. The end result may be what Cass Sunstein terms "cyberbalkanization," where the media commons is largely supplanted by a "daily me" in which consumers encounter only the news and information they want, most of which tends to confirm rather than challenge their preexisting attitudes. Whether or not the media commons disappears entirely, there is little question that technological innovations and shifts in audience behavior are changing the way citizens consume news, with content growing increasingly personalized and subject to individual preferences regarding what, when and where they entertain themselves or expose themselves to politically themed information.

Of course, effective presidential leadership requires both exciting the base *and* building coalitions—and there is no reason to suppose that future presidents will succeed, at least over the longer term, by emphasizing one over the other. Along with, and perhaps in part *because of,* the three medias, politics in America are at a crossroads. Traditional communications channels are increasingly foreclosed, even as new ones emerge. Different channels, in turn, reach different audiences, and so privilege different communication strategies, different forms of leadership, and ultimately different policies. Given the enormity and speed of the changes in this marketplace, the potential consequences for democratic participation and the strategic landscape for politicians, the evolution of the communication environment within which our politics are contested seems likely to play a central role in shaping the future course of American democracy.

Notes

1. Audience size estimated by nielsenwire.com
2. Barack Obama, e-mail to supporters, September 9, 2009.
3. Matthew A. Baum and Tim Groeling, *War Stories: The Causes and Consequences of Citizen Views of War* (Princeton: Princeton University Press, 2010).
4. Though I do not focus on it here, most of the arguments I make concerning partisan political blogs apply to political talk radio as well.
5. Matthew A. Baum and Sam Kernell, "Has Cable Ended the Golden Age of Presidential Television?" *American Political Science Review* 93 (March 1999): 1–16; Emily Guskin, Mark Jurkowitz and Amy Mitchell, "The State of the News Media 2013," *The Pew Research Center's Project for Excellence in Journalism*, available at: http://stateofthemedia.org/2013/network-news-a-year-of-change-and-challenge-at-nbc/network-by-the-numbers (Accessed 10/30/14).
6. Pew Research Center for the People and the Press, "Biennial Media Consumption Survey 2012" (May 9–June 3, 2012), available at: http://www.people-press.org/files/legacy-questionnaires/News%20Consumption %20topline%20for%20release.pdf (Accessed 10/30/14).
7. Samuel Kernell and Laurie L. Rice, *Cable and Partisan Polarization of the President's Audience* (Unpublished Manuscript, University of California, San Diego, 2010).
8. Baum and Groeling, *War Stories*.
9. Daniel Hallin, *We Keep America on Top of the World: Television Journalism and the Public Sphere* (London: Routledge, 1994).
10. John Consoli, "Obama Drama: Nets Take a Stand Against Primetime Pre-emptions," *The Hollywood Reporter* (May 7, 2009). Available at: http://www.hollywoodreporter.com/news/obama-drama-83575 (Accessed 10/30/14).
11. Consoli, "Obama Drama."
12. Baum and Groeling, *War Stories*.
13. Baum and Groeling, *War Stories*.
14. Reported in Kernell and Rice, *Cable and Partisan Polarization*, and Will Feltus, "Cable News Bias? Audiences Say 'Yes.'" *National Media Research, Planning, and Placement* (2009).
15. Matthew Gentzkow and Jesse M. Shapiro, "Ideological Segregation Online and Offline," NBER Working Paper 15916 (April 2010), available at: http://www.nber.org/papers/w15916.pdf
16. Michael J. LaCour, "Balanced News Diet, Not Selective Exposure: Evidence from Direct Measurement of Media Exposure," typescript, University of California, Los Angeles, 2013; Matthew S. Levendusky, *How Partisan Media Polarize America* (Chicago, IL: University of Chicago Press, 2013).
17. David All, "Is Yahoo!'s Online Debate Going to be Fair and Balanced?", available at: http://techpresident.com/blog-entry/yahoo's-online-debate-going-be-fair-and-balanced (Accessed 10/30/14).
18. Sounman Hong, "Who Benefits from Twitter? Social Media and Political Competition in the U.S. House of Representatives," typescript, Harvard Kennedy School, 2011.

19. Appearances by presidential aspirants on *daytime* talk shows also attract large audiences. For instance, 8.7 million households watched presidential candidate Al Gore's September 11, 2000 appearance on *The Oprah Winfrey Show*.

20. Matthew A. Baum, *Soft News Goes to War: Public Opinion and American Foreign Policy in the New Media Age* (Princeton, NJ: Princeton University Press, 2003).

21. Matthew A. Baum, "Talking the Vote: Why Presidential Candidates Hit the Talk Show Circuit," *American Journal of Political Science* 44 (April 2005): 213–234.

22. Baum and Groeling, *War Stories*.

23. Matea Gold, "Candidates Embrace the Chat: Daytime Gabfests and Latenight Comedy TV Become Essential Stops on the Presidential Trail to Reach 'Regular Folks'," *New York Times*, September 29, 2007.

24. Matthew A. Baum, "Sex, Lies and War: How Soft News Brings Foreign Policy to the Inattentive Public," *American Political Science Review* 96 (March 2002): 91–109; Baum, *Soft News Goes to War*; Patricia Moy, Michael A. Xenos and Verena K. Hess, "Communication and Citizenship: Mapping the Political Effects of Infotainment," *Mass Communication and Society* 8 (May 2005): 111–131; Liesbet Van Zoonen, Floris Muller, Donya Alinejad, Martijn Dekker, Linda Duits, Pauline van Romondt, and Wendy Wittenberg, "Dr. Phil Meets the Candidates: How Family Life and Personal Experience Produce Political Discussions," *Critical Studies in Mass Communication* 24 (October 2007): 322–338.

25. Baum, *Soft News Goes to War*; Matthew A. Baum, "Soft News and Political Knowledge: Evidence of Absence or Absence of Evidence?" *Political Communication* 20 (April 2003): 173–190; Paul Brewer and Xiaoxia Cao, "Candidate Appearances on Soft News Shows and Public Knowledge About Primary Campaigns," *Journal of Broadcasting and Electronic Media* 50 (March 2006): 18–35; Dannagal G. Young and Russell M. Tisinger, "Dispelling Late-Night Myths: News Consumption among Late-Night Comedy Viewers and the Predictors of Exposure to Various Late-Night Shows," *The Harvard International Journal of Press/Politics* 11 (Summer 2006): 113–134; Dannagal G. Young, "Daily Show Viewers Knowledgeable about Presidential Campaign, National Annenberg Election Survey Shows," Issue Paper (Philadelphia, PA: Annenberg Public Policy Center, 2004).

26. Matthew A. Baum, "Circling the Wagons: Soft News and Isolationism in American Public Opinion," *International Studies Quarterly* 48 (June 2004): 313–338; Matthew A. Baum, "Talking the Vote: Why Presidential Candidates Hit the Talk Show Circuit," *American Journal of Political Science* 44 (April 2005): 213–234; Paul Brewer and Emily Marquardt, "Mock News and Democracy: Analyzing The Daily Show," *Atlantic Journal of Communication* 15 (November 2007): 249–226; Geoffrey Baym, "The Daily Show: Discursive Integration and The Reinvention of Political Journalism," *Political Communication* 22 (July–September 2005): 259–276.

27. Jody Baumgartner and Jonathan Morris, "The Daily Show Effect: Candidate Evaluations, Efficacy and American Youth," *American Politics Research* 34 (May 2006): 341–367; Markus Prior, *Post-Broadcast Democracy: How Media Choice Increases Inequality in Political Involvement and Polarizes Elections* (Cambridge, NY: Cambridge University Press, 2007); Baum, "Talking the Vote"; Matthew A. Baum and Angela Jamison, "The Oprah Effect: How Soft News Helps Inattentive Citizens Vote Consistently," *Journal of Politics* 68 (November 2006): 946–59.

28. Matthew A. Baum and Angela Jamison, "Soft News and The Four Oprah Effects," *Oxford Handbook of American Public Opinion and the Media*, Jacobs, Lawrence and Robert Shapiro, eds., Ch. 8 (Oxford: Oxford University Press, 2011), pp. 121–137.

29. Michael Xenos and Amy Becker, "Moments of Zen: Effects of the Daily Show on Information Seeking," *Political Communication* 26 (July 2009): 317–332.

30. For example, in their famous "Middletown" study of what they regarded as a typical American city in the 1920s, Robert and Helen Lynd found that "The local morning paper distributes 8,851 copies to the 9,200 homes of the city, and the afternoon paper 6,715, plus at least half of an additional 785 sold on the street and news-stand. In addition, the circulation of out-of-town-papers{ ... } now totals 1200 to 1500 a day." See Robert Lynd and Helen Merrell Lynd, *Middletown: A Study in Modern American Culture* (Orlando, FL: Harcourt Brace, 1929).

31. Markus Prior, *Post-Broadcast Democracy: How Media Choice Increases Inequality in Political Involvement and Polarizes Elections* (Cambridge, NY: Cambridge University Press, 2007).

32. Baum and Groeling, *War Stories.*

33. Gary C. Jacobson, *A Divider, Not a Uniter: George W. Bush and the American People* (New York: Pearson Longman, 2006).

34. E.g., Steven Kull, Clay Ramsay, and Evan Lewis, "Misperceptions, the Media, and the Iraq War," *Political Science Quarterly* 118 (Winter 2003–2004): 575–90; Stefano Della Vigna and Ethan Kaplan, "The Fox News Effect: Media Bias and Voting," Manuscript (March 30, 2003), Berkeley, CA; Gary C. Jacobson, "The War, the President, and the 2006 Midterm Congressional Elections," paper presented to the annual meeting of the Midwest Political Science Association (April 12–15, 2007), The Palmer House Hilton, Chicago, IL.

35. Jacobson, "The War, the President."

36. Angus Campbell, Philip E. Converse, Warren E. Miller, and Donald E. Stokes, *The American Voter* (New York: Wiley, 1960).

37. Baum and Groeling, *War Stories.*

Chapter 16

Public Opinion and Public Policy

Andrea Louise Campbell and Elizabeth Rigby

The relationship between public opinion and public policy is a two-way street.[1] In one direction, we observe public preferences influencing government activity and policy outcomes, as we would expect in a democracy. That said, the correspondence between what the public says that it wants and what it gets out of government varies across time and across issues. Moreover, some groups in society—the economically privileged and the highly politically active, for instance—tend to get more of their preferences fulfilled than do others, raising concerns about the policy consequences of economic and political inequality.

In the other direction, we see public policy influencing public opinion. As previous chapters revealed, there are many factors shaping the public's preferences. Here we add existing policy to the list. What Americans think the government should do now and in the future depends in part on how they regard what government has done in the past. Hence government policy is highly consequential because it influences what the public desires subsequently, shaping future policy outcomes.

This chapter explores existing scholarship on this two-way relationship between public opinion and public policy. It then utilizes a case study of the Affordable Care Act—the 2010 federal health reform bill nicknamed "ObamaCare"—to demonstrate both the ways in which public opinion can shape policy outcomes and the ways in which the influence of the public is constrained when it comes head to head with the preferences of powerful interest groups and lawmakers themselves. The case of healthcare reform also sheds light on how public policies may or may not influence subsequent public opinion and the political environment in which future policymaking takes place. Although there is still much to learn about the relationship between public opinion and public policy, we can begin to assess how well our democracy in practice measures up to the ideal extolled by democratic theorists.

Public Opinion as an Influence on Public Policy

A hallmark of democratic governance is the notion of popular sovereignty, the idea that government policy should reflect the preferences of its citizens. As John

Stuart Mill said, "There is no difficulty in showing the ideally best form of government is that in which the sovereignty, or the supreme controlling power in the last resort, is vested in the entire aggregate of the community."[2] The founders may have expressed skepticism about the capacities of ordinary citizens and the role of public opinion, designing a number of institutional barriers to its direct effects,[3] but modern theorists such as V.O. Key Jr. firmly emphasize the central role of the public and its preferences: "Unless mass views have some place in the shaping of policy, all the talk about democracy is nonsense. As Lasswell has said, the 'open interplay of opinion and policy is the distinguishing mark of popular rule.'"[4] As another modern theorist, Robert Dahl, put it, democratic governance is prefaced on "the continuing responsiveness of the government to the preferences of its citizens, considered as political equals."[5] And empirical social scientist Chris Achen considers one of the central features of democratic theory to be "*control of outcomes*" (emphasis in the original).[6] Thus if the American democratic state is functioning as expected, there should be a robust correspondence between the public's professed preferences and public policy.

Political scientists have spent decades examining whether in fact public opinion does influence policy outcomes. The basic finding is that representation occurs, and seems to occur fairly often, at the aggregate level, although there is important variation across issues and different kinds of individuals.[7] Notably, the public is more likely to see its views reflected on highly salient issues, and the preferences of some citizens, particularly the well-resourced and organized, are better represented than others.

There are several pathways by which public opinion shapes public policy: electoral accountability, politicians' view of their job, and group-based pressures and political parties.[8] Elections are a chief mechanism by which voters can make their views felt, elevating to office those who promise to reflect their views and removing politicians who have failed to do so.[9] A piece of evidence supporting this mechanism is that overall responsiveness tends to increase as elections draw nearer, presumably as a consequence of politicians attempting to curry favor with voters.[10] Another possibility is that voters choose representatives who are like them and who in turn pass policies congruent with their supporters' preferences. A second mechanism is that elected officials feel under "social pressure" to respond to their constituents, acting either as delegates or trustees.[11] Delegates respond to specific instructions from constituents while trustees pursue policies they judge to be best for those they represent.[12] A third link between public opinion and public policy is the role of political parties and interest groups. Parties are crucial aggregators of interests in American politics, but there is concern that, with the rise of candidate-centered elections and the importance of money in campaigning, parties represent the interests of the well-heeled and ideologically extreme more than those of broader publics.[13] Interest groups are the other important opinion aggregators, and the influence of interest groups on representation has been much debated as well. Early pluralist thinkers such as David Truman and Robert Dahl believed that organized groups, which would naturally emerge in response to political issues, enhanced representation, while later critics such as E. E. Schattschneider argued that the privileged were far more likely to organize and that many interests are in fact left without representation.[14] Contemporary research is divided, with some scholars believing that representation is enhanced in policy areas that are thickly populated by interest groups,[15] and with others arguing that "special interests" undermine the relationship between public opinion and public policy rather than reinforce it, exacerbating inequalities in representation.[16] Most of this latter research focuses on the skewed distribution of the "pressure system" in favor of business interests and the affluent and well-educated, and predicts that these compositional biases will lead to unequal policy outcomes.[17]

Scholars have employed several different approaches in measuring the relationship between public opinion and public policy. Virtually all of these approaches measure public opinion with responses to surveys, either opinion on specific issues[18] or aggregate measures of policy liberalism or "mood" that combine many survey items and issues.[19] Measures of the outcome, public policy, include specific policy outcomes,[20] roll-call votes,[21] or "policy liberalism," the latter typically an aggregate measure across issues, such as the net liberal direction of *Congressional Quarterly* key votes.[22] "Responsiveness" is then usually assessed by examining the correspondence between public opinion and policy outcomes in some space or time. Analysis proceeds in one of several different ways.[23] The earliest empirical studies began by looking across different units such as Congressional districts,[24] then later cities[25] and states,[26] and assessing the cross-sectional relationship between public opinion and public policy within each of those units. A second approach looked over time and across issues to see whether policy moved in a direction favored by the majority of Americans.[27] A third approach examined changes in public opinion and sought to discern whether changes in policy followed, either on specific issues[28] or in responses to changes in the aggregate "public mood."[29]

Overall, the magnitude of representation found in these studies is quite substantial. Comparing national surveys with policy outcomes, Monroe determined that policy was consistent with opinion 63 percent of the time between 1960 and 1979 and 55 percent of the time between 1980 and 1993. Page and Shapiro similarly found that policy change is consistent with the direction of opinion change about two-thirds of the time.[30] Erikson, Wright, and McIver found a very strong relationship between state policy and state opinion liberalism in their cross-sectional study, and Stimson, MacKuen, and Erikson discerned a nearly "one-to-one translation of preferences into policy" in their examination of congruence between policy change and policy mood, with the greatest congruence in elected institutions such as Congress and the least with non-electoral institutions such as the Supreme Court.[31]

The apparently robust policy–opinion relationship notwithstanding, a number of important methodological and substantive issues remain. One concern is that scholars typically utilize survey results to define "public opinion,"[32] whereas there are "at least" three other sources of public preferences that guide policymakers: activated public opinion, referring to the views of those "actively participating in political life" through political participation, organizational memberships, and social movements; latent public opinion, or the "underlying values and fundamental preferences of citizens" such as the desire for good economic performance; and perceived majority opinions, or the "assumed preferences of citizens . . . which may or may not accurately reflect actual preferences."[33] The reliance on surveys not only may mis-measure public opinion by failing to include these other sources but also may artificially inflate the congruence between opinion and policy because only the most salient issues get included on surveys. Moreover, Adam Berinsky argues that survey analysis may not be representative of actual public opinion because it excludes certain interests (those who say "don't know," who turn out to be systematically different from those who do respond).[34]

A related concern arises around the sampling of issues, which is that the way in which researchers go about their work may inflate the relationship as well. Does one choose what questions individuals get surveyed on and match to policy, or choose some policies and match to survey responses? Paul Burstein asserts that the former practice—widely utilized in this literature—leads to bias because surveys ask about the most salient issues, and salience leads to better representation. Indeed, when he takes a random sample of Congressional votes and then looks at corresponding polls, he finds less responsiveness than do other scholars.[35] It also appears that the greater the level of aggregation (e.g. looking at an aggregated public mood indicator rather than opinion on individual policies), the greater the correspondence with policy outcomes (e.g. Erikson, MacKuen, and Stimson's one-to-one relationship versus Monroe's 55 percent). When Lax and Phillips look at state-level support for 39 specific policies across eight different policy areas, including abortion, law enforcement, healthcare, and education, they identify what they call a "democratic deficit" in which only half of the time does a state's policy match up with the preferences of the majority of the people in that state.[36] It is difficult to know which measure of representation is "better," or whether the public feels better represented when its overall mood is reflected in policy or its opinion on specific issues.[37]

We might also wonder whether public opinion is an independent force or is itself shaped by political elites. The causality question—who leads whom?— arises.[38] The more problematic version is that elites can manipulate public opinion through misinformation campaigns.[39] Somewhat more benign is the "crafted talk" argument—that politicians pursue their own policy goals and use public opinion polls to identify the "language, symbols, and arguments that will 'win' public support for their policy objectives."[40] Certainly framing effects are common in public opinion, with different question wordings and contexts— whether within the survey itself or in the real world—having significant effects on reported opinions.[41] Most likely the relationship between public opinion and public policy is reciprocal, with political elites having an ear to the ground to discern what issues will play well with the public.[42] Or as Stimson, MacKuen, and Erikson put it in their model of "dynamic representation": "[l]ike antelope in an open field, [policy-makers] cock their ears and focus their full attention on the slightest sign of danger" in the form of electoral consequences arising from failures of representation.[43]

Beyond these measurement issues are substantive concerns about the preference–policy relationship. One is whether responsiveness has changed over time. Morris Fiorina argues that there is now a "disconnect" between citizens and the "political class"—because political elites are far more polarized than are the moderate voters they purport to represent and because such elites set the political agenda and pursue their own issue priorities.[44] In contrast, Paul Quirk argues that responsiveness has improved over time, indeed problematically so, with too much deference to mass opinion, which is often uninformed or even biased by a misleading information environment. He argues that "politicians do pander," aided by the erosion of institutional protections against the "excess of democracy" the Founders warned against: the elimination of indirect election of the Senate; the Congressional sunshine laws of the 1970s; the rise of the "plebiscitary presidency"; and the growth in the use of the initiative and referendum.[45]

Empirically, the lion's share of evidence points toward rising responsiveness for several decades into the 1970s[46] and steep declines thereafter,[47] squaring with Fiorina's account. As mentioned, Monroe's studies show a decline in the congruence between majority preferences and government policies between 1960–1979 (63 percent) and 1980–1991 (55 percent).[48] Jacobs and Shapiro find that the consistency between public opinion and policy change for a basket of social welfare and crime issues fell from 67 percent in 1984–1987 to 40 percent in 1988–1991, to just 37 percent in 1992–1994.[49] Using a sample of more than 1,700 policy questions, Gilens finds that between 1981 to 2002, 59 percent of survey items revealed majority support for change, but only 35 percent of policy changes took place.[50]

Jason Barabas worries that scholars' ability to assess trends in responsiveness might be affected by data availability: the proportion of all survey questions asking about policy preferences or the national issue agenda declines over time. Controlling for these changes, however, he reaches the same conclusion: democratic responsiveness has been declining since the 1970s for observable issues, although "it is impossible to tell" for huge portions of the national policy agenda that are excluded from surveys.[51]

Another concern is the important question of inequality and *whose* preferences are represented in policy outcomes. Early work on the opinion-policy relationship ignored questions of inequality and examined public opinion as a whole.[52] More recently, scholars have taken up the crucial question raised by the democratic theorists—"How does a 'democratic' system work amid inequality of resources?"[53]—and studied whether the affluent or the highly participatory are better represented than are the poor or the politically quiescent.[54] Martin Gilens examines hundreds of survey questions on proposed policy changes between 1981 and 2002 and finds that most of the time policy does not change, reflecting the status-quo bias built into American governing institutions. However, when policy does change and policy preferences differ across income groups, policy outcomes strongly reflect the preferences of the most affluent—those at the 90th income percentile—but neither those of the poor nor middle-income Americans.[55] Similarly, Larry Bartels finds in an examination of Senatorial roll call votes that the preferences of the affluent were weighted 50 percent more than those of middle income citizens, while the preferences of the poor were not reflected in their Senators' voting behavior at all.[56] Lawrence Jacobs and Benjamin Page show that foreign policy (as measured by foreign policy opinion among policymakers) more closely matches the preferences of business leaders and experts than those of the public.[57] James Druckman and Lawrence Jacobs examine internal White House polls and find that Ronald Reagan's positions on core economic issues (taxes, spending, and Social Security reform) corresponded much more to the policy preferences of affluent poll respondents than to those of the typical respondents.[58] And in a second look at the strong aggregate correlation between state-level opinion and policy, Elizabeth Rigby and Gerald Wright examine the responsiveness of state-level policy to different income groups and find evidence of inequality in economic policy in poor states. In wealthy states, there are few differences in economic policy preferences across income groups and so, therefore, no potential for inequality in responsiveness. However, in poorer states, the preferences of the affluent do differ from those of middle- and low-income residents, and there is a pronounced gradient in responsiveness, with policy corresponding closely with the preferences of the affluent and falling off for middle- and lower-income groups.[59]

The mechanisms by which the affluent prevail in getting their policy stands reflected in policy deserve more research, although there is support for the electoral accountability path, with scholars finding that those who are politically active appear to be better represented. The preferences of voters are better reflected in Senatorial roll-call voting than are the preferences of non-voters,[60] as well as in campaign stances adopted by Democratic and Republican candidates in state and federal races.[61] Social welfare programs are less generous in states where the poor constitute a smaller proportion of those who turn out to vote.[62] Another hypothesized pathway is through interest groups: since the well-heeled are more likely to be organized, perhaps interest groups acting on their behalf amplify their influence on policy outcomes. Recent research by Martin Gilens, however, suggests that interest groups and the affluent operate independently; interest groups sometimes share the preferences of the affluent and sometimes they do not. And quite often interest groups represent different segments of the affluent, cancelling out the role of resources in determining policy change.[63] The affluent are far more likely to see their preference enacted when interest groups push in the same direction, but they prevail even without the assistance of organized groups.[64]

Some dissenters argue that policy preferences do not differ much across income groups and hence inequality in representation is of little concern.[65] When asked whether they believe the government is spending too much, too little, or about the right amount on cities, crime, defense, education, the environment, foreign aid, health, and welfare, respondents of different income levels differed substantially only on their welfare attitudes. However, these researchers divide respondents into three income groups only, which may mask the distinctive preferences of the truly affluent, and they rely primarily on General Social Survey (GSS) spending questions that are broad and unsurprisingly elicit similar reactions from different income groups.[66] Analyses of other data reveal that there are large differences in preferences on redistributive issues across income groups, differences that are greater than those by education or gender.[67] Moreover, it is important to differentiate between economic and social policy. Because the affluent display cross-cutting preferences—they are economic conservatives but social liberals—using summary scores like ideology clouds analysis.[68] When policies are divided into economic or social issue areas, or when individual policies are examined, inequalities in responsiveness by income emerge.

Finally, Larry Bartels asks whether we are measuring the right thing by looking at responsiveness rather than congruence, that is, change versus level.[69] Many studies examine whether change in policy follows change in opinion, that is, how responsive policy is to marginal changes in public preferences. However, Bartels examines preferred levels of government spending across countries and finds large discrepancies between perceived and preferred levels of spending, with governments spending far less than their publics desire. In a related vein, Cook and Barrett found a significant mismatch between the spending preferences of the public and members of Congress, with the public far more expansive.[70] It could be that policymakers recognize fiscal constraints on spending or tradeoffs across programs that publics do not, but this discrepancy between desired and actual spending does raise questions about how to measure the relationship between public opinion and public policy, and also about how much responsiveness is desirable. Policymakers could respond to demands for more spending, but pay the price later when voters become restless about the scope of government or ensuing tax increases or deficits.[71]

Policy Effects on Public Opinion

A smaller and more recent literature examines the effect of public policy on public opinion. Political scientists have long known that preferences are shaped by many influences, including childhood socialization, group memberships, identity, media, the political environment, and elite leadership. Yet there is the additional possibility that the public reacts to public policies themselves, recognized at least as early as Schattschneider's exhortation that "new policies create new politics." Only recently have scholars started to examine this effect empirically, which reverses the causal arrow to run from policy to opinion.

One version of this effect is the literature examining trends in attitudes over time and reactions to existing policies. Christopher Wlezien identified a "thermostatic" pattern in public opinion whereby the public's preferences for more or less spending on defense and several social policy areas is negatively related to recent policy. That is, when appropriations increase, the public becomes more likely to say spending in that area should be decreased, and vice versa.[72] James Stimson similarly argues that aggregate public opinion trends reveal a public that seems to drift away from the policy stances of the president it has most recently elected.[73]

The policy feedbacks literature takes this notion that existing policy can affect subsequent attitudes even further, asserting that these effects cycle back into the political system creating a policy–preference spiral in which policies affect preferences, which affect subsequent policies, and so on.[74] Early theorists in this area, such as Helen Ingram and Anne Schneider, and Paul Pierson, suggested that the ways in which policies are designed—what they do, for whom, and by what means—affect the attitudes of the public and the particular groups targeted by the policies.[75] For example, Julianna Pacheco examined public opinion on smoking and found that these attitudes shifted after enactment of smoking bans in restaurants. Survey respondents view smokers more negatively and believe secondhand smoke is more dangerous after the enactment of these bans—with policy apparently educating, changing social norms, and/or altering the stereotypes associated with population subgroups.[76]

A good deal of empirical work has examined the variation in policy feedback for differently-designed policies, showing for example that although Social Security and "welfare" are both anti-poverty programs, they have very different designs and therefore very different impacts on attitudes. Social Security is a universal program with contributory payroll tax financing. Virtually all seniors receive monthly pension benefits; they feel these benefits are earned; and the program's administration is based on well-defined rules and has a pro-client orientation in seeking to assist its clients to get the benefits to which they have contributed. The poor benefit because the Social Security formula redistributes from high- to low-income earners and pulls most seniors out of poverty, but in a hidden and non-stigmatizing way.[77] In contrast, welfare or AFDC/TANF is a means-tested program for poor families financed out of general tax revenues. Benefits are not high enough to pull families above the poverty line and are awarded not by automatic formula but by case workers who appear to clients to have great discretion and indeed arbitrary and capricious powers.[78] These differing policy designs have vastly different effects on client attitudes. Senior citizens have high levels of political efficacy and political interest and strong feelings about the nature of government provision, rejecting alternative models such as Social Security private accounts and Medicare vouchers which would change the design of their programs in ways they view as inimical to their interests. Welfare recipients have lower levels of political efficacy and interest than even their low levels of income and education would predict due to their policy experiences. They come to view the entire government as being as arbitrary and capricious as "the welfare," and largely fail to participate in politics.[79]

Another example of the effects of program designs on public opinion comes from the "tax expenditure" system. Many social policies in the United States are direct spending programs in which the government directly spends money to provide cash or in-kind benefits. Examples include Social Security, Medicare, welfare, food stamps, unemployment insurance, and public housing. But many other social policies are delivered indirectly through the tax code in the form of tax credits or tax exemptions. These tax expenditures provide a benefit or subsidize an activity by reducing or eliminating income taxes on the money an individual spends. Examples include the home mortgage interest deduction, whereby homeowners can deduct the interest on their home loan from their taxable income, and the tax exclusion for employer-provided health insurance, in which neither employers nor employees pay taxes on the amount they contribute for the employees' health insurance.

This "hidden welfare state" is nearly as large as the visible welfare state,[80] and yet scholars have long speculated that it would have very different effects on public attitudes, that individuals receiving a benefit that does not come as a visible cash payment or service but rather as a saving on their taxes would not perceive it as a government benefit. New data demonstrate that this is in fact the case. Beneficiaries of the home mortgage interest deduction (an indirect program) are far less likely to say that the program "helped them a lot" than are beneficiaries of government-provided housing (a direct program). Similarly, beneficiaries of a Hope or Lifetime Learning tax credit for higher education are far less likely to say that the program helped them a lot than are beneficiaries of direct student loans.[81] Thus the government foregoes billions of dollars in tax revenues to provide benefits which many do not perceive as government benefits. The impact of these policy designs on public attitudes is extremely consequential. Americans recognize that the government spends a great deal of money on the young through public education and on the old through Social Security and Medicare. The government also "spends" billions on those between ages 18 and 65, but much of this is in the form of tax expenditures, which, because they are hidden, people don't recognize as government benefits and think government does little for them. This feeds skepticism about government and makes it more difficult to implement further government programs. Hence public policies and their designs have enormous effects on public opinion.

Public Opinion and Healthcare Reform

The interplay between public opinion and public policy is complex. We wonder how much influence the public's preferences have in shaping policy outputs, especially in issue areas where other powerful actors may have different preferences. In turn we wonder how policy outcomes affect subsequent opinion and the possibilities for further policymaking. The passage of the Affordable Care Act (ACA) of 2010 and its subsequent implementation represent a useful case study in examining the relationship between public opinion and public policy, illustrating many of the dynamics discussed above (although a single case study cannot necessarily test them definitively).

In March 2010, Congress passed and President Obama signed the Patient Protection and Affordable Care Act (now referred to as the ACA, or "ObamaCare"). After decades of failed efforts to reform America's health-care and health insurance system, this law finally did so after more than a year of intense negotiation among policymakers, interest groups, and other stakeholders.

The impetus for the ACA was not public opinion per se but rather a policy conviction among Obama and his advisors. The policy situation was this: about 83 percent of Americans had health insurance either through their employer (just over half) or through a public program such as Medicare or Medicaid (around 30 percent). However, one in six Americans lacked insurance altogether, a number that had been edging up over time as more employers stopped offering coverage. Not only were the ranks of the uninsured growing, but also coverage in those employer-provided insurance plans was deteriorating, with patients confronting increased premiums and out-of-pocket spending, narrower doctor and hospital networks, and thinner benefits. "Underinsurance" was an increasing problem as well, with people thinking they had good coverage until a severe accident or illness or life event revealed shortcomings such as annual or lifetime caps on their insurance benefits, lack of maternity coverage, or coverage for in-patient procedures only, not out-patient procedures, where the majority of surgeries and chemotherapy now take place. Some estimates put the underinsured number at 25 million, on top of the 50 million uninsured.[82] Little wonder that medical expenses were a leading cause of personal bank-ruptcy.[83] With Obama centering his presidential campaign around a concern with economic inequality, addressing problems in health insurance, a major source of financial insecurity for ordinary Americans, made a great deal of sense. In September 2009, President Obama promised a Joint Session of Congress, "I am not the first president to take up this cause, but I am determined to be the last."[84]

There was a powerful political motivation behind healthcare reform as well. If successful, reform would not only give Obama a place in history, but also secure new groups of thankful voters for the Democratic party, as social welfare programs of the New Deal had done decades earlier. Or at least, that was the fear among Republican opponents of reform. Back in 1993, when another Democratic president, Bill Clinton, attempted health reform, Republican strategist William Kristol wrote a famous memo entitled "Defeating President Clinton's Health Care Proposal," in which he stated:

[the law's] passage in the short run will do nothing to hurt (and everything to help) Democratic electoral prospects in 1996. But the long-term political effects of a successful Clinton health care bill will be even worse—much worse. It will relegitimize middle-class dependence for "security" on government spending and regulation. It will revive the reputation of the party that spends and regulates, the Democrats, as the generous protector of middle-class interests. And it will at the same time strike a punishing blow against Republican claims to defend the middle class by restraining government.

Observers of the Obama healthcare episode made much the same point: *New York Times* columnist Eduardo Porter noted that Republican opposition to the ACA arose from a fear that the "law has many provisions that are likely to improve life for millions of Americans, including a big portion of what we know as the working middle class," who in turn "might be grateful to Democrats for the benefit."[85]

However, the electoral fears of Republicans notwithstanding, public opinion actually posed a potentially serious barrier to healthcare reform. For one thing, although 2008 was a historic year in which the nation elected its first African American president, including support from states that had been voting Republican, the political environment presented a number of challenges. Although Democrats controlled both houses of Congress, political polarization between Democratic and Republican lawmakers was ever-widening. Further-more, Obama was attempting healthcare reform at an historic low point in trust in government. Only 19 percent of Americans reported trusting government to do the right thing most or all of the time, the lowest level since government trust was first measured in 1958.[86]

Moreover, public opinion with regard to healthcare was not necessarily propitious. The same pattern of public attitudes appeared in 2009–2010 in the run-up to the ACA as had obtained in 1993–1994, during the Clinton reform attempt: polls showed that many Americans thought the healthcare and health insurance systems were broken and supported reform, but large majorities liked their own health insurance arrangements and feared change above all. For example, in 2009, just 26 percent of Americans rated the current national healthcare insurance system as excellent or good.[87] However, 67 percent of those respondents viewed their own health insurance coverage as excellent or good.[88] Such attitudes helped deep-six the Clinton reform effort; many worried that they would do the same thing to the Obama initiative.

Previous successful healthcare reforms enjoyed majority support among the public. Polls showed that providing government-funded health insurance to senior citizens—Medicare—was supported by two-thirds of Americans in the years leading up to the program's 1965 passage.[89] More than 80 percent of Americans supported the Children's Health Insurance Program when it was passed in 1997.[90] The extension of prescription drug benefits to senior citizens in 2003 was also very popular—supported by 89 percent of adult respondents in one indicative poll[91]—even if the public didn't get all of the policy details it wanted.

What Obama was attempting to do would affect far more people than this previous legislation targeted at popular groups such as senior citizens and children. Further, many Americans were suspicious of those lacking health insurance, and tended to assume that most were non-workers, when in fact the uninsured population was dominated by young people, those forced into retirement too early for Medicare, and people from working households whose employers did not offer insurance or who found the insurance too expensive.[92]

The question became how to craft legislation for a reform that Americans wanted in an abstract sense, but which history had shown they would quickly oppose if it proved inimical to their interests. The solution was to avoid changing the manner in which all Americans get their health insurance, as the Clinton reform would have done, and instead fashion a patch on the existing system, extending insurance to the uninsured while keeping intact the arrangements of the insured.[93] Thus the Affordable Care Act extends coverage to the uninsured by requiring employers above a certain size to offer insurance to their employees (the employer mandate) and requiring Americans to have insurance (the individual mandate), a requirement facilitated by expanding Medicaid (which the Supreme Court later undercut by making it optional for the states) and setting up health insurance exchanges on which individuals and small employers could shop for insurance at group rates, with a sliding scale of subsidies for families up to 400 percent of the federal poverty line. Americans who already had health insurance through their employer, Medicare or Medicaid would maintain those arrangements. The law also included a number of provisions meant to curb the worst practices of private insurers in the pre-reform era, such as banning annual or lifetime caps on health claims, preventing the rescission of coverage except in cases of fraud, and preventing preexisting condition exclusions. Insurers must also extend coverage to people up to age 26 under their parents' plan and must limit the amount spent on administration, marketing, and profit rather than health claims.

Thus public opinion prevailed in an overall sense. It induced the ACA's framers to design a reform to minimize opposition among the insured by essentially leaving them alone, and perhaps even improving their insurance. In addition, in a country skeptical of government, the reform gives a big role to private insurers (the insurance plans on the exchanges are from private health insurers, and most states enroll most of their Medicaid recipients in private managed care plans). No health policy expert starting from scratch would ever invent the complicated work-around which is the ACA—it's "an ugly patch on an ugly system," in the words of Princeton health economist Ewe Reinhardt[94]— but it was a politically feasible reform, largely because of the ways it addressed the public's main concerns around health reform.

Where public opinion failed to prevail was in some of the policy details. For example, sizable majorities of 50 to 60 percent favored a "public option," in which a government insurance plan much like Medicare would be available on the health exchanges in addition to the private plans.[95] However, insurers strongly opposed the public option, fearing that it could easily become the default option for consumers flummoxed by choice, and bloom into single-payer government health insurance for all in the long run. In the face of this interest group opposition, the public option was dropped. Similarly, other proposals were favored by majorities of Americans, such as allowing 55- to 64-year-olds to buy into Medicare, limiting malpractice awards, and allowing the reimportation of cheaper prescription drugs from Canada (American drug prices are the highest in the world).[96] Yet, all of these provisions were opposed by important health industry interest groups, and none were included in the final law. Public opinion might serve as a general guide to reform, but on policy specifics where interest groups have other preferences, they usually prevail.

Although the legislation did not include these options preferred by majorities of Americans, the influence of public opinion is again evident in the record of implementation of the ACA at the state level. Both as written and as later modified by the Supreme Court, the ACA gives considerable latitude to the states to implement health reform. For example, states decide whether to expand Medicaid, and whether to create their own insurance exchanges or let the federal government do this for them.

The influence of public opinion is seen in the congruence between policy preferences among state residents and state leaders' choices in ACA implementation. Across the states, support for (vs. opposition to) the ACA varies tremendously—with one estimate ranging from 35 percent in Utah to 59 percent in New York. This variation in public opinion helps explain important differences in states' ACA implementation—although party control of the state legislature is the main explanatory factor, accounting for nearly 50 percent of the differences in state implementation responses, while public opinion differences account for about 15 percent of the variation.[97] The role of public preferences is evident in that states with greater public support for the ACA were more likely to move forward to implement state-based health insurance exchanges[98] and Medicaid expansions[99] as specified in the federal legislation. An additional examination of regional variation in ACA implementation concluded that inter-regional differences in support or opposition to the ACA are based not on differences in insurance status (the percentage uninsured does vary dramatically from state to state) but are rather due to ideological and partisan differences among the regions.[100]

Public opinion on the ACA also highlights the way that Americans' policy positions are shaped by the political discourse they encounter. One prominent feature of public opinion toward the ACA is that individuals liked particular parts of the bill far more than the overall package. When told about key provisions of the bill, most Americans reported being more likely to support keeping the bill (versus repealing it).[101] For example, being informed that the law provides tax credits to small businesses led 82 percent of respondents to be more likely to support keeping the law—with similar responses to information on provisions that improve the Medicare prescription drug benefit (76 percent), provide subsidies to make insurance affordable for low- and moderate-income families (72 percent), and increase the Medicare payroll tax on the wealthy (58 percent). The one key exception is learning that the bill includes an individual mandate that requires Americans to be insured, which makes only 27 percent of respondents more likely to support keeping it—and 67 percent more likely to support repealing the ACA. Jacobs and Skocpol called this ambivalence about ObamaCare, but support for its key features, a "schizophrenic response."[102]

The public was also susceptible to framing effects. Opinions on the ACA are even more polarized when public opinion researchers ask about "ObamaCare." When asked about the ACA, 22 percent expressed support and 37 percent expressed opposition. This divergence was more extreme when respondents were asked about the same question but the term "ObamaCare" was used—more people supported the law (29 percent) but also more people opposed it (46 percent). The greater gap may be due to greater familiarity with "ObamaCare": 30 percent of the public didn't know what the ACA was, but only 12 percent reported not knowing about ObamaCare.[103]

What about the other direction of causality, policy change in turn affecting public opinion? The policy feedbacks literature would suggest that changing the structure of the U.S. healthcare system would shape American public opinion on this issue. We might expect at minimum that as Americans begin to sign up for insurance through Medicaid or the health exchanges that their opinion toward the reform would grow more positive. Ditto for the millions of Americans who now no longer have to fear preexisting condition exclusions or lifetime or annual limits on benefits. More profoundly, we might imagine that seeing the ACA at work, or receiving government subsidies on the exchanges, might enhance regard for government or possibly for the Democratic party, which forged the reform.

However, little evidence of attitudinal change arising from this policy reform has emerged. In terms of attitudes toward the reform as a whole, support for the ACA was weak to begin with, and has not increased. Upon passage, just 49 percent of Americans reported that they thought health reform was a "good thing." Perhaps unsurprisingly, given that the ACA was passed with no Republican votes in the Senate or House, this view was quite polarized by party—endorsed by 79 percent of Democrats but only 14 percent of Republicans. Further, although 35 percent indicated that the best description of their reaction to the ACA's passage was to be pleased, more Americans were "angry" (19 percent) than were "enthusiastic" (15 percent) about the bill's passage. Even among Democrats, only 29 percent of respondents indicated that they were excited about the bill.[104]

Since implementation has begun, attitudes have not yet shifted. Polls from 2014, four years after enactment, reveal that public opinion was still divided, with 35 percent of Americans favorable, 47 percent unfavorable, and a large contingent (19 percent) still expressing no opinion on the ACA.[105] A Gallup Poll from Spring 2014, after the first enrollment period closed with eight million new enrollees, found little change in how Americans viewed the impact of the ACA on their own lives. Most Americans (59 percent) reported that the law had no effect. Among those who perceived an effect, more felt the law hurt them (24 percent) than helped them (14 percent). However, among the small proportion of the respondents who reported that they obtained a new health insurance policy in 2014, more viewed the ACA as likely to help them (27 percent) than did those who maintained the same insurance policy as in the past (of whom only 11 percent viewed the law as helping them).[106]

Perhaps as more people experience changes in their insurance status or benefits owing to the ACA, attitudes toward the reform will become more positive; perhaps even attitudes toward government will shift as well. However, there are a number of aspects of the ACA's design that may thwart the development of feedback effects, particularly the fact that the expansion utilizes private insurers rather than public, minimizing the visibility of the government's role. Ironically, the well-publicized early implementation failures of the healthcare.gov portal which the federal government ran on behalf of 34 states may have raised the public visibility of this submerged, market-based government program. The Kaiser Health Tracking Poll found that in January 2014, after the troubled roll-out of healthcare.gov, 68 percent of Americans were aware that the ACA created health insurance exchanges, up ten percentage points from a year earlier.[107] Similarly, the efforts by reform opponents to attack the ACA may have heightened public awareness of its existence and key features: enrollment in the ACA is higher in states where more money was spent on television ads attacking the reform.[108]

Although ACA implementation may increase knowledge and awareness, whether it shifts underlying attitudes is an altogether different question. Partisanship and ideology tend to have strong effects on issue attitudes (although sometimes personal experience can make a dent). However, another example of the failure of a major policy design change to change attitudes suggests just how durable they are. In 1996 welfare was transformed in fundamental ways. The AFDC program was replaced with TANF, stripping welfare of its entitlement status and placing new work requirements and lifetime limits on the program, provisions that were very popular with the public. Hypotheses arising from the feedbacks literature would suggest that the new design of welfare, especially because it implemented changes the public desired, would change attitudes about welfare and welfare recipients. No longer could a recipient be on welfare for a lifetime, and now recipients would have to work to receive benefits. Despite these changes in policy design, however, no attitudinal change occurred: Americans are no more favorably disposed toward welfare than they were before the reform.[109] The lack of change in attitudes suggests the considerable influence of other factors beyond public policy, such as childhood socialization, ideological commitments, media messages, and so on. It may also be the case that attitudinal change is a long-term process. Perhaps we will not observe new attitudes toward the ACA until more Americans have grown up into a world where its provisions are the norm.

Conclusion

Thanks to the work of many scholars over time, we know more and more about the relationship between public opinion and public policy. Although there are many areas where more research is needed, we can draw a number of conclusions with confidence.

Among the myriad influences on public policy—the ideological and policy preferences of lawmakers, the desires of organized interests, norms and models arising from existing policy, budget constraints imposed by ongoing governmental operations, and so on—public opinion does play a role. But this role is constrained in important ways. The public has its greatest influence on salient issues; in more esoteric realms in which the public cannot discern its interest or believes it has none, other elite-level influences tend to prevail. Where the public does have influence, it usually shapes the general direction of policy rather than fine-grained specifics, where again, other interests tend to stipulate the details. And the consensus among many scholars is that inequality in representation is a significant problem, one that threatens to undermine the very legitimacy of democratic governance. Democratic theory is predicated on the equal distance of all citizens from government, but clearly some citizens are viewed as more central, and their preferences tend to prevail over those of the less privileged and less participatory.

Important too is the influence of existing policy on the public's attitudes (precisely because those attitudes tend to feed back into the political system, determining the possibilities for future policymaking). The observation that public opinion reacts in thermostatic fashion, moving away from the status quo to prefer, say, more or less spending or a stronger or weaker role for government than exists at the moment, begs the question: is government doomed perpetually to disappoint its citizens? Or is the very fact of opinion and policy tacking from side to side ideologically a measure of responsiveness? What we do know is that public policy is only one of many influences on public preferences, and changing policy does not always succeed in winning over the public, whether because other influences remain dominant, or simply because the public does not realize the policy change took place.

Thus the relationship between public opinion and public policy looks to be a variable one, stronger on some issue areas and for some subgroups in society, weaker in other areas and for less privileged groups. As with other aspects of public opinion, the public's widespread lack of knowledge and inattentiveness to politics undercuts its ability to shape policy outcomes, something that ultimately only the public can choose to change.

Notes

1. Many thanks to Blair Read and Mike Sances for their superb research assistance.
2. John Stuart Mill, *Considerations on Representative Government* (Chicago: Henry Regnery, 1962), p. 57.
3. See Alexander Hamilton, James Madison, and John Jay, *The Federalist* (New York: Anchor, 1961).
4. V. O. Key (Jr.), *Public Opinion and American Democracy* (New York, NY: Alfred A. Knopf, 1964), p. 7.
5. Robert A. Dahl, *Polyarchy: Participation and Opposition* (New Haven: Yale University Press, 1971), p. 1.
6. Christopher Achen, "Measuring Representation," *American Journal of Political Science* 22 (1978): 475–510.
7. For valuable overviews of this literature, see Robert Y. Shapiro, "Public Opinion and American Democracy," *Public Opinion Quarterly* 75 no. 5 (2011): 982–1017; Paul Burstein, "The Impact of Public Opinion on Public Policy: A Review and an Agenda," *Political Research Quarterly* 56 (2003): 29–40 and *American Public Opinion, Advocacy, and Policy in Congress: What the Public Wants and What It Gets* (New York: Cambridge University Press, 2014); Carroll J. Glynn, Susan Herbst, Garrett J. O'Keefe, Robert Y. Shapiro, and Lawrence R. Jacobs, "Public Opinion and Policy Making," in *Public Opinion*, eds. Carroll J. Glynn, Susan Herbst, Garrett J. O'Keefe, and Robert Y. Shapiro (Boulder, CO: Westview Press, 1999), pp. 299–340; and Jeff Manza and Fay Lomax Cook, "A Democratic Polity? Three Views of Policy Responsiveness to Public Opinion in the United States," *American Politics Research* 30 (2002): 630–667.
8. Glynn et al., "Public Opinion and Policy Making."
9. Anthony Downs, *An Economic Theory of Democracy* (New York: Harper, 1957).
10. Edward R. Tufte, *Political Control of the Economy* (Princeton: Princeton University Press, 1978).
11. Glynn et al., "Public Opinion and Policy Making."
12. Douglas R. Arnold, *The Logic of Congressional Action* (New Haven: Yale University Press, 1990).
13. Morris P. Fiorina, *Disconnect: The Breakdown of Representation in American Politics* (Julian J. Rothbaum Distinguished Lecture Series) (Norman: University of Oklahoma Press, 2009).
14. David B. Truman, *The Governmental Process: Political Interests and Public Opinion* (New York: Knopf, 1951); Robert A. Dahl, *Who Governs? Democracy and Power in an American City* (New Haven: Yale University Press, 1961); E.E. Schattschneider, *The Semi-Sovereign People: A Realist's View of Democracy in America* (Austin: Holt, Rinehart and Winston, 1960).
15. Burstein, "The Impact of Public Opinion on Public Policy."
16. Jacob Hacker and Paul Pierson, "Winner-Take-All Politics: Public Policy, Political Organization, and the Precipitous Rise of Top Incomes in the United States," *Politics & Society* 38 (June 2010): 152–204.
17. Schattschneider, *The Semi-Sovereign People*; Frank R. Baumgartner and Beth L. Leech, *Basic Interests: The Importance of Groups in Politics and in Political Science* (Princeton, NJ: Princeton University Press, 1998).

18. Benjamin I. Page and Robert Y. Shapiro, *The Rational Public: Fifty Years of Trends in Americans' Policy Preferences* (Chicago: University Of Chicago Press, 1992); Alan D. Monroe, "Consistency between Policy Preferences and National Policy Decisions," *American Politics Quarterly* 7 (1979): 3–18; Alan D. Monroe, "Public Opinion and Public Policy, 1980–1993," *Public Opinion Quarterly* 62 (1998): 6–28; Martin Gilens, "Inequality and Democratic Responsiveness," *Public Opinion Quarterly* 65 (2005): 778–796.

19. James A. Stimson, Michael B. MacKuen, and Robert Erikson, "Dynamic Representation," *American Political Science Review* 89 (1995): 543–565; James Stimson, *Tides of Consent: How Public Opinion Shapes American Politics* (New York: Cambridge University Press, 2004).

20. Page and Shapiro, *The Rational Public*; Monroe, "Consistency between Policy Preferences and National Policy Decisions"; Monroe, "Public Opinion and Public Policy, 1980–1993"; Gilens, "Inequality and Democratic Responsiveness."

21. Warren E. Miller and Donald E. Stokes, "Constituency Influence in Congress," *The American Political Science Review* 57 (1963): 45–56; Larry Bartels, *Unequal Democracy: The Political Economy of the New Gilded Age* (Princeton, NJ: Princeton University Press, 2008).

22. Stimson, MacKuen, and Erikson's policy liberalism measures include: for Congress the net liberal direction on *Congressional Quarterly* key votes, the size of the liberal coalition on those votes, and interest group ratings of members; for the President the liberalism of his support coalition in Congress, the liberalism of the President's stand on key votes, and solicitor general briefs; for the Court a content-analysis-based measure of net liberalism of majority opinions. See Stimson, MacKuen, and Erikson, "Dynamic Representation."

23. Larry Bartels distinguishes between responsiveness—a change in policy following a change in opinion—and policy congruence—a static measure of correspondence between preferences and policy as will be discussed below. See also Christopher Achen's discussion of three theoretically and empirically distinct measures of representation in Achen, "Measuring Representation"; Larry Bartels, "The Opinion-Policy Disconnect: Cross-National Spending Preferences and Democratic Representation," paper prepared for presentation at the Annual Meeting of the American Political Science Association, Boston, August 2008.

24. Miller and Stokes, "Constituency Influence in Congress."

25. Jeffrey M. Berry, Kent E. Portney, and Ken Thomson, *The Rebirth of Urban Democracy* (Washington, DC: Brookings, 1993).

26. Robert S. Erikson, John P. McIver, and Gerald C. Wright, *Statehouse Democracy: Public Opinion and the American States* (New York: Cambridge University Press, 1994).

27. Monroe, "Consistency between Policy Preferences and National Policy Decisions"; Monroe, "Public Opinion and Public Policy, 1980–1993."

28. Page and Shapiro, *The Rational Public*.

29. Stimson, MacKuen, and Erikson, "Dynamic Representation."

30. Benjamin I. Page, and Robert Y. Shapiro, "Effects of Public Opinion on Policy," *American Political Science Review* 77 no. 1 (1983): 175–190.

31. Stimson, MacKuen, and Erikson, "Dynamic Representation."

32. We might wonder whether there is indeed a "public opinion" to translate into public policy in the first place, with skeptics examining individual-level opinion arguing that citizens have reasons to be rationally ignorant about politics (Downs, *An Economic Theory of Democracy*) and lack true attitudes on many issue areas (Philip E. Converse, "The Nature of Belief Systems in Mass Publics," in *Ideology and*

Discontent, ed. David Apter (New York: Free Press, 1964), pp. 206–261). Aggregating opinions across many individuals, as most scholars in this arena do, in theory leads to the canceling out of individual-level error in opinion (see Benjamin I. Page and Robert Y. Shapiro, *The Rational Public*).

33. Manza and Cook, *A Democratic Polity?*, pp. 632. On latent public opinion, see also John R Zaller, "Coming to Grips with V. O. Key's Concept of Latent Opinion," in *Electoral Democracy*, eds. Michael MacKuen and George Rabinowitz (Ann Arbor, MI: University of Michigan Press, 2003), pp. 311–336.

34. Adam J. Berinsky, *Silent Voices: Public Opinion and Political Participation in America* (Princeton: Princeton University Press, 2005).

35. Paul Burstein, "Why Estimates of the Impact of Public Opinion on Public Policy Are Too High," *Social Forces* 84 (2006): 2273–2290.

36. Jeffrey R. Lax and Justin H. Phillips, "The Democratic Deficit in the States," *American Journal of Political Science* 56 (2012): 148–166.

37. We do know that many Americans do not think their opinions generally matter for policy outcomes. Large majorities say that Congress is "generally out of touch with average Americans" and that "people in government" do not "understand what most Americans think." See Steven Kull and Clay Ramsay, "How Policymakers Misperceive U.S. Public Opinion on Foreign Policy," in *Navigating Public Opinion*, eds. Jeff Manza, Fay Lomax Cook, and Benjamin I. Page (Oxford: Oxford University Press, 2002), pp. 201–218.

38. For discussions of the causality question, see Gilens, "Inequality and Democratic Responsiveness," pp. 789–793; Brandice Canes-Wrone, *Who Leads Whom?: Presidents, Policy, and the Public* (Chicago: University of Chicago Press, 2005); Kim Quaile Hill and Angela Hinton-Andersson, "Pathways of Representation: A Causal Analysis of Public Opinion-Policy Linkages," *American Journal of Political Science* 39 (1995): 924–35; Stimson, Erikson, and MacKuen, "Dynamic Representation," p. 546.

39. Page and Shapiro, *The Rational Public*, Chapter 9.

40. Lawrence Jacobs and Robert Y. Shapiro, "Politics and Policymaking in the Real World: Crafted Talk and the Loss of Democratic Responsiveness," in *Navigating Public Opinion*, eds. Jeff Manza, Fay Lomax Cook, and Benjamin I. Page (Oxford: Oxford University Press, 2002), pp. 54–75.

41. James Druckman, "The Implications of Framing Effects for Citizen Competence," *Political Behavior* 23 (2001): 225–256.

42. Hill and Hinton-Andersson, "Pathways of Representation."

43. Stimson, MacKuen, and Erikson, "Dynamic Representation," p. 559.

44. Fiorina, *Disconnect: The Breakdown of Representation in American Politics*.

45. Paul J. Quirk, "Politicians Do Pander: Mass Opinion, Polarization, and Law Making," *The Forum* 7 (2009), http://www.bepress.com/forum/vol7/iss4/art10/

46. Stephen Ansolabehere, James M. Snyder (Jr.), and Charles Stewart III, "Candidate Positioning in U.S. House Elections," *American Journal of Political Science* 45 (2001): 136–59; Page and Shapiro, "Effects of Public Opinion on Policy."

47. Ansolabehere, Snyder, and Stewart, "Candidate Positioning in U.S. House Elections"; Monroe, "Public Opinion and Public Policy, 1980–1993."

48. Monroe, "Consistency between Policy Preferences and National Policy Decisions"; Monroe, "Public Opinion and Public Policy, 1980–1993."

49. Lawrence R. Jacobs, and Robert Y. Shapiro, "The Myth of the Pandering Politicians," *The Public Perspective* 8 (April/May 1997): 3–5.

50. Gilens, "Inequality and Democratic Responsiveness," p. 784.

51. The proportion of policy-related questions among survey questions archived at the Roper Center at the University of Connecticut declined from 15.6 percent in the 1980s to 9.4 percent in the 2000s. Jason Barabas, "Democracy's Denominator: Public Opinion on the National Policy Agenda and Evidence of Declining Responsiveness," unpublished article, Stony Brook University, June 2014.

52. Miller and Stokes, "Constituency Influence in Congress"; Page and Shapiro, "Effects of Public Opinion on Policy."

53. Dahl, *Who Governs?*, p. 3.

54. See also the report of the APSA Task Force on Inequality and American Democracy, *American Democracy in an Age of Rising Inequality: Report of the American Political Science Association Task Force on Inequality and American Democracy* (Washington, DC: American Political Science Association, 2004), available at: http://www.apsanet.org/imgtest/taskforcereport.pdf

55. Martin Gilens, *Affluence and Influence: Economic Inequality and Political Power in America* (Princeton, NJ: Princeton University Press, 2013).

56. Bartels, *Unequal Democracy*, Chapter 9.

57. Lawrence R. Jacobs and Benjamin I. Page, "Who Influences U.S. Foreign Policy?" *American Political Science Review* 99, no. 1 (2005): 107–123.

58. James Druckman and Lawrence R. Jacobs, "Segmented Representation: The Reagan White House and Disproportionate Responsiveness," in *Who Gets Represented?*, eds. Peter Enns and Christopher Wlezien (New York: Russell Sage Foundation, 2011), pp. 166–188.

59. Elizabeth Rigby and Gerald C. Wright, "Whose Statehouse Democracy? Policy Responsiveness to Poor versus Rich Constituents in Poor versus Rich States," in *Who Gets Represented?*, eds. Peter Enns and Christopher Wlezien (New York: Russell Sage Foundation, 2011), pp. 189–222.

60. John D. Griffin and Brian Newman, "Are Voters Better Represented?" *The Journal of Politics* 67, no. 4 (2005): 1206–1227.

61. Elizabeth Rigby and Gerald C. Wright, "Political Parties and Representation of the Poor in the American States," *American Journal of Political Science* 57 (2013): 552–565.

62. Kim Quaile Hill and Jan E. Leighley, "The Policy Consequences of Class Bias in State Electorates," *American Journal of Political Science* 36 (1992): 351–65; William W. Franko, "Political Inequality and State Policy Adoption: Predatory Lending, Children's Health Care, and Minimum Wage," *Poverty & Public Policy* 5 no. 1 (2013): 88–114.

63. Frank R. Baumgartner, Jeffrey M. Berry, Marie Hojnacki, David C. Kimball, and Beth L. Leech, *Lobbying and Policy Change: Who Wins, Who Loses, and Why* (Chicago: University of Chicago Press, 2009).

64. Gilens, *Affluence and Influence.*

65. Stuart N. Soroka and Christopher Wlezien, "On the Limits to Inequality in Representation," *PS: Political Science and Politics* 41 (2008): 319–327.

66. Martin Gilens, "Preference Gaps and Inequality in Representation," *PS: Political Science and Politics* 42 (2009): 335–341.

67. Patrick Flavin, "Income Inequality and Policy Representation in the American States," *American Politics Research* 40 no. 1 (2012): 29–59.

68. Rigby and Wright, "Whose Statehouse Democracy?"

69. Bartels, "The Opinion-Policy Disconnect."

70. Fay Lomax Cook and Edith J. Barrett, *Support for the American Welfare State: The Views of Congress and the Public* (New York: Columbia University Press, 1992).

71. Zaller, "Coming to Grips."

72. Christopher Wlezien, "The Public as Thermostat: Dynamics of Preferences for Spending," *American Journal of Political Science* 39 no. 4 (1995): 981–1000. See Christopher Ellis and Christopher Faricy, "Social Policy and Public Opinion: How the Ideological Direction of Spending Influences Public Mood," *Journal of Politics* 73 no. 4 (October 2011): 1095–1110 for a subsequent refinement: they find that the public moves in a conservative direction after increases in direct social spending but in a liberal direction after increases in indirect social spending carried out through the tax code.

73. James Stimson, *Tides of Consent: How Public Opinion Shapes American Politics* (New York: Cambridge University Press, 2004).

74. For reviews of the literature on policy feedbacks, see Andrea Louise Campbell, "Policy Makes Mass Politics," *Annual Review of Political Science* 15 (2012): 333–51; and Suzanne Mettler and Joe Soss, "The Consequences of Public Policy for Democratic Citizenship: Bridging Policy Studies and Mass Politics," *Perspectives on Politics* 2 no. 1 (2004): 55–73.

75. Helen Ingram and Anne Schneider, "Constructing Citizenship: The Subtle Messages of Policy Design," in *Public Policy for Democracy*, eds. Helen Ingram and Steven Rathgeb Smith (Washington, DC: Brookings, 1993); Paul Pierson, "When Effect Becomes Cause: Policy Feedback and Political Change," *World Politics* 45 (1993): 595–628.

76. Julianna Pacheco, "Attitudinal Policy Feedback and Public Opinion: The Impact of Smoking Bans on Attitudes towards Smokers, Secondhand Smoke, and Antismoking Policies," *Public Opinion Quarterly* 77 no. 3 (Fall 2013): 714–34.

77. Andrea L. Campbell, *How Policies Make Citizens: Senior Political Activism and the American Welfare State* (Princeton: Princeton University Press, 2003).

78. Joseph Soss, "Lessons of Welfare: Policy Design, Political Learning, and Political Action," *American Political Science Review* 93 (1999): 363–80.

79. Campbell, *How Policies Make Citizens*; Soss, "Lessons of Welfare."

80. Christopher Howard, *The Hidden Welfare State: Tax Expenditures and Social Policy in the United States* (Princeton, NJ: Princeton University Press, 1997).

81. Suzanne Mettler, *The Submerged State: How Invisible Government Policies Undermine American Democracy* (Chicago: University of Chicago Press, 2011). For a cross-national examination of the attitudinal implications of welfare state program visibility, see Jane Gingrich, "Visibility, Values, and Voters: The Informational Role of the Welfare State," *Journal of Politics* 76 no. 2 (April 2014): 565–80.

82. Cathy Schoen, Sara R. Collins, Jennifer L. Kriss, and Michelle M. Doty, "How Many Are Underinsured? Trends among U.S. Adults, 2003 and 2007," *Health Affairs* 27 (July 2008): w298–w309.

83. David U. Himmelstein, Elizabeth Warren, Deborah Thorne, and Steffie Woolhandler, "Illness and Injury as Contributors to Bankruptcy," *Health Affairs* (February 2005): w5–w63.

84. President Barack Obama, Speech to Congress, "Obama's Health Care Speech to Congress," September 9, 2009.

85. Eduardo Porter, "Why the Health Care Law Scares the G.O.P.," *New York Times*, October 1, 2013.

86. Gallup Poll, "Trust in Government," September 2013, available at: http://www.gallup.com/poll/5392/trust-government.aspx

87. Gallup Poll, "Americans Maintain Negative View of Healthcare Coverage," November 2011, available at: http://www.gallup.com/poll/150788/Americans-Maintain-Negative-View-Healthcare-Coverage.aspx

88. Gallup Poll, "In US, More Rate Own Healthcare Quality and Coverage as Excellent," November 2011, available at: http://www.gallup.com/poll/150806/rate-own-health care-quality-coverage-excellent.aspx

89. Michael E. Schiltz, *Public Attitudes toward Social Security, 1935–1965*, Social Security Administration, Office of Research and Statistics, Research Report No. 33 (Washington, DC: U.S. Government Printing Office, 1970), p. 140.

90. Washington Post/Kaiser Family Foundation Harvard Gender Poll, August 14–September 14, 1997.

91. ABC News Poll, May 7–May 9, 2000 and based on 1,013 telephone interviews, sample: national adult, [USABC.051000.R6], accessed from the Roper Center Public Opinion Archives July 2, 2010.

92. Kaiser Commission on Medicaid and the Uninsured, "The Uninsured, A Primer: Key Facts about Health Insurance on the Eve of Health Reform," October 2013.

93. Lawrence R. Jacobs and Theda Skocpol, *Health Care Reform and American Politics: What Everyone Needs to Know* (New York: Oxford University Press: 2012).

94. Quoted in *The Economist*, "Will It Get Better?" October 5, 2013.

95. Jacobs and Skocpol, *Health Care Reform and American Politics*.

96. Robert J. Blendon and John M. Benson, "Public Opinion at the Time of the Vote on Health Care Reform," *New England Journal of Medicine* 362 no. 16 (2010): e55.

97. Elizabeth Rigby, "State Resistance to ObamaCare," *The Forum: Journal of Applied Research in Contemporary Politics* 10 no.2 (2012), available at: http://www. degruyter.com/view/j/for.2012.10.issue-2/1540-8884.1501/1540-8884.1501.xml? format=INT

98. Elizabeth Rigby and Jake Haselswerdt, "Hybrid Federalism, Partisan Politics, and the Early Implementation of State Health Insurance Exchanges," *Publius: The Journal of Federalism* 43 no. 3 (2013): 368–391.

99. Colleen Grogan and Sungguen Park, "Expanding Access to Public Insurance in the States: Public Opinion and Policy Responsiveness," paper presented at Association for Public Policy Analysis and Management, November 2013.

100. Mollyann Brodie, Claudia Deane, and Sarah Cho, "Regional Variations in Public Opinion on the Affordable Care Act," *Journal of Health Politics, Policy, and Law* 36 no. 6 (2011): 1097–1103.

101. Lawrence R. Jacobs and Suzanne Mettler, "Why Public Opinion Changes: The Implications for Health and Health Policy." *Journal of Health Politics, Policy, and Law* 36 (2011): 917–933.

102. Jacobs and Skocpol, *Health Care Reform and American Politics*, p. 121.

103. CNBC, Third-quarter All-America Economic Survey, September 2013, available at: http://www.cnbc.com/id/101064954

104. Gallup Poll, "By Slim Margin, Americans Support Health Care Bill Passage," March 2010, available at: http://www.gallup.com/poll/126929/slim-margin-americans-support-healthcare-bill-passage.aspx

105. Kaiser Family Foundation, "Kaiser Health Tracking Poll August-September 2014," available at: http://kff.org/health-reform/poll-finding/kaiser-health-tracking-poll-august-september-2014/

106. Gallup Poll, "Few Americans Say Health Care Law Has Helped Them," May 2014, available at: http://www.gallup.com/poll/170756/few-americans-say-healthcare-law-helped.aspx

107. Kaiser Family Foundation, "Kaiser Health Tracking Poll January 2014," available at: http://kaiserfamilyfoundation.files.wordpress.com/2014/01/8545-t1.pdf

108. Niam Yaraghi, "Have the Anti-Obamacare Ads Backfired?" Tech Tank: Improving Technology Policy,Washington, DC, The Brookings Institution.

109. Joseph Soss and Sanford F. Schram, "A Public Transformed? Welfare Reform as Policy Feedback," in *Remaking America: Democracy and Public Policy in an Age of Inequality*, eds. Joseph Soss, Jacob S. Hacker, and Suzanne Mettler (New York: Russell Sage, 2007), pp. 99–118.

Conclusion

Assessing Continuity and Change

David O. Sears

Formal academic survey research on public opinion about politics began in the 1940s. In the early years, several milestone projects were published that not only set the agenda for later researchers, but pointed the way. Here we are, seven decades later, and research has burgeoned in the interim. The authors of this collection have done a wonderful job, in my judgment, of summarizing the current state of the art (and science).

The question I have set for myself in this concluding chapter is to assess the "new directions" part of the title. Pioneers sometimes stake out the territory so thoroughly that little remains for those who follow but to fill in the gaps with predictable results. If that has been the case, surely great disappointment would reign in the halls of the National Science Foundation.

But sometimes the founding paradigm(s) are challenged by new perspectives. And sometimes the external environment changes in ways that force us to rethink the conventional wisdom. In some cases, even, the pioneers may have had it wrong. After all, Europeans named native Americans "Indians" believing they had reached "India," not North America. And sometimes vast territories are ignored by pioneers and only later become recognized for what they are. Sixteenth and seventeenth century maps of North America remain exquisitely detailed and accurate for the Atlantic coastline, and even a few miles inland, but beyond that, it was all terra incognita.

So I will attempt to assess the relative balance of continuity and change in the chapters of this volume. As might be expected, all of these possibilities are true in some respects. I hope I can do justice to the nuanced and extensive treatments of the topics covered by the authors. For convenience I have grouped the research covered in this volume into six categories: voting behavior; campaigns and media effects; personality, motivation, and emotion; social groups in mass politics; the effects of changes in society exogenous to academic research on politics; and the implications of this research for the quality of democratic governance.

The Pioneers

The earliest major academic studies of public opinion and voting behavior were, of course, those of Paul Lazarsfeld and his sociological colleagues at Columbia University. They conducted studies of two medium-sized communities, and emphasized the stability through presidential campaigns of voting preferences rooted in demographic differences and primary group relationships. They found disappointingly slim returns from an ambitious examination of propaganda and media influence.[1] Those latter findings were later generalized by Klapper's influential 1960 literature review on the effects of mass communications. He concluded that under normal circumstances they effectively reinforced prior attitudes rather than changing them very much, a viewpoint that later became known as the "minimal effects model."[2] In my classes I usually contrast this view with a slim 1939 volume called *The Fine Art of Propaganda* which in a more qualitative style detailed the "tricks of the trade" that purportedly gave artful propagandists like Father Charles Coughlin and Joseph Goebbels powerful sway over gullible mass publics.[3] A similar contrast is given broader historical perspective by Herbst in this volume.

A radically different style of research using nationally representative sample surveys came to some overlapping, and some different, conclusions with the publication in 1960 of *The American Voter*. It developed a systematic theory of voting behavior later known as "the Michigan School," since all four authors were professors at the University of Michigan. This early work largely replaced sociology with both political science and psychology as the starring players in the story, but with a similar underlying theme: that individual voting preferences were not easily changed. The primary reason they gave, however, was that voting choices and many other features of political opinion were organized by a powerful attachment to a political party, i.e., "party identification," that was acquired early in life, most often from parents, and that rarely changed very much in later years.[4]

In terms of information processing, it seems apparent that the pioneers relied principally on the cognitive consistency theories that were just being developed at the time, though not explicitly referencing them.[5] Public opinion about issues and candidates was viewed as strongly influenced by demographics or party identification, and the media frequently simply reinforced prior attitudes because of selective exposure and interpretation.

In both early versions of the voting literature, social groups were central players, especially as being the fundamental grounding for partisan preferences. However the pioneers did not take a uniform view of how they operated in politics. *The People's Choice* took objective demographic categories—membership groups such as social class or religious denomination—as key influences on the vote.[6] *Voting* broadened that perspective to examine the direct social influence of primary groups, especially in the families and the workplaces of the moderate-sized community it studied.[7] *The American Voter* adopted the more social psychological concept of reference groups, measured with subjective orientations such as group identification and perceived group norms, as a way to analyze the political impact of social class, labor unions, and religion.[8]

In that era, the study of personality was a flourishing field within the discipline of psychology. Personality assessment had been the dominant activity of clinical psychologists, psychoanalytic theory was much in vogue among intellectuals, and personality was such a strong focus of attention that the premiere journal for social psychologists was renamed *The Journal of Personality and Social Psychology*. Perhaps the most visible research project for psychologists with an interest in politics was Adorno et al.'s *The Authoritarian Personality*, using both depth interviews and questionnaires to develop the thesis that anti-Semitism (and a variety of other unsavory political attitudes) had its immediate roots in personality dispositions.[9] In political science, Herbert McClosky developed a pioneering analysis linking political conservatism to a variety of unappealing personality traits.[10] However neither the Columbia nor the Michigan schools, different as they were, paid much attention to personality variables. Nonetheless the personality and politics paradigm was, to political scientists, perhaps the most visible application of psychology to the general domain of political behavior.[11]

Finally, because of the apparent indifference of the voters to much of the substance of political campaigns, except perhaps as rationalizations for standing partisan decisions made much earlier, both the Columbia and Michigan studies created great complications for those who wished to defend democratic citizenries' capabilities for governing their own affairs. These studies were widely interpreted as sharply questioning the competence of democratic citizens to govern themselves. They concluded that the public has, on average, modest information about politics, fairly inconsistent issue preferences, not especially stable political attitudes, and impoverished understanding of conventional political ideologies.[12]

Voting Behavior

One consequence of the pioneers' efforts in the area of voting behavior was a growing gap between the political behavior academics, who saw relatively little impact of campaigns, and media commentators and campaign consultants, whose livelihood depended on asserting their effectiveness. To what extent and where do we see continuity and change? Here I am relying principally on the chapters by Baum, Hetherington, and Sides and Haselswerdt.

For one thing, individual voters' preferences in presidential elections remain highly predictable from measures that can be assessed long before the traditional start of general election campaigns after Labor Day, on the basis of their demographics and party identification. In a way the case for that predictability is even stronger today than it was decades ago, given the subsequent discovery that self-described "Independents" leaning to one party or the other resemble partisans more than they do "Independents" with no such leanings (Sides), and the more consistent "sorting" (of which more below) of voters into the parties that best fit their ideologies. Moreover, party identification is the most stable of political attitudes, and the most powerful influence on other attitudes (Hetherington). It remains the single most important individual attitude in American mass politics.

However party identification is not so tidily ascribed to parental influence as once thought, for several reasons. Some parents are disengaged from politics, and have little lasting influence on their children's politics. The embeddedness of party identification in social groups, such as racial or religious groups, means that some will realign their party identifications more appropriately with other group attachments later in life. And there is evidence that the individual's early political experiences, like living through the Great Depression and the New Deal, may foster some departures from parental norms, as discussed by Hetherington. Moreover, Gonzalez and colleagues suggest that party identification and other fundamental political predispositions may be "heritable to a point and therefore not entirely socialized."

Campaigns and Media Effects

The Sides and Haselswerdt chapter is a particularly useful analysis of current perspectives on campaign influences. Reinforcement remains more common than persuasion in presidential elections. Generally speaking, each side's partisans mostly perceive their own candidates to have been the "winner" in presidential debates. Only rarely does one candidate outperform the other enough to overcome that bias, as in the case of the first 2012 debate. Off-year elections in particular continue to show frequent strong tilts away from the party of the White House incumbent, as in 2006, 2010, and 2014.

A major new player in the understanding of voting behavior is the perceived performance in office of the incumbent.[13] A healthy economy and a nation at peace particularly benefit the incumbent party, as Sides and Haselswerdt note. But they caution us that such "retrospective voting" may not always be as rational as it seems. The president may actually not have much influence over the economy, and politically-irrelevant factors such as local football victories or droughts also affect incumbents' fates. Moreover, as Schildkraut notes, a substantial literature suggests that the putatively "rational" influence of economic self-interest over voters' decisions usually weighs in less heavily than other political predispositions and perceived benefits to the collective interest.

Another break with the past has come from the changing conceptions of human information processing originating in cognitive psychology. The widely used idea of "motivated reasoning" is in large part an evolved version of those earlier consistency theories. Gonzalez and colleagues, for example, allude to those theories' assertion of the dominance of affect over cognition, and the widespread role of cognition as mere rationalization. "Dual process" theories have also become staples of cognitive psychology, though in various versions.

One is that ordinary citizens most commonly engage in habit-driven peripheral (or heuristic) processing, and reserve the more effortful central (or systematic) processing for a few most important tasks (Mondak and Hibbing). Anger may trigger the former, and fear the latter (Brader and Wayne). Another is the contrast of Kahneman's "System 1" (fast, emotional, intuitive, often non-conscious, often influenced by subtle contextual factors) with "System 2" processing (slow, deliberate, more logical; see Gonzalez and colleagues).[14]

Moreover, researchers pay more attention today than did the pioneers to lower profile elections, such as primaries, sub-presidential elections, or ballot propositions. Persuasion via the media seems to be more common in those cases than in presidential general elections. Perhaps Klapper would have anticipated that from his lesser-known principle,[15] that change is more common when "mediating factors," such as group norms, party identification, and selective reception are absent. In such cases the voter's policy preferences and personality may have more influence, even though party identification still dominates when relevant. A surrogate for media attention, the amount of money spent by a campaign, similarly seems to have more influence on down-ballot races, and for congressional challengers. Spending at the end of a campaign may have special impact, such as by the Bush campaign in Florida in 2000. Priming attention to the economy in particular can influence the outcome. Get-out-the-vote campaigns can also influence the outcome sometimes, though in 2012 apparently limited mainly to Florida. These days scholars and others have developed an appreciation for the fact that the institution of the Electoral College tends to turn presidential elections into something like 50 state-wide elections rather than a single national referendum. In recent years only a few of those state-wide elections have been competitive.

In the end, party identification, a highly stable attitude, remains by far the single most powerful influence on individual voting decisions, especially in presidential elections. But the conditions under which campaigns, as principally conveyed through the media, have important effects are clearer now than they were in the 1950s and 1960s. In that sense the gap between academics' tendency to downplay the effectiveness of campaigns, and campaign consultants' trumpeting of their own successes, seems to have diminished. Money and tactics play a role in campaigns, but voters are far more than passive recipients of ads and strategies, contrary to the view developed in *The Fine Art*.

The Baum chapter more directly presents a contemporary view of media influence in politics. Nevertheless, there is much that is familiar from the earlier reign of the minimal effects model. The old idea of selective exposure is back with a vengeance, with slumping audiences for nominally neutral mainstream media such as newspapers and network news, and increased attention to highly partisan new media such as cable television and the blogosphere. Selective interpretation, reflected in partisan credibility assessments, catches whatever slips through the selective exposure net, leading to further reinforcement of the voter's prior preferences. That would be a familiar world for the old advocates of the minimal effects model. Nevertheless, we are cautioned, the audience for the new media tends disproportionately to be highly ideological and small. As Baum says, that makes them better for preaching to the choir than for converting the flock. Social media also seem to be subject to some selectivity in exposure and interpretation, though perhaps more complexly since they are used primarily for non-political purposes.

What has changed in public response to the media, then? There is perhaps greater recognition of individual differences in such obstacles to persuasion, with stronger partisans considerably more selective in exposure and interpretation than weaker partisans (though with the complication that the latter are less likely to pay attention to politics). On the other hand, the large audiences for normally apolitical entertainment television are quite vulnerable to political persuasion on the rare occasions when politics arises, given the absence of those pesky "mediating factors." Zaller's "RAS" model nicely balances reception and acceptance as sometimes conflicting influences on persuasion.[16] There also is greater appreciation for elites' and campaigns' ability to prime the issues they "own" and thereby swing things their way. Vavreck has supplied a useful analysis of how differently the 2000 Gore and 2008 Obama campaigns dealt with the economy, with the former passing up the opportunity to boast about the strong Democratic record,[17] and the latter pounding on the dismal Republican record.

Another change is greater attention to elites' behavior as a central factor in the mass public's response. In the pioneers' day, there was considerable ideological overlap between the two parties, at both the elite and mass level. Hetherington's chapter reviews the profound changes in party elites over the past half century, describing the general consensus that they are far more politically polarized than used to be the case. There is some dispute about whether the mass public has become more polarized as well, but little argument about the fact that the public has in response sorted itself into ideologically more consistent camps, with the Democrat base becoming more liberal on average, and Republicans more consistently conservative. This sorting process seems to have penetrated far beyond partisan politics even into preferences for different sports (Republican as NASCAR fans, and Democratic as soccer fans) or entertainment shows.

Why have voters more consistently sorted themselves out by party? Partly it is because elites are more polarized, and so offer voters more polarized choices, as Fiorina says. Cable and the internet, which over-represent the politically attentive, facilitate sorting, despite their relatively small audiences. But hot button issues, especially those with a link to race (such as black candidates or affirmative action or welfare) or religiously-based moral traditionalism (such as abortion or gay rights) have become more prominent, which excites the base and attracts the cross-pressured. The civil rights movement, once it had finally been endorsed by the Democratic White House in 1963, broke the back of the old anomalous race-centered solidly Democratic Party in the South, sorting most white Southerners into the Republican Party and almost all black Southerners into the Democratic party.

The political implications of this elite polarization and public sorting are profound. As Hetherington points out, an elite committee of the APSA in 1950 advocated the strengthening of the two major political parties, which at the time were often charged to be so similar that they were described as "Tweedledee and Tweedledum." APSA! Be careful what you wish for! The increased strength of party loyalty at all levels has had a paralyzingly powerful impact in Congress and legislative halls in state capitals all over the country. Yet Baum reminds us that the parties and media were also highly polarized a century ago, so perhaps the anomaly is the period immediately after the Second World War. That is when empirical research on political behavior first began to flourish, and so perhaps that era looms larger in the research literature than it should.

Groups in Politics

Another theme in this volume concerns groups in politics, as reflected in the chapters by Erica Czaja, Nancy Burns, David Campbell, Deborah Schildkraut, and their colleagues. Again we see both clear continuities and some marked changes.

The pioneers had social groups squarely in their focus. But they concentrated on those that were most influential in the New Deal and immediate post-New Deal eras—social class, religious denomination, and labor unions. In the 1950s blacks were almost politically invisible, largely prevented from voting in the South and concentrated in a few large metropolitan areas in the North, often with low participation rates.[18] The Columbia studies focused on moderate-sized communities with few blacks, and blacks made only a cameo appearance in *The American Voter*. Nor did ethnicity receive much attention in those early works, despite the prominence of European ethnic groups in the political machines and ticket-balancing of the day. Women were generally assumed simply to double their husbands' votes. Religion was thought to influence politics primarily through the partisan allegiance of Catholics and Jews to the New Deal Coalition, and Northern Protestants to the Republicans. Religiosity did receive modest attention in *The American Voter*, but the real spotlight on that variable came only in the Michigan team's later account of the 1960 election, which presciently put the spotlight on variations in religious observance separately among Protestants and Catholics.[19] With the exception of *The American Voter*'s interest in labor unions, interest groups received little attention as proactive motivators, organizers, and mobilizers.

Much has changed in how groups are treated in the public opinion literature, principally because the political reality has changed. Race, ethnicity, gender, and religious observation have become more central to American politics, and justifiably have a large footprint in this volume. The politics of the 1960s were full of mobilization of groups in the mass public. The civil rights struggle received the earliest attention, especially with the passage of the Civil Rights Act in 1964 and the Voting Rights Act in 1965. Accordingly the Michigan account of the 1964 election put race front and center.[20] The massive immigration of Latinos and Asians that started in the 1960s has substantially changed the demography of the nation. The civil rights movement was soon followed by a resurgent feminist movement, Chicano and Asian American movements, and later the Christian Right, and lower-keyed advocacy on behalf of the elderly, disabled, gun owners, immigrants, children, and animals.

The grassroots civil rights movement of the 1950s and early 1960s was the model for the entry of these other groups into mass politics. So, for example, the key concepts that Czaja, Junn, and Mendelberg use for understanding non-European ethnic groups such as Hispanics and Asians are drawn from research focusing on black activism: prejudice and discrimination, identity, linked fate, the black utility heuristic, and group consciousness more generally. Schildkraut reports that Latinos and Asian Americans with strong group consciousness have less restrictive attitudes toward immigration. Burns et al. find that gender solidarity affects gender-related policy attitudes, though it affected support for Hillary Clinton only when she was most politically salient.

Nonetheless, blacks seem to me not to be as helpful a model for understanding other groups in politics—even other racial and ethnic groups—as one might think. We use the term "black exceptionalism."[21] Historically, the life circumstances of blacks in the United States have always been quite unique, and in our view those exceptional circumstances continue to make black public opinion distinctive today. When group consciousness is defined in terms of group identification, common fate, and anger, blacks' is more prevalent, is stronger, and has more influence over attitudes about issues that affect them collectively than is the case for women. Burns et al. quite reasonably ascribe that difference to the contrast between the segregation of blacks from whites and the intimate relations that most women and men have with each other, arguing that intimate relations with an outgroup impair both ingroup solidarity and hostility toward the outgroup, whereas separation stimulates them. I would add that the two groups' histories are quite different. One recent political consequence is that racial resentment was a stronger influence on matchups between Obama and Hillary Clinton during the 2008 primary season than was gender resentment.[22]

The examination of Asians and Latinos by Erica Czaja, Jane Junn, and Tali Mendelberg yields further evidence of black exceptionalism. As already mentioned, they borrow the language of black group consciousness.[23] Strong ethnic identity and linked fate predict those other groups' support for less restrictive immigration laws, according to Deborah Schildkraut. But in other respects they do not follow the black model. US-born Latinos and Asian Americans are closer to whites' more restrictive attitudes. Asians are much less likely to use the pan-ethnic term "Asian American" to describe their own identities than blacks are to use "African American."[24]

Blacks are distinctive in their partisanship as well. The acquisition of partisan identification among Latinos and Asians depends more on the length of time they have been in the country than the standard processes of socialization described by *The American Voter*, which continue to dominate among both blacks and whites. Moreover, blacks are the most homogeneously Democratic group in the nation. Both Asians and Latinos are considerably more divided, with Japanese Americans and Mexican Americans quite Democratic, and Vietnamese and Cuban Americans quite Republican. SES does not create divisions in African Americans' strong support for policies benefitting blacks, but higher social class does reduce Asians' and Latinos' support for policies particularly benefitting their groups. And Czaja, Junn, and Mendelberg and Schildkraut add a focus on understanding the political incorporation of Latinos and Asians, not so much an issue for blacks today or European ethnic groups in the 1950s. The long and frustrating efforts of African Americans to become integrated into the broader society also contrast with Latinos' and Asian Americans' greater success at integration into various facets of the mainstream, at least in the generations after immigration.

Finally, links between party and a social group have proven mostly quite durable, even if not static, over the half century since the pioneers' day, as Burns et al. say. For example, the racial divide in partisanship has expanded sharply since the 1950s, reaching an all-time high in 2008, presumably due to the unique circumstance of an election pitting a black candidate against a white one.[25] A persistent gender gap in partisanship has developed, though it is far smaller than the racial divide. David Campbell, Geoffrey Layman, and John Green highlight the shift of religious cleavages in partisanship from following denominational lines to separating people in every denomination based on their religiosity. They also provide a useful caution about oversimplifying the link of group membership to issue positions. Religiosity is not always associated with conservative issue attitudes (yes on abortion, no on immigration), any more than that blacks are more liberal than whites on all issues (yes on affirmative action, no on gay marriage).

Perhaps the most dramatic example of a mass group shift in partisanship is one that, somewhat surprisingly, does not show up in this volume. In the immediate postwar period, the former Confederacy was almost solidly Democratic in presidential elections, whereas today it is heavily Republican. Why? Several reasons are usually given. The switch originally had much to do with the South's peculiar historical circumstance surrounding race. Slavery, and later legalized discrimination, was embedded more deeply in local institutions, and for longer, there than elsewhere. During the 1960s and 1970s the national Democratic party abandoned its long-time protection of Southern white supremacy, with the consequence that the more racially conservative white South gradually shifted overwhelmingly to the Republican Party.[26] The current attachment of the white South to the Republicans is, however, ascribed by others to the region's growing affluence and its more widespread religious conservatism.[27]

The pioneers did not directly address nativism or racial prejudice. But much subsequent research has ascribed whites' race-relevant policy and candidate preferences to modern forms of racial prejudice, variously dubbed "symbolic racism" or "racial resentment."[28] For example, racial resentment had stronger effects on opposition to Barack Obama in 2008 than on opinions about earlier, ideologically indistinguishable, white liberal candidates, and was stronger regarding healthcare policies associated with Obama than those associated with, say, Hillary Clinton.[29] Hetherington shows that racial resentment is linked to Republican Party identification, and Barreto and Parker argue that it may be involved in support for the Tea Party. Burns and colleagues extend a similar argument to modern sexism, which is linked to support for the war in Iraq, opposition to abortion, and opposition to legislation against job discrimination. Schildkraut has developed a measure of "immigrant resentment," which is linked to restrictive attitudes toward immigration.

Personality, Motivation, and Emotion

Personality, motivation, and emotion were central topics for personality and social psychologists in the 1950s and early 1960s. *The Authoritarian Personality* by Adorno and colleagues was the most visible example. However such analyses soon fell out of favor. *The Authoritarian Personality* was excoriated by sociological critics steeped in the ways of survey research, a bashing from which it never fully recovered.[30] *The American Voter* scarcely mentions personality at all as a factor in presidential voting. Philip Converse challenged the presumption that wide-ranging ideological belief systems were widespread in the mass public, shedding some doubts about bold claims that such quasi-political attitudes as ethnocentrism, xenophobia, or authoritarianism were strongly grounded in personality.[31] Within the discipline of psychology, Walter Mischel published a widely heralded challenge to the notion that personality traits had powerful trans-situational effects on behavior, dampening the interest of many psychologists in pursuing them.[32] The "cognitive revolution" in social psychology soon followed, seeking purely cognitive, non-affective, non-dispositional explanations for errors and biases in judgment. Indeed perceiving stable, consistent personality traits was itself ascribed to cognitively-based biases in perceivers' judgments, described as the "fundamental attribution error."[33]

As often happens, personality analyses cycled back into vogue in the 1990s with the growing attention to the "Big Five" personality inventory.[34] As Federico indicates, a revisionist "right-wing authoritarianism" surfaced in public opinion research, though centered more in social learning theory than in psychoanalytic theory.[35] The old link between conservatism and intolerance of ambiguity reemerged in work by Jost and his colleagues that treated political conservatism as reflecting motivated reasoning, easing anxieties stemming from ambiguity and uncertainty.[36]

These forays into the personality determinants of ideology have come more from psychology than from political science. In general they assume the widespread existence of an underlying left-right ideological dimension in the mass public (or perhaps two partially independent sub-dimensions, of equality vs. inequality and openness vs. order). Psychologists have generally not integrated that assumption with the long line of public opinion research, going back to Converse's classic work, questioning the coherence of public opinion and the understanding of conventional political ideologies in the general public.[37] For example, the "top of the head" view of survey responses promoted by Zaller and Feldman would not lead us to expect strongly coherent policy preferences emerging from either ideology or personality.[38]

Federico acknowledges that citizens' preferences are usually not firmly based in ideological commitments, and that any sub-dimensions of ideology are likely to be more coherently reflected in the thinking of elites and the attentive public than in that of the average voter. Similarly, Gonzalez, Smith, and Hibbing qualify their assertions about the biological basis of public opinion somewhat by speculating that biology may matter more for broad, general orientations and predispositions than for specific issue positions. But squaring the two views of ideology in the mass public is a project for the future. I find the role of personality in public opinion difficult to assess absent more precise integration of those two literatures. One possible avenue of reconciliation may lie in Converse's later observation that information has a low mean but high variance in the general public.[39]

Finally, the attention to discrete emotions in the Brader and Wayne chapter is another clear "new direction." In the pioneers' day, affect in public opinion was generally treated as a single bipolar dimension ranging from positive to negative, with qualitatively different emotional reactions treated as slight variations on the more fundamental evaluative dimension.[40] Now more complex theories of emotion with roots in contemporary biological and evolutionary theorizing, such as theories of "fight or flight," have led to a richer view of emotional functioning. The case Ted Brader and Carly Wayne make for the differential political effects of diverse emotions is impressive. They can differentially affect exposure to and learning of information, party loyalty, style of information processing, and even political participation.

The increased attention to group-based politics noted earlier surfaces here in a link between group identifications or animosities and a variety of group-based emotions. Moreover, different groups may evoke quite different emotions. African Americans may often evoke anger and resentment among whites, and gays and lesbians, disgust.

Exogenous Changes

Not all changes in today's account of public opinion come from fresh theories or new empirical findings. To some extent change is also produced by factors quite exogenous to academic research. Three such changes are examined in this volume: increased rate of immigration (Erica Czaja, Jane Junn, and Tali Mendelberg, and Deborah Schildkraut), the structure of the media (Matt Baum), and technological changes that have influenced methods of collecting data on public opinion (D. Sunshine Hillygus).

Change in the ethnic composition of the nation has been perhaps the most dramatic external change that has directly affected public opinion. Extensive immigration from Latin America and Asia has resulted in a rapid diversification of the nation. A renewal of massive immigration was not dreamed of by the pioneers of our field, and was even unanticipated by those who wrote the enabling legislation in the mid 1960s. I have already discussed ways in which modeling an analysis of Latinos and Asians on African Americans, the major racial minority group extant in the 1950s, may go awry. Arguably a closer analogue would be the European immigrants of a century ago, and their descendants. Generation in the United States would be a stronger predictor of many political outcome variables than the subjective orientations so important in analyses of black opinion, consistent with what Czaja, Junn and Mendelberg have written. It is more of an open question as to whether Latinos and Asians as the objects of others' opinions can be understood in the same terms as African Americans.[41]

In some ways the immigration of Latinos has become the hot button issue in the current era that civil rights for blacks once was. Barreto and Parker describe the Tea Party rhetoric depicting undocumented immigrants as constituting a multi-faceted threat to America, to both the economy and to the traditional white-dominated culture. Yet Deborah Schildkraut describes public opinion about immigration as complex, as ambivalent at both the individual and aggregate level and in flux over time. Today public opinion seems to support a "path to citizenship" despite the Tea Party and congressional inaction. Varying the framing of immigration sometimes affects public opinion about it, and sometimes does not. Much of the support for restrictive policies seems to come from resentment over immigrants perceived as not assimilating, and so representing a cultural threat, rather than an economic threat to whites' self-interest. Hopkins chimes in with the finding that rapid growth in the number of immigrants in a locality seems to create anxiety primarily when the media send forth threatening messages about immigration.[42]

Changes in the media over time represent another important exogenous change. One central set of changes has been in the way the public gets political news. Both the diminished newspaper readership and audiences for network news programs have had non-trivial effects. Newspapers and network news have generally reflected somewhat balanced and moderate political viewpoints, and attracted broad audiences across the political spectrum, at least in the period since the Second World War. Instead now there are surging numbers of cable outlets, political blogs on the Internet, and high profile radio talk shows. Moreover the audiences for the new media tend to be small. They prominently feature stridently partisan political views, and seem to invite highly selective exposure. Matt Baum would also include the growing importance of the more sporadically presented "soft news" in entertainment programs such as *Saturday Night Live*, Oprah, David Letterman, or Jon Stewart.

These changes probably have not greatly enlarged the store of political information in the general public, nor led to more informed political choices. Rather, they have at least been accompanied by, if not created, increased polarization, certainly of elites and of the more politically attentive members of the public. They are part of what Herbst notes is the yin and yang of the atomized, as opposed to communal, public, perhaps reflecting a swing back to the latter. Audiences for political cable or radio talk shows or for particular blogospheres are members of new communities, if often imagined ones rather than face to face, quite unlike newspaper readers or the viewers of network news, who remain very much on their own in trying to make sense of the complexities of the political world.

Exogenous changes have also affected the gathering of the data on public opinion that we all rely on. Here too we see a blend of continuity and change. Initially quota sampling, community-based samples, and face to face interviewing were the norm, at least for academic surveys. After the debacle of the mis-called 1948 election, all that evolved into probability sampling of national samples. Later on, RDD telephone surveys began to replace face to face home interviews as their cost began to escalate. But then response rates for telephone surveys began to fall precipitously. Today, as Hillygus says, there is a proliferation of polls, but people have become harder to reach by telephone. As a result we must choose between poor response rates using telephone samples or online samples, where sometimes even the concept of a response rate may not apply.

Encouraging research progress has been made in identifying the sources of error in public opinion surveys beyond sampling error. D. Sunshine Hillygus touches on some and on the notion of "total survey error," and is justly critical of the media for publishing polls without mentioning the numerous other possible sources of error.

She draws the wise conclusion that every survey is flawed in some way or another, though some less than others, which she memorably describes as the "gold" vs. the "tin" standards of survey excellence. However, it is usually impossible to assess the actual bias introduced by any given factor in any given survey in the absence of a control group. We can, of course, cite other (sometimes experimental) research that has assessed the biasing effects of that factor elsewhere. However the best we usually can do is speculate about how much the procedures used in any given survey induced biases due to any one factor. So the acid test, in my view, is whether or not the same results are replicated in surveys using different methods.

Hillygus does apply this criterion of replication with telling effect when assessing the effects of falling response rates for telephone surveys. Some careful studies have shown that survey findings are quite similar if otherwise identical surveys are allowed to have either higher or lower response rates. So dwindling survey response rates may not be as severe a problem as feared a couple of decades ago. At least that is the current wisdom.

What about online surveys? She compares "opt-in" versions in which self-selected respondents choose to participate, and then are weighted according to their population frequencies, with "opt-out" versions, in which respondents are pre-selected for the sample but can refuse to participate. She favors the latter for using probability sampling, and rejects the former for using a distant (but far more sophisticated) cousin of the quota sampling discredited as a result of the 1948 debacle (remember the *Chicago Tribune* headline, "Dewey beats Truman"). She does note, however, that both tend to yield similar results for vote choice, if not for indicators of political engagement.

I would have liked to see the replication criterion applied to this comparison, perhaps for selfish reasons. Our analysis of the 2008 presidential election used both the online "opt-in" CCAP survey, with over 18,000 cases, and the erstwhile "gold standard" ANES, based on a far smaller sample.[43] The major findings are almost identical. The exception concerns the findings for Latinos, where the far smaller ANES subsample may have yielded less than perfectly reliable findings. In this study, opt-in seems to have been just fine, at least for the analysis of voting behavior. However, my instincts, like hers, would support caution about allowing respondents to self-select into any survey based on its topic if it centrally involves interest in politics and information. Alas, that also includes telephone surveys and the ANES to a significant degree these days.[44]

Czaja, Junn, and Mendelberg's chapter highlights another impact of exogenous changes on survey methodology. The proportion of Americans with Asian or Latino ancestry has skyrocketed. Such groups still do not show up in sufficient numbers to yield reliable results in most national probability samples. The standard solution is to oversample such small subpopulations. That works fairly well for African Americans, who are both highly residentially segregated and a rather attitudinally homogeneous subpopulation, at least on partisan and racial issues. For either face to face or telephone surveys, oversampling them is easy and likely to yield relatively unbiased results.

But what about Latinos and Asians? Oversampling may not be so easy and/or safe. As Czaja, Junn, and Mendelberg point out, both groups are far more dispersed than are blacks, and geographical dispersion is likely to be correlated with other key variables, such as generation in the United States, language preferences, national origins, and political attitudes. One would not expect an oversampling of Latinos in Miami to look politically like those in Los Angeles or San Antonio. So oversampling Latinos and Asians is a trickier business than oversampling blacks.

A final exogenous change is the development of new, more biologically-based measures of public opinion. Frank Gonzalez and colleagues draw our attention to some limits to the value of standard survey self-reports, insofar as genetic inheritance may play a role in public opinion. Electrodermal activity, chemical substances in the body, eye movements, facial muscles, and brain scanning may all represent new and more indirect ways of measuring an individual's attitudes. To be sure, the use of such biological markers in public opinion research is in its infancy, so their true potential is unknown at this time. But stay tuned. And heed the authors' wise words toward the end of their essay about the "concerns" many traditional scholars have about biological approaches to public opinion. They come in the early stages of the debates that no doubt will become more common in coming years.

Democratic Governance

The basic precept of democratic governance is the continuing responsiveness of government to the people. That means there should be some dependence of public policy on public opinion, though of course political theorists as well as politicians differ about how tight they believe the link should be. Martin Gilens' chapter, for example, makes a useful distinction between "ideal" and "minimalist" criteria for satisfactory democratic citizenship.

Early research on political behavior questioned the competence of the public to guide public policy. The Michigan school in particular believed that the public possesses inadequate information, partisan preferences that are indifferent to contemporary realities, and a weak understanding of fundamental ideological principles.[45] Mitigating those shortcomings was the idea that voters could take cues from elites, in essence developing "ideology by proxy." Alternatively, voters might develop specialized expertise, such that for every issue there might be an interested and informed "issue public." The issue publics for different issues might not overlap very much, so that the public as a whole might show generally poor information levels, but still exercise some wise judgment in specific issue areas.[46]

At the same time Downs and Key took contrarian positions. Key famously maintained that "voters are no fools," and Downs asserted in a variety of ways that voters actually resembled rational thinkers more than the behavioral pioneers believed.[47] They, of course, foreshadowed the later development of portraits of democratic voters developed by rational choice theorists.[48]

Today, perhaps, the conventional wisdom is that "the miracle of aggregation" leads public opinion as a whole to look a good bit more rational than a cold-eyed examination of individual attitudes would suggest. Perhaps public opinion is "enlightened enough," in Gilens' words. He notes that deliberative polls often find rather little change in public opinion after ordinary people have been exposed to intensive bursts of information and have had a chance to discuss it. Second, simulations of a public composed of the well-informed, produced by imputing the preferences that the poorly informed *would* have if they were better informed, yield estimates of public opinion close to the aggregate opinion of the actual public. Third, framing and question wording effects obtained in artificial survey experiments sometimes give the impression that the public emotionally overreacts to the particularly loaded symbols they are presented with, such as "welfare" or "death tax," ignoring the realities of the policies they purportedly refer to. But as Gilens says, such dramatic examples may not be typical, they may lead the public to think about quite different policies rather than being swayed in their attitudes about a given policy, and such swings may not be especially robust in the face of competing rhetoric from other elites. The suggestion is that public opinion, at least in the aggregate, may resemble what a much more informed citizenry would prefer, with the "signal" of the informed coming through despite the "noise" of the rabble.

That may be too generous, however, for several reasons. The inescapable fact remains that once having looked inside the sausage factory of individual opinions, we cannot easily forget the grim reality we have seen. Relatively few members of the general public are well informed about politics, or have consistent and stable preferences on most issues. Second, the best informed are the *most* likely to disregard facts inconveniently inconsistent with their priors.[49] Third, partisan elites are constantly trying to manipulate the public, and often successfully. Just as often, however, they are pandering to an ill-informed and emotional public, which is no better for rational public policies. When they are not engaged in manipulation or pandering, they may be engaged in deception for partisan advantage. Andrea Campbell illustrates that vividly in her case study of Obamacare. Perhaps public opinion influenced the general direction of public policy, but in terms of the actual impact of the policy on citizens' lives, the devil truly was in the details. And fourth, there is the problem of social inequality, as Gilens' and Andrea Campbell and Elizabeth Rigby's chapters so tellingly indicate. The well-off are not only more powerful but are more politically competent than the little guy. And they have disproportionate influence over who decides on the details.

The pioneers would have found familiar landscape in those observations. But we do have some "new directions" in democratic governance as well, emphasized by Baum. He suggests that political consensus is more difficult to achieve today than it was, given some important political changes. One is the strikingly increased elite polarization. Political machines are far weaker, so deal-making is more complicated. The media environment has changed as well. The traditional news media are less important, replaced to some extent by the more polarizing new media. Media audiences have fragmented, becoming smaller, politically narrower, and more partisan. A shrinking "media commons" is replaced with increased selective exposure and selective interpretation. "Cyberbalkanization" seems to be growing instead. The proportion of the population voting is also far higher than it was a century ago, making the task of persuasion more difficult.

And the goal of achieving national consensus and unity may be especially difficult for the individual whose job that is, the president. The ground on which presidents stand has shifted, in Baum's felicitous terms, making the task of sustaining bipartisan consensus more daunting, even in time of war. It has become harder for the president to mobilize the public, for better or worse. The content of the media has changed as well, becoming more negative and skeptical. Presidents have less direct access to the public, as the media increasingly feature journalists' own interpretations, rather than presenting presidential speeches and news conferences in the leaders' own words.

But then let us remember that the Founders expected that democracy would be disputatious. They were not rebelling against a Europe filled with benign leaders who thoughtfully and responsively considered the preferences of all the people. They were rebelling against selfish autocrats who rolled roughshod over ordinary people. They did not expect democracy to be pretty or that all interested parties would pull together cooperatively all the time. The ills of our democracy are what they are, and the public bears some responsibility for them, engaging in sins of commission and omission alike. And it seems inevitable, if regrettable, that democratic systems are no cure-all for the natural differences in wealth and power that develop in any human society. Nevertheless, almost all public opinion scholars today would no doubt fall back on Winston Churchill's famous dictum, that "democracy is the worst form of government except for all the others that have been tried."

In all these areas, I am impressed by the authors' abilities to layer the "new directions" that the study of public opinion has taken on top of the foundations laid down by the pioneers half a century ago. It has been my privilege to add these few comments to what they have achieved.

Notes

1. Berelson, Bernard R., Paul F. Lazarsfeld, and William N. McPhee, *Voting: A Study of Opinion Formation in a Presidential Campaign* (Chicago: University of Chicago Press, 1954); Lazarsfeld, Paul F., Bernard Berelson, and Hazel Gaudet, *The People's Choice*, 2nd ed. (New York: Columbia University Press, 1948).
2. Klapper, Joseph T., *The Effects of Mass Communications* (Glencoe, IL: Free Press, 1960).
3. Lee, Alfred McClung and Elizabeth Briant Lee, eds., *The Fine Art of Propaganda: A Study of Father Coughlin's Speeches* (New York: Harcourt, Brace, 1939).
4. Campbell, Angus, Philip E. Converse, Warren E. Miller, and Donald E. Stokes, *The American Voter* (New York: Wiley, 1960).
5. E.g., Festinger, Leon, *A Theory of Cognitive Dissonance* (Evanston, IL: Row, Peterson, 1957).
6. Lazarsfeld, Berelson, and Gaudet (1948).
7. Berelson, Lazarsfeld, and McPhee (1954).
8. Campbell, Angus, Gerald Gurin, and Warren E. Miller, *The Voter Decides* (Evanston, Illinois: Row, Peterson, 1954); and Converse, Philip. E., "The Nature of Belief Systems in Mass Publics," in David E. Apter (ed.), *Ideology and Discontent* (New York: Free Press of Glencoe, 1964), pp. 206–261.
9. Adorno, Theodor W., Else Frenkel-Brunswik, D. J. Levinson, and R. N. Sanford, *The Authoritarian Personality* (New York: Harper and Row, 1950).

10. McClosky, Herbert, "Conservatism and Personality," *American Political Science Review 52 (1958): 27–45.*
11. Greenstein, Fred I., *Personality and Politics: Problems of Evidence, Inference, and Conceptualization* (Princeton: Princeton University Press, 1969).
12. Berelson, Lazarsfeld, and McPhee (1954), and Converse (1964).
13. Fiorina, Morris P., *Retrospective Voting in American National Elections* (New Haven, CT: Yale University Press, 1981); Miller, Warren E., and J. Merrill Shanks, *The New American Voter* (Cambridge: Harvard University Press, 1996).
14. Kahneman, Daniel, *Thinking Fast and Slow* (New York: Farrar, Straus, and Giroux, 2011).
15. Klapper (1960).
16. Zaller, John, *The Nature and Origins of Mass Opinion* (New York: Cambridge University Press, 1992).
17. Vavreck, Lynn, *The Message Matters: The Economy and Presidential Campaigns* (Princeton, NJ: Princeton University Press, 2009).
18. Today, of course, blacks' pivotal roles in the desegregation of the armed forces and in Harry Truman's victory in 1948 are more widely recognized.
19. Converse, Philip. E., Angus Campbell, Warren E. Miller, and Donald E. Stokes, "Stability and Change in 1960: A Reinstating Election," *American Political Science Review* 55 (1961): 269–280.
20. Converse, Philip. E., Aage R. Clausen, and Warren E. Miller, "Electoral Myth and Reality: The 1964 Election," *American Political Science Review* 59 (1965): 321–336.
21. Sears, David O., and Victoria Savalei, "The Political Color Line in America: Many Peoples of Color or Black Exceptionalism?" *Political Psychology* 27 (2006): 895–924.
22. Tesler, Michael and David O. Sears, *Obama's Race: The 2008 Election and the Dream of a Post-Racial America* (Chicago: University of Chicago Press, 2010).
23. Dawson, Michael C., *Behind the Mule: Race and Class in African American Politics* (Princeton: Princeton University Press, 1994).
24. Sears, David. O., Mingying Fu, P. J. Henry, and Kerra Bui, "The Origins and Persistence of Ethnic Identity among the 'New Immigrant' Groups," *Social Psychology Quarterly* 66 (2003): 419–437.
25. Tesler and Sears (2010).
26. Valentino, Nicholas A., and David O. Sears, "Old Times There Are Not Forgotten: Race and Partisan Realignment in the Contemporary South," *American Journal of Political Science* 49 (2005): 672–688.
27. Black, Earl, and Merle Black, *The Rise of Southern Republicans* (Cambridge: Harvard University Press, 2002).
28. Sears, David O., and P. J. Henry, "Over Thirty Years Later: A Contemporary Look at Symbolic Racism," in Mark Zanna (ed.), *Advances in Experimental Social Psychology*, Vol. 37 (San Diego: Elsevier Academic Press, 2005), pp. 95–150; Kinder, Donald R. and Lynn Sanders (1996).
29. Tesler and Sears (2010); Michael Tesler, "The Spillover of Racialization into Health Care: How President Obama Polarized Public Opinion by Racial Attitudes and Race," *American Journal of Political Science* 56 (2012): 690–702.
30. Hyman, Herbert H., and Paul B. Sheatsley, "The Authoritarian Personality: A Methodological Critique," in R. Christie and M. Jahoda (eds.), *Studies in the Scope and Method of the Authoritarian Personality* (Glencoe, IL.: The Free Press, 1954).
31. Converse, P. E. (1964).
32. Mischel, Walter, *Personality and Assessment* (New York: John Wiley and Sons, 1968).
33. Jones, Edward E. and Victor A. Harris, "The Attribution of Attitudes," *Journal of Experimental Social Psychology* 3 (1967): 1–24.

34. Goldberg, Lewis R., "An Alternative 'Description of Personality': The Big-Five Factor Structure," *Journal of Personality and Social Psychology* 59 (1990): 1216–1229.

35. Altemeyer, Bob, *Enemies of Freedom: Understanding Right-wing Authoritarianism* (San Francisco: Jossey-Bass, 1988).

36. Jost, John T., Jack Glaser, Arie Kruglanski, and Frank Sulloway, "Political Conservatism as Motivated Social Cognition," *Psychological Bulletin* 129, no. 3 (2003): 339–375.

37. Converse, Phillip E. (1964).

38. Zaller, John, and Stanley Feldman, "A Simple Theory of the Survey Response: Answering Questions Versus Revealing Preferences," *American Journal of Political Science* 36 (1992): 569–616.

39. Converse, Phillip E., "Assessing the Capacity of Mass Electorates," *Annual Review of Political Science* 3 (2000): 331–353.

40. Osgood, Charles E., George J. Suci, and Percy H. Tannenbaum, *The Measurement of Meaning* (Urbana: University of Illinois Press, 1957); and Rosenberg, Seymour and Andrea Sedlak, "Structural Representations of Implicit Personality Theory," in *Advances in Experimental Social Psychology*, ed. Leonard Berkowitz, Vol. 6 (New York: Academic Press, 1972).

41. Citrin, Jack, and David O. Sears, *American Identity and the Politics of Multiculturalism* (New York: Cambridge University Press, 2014); Sears et al. (2003); and David O. Sears and Victoria Savalei (2006).

42. Hopkins, Daniel J., "Politicized Places: Explaining Where and When Immigrants Provoke Local Opposition," *American Political Science Review* 104, no. 1 (2010): 40–60.

43. Tesler, M. and D. O. Sears (2010).

44. On the robustness of survey findings despite major changes in American society and survey procedures, I might also mention the replication of the great majority of findings from *The American Voter* (1960), using data collected in the 1950s, in *The American Voter Revisited* (2008), using data collected over the half century since.

45. Berelson, Bernard R., Paul F. Lazarsfeld, and William N. McPhee (1954); Converse, Philip E. (1964); Lewis-Beck, Michael S., William G. Jacoby, Helmut Norpoth, and Herbert E. Weisberg, *The American Voter Revisited* (Ann Arbor: University of Michigan Press, 2008).

46. Campbell, Converse, Miller, and Stokes (1960); and Converse, Philip E. (1964).

47. Downs, Anthony, *An Economic Theory of Democracy* (New York: Harper-Row, 1957); and Key, V. O., Jr., *The Responsible Electorate* (Cambridge: Harvard University Press, 1966).

48. Fiorina, Morris P. (1981); Benjamin I. Page and Robert Y. Shapiro, *The Rational Public: Fifty Years of Trends in Americans' Policy Preferences* (Chicago: University of Chicago Press, 1992); and Popkin, Samuel, *The Reasoning Voter: Communication and Persuasion in Presidential Campaigns*, 2nd edition (Chicago: University of Chicago Press, 1994).

49. Zaller (1992).

Index